for ♂

Calais, Vermont

April 29th, 1991

BONNIE
PRINCE CHARLIE

BONNIE
PRINCE CHARLIE

Fitzroy Maclean

ATHENEUM   New York   1989

First published in Great Britain in 1988 by
George Weidenfeld & Nicolson Limited, London.

The maps of Prestonpans, Falkirk and Culloden by Arthur Banks are
from *Ships of the '45* by J. S. Gibson and reproduced by kind permission of Century Hutchinson Ltd. The map of the Prince's travels in
Britain is from *Bonnie Prince Charlie* by Rosalind K. Marshall and
reproduced by permission of HMSO Books, Crown copyright 1988.

Atheneum
Macmillan Publishing Company
866 Third Avenue, New York, N.Y. 10022

Library of Congress Cataloging-in-Publication Data
Maclean, Fitzroy, 1911–
    Bonnie Prince Charlie / by Fitzroy Maclean.
        p.   cm.
    Bibliography: p.
    Includes index.
    ISBN 0-689-12047-8
    1. Charles Edward, Prince, grandson of James II, King of
England, 1720–1788. 2. Jacobite Rebellion, 1745–1746.
3. Great Britain—Princes and princesses—Biography.
4. Scotland—History—18th century. I. Title.
DA814.A5M35 1989
941.07'2'0924—dc19   88-31165   CIP
[B]

Macmillan books are available at special discounts for bulk purchases
for sales promotions, premiums, fund-raising, or educational use.
For details, contact:
Special Sales Director
Macmillan Publishing Company
866 Third Avenue
New York, N.Y. 10022

10 9 8 7 6 5 4 3 2 1

Printed in the United States of America

For dear Rhoda

The adventurous Prince, as is well known, proved to be one of those personages who distinguish themselves during some single and extraordinarily brilliant period of their lives, like the course of a shooting star, at which men wonder, as well on account of the briefness as the brilliancy of its splendour.

Sir Walter Scott
Introduction to Redgauntlet

CONTENTS

ILLUSTRATIONS

Prince Charles Edward and Henry Stuart (*courtesy of the Duke of Buccleuch*)

Prince James Edward Stuart (*National Portrait Gallery, London*)

Princess Clementina Sobieska (*National Galleries of Scotland*)

Prince Charles and Antoine Walsh on the shore of Lochnanuagh, July 1745 (*Robert Harding Assocs/National Galleries of Scotland*)

Duncan Forbes, Lord President of Scotland (*National Galleries of Scotland*)

The entry of Prince Charles into Edinburgh, 1745 (*BBC Hulton Picture Library*)

William, Duke of Cumberland by Morier (*Reproduced by gracious permission of H. M. The Queen*)

Prince Charles Edward Stuart by Blanchet (*Reproduced by gracious permission of H. M. The Queen*)

The March to Finchley by William Hogarth (*Witte Collection, Courtauld Institute of Art, London*)

The Battle of Culloden, 1746, by Morier (*Reproduced by gracious permission of H. M. The Queen*)

The Battle of Culloden by Holford (*Weidenfeld Archives*)

Henry, Cardinal York (*National Portrait Gallery, London*)

Lord George Murray (*From the Duke of Atholl's Collection at Blair Castle, Perthshire*)
Clementina Walkinshaw by Ramsay (*Derby Art Gallery*)
Charlotte, Duchess of Albany by Hamilton (*National Galleries of Scotland*)
Flora MacDonald by Ramsay (*National Galleries of Scotland*)
The Hôtel de Guéméné, Place des Vosges, Paris (*Author's collection*)
Louise de Montbazon, after Lancret (*Bibliothèque Nationale, Paris*)
Louise of Stolberg (*Trustees of Stonyhurst College*)
Charles Edward Stuart in later life by Hamilton (*National Galleries of Scotland*)

Maps

ACKNOWLEDGEMENTS

In the first place my gratitude is due to H. M. The Queen for permission to examine and make use of the Stuart Papers at Windsor. I should also like to express my indebtedness to John Prebble for his classic account of Culloden and its aftermath; to Dr Bruce Lenman for his stimulating study of the Jacobite Risings; to Dr Frank McLynn for his masterly work on different aspects of the Jacobite scene; to James Lees-Milne for his most readable account of *The Last Stuarts*; and finally to Professor L. L. Bongie for his brilliantly researched *Love of a Prince* and in particular for his rediscovery of Louise de Montbazon's long neglected letters at Windsor. But, on this whole subject, no one, surely, has hit the historical nail on the head more disturbingly than Professor A. J. F. Youngson in *The Prince and the Pretender*. Indeed, had I read this sooner, it might well have deterred me altogether from my present excursion into the minefield of popular biography.

F.M.

FOREWORD

Going through a deedbox of recently inherited family papers late one night some twenty-five or more years ago, I came quite unexpectedly on a small, twice-folded sheet of frayed and yellowing paper bearing in faded ink the inscription 'Prince Charles Edward 1745 – given to my Grandfather's care by another Jacobite gentleman who was afraid to have the portrait found on him.'

The little packet was no more than a couple of inches long. What kind of portrait could it contain? Carefully unfolding first one and then a second flimsy layer of paper, I came at last to two tiny representations of the Prince, a fraction of an inch square, bearing, on either side of his head, the letters 'P.C.' for Prince Charles. All at once I felt immensely excited. Clearly these were secret tokens carried on their person by loyal Jacobites – in the back of a watch or some such safe place – and discreetly displayed to like-minded persons, whom, rightly or wrongly, they thought they could trust.

At once I felt myself carried back two centuries to the anxious weeks and months before and after the Rising, when, apart from the hazards of the battlefield, any chance indiscretion could lead to hanging, drawing and quartering at Tyburn or on Tower Hill.

Not unnaturally, the sudden discovery of this direct personal link with the Rising of 1745 and with my own kinsmen, who were involved in it and for so long went in fear of their lives, caught my imagination and also made me realize how little, though coming of sound Jacobite stock, I really knew of the Rising and of the events that preceded and followed it. Here, I decided, was a gap in my knowledge that required to be remedied.

In the quarter of a century that followed my researches have taken me from the Palazzo San Clemente in Florence and the Basilica dei Santissimi Apostoli in Rome to Glen Corradale in South Uist and 'Lady Clan's' pleasant parlour at Nunton on Benbecula, where 'Betty Burke's' blue-sprigged gown was so hurriedly cobbled together, and from the stricken field of Culloden to the upper floors of the great Hôtel de Guéméné on the Place des Vosges. Here and there, in drenching rain on precipitous hillsides and dodging in little boats from island to island and bay to bay, I have found echoes of my own long past experience of such things, memories too of the shared hazards and hardships of guerilla war and of the lasting loyalties they engender.

The result is the present book, published to mark the two hundredth anniversary of Bonny Prince Charlie's death. I can only hope that some at any rate of my readers will enjoy reading it as much as I have enjoyed researching and writing it.

Dates

During the first half of the eighteenth century Great Britain retained the Old Style Julian calendar, while the Roman Catholic countries of Europe adopted the New Style Gregorian system, which left Old Style British dates ten days behind. I have accordingly used Old Style for the period when Prince Charles was in Great Britain and New Style for when he was on the Continent.

Fitzroy Maclean
Strachur, Argyll

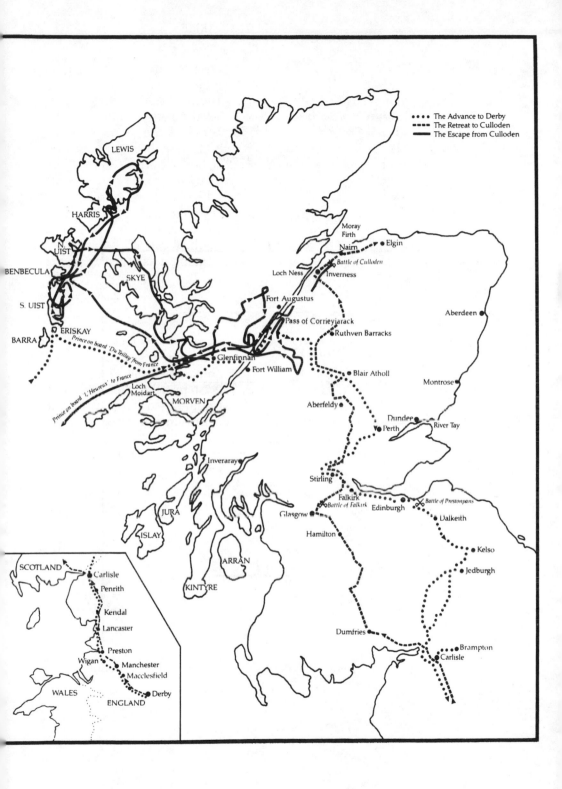

The Advance to Derby
The Retreat to Culloden
The Escape from Culloden

LEWIS

HARRIS

Moray
Firth

Nairn ● Elgin

N.
UIST

BENBECULA

SKYE

Loch Ness

Battle of Culloden

Inverness

S. UIST

Fort Augustus

Aberdeen ●

BARRA

ERISKAY

Pass of Corrieyiarack

Ruthven Barracks

Prince on board 'Du Teillay' from France

Glenfinnan

Fort William

Blair Atholl

Prince on board 'L'Heureux' to France

Loch
Moidart

MORVEN

Aberfeldy

Montrose

Dundee

Perth

River Tay

Inveraray ●

Stirling

JURA

Falkirk

Battle of Prestonpans

Battle of Falkirk

Edinburgh

ISLAY

Glasgow ●

Dalkeith

ARRAN

Hamilton ●

Kelso ●

KINTYRE

Jedburgh ●

SCOTLAND

Carlisle

Penrith

Dumfries

Brampton

Carlisle

Kendal

Lancaster

Preston

Wigan

Manchester

Macclesfield

WALES

ENGLAND

Derby

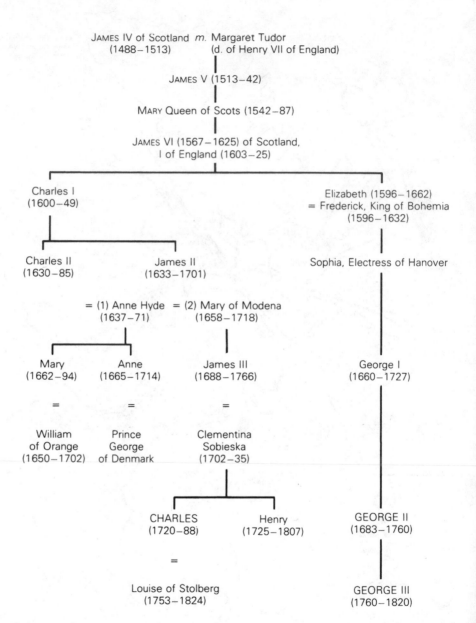

JAMES IV of Scotland *m.* Margaret Tudor
(1488–1513)   (d. of Henry VII of England)

JAMES V (1513–42)

MARY Queen of Scots (1542–87)

JAMES VI (1567–1625) of Scotland,
I of England (1603–25)

Charles I
(1600–49)

Elizabeth (1596–1662)
= Frederick, King of Bohemia
(1596–1632)

Charles II
(1630–85)

James II
(1633–1701)

Sophia, Electress of Hanover

= (1) Anne Hyde   = (2) Mary of Modena
(1637–71)   (1658–1718)

Mary
(1662–94)

Anne
(1665–1714)

James III
(1688–1766)

George I
(1660–1727)

=

=

=

William
of Orange
(1650–1702)

Prince
George
of Denmark

Clementina
Sobieska
(1702–35)

CHARLES
(1720–88)

Henry
(1725–1807)

GEORGE II
(1683–1760)

=

Louise of Stolberg
(1753–1824)

GEORGE III
(1760–1820)

PART I

BORN TO BE KING

Reared from infancy never to forego the desire
or the hope of recovering the Crown.

Giulio Cesare Cordara

CHAPTER ONE

Charles Edward Louis John Casimir Silvester Severino Maria Stuart, to be known to his own and succeeding generations as Bonnie Prince Charlie*, was born at the Palazzo Muti in Rome on the last day of December 1720, son of the titular King James VIII of Scotland and III of England or, as his Whig opponents preferred to call him, the Old Pretender, and of his bride of the previous year, Clementina Sobieska, granddaughter of the resoundingly heroic King John Sobieski of Poland, who, thirty-seven years earlier had driven back the Turks from the walls of Vienna. The birth took place in the presence of half a dozen cardinals and a great number of other local dignitaries, and the baby was baptized according to the Roman rite by the Bishop of Montefiascone, who the year before had officiated at his parents' marriage. The guns from the neighbouring Castel Sant' Angelo thundered out a royal salute and the Pope himself called at the Palazzo Muti to give his blessing.

On the night of Charles's christening a new star of extreme brilliance is said to have appeared in the heavens, while in Germany a great storm laid waste the Electorate of Hanover. Although the British Government's agent in Rome, Baron Philipp von Stosch from Brandenburg, an occasional dealer in antiques, otherwise known as John Walton, sought to minimize the event by reporting to his masters that the baby was malformed and that his mother could never bear another child, the birth of a healthy heir to the House of Stuart was bound to be as much of a blow to the adherents of Hanover as it was a matter for congratulation and encouragement to the upholders of the Jacobite cause. 'The most acceptable news which can reach the ears of a good

*From the Gaelic Tearlach or Charles.

3

Englishman,' declared Dr Attenbury, the Bishop of Rochester, a leading English Jacobite. And little King Louis xv of France, by now just ten, is said to have jumped for joy and clapped his hands on hearing the news.

For the baby's father, on whom Jacobite hopes had hitherto centred, life during the past thirty years had held many disappointments. Born in London at St James's Palace in June 1688, barely six months before his own father's precipitous departure for France and for exile, he had on the latter's death in September 1701 been in his turn proclaimed King at St Germain, where, by courtesy of Louis xv of France, the exiled court were now established and whence they kept in touch as best they could with their still quite numerous and not uninfluential supporters in England and Scotland. But when six months later the death of James's brother-in-law, William of Orange, had again left both thrones vacant, the succession had passed quietly and without great question to his Protestant half-sister Anne.

Like his father, James was a Roman Catholic and the fact was that neither the people of England nor those of Scotland wanted another Catholic king. Already in 1701, following the death of Anne's last surviving child, an Act of Settlement had hurriedly been pushed through Parliament, providing that on her death the succession should pass to the remote but reassuringly Protestant Electress Sophia of Hanover, a granddaughter, through her mother, of King James vi and i. With the union of the two countries in 1707, parallel legislation had been passed in Scotland. And, when the Electress had died in June 1714, her place as heir apparent had passed to her son George, a not very prepossessing German princeling, unable to speak English.

Being both a Stuart and a Protestant, as well as British born and bred, Anne, though lacking charm, had proved reasonably acceptable to the majority of her subjects. For her appointed successor there was but little enthusiasm save amongst those who, for reasons of their own, calculated that a foreign monarch, speaking no English and primarily concerned with the affairs of his native Hanover, could prove a useful tool in the right hands. In Scotland, in particular, dislike of the union with England had by this time substantially increased support for the Jacobite cause. 'The Jacobites', wrote Parson Wodrow of Eastwood, 'are mighty uppish.' And so, as Anne herself, predeceased by all her seventeen children, lay dying in that same summer of 1714, it could be said without exaggeration that the question of the succession was once again wide open.

Had James been prepared to change his religion, the throne could almost certainly have been his for the taking. But this he would not do and most people did not know which they liked less, the prospect of a Catholic king or of being handed over 'as a province to a despicable German Electorate'. And so the majority went quietly about their business and, when it came to the point, the matter was quickly settled by prompt political action on the part of the Whig leaders. No sooner was Anne dead than the Elector of Hanover was at once proclaimed King in London; in Edinburgh the Duchess of Argyll gave a great ball to celebrate the occasion; and, before the Jacobites had managed to make any kind of a move, the reign of George I had begun.

On reaching England in September 1714, George of Hanover, who, it must be said, regarded his accession to the British throne without enthusiasm, made little effort to endear himself to his new subjects. Conscious that he owed his crown to one political party, he governed from the first as a party monarch. When some of the leading Tories and even some former Jacobites sought to ingratiate themselves with him, he rudely rebuffed their advances. Soon he and the House of Hanover were less popular than ever, particularly in Scotland, where the recent union still rankled and a variety of scurrilous songs were current about the 'wee, wee German lairdie' who now occupied the throne of the Stuart kings.

It is therefore scarcely surprising that James, by this time twenty-seven years old, should have come to the conclusion that now, if ever, was the moment for him to try to regain his kingdom. Though uninspiring in other respects, he did not lack courage. He had seen action against the English at Oudenarde, Lille and Malplaquet and in 1708 had actually set out for Scotland with a sizeable French naval expedition which, after a bad storm and a skirmish with the English Admiral Byng, had, despite his protests, been forced to put back to France without ever setting him ashore. Accordingly, in the summer of 1715, contact was made with the Jacobites in the South and West of England and another naval expedition was mounted by the French. At the same time James wrote to the Earl of Mar, with whom he was in secret correspondence, inviting him to raise the loyal clans on his behalf in Scotland.

'Bobbing John', as Mar was known to his contemporaries, had served as Secretary of State for Scotland under Queen Anne and had at the beginning of the new reign done his best to ingratiate himself with George I. But, like others, he had been rebuffed. It was thus that, on receiving James's letter, he promptly disguised himself as a workman and travelled north to Braemar, where on 25 September he raised the Royal Standard and boldly proclaimed James King.

At first the venture showed every sign of succeeding. Within a few days Mar had been joined by some 3,000 loyal Jacobites and soon had under his command an army more than twice the size of the small

Government force which stood against him, commanded by the staunchly Whig Duke of Argyll. Before long Perth and large parts of the Highlands were in Jacobite hands. The outlook was extremely promising.

This is not the place to tell in detail the history of the 'Fifteen. It is enough to say that its early promise was not fulfilled. The French ships bound for the south of England were dispersed by an untimely gale and the plans for a rising there came to nothing. In Scotland Mar proved disastrous as a military leader. While Argyll, a good and relatively experienced general, very sensibly stayed in Stirling, only once moving out to defend Edinburgh against a not very determined Jacobite attack. Bobbing John, in spite of the opportunities open to him, simply lingered on in Perth. Finally, after six weeks of inactivity, the two armies decided to try their luck and on 13 November encountered each other at Sheriffmuir on the bare windswept uplands a couple of miles north-east of Dunblane. The ensuing battle, though bloody, was indecisive. But when it was over Mar fell back again on Perth, while Argyll, for his part, remained firmly before Stirling, thus effectively blocking the road south by which the Jacobites might have hoped to advance. And so, strategically, the result was a gain for the Government. From the north of England, meanwhile, where the response of the English Jacobites had been disappointing, came the news that a Jacobite force had surrendered to Government troops at Preston in Lancashire.

As Argyll rightly appreciated, the deadlock which now ensued favoured the Government. While the Government forces received a steady flow of regular reinforcements, many of Mar's Highlanders, homesick and disappointed at the way things were going, began to melt back into the hills and glens. 'Amongst many good Qualities,' remarked Lord Mar later, speaking from unhappy experience, 'the Highlanders have one unlucky Custom, not easy to be reform'd, which is that generally after an Action they return Home.' Soon Argyll, once so much the weaker numerically, outnumbered his opponent by three to one.

By the end of the year all hopes of a Jacobite victory had vanished. Late in December, James, after a difficult journey, finally arrived at Peterhead to take command of his troops in person. He was in poor health; the weather was bitterly cold; and some gold sent from Spain had been lost at sea. 'For me,' he told his assembled officers, 'it is no new thing to be unfortunate, since my whole life from my cradle has been a constant series of misfortunes.' Clearly 'Old Mr Melancholy', as the Whigs unkindly called him, was not the leader to rally the spirits of men already discouraged and depressed. 'Some said', wrote an eyewitness, 'the circumstances he found us in dejected him; I am sure the figure he made dejected us.'

The order was now given for a general retreat northwards and, on reaching Aberdeen, James's troops were dismayed to receive from the King a 'Letter of Adieux to the Scotch', thanking them for their services, informing them that he and Mar had set sail for France and advising them to shift for themselves as best they could. The rising, so far as James was concerned, was over. Disconsolately his followers shifted for themselves, some more successfully than others, while the Government, alarmed by what had occurred, took a series of measures calculated to prevent any recurrence of trouble in the Highlands. In addition to a good number of executions and the attempted disarmament of the Highland clans, these included the building of a system of strategic roads designed to facilitate troop movements from one part of the Highlands to another. The task was assigned to George Wade, an English general, who between 1725 and 1740 completed some 250 miles of roads. One, running the length of the Great Glen, linked Fort William with Inverness, another Perth with Inverness and yet another Stirling with Inverness, while a fourth ran from Dalwhinnie in the Grampians across the headwaters of the Spey and climbed 2,500 feet in a series of zigzags to the Pass of Corryarrack before descending to Fort Augustus. Though parts of the Highlands, the west in particular, remained as impenetrable as ever, there could be no doubt that General Wade's roads did much to open up the area as a whole. 'If you'd seen these roads before they were made,' ran a jingle, 'you'd lift up your hands and bless General Wade.'

For James, after this fresh setback, the outlook was anything but promising. The death of Louis XIV of France in September 1715, at the very outset of the rising, had deprived him of his principal friend and protector. The Treaty of Utrecht, which restored peace in Europe, contained a provision expressly binding the French Government to deny him permission to live in France, and on his return from Scotland, early in 1716, the reception he met from the Duke of Orleans, now Regent of France, was openly discouraging: politely but firmly he was told to leave French territory. With what was left of his entourage, he moved to Avignon, then still under Papal rule. But even now George I's Government, who did not want him anywhere in France, let the Pope know that, if he were allowed to stay there, they would bombard the Papal port of Civitavecchia from the sea. And so, from Avignon, James made his way to Italy, eventually coming to rest in June 1717 at Urbino, in the Papal States, where the Pope placed at his disposal the magnificent if chilly pink and brown Palazzo Ducale, looking out from its hilltop across the olive and vine-covered hills of the Marche.

Despite his many misfortunes, James still believed in the possibility of a restoration. But the experience of the 'Fifteen had convinced him that any new attempt to win back his kingdom must have effective foreign support. The attitude of the Regent had made it clear enough that he could not expect such support from France, while what at first seemed a promising scheme to obtain help from King Charles XII of Sweden came to nothing. But in the summer of 1718 James found a new sponsor. A realignment, indeed a reversal, of alliances had taken place in Europe, for although France and England were on better terms with each other, the relations of both with Spain had deteriorated. The Treaty of Utrecht, which had largely resolved their mutual differences, had deprived Spain of her possessions in Italy and the Netherlands. This had caused Philip V's Government to review their position and, on a number of grounds, Cardinal Alberoni, Philip's exceptionally able Minister, had arrived at the conclusion that, in the prevailing international situation, a Stuart restoration in Britain would be in his country's best interest. He accordingly informed James of his readiness to send a Spanish army to invade Great Britain. Discussions between the Spanish Government and the exiled Jacobite court were opened and plans made. By mid-January 1719 both Great Britain and France had declared war on Spain. In March, after further discussion and preparation, James left for Spain with the object of accompanying the proposed expedition.

The major part of the expeditionary force, consisting of five warships and twenty-two transports carrying 5,000 men under the command of the Jacobite Duke of Ormonde and weapons for 30,000 more, was destined for the West of England where it was firmly hoped there would be a strong response to a Jacobite call to arms. A much smaller force, under three prominent Scottish Jacobites, George Keith, the Earl Marischal, the Mackenzie Earl of Seaforth, and the Marquess of Tullibardine, was to go to Scotland to raise the loyal clans. But yet again James was dogged by ill luck. On 29 March a storm dispersed the main expedition and the idea of invading England was abandoned. The smaller expedition, which had left independently, eventually reached Loch Alsh in Kintail on the West Coast of Scotland, where in April some arms and a few hundred Spanish soldiers were duly landed at Eilean Donan.

This was Mackenzie country. Lord Seaforth now put himself at the head of his clan. A delay of some weeks ensued while the neighbouring clans debated whether or not to rise and the Government mustered some regular troops, a few Swiss and Dutch mercenaries and a number of Whig clansmen to help handle the situation. Finally on 10 June, James's thirty-first birthday and almost two months after the landing,

8

a minor engagement took place in nearby Glenshiel. In the course of this a Government force of about 1,000 from Inverness, capably led by Major-General Joseph Wightman, used their four small mortars to good effect on Eilean Donan Castle; the Spaniards, after withstanding the mortar fire as long as they could, surrendered; a landing party from one of five Government ships, which had by now appeared on the scene, captured the castle; the loyal clans faded back into the hills, taking with them such arms as they could for possible future use; and Lord Seaforth and his companions took ship to Spain. 'Farewell to Mackenzie, High Chief of Kintail', sang his loyal clansmen gloomily as their Chief departed, the chorus of their sad little song neatly matching the double pull upon the oars of his departing galley. Or so it is said.

James, in the meanwhile, had been hovering about uneasily in Spain, waiting to sail. On learning what had happened, he returned somewhat disconsolately to Italy, where, in his absence, he had been married by proxy.

James's bride had been picked for him the year before by Charles Wogan, a dashing young Irish adventurer who had fought as a boy in the 'Fifteen, later escaping from Newgate Prison, and who, after an extensive tour of Europe, had in the end recommended the sixteen-year-old Clementina Sobieska as the prettiest and in other respects the most suitable of Prince James Sobieski's three available daughters. Of Clementina's two sisters the elder, Casimire, Wogan reported, was 'astonishingly solemn'; the next, Charlotte, was 'beyond all measure gay'; while Clementina herself was 'sweet, amiable, of an even temper and only gay in season'. In addition to these assets, Clementina brought with her a dowry of 25 million francs and the immensely valuable Sobieski rubies. On the strength of the description brought back to him by the discerning Wogan, James readily accepted the latter's choice.

Pressure was now brought to bear from London on Clementina's cousin, the Emperor, to forbid the marriage. This he did, with the result that she and her mother were arrested and held prisoner in a convent in Innsbruck on their way to Italy. But in the end, thanks to a series of ingenious stratagems worthy of a French farce and to the cooperation of an obliging lady's maid called Jeanneton, who at the last moment had been left behind in the convent in place of Clementina, the bride and her mother had been rescued in the middle of the night in a snowstorm by Wogan and three other Irishmen, Gaydon, Misselt and a blue-eyed giant called O'Toole; carried across the Brenner 'in a strong coach', and, after 'a Melancholy Variety of Ugly Accidents', brought safely to Bologna, where on 9 May 1719, the marriage by proxy took place and whence Clementina continued her journey to Rome.

James himself did not return to Italy from Spain until the end of August when a second marriage ceremony took place and James duly knighted the four Irishmen. The Pope, who still recognized James as legal king of Great Britain and Ireland, now placed at his disposal the Palazzo Muti, a capacious but, compared to the Palazzo Odescalchi next door, relatively undistinguished late Renaissance palace tucked away at one end of the Piazza dei Santissimi Apostoli and closely adjoining the colonnaded basilica of that name, newly rebuilt in the baroque manner. It was here that sixteen months later the long-awaited heir to the House of Stuart was born, while a Papal guard kept watch outside.

Despite the gloomy prognostications of Baron von Stosch, Charles quickly grew into a sturdy infant. 'Really a fine, promising child,' wrote the Duke of Marlborough's son, Lord Blandford, who saw him while on a visit to Rome in May 1721 and, by his own admission, kissed the little Prince's hand. Whereupon the young Whig nobleman was told by Clementina amid much laughter and what Charles Wogan would have called seasonable gaiety that 'the day would come that he should not be sorry to have made so early an acquaintance with her son'. Before leaving England Lord Blandford had been strongly urged to avoid all contact with the exiled court while in Rome. But his curiosity seems to have got the better of his discretion and in the end he became a frequent guest at the Palazzo Muti, where, he reports, 'there is every day a regular table of ten or twelve covers well served ... supplied with English and French cookery, French and Italian wines'. He was impressed, too, by James himself. 'He talks', he wrote, 'with such an air of sincerity that I am apprehensive I should become half a Jacobite, if I continued following these discourses any longer.'

Others who frequented the exiled court were likewise much taken with the little Prince's sturdiness and other qualities. In 1723 Colonel John Hay, a brother of Lord Kinnoul who had been out in the 'Fifteen and was now a member of James's household, described Charles as 'the finest child in the world, healthy and strong, speaks everything and runs about from morning till night'. 'He is a great musician,' wrote Hay the following year, 'and plays on his violin continually: no porter's child in the country has stronger legs and arms, and he makes good use of them, for he is continually in motion. You may easily imagine what amusement he gives to his Father and Mother; and indeed they have little other diversion.'

Inevitably the Prince's upbringing presented problems. James held decided views on the qualities required of a royal governess or nurse. When the baby was only four months old, he sent for Mrs Sheldon, the daughter of one of his father's equerries, in place apparently of a first nurse, Mrs Hughes, whom he now judged 'not bigg enough' for the task. 'The qualities of a person for so important a charge', he wrote to Mar on 1 April 1721, 'are obvious. The better born she be, the better, but what is above all requisite is prudence, a reasonable knowledge of the world, and a principle of obedience, attachment and submission to me, which may put her above private envies or factions.'

In practice it did not work out like that. First Mrs Hughes and then Mrs Sheldon, who quickly managed to ingratiate herself with Clementina, displayed a marked talent for mischief-making and intrigue, causing in their petty way endless trouble between James and his wife. There was even talk of a wild scheme, in which Mrs Hughes seems to have been involved, to send the infant Prince, or possibly a look-alike, to Scotland. Before long John Hay had 'a notion of the impossibility of women's ever agreeing together' and in February 1722 he reported to Mar that the King 'is resolved to meddle no more in these matters'.

But James, who was conscientious to a fault, could not but concern himself with his son's education. And once again this brought him into conflict with his teenaged wife, whose sweetness, amiability and even temper were by this time beginning to wear a trifle thin. Devout Roman Catholic though he was, James wisely believed that, as the future monarch of a Protestant country, Charles should grow up with Protestants round him as well as Catholics. 'It should never be my business', he wrote, 'to become an Apostle, but a good King of all my subjects.' Clementina, though she seems to have taken a different line with Lord Blandford, wanted her son's education to be entrusted exclusively to Roman Catholics. Egged on by the strongly Catholic Mrs Sheldon, who had become her confidante and whom James now dismissed, she conceived a strong dislike for the three principal members of her husband's household, all of whom were in one way or another concerned with Charles's education. These were John Hay, whom James had created Earl of Inverness and appointed his Secretary of State in Exile in place of Mar; Hay's wife Marjorie or Marcelle, a daughter of Lord Stormont, whom the vigilant Baron von Stosch, malicious as ever, describes as 'a mere coquette, tolerably handsome, but withal prodigiously vain and arrogant'; and finally Mrs Hay's brother, James Murray, who now became Charles's governor or tutor, receiving the Earldom of Dunbar. Though later to turn Catholic, all three were at this time still Protestants, though Sir Thomas Sheridan, thought to be the son of a bastard daughter of James VII and II, who now became Charles's sub-governor, was a strong Catholic. By special dispensation of the Pope, James also kept in Rome two Protestant chaplains and a Protestant chapel, for the benefit of the Protestant members of his entourage. It was thus perhaps only natural that when at the age of four Prince Charles noisily refused to kneel when presented to the new Pope in the gardens of the Vatican, some saw in this a sign of precocious Protestantism.

Clementina, who in March 1725 had belied the prophecies of Baron von Stosch by giving birth to another healthy son, christened Henry Benedict by the Pope himself, now declared somewhat dramatically that James was having her children brought up as Protestants and that she would herself sooner stab them to death than allow this to happen. At the same time she announced, with how much truth it is impossible to say, that the 'tolerably handsome' Lady Inverness had become her husband's mistress and that, unless he at once dismissed the Hays and James Murray and reinstated Mrs Sheldon, she would leave him. Characteristically James replied with a long, carefully reasoned but not very tactful letter, explaining that he had endured her 'poutings' patiently, informing her that he 'awaited her submission with open arms', and inviting her to 'return to reason, to duty, to yourself and to me'. To this Clementina predictably retorted that she would 'rather suffer death than live with people that have no religion, honour or conscience', and on 15 November left the Palazzo Muti to take refuge in the architecturally attractive and pleasantly situated Convent of St Cecilia on the other side of the Tiber.

Not surprisingly the scandal caused by Clementina's dramatic departure echoed round Europe, greatly to the delight of James's enemies and to the dismay of his friends. Nor were things improved by his decision to publish his private correspondence with his wife, a gesture which, as one of his supporters hastened to point out, was not 'very suitable to the King's dignity'. In Rome there were, needless to say, many who inclined to take Clementina's side and believe her version of the story, and on the day after she left Palazzo Muti Pope Benedict himself sent round a Bishop to inform James that His Holiness would tolerate neither the education of the two little princes as Protestants nor his 'concubinage with Lady Inverness'. This was too much for James, who, in reply, robustly invited His Holiness to mind his own business, remarking that, had he taken his message seriously, the Bishop would have 'run the risk of leaving the house by the window instead of the staircase'.

But James was to be given no peace. The Pope's message was followed by a long and no less offensive communication from the Queen of Spain. As for Cardinal Alberoni, the sponsor of the ill-fated venture of 1719, he actually came in person to protest and, on being told by the King that he was forgetting himself, rose to his feet in a fury, tearing his Cardinal's robes on the arms of his chair as he did so and finally leaving with the wounding retort that, having always spoken the truth in the presence of the most powerful sovereigns, he was not to be intimidated by a king without a country. In the lovely cloisters of St Cecilia, meanwhile, or so Baron von Stosch was informed by the brother of one of the nuns, 'the Princess wept freely and used very exaggerated language in her first explosion of anger', thereby 'filling the Convent with alarm'. 'I cannot answer for myself,' wrote James in despair, 'that I may not finally take some violent step to release myself from the infamous tyranny of a wife ... who knows how to cover her true positions to the public by the finest dissimulation and hypocrisy.' Gone by now was that attractive 'gaiety in season' by which Charles Wogan had set such store.

Despite more or less helpful attempts at mediation by various well-wishers, including the Pope (on whom James, it must be remembered, depended for his pension), the months went by and Clementina did not return. The scandal grew ever greater. Nor did James help matters by appearing publicly at the opera with the coquettish Lady Inverness. By the end of March 1727, James, whose dynastic hopes were momentarily raised by the death in that year of George I, and John Hay had reluctantly decided that they must part. Another Jacobite exile, Sir John Graeme, took the latter's place as Secretary of State and in August James and his consort were finally reconciled. Clementina had gained her point in the end. But her nerves and temper were still badly frayed; her health soon broke down completely; she became with time more unbalanced and more devout than ever, even causing gossip among the scandal-loving Romans by driving out in public with the new Pope Clement XIII, for whom she had conceived a purely spiritual passion. By October 1730, James, in despair, was wishing that he could find some 'prudent means of separation'.

Such was the ambiance in which little Prince Charles was brought up, against the wider background of Papal Rome, an ambiance of tension, mischief-making and intrigue, of petty plots and squabbles between scheming governesses and priests and idle, frustrated exiles. 'No place for an honest man,' was the Earl Marischal's brusque description of the Palazzo Muti. And it is not hard to see what he meant.

But Charles, for all this, grew up a bright, good-looking, active little boy, spending his summers in better air at the Palazzo Savelli on its hillside at Albano looking out across open country to the Mediterranean. 'The Prince of Wales', wrote his cousin the Duke of Liria, son of James's natural brother the Duke of Berwick, 'was now six and a half and, besides his great beauty, was remarkable for dexterity, grace and almost supernatural address. Not only could he read fluently, he could ride, could fire a gun; and, more surprising still, I have seen him take a cross-bow and kill birds on the roof and split a rolling ball with a bolt ten times in succession. He speaks English, French and Italian perfectly and altogether is the most ideal Prince I have ever met in my life.' And a few months later James Edgar, a member of James's household, gave an equally enthusiastic description. 'The eldest', he wrote, 'improves daily in body and mind to the admiration and joy of everybody. As to his studies, he reads English now correctly, and has begun to learn to write. He speaks English perfectly well and the French and Italian very little worse. He has a stable of little horses and every day almost diverts himself by riding. Chevalier Geraldin is his riding master. He is almost alert in all his exercises, such as shooting, the tennis, shuttlecock, etc. And a gentleman in town has prepared a *caccia* of pigeons and hares to be shot by him this afternoon. You would be surprised to see him dance, nobody probably does it better, and he bore his part at the balls in the carnival as if he were already a man.' In the evening, when there were no blackbirds for him to aim at, he would practise his marksmanship on the bats as they skimmed silently across the twilight sky. From Paris two dozen shuttlecocks and two racquets were ordered for him. But 'his favourite diversion', we learn, was 'the Golf' while another correspondent was told that 'it would very agreeably surprise you to see him play so well at it'.

In the summer of 1727, after his mother's eventual return to the Palazzo Muti, Charles, in a large, clear hand, wrote his first letter to his father who, on learning of George I's death, had gone to France to see how the land lay – only to be tactfully but promptly sent back again by the French Government.

Dear Papa,
    I thank you mightily for your kind letter. I shall strive to obey you in all things. I will be very dutifull to Mamma, and not jump too near her. I shall be much obliged to the Cardinal for his animals. I long to see you soon and in good health.
                    I am, dear Papa,
             Your most dutifull and affectionate son,
                            Charles P.

But, in contrast to his younger brother Henry, Charles seems to have had no great liking for learning or scholarship or indeed for writing letters. 'It is impossible to get him to apply to any study as he ought to do,' complained James Murray. His taste inclined on the whole to less intellectual pursuits. Although English was regularly spoken at the Palazzo Muti, Charles was to speak it all his life with a distinct foreign accent, while his spelling, in English, French and Italian alike, was deplorable. In 1728 a Mr Stafford became his tutor with

James Murray still in the offing. Five years later, in 1733, we hear from that shrewd observer, the Earl Marischal, that he has 'got out of the hands of his governors'. And in October of the same year Baron von Stosch, with his ear to the ground as usual, sent back to London sensational reports of the teenage Prince threatening James Murray with violence and having consequently been confined to his room and deprived of all offensive weapons. 'He had,' noted another, less prejudiced, observer, 'an overmastering passion for the profession of arms' – in many ways an advantage, but on occasion clearly an embarrassment.

The year 1734 was to be a landmark in Charles's life. In an attempt to drive the Emperor Charles VI from his kingdom of Naples and Sicily, the Spaniards under Don Carlos, the younger son of the King of Spain and now himself the self-declared King of Naples, were at this time besieging the Emperor's troops in Gaeta. In June Charles received from his cousin the Duke of Liria, who had recently succeeded his father as Duke of Berwick and was now serving with the Spanish army in Italy, an invitation to visit him at the front less than a hundred miles south of Rome. The fourteen-year-old Prince was naturally delighted and even his father, recalling his own warlike exploits, seemed pleased at the prospect. 'He is to be absolutely incognito', James wrote on 24 July, 'under my old name the Chevalier de St George.' The Pope, James recorded, was *attendri* when Charles took leave of him, 'but', James adds sadly, 'gave me no money on this occasion'.

Charles left Rome for Gaeta on 30 July and James sent him 'my blessing, with all the tenderness I am capable of', and hoped that he might 'one day be both a great and a good man'. With the Prince went James Murray and Thomas Sheridan, four servants, a surgeon and two friars, the latter presumably to attend to his spiritual welfare.

On his arrival Charles was received by Don Carlos with royal honours as Prince of Wales, at once appointed a General of Artillery and paid a welcome 1,000 crowns a month. That the young Prince took his military duties seriously soon became evident. No sooner had he arrived than he was begging to be allowed to go into the firing line and, when Gaeta surrendered on 6 August, he was actually serving in the trenches before the town.

'The siege of Gaeta is now over, blessed be God,' wrote the Duke of Berwick to his half-brother. 'Though a very short one, I suffered more whilst it lasted than in any siege I had been heretofore at. You may easily imagine the uneasiness I talk of was my anxiety and concern for the person of the Prince of Wales. The King, his father, had sent him hither under my care to witness the siege, and laid his commands on me not only to direct him, but even to show him everything that merited his attention. And I must confess that he made me pass some uneasy moments as ever I met with from the crossest accidents of my past life. Just at his arrival I conducted him to the trenches, where he showed not the least concern at the enemy's fire, even when the balls were hissing about his ears. I was relieved the day following from the trenches, and as the house I lodged in was very much exposed, the enemy discharged at once five pieces of cannon against it, which made me move my quarters. The Prince arriving a moment after would at any rate go into the house, though I did all I could to dissuade him from it, by representing to him the danger he was exposing himself to, yet he stayed in it a very considerable time with an undisturbed countenance, though the walls had been pierced through with the cannon balls. In a word, this Prince discovers that in great Princes whom nature has marked out for heroes, valour does not wait for number of years. I am now, blessed by God, rid of all my uneasiness, and joyfully indulge myself in the pleasure of seeing the Prince adored by officers and soldiers. His manner and conversation are really bewitching, and you may lay your account that were it otherwise I would not have kept it a secret from you. We set out for Naples in a day or two, where I am pretty certain His Royal Highness will charm the Neapolitans as much as he has done our troops. The King of Naples [Don Carlos] is much taken with his polite behaviour, and there is not the least necessity of suggesting to him what is either proper for him to do or to say. I wish to God that some of the greatest sticklers in England against the family of the Stuarts had been eye-witnesses of this Prince's resolution during that siege, and I am firmly persuaded that they would soon change their way of thinking. In his very countenance I discover something so happy that presages to him the greatest felicity.'

Following the fall of Gaeta Charles went on by sea to Spanish-occupied Naples at the invitation of Don Carlos. On the way there, it is said, his hat blew off into the sea, but when the crew started lowering a boat to pick it up, he told them to leave it, as he 'should be obliged before long to go and fetch himself a hat in England' – an early hint of a purpose that from now onwards would continually be uppermost in his mind.

In Naples he was made much of by Don Carlos and his nobles, provided with a royal escort of fifty soldiers, an officer and a flag, and sent home early in September 'rich and opulent with two splendid horses given him by the King of Naples and numerous jewels'.

Not unnaturally the fourteen-year-old's military experiences seem to have gone straight to his head. While in camp, he had made himself ill by overeating and had written to his father only one short note,

16

which was so full of spelling mistakes that he had had to copy it out again. ('Wonderfully thoughtless for one of his age', wrote his father.) Back in Rome he was reprimanded by James, who had already written suggesting that he should be 'more temperate in his dyet'. As a result 'he was in penance again yesterday, but things went better today'. But for the fourteen-year-old Charles the siege of Gaeta marked the end of childhood and the beginning of manhood. 'Everybody', wrote Baron von Stosch, 'says that he will be in time a far more dangerous enemy to the present establishment of the Government of England than ever his father was.'

For some years now Charles's parents had been more or less re-conciled and were again living quite peaceably together at the Palazzo Muti or in the summers at the Palazzo Savelli on the hillside at Albano. Clementina was by this time even on reasonably friendly terms with the Hays. That September she drove out to meet Charles on his return from Gaeta, bringing with her his brother Harry, who, though only nine, was deeply indignant at having missed the fighting.

But already the Queen's asthma had become worse and her husband feared the winter for her. By the end of 1734 she was going downhill fast. Her health, James wrote early in January 1735, 'grows worse and worse, as she is now at the last extremity'. 'The Queen', he wrote on 12 January, 'received the *viatique* this morning. She is perfectly in her senses, and dies with a tranquillity, a piety, and a peace which is, with reason, a great comfort to me in my present situation.' To the end, James and both Princes were continually with her, praying at her bedside. On 18 January she died, at the age of thirty-three, leaving in her will a small gift to the Hays. Her funeral at St Peter's was a magnificent one. Pope Benedict himself bore the expense; it was attended by no less than thirty-two Cardinals; and the candles burnt weighed no less than 13,000 pounds. Later the Pope erected a fine monument to her and for many years miracles of healing were attri-buted to her intercession. Her heart the Franciscans enshrined sep-arately in a fine Baroque urn supported by hovering cherubs in the Basilica dei Santissimi Apostoli, only a hundred yards or so from the gloomy palace which for the past fifteen years had been her home.

Charles was by now fifteen. For the time being there was little he could do besides amuse himself and continue his education. 'Make my compliments to him', wrote the soundly Jacobite and notoriously dissolute Duke of Wharton in a message to James Murray, 'and desire him that he will not only train the Prince for glory, but likewise give him a polite taste for pleasurable vice.' There is, however, no indication that this sage advice was ever taken.

In the spring of 1737, with the idea of widening his horizons, James sent Charles on a tour of the states of northern Italy, during the whole of which his movements were watched with close attention by Baron von Stosch and other agents of the British Government. With him went James Murray, to whom he seems to have been consistently rude, old Sir Thomas Sheridan, two younger companions, Henry Goring and Francis Strickland, and a suite of twelve attendants, of whom at least five were in livery. Though he travelled nominally incognito as Count of Albany, his identity was an open secret and his tour soon developed into a triumphal progress. This time the Pope, on bidding him farewell, had made a handsome contribution to his expenses, enabling him to do things in proper style. At Bologna, where he spent two days, he was greeted by a deputation from the Senate; a guard of honour was placed at his disposal and a great ball given for him at the Palazzo Tibbia. At Piacenza, at Genoa and at Milan there were no less lavish entertainments and again he was the centre of interest. He had, we are told, become 'the fashionable idol at the moment'.

From Milan Charles went to Venice where he was accorded the full honours due to royalty. He was received by the Doge in person and attended the Assembly of the Grand Council, and throughout his stay the French Ambassador's gorgeous gondola was placed at his disposal. His next stopping-place was Florence, the capital of the Grand Duchy of Tuscany, where he arrived on 23 June to stay at the Palazzo Corsini. But by this time the British Government were seriously disturbed at the success Charles was having and had begun to react. The Venetian Envoy in London was given three days in which to leave England; a sharp reprimand was administered to the Republic of Genoa; and, before Charles's arrival in Florence, Mr Fane, the British Minister there, called on the Grand Duke's Secretary to make a formal request that his visit should not be made the occasion of official celebrations. Having received the assurances he had asked for, Mr Fane was nevertheless distressed to learn that on Charles's arrival the Grand Duke's state coaches had after all been sent out to meet him. This, he was assured, on hurrying round again to protest, had been a mistake and in the event the Grand Duke did not receive Charles. But, though the Grand Duke reluctantly agreed to remain aloof, the enthusiastic reception the Prince was given by the rest of Florentine society more than made up for this and Charles's journey back to Rome by way of Lucca, Pisa and Leghorn continued triumphal. For once Charles sent back occasional letters to his father. 'I am pleased with your writing,' wrote the latter. 'A little custom and application will soon make you write well, both for spelling and sense.'

Charles was by now almost eighteen and remarkably handsome. His long hair had been cut and replaced by a wig and on his seventeenth birthday he had been shaved for the first time. From his earliest childhood he had been brought up to regard himself as the rightful heir to the British throne. In the words of the Jesuit Cordara, he had been 'reared from infancy never to forego the desire or the hope of recovering the Crown'. Nothing interested him so much as tales of his grandfather's campaign in Ireland in 1690, of the 'Fifteen and the loyalty of 'his brave Scotch'. As he had shown at Gaeta, he himself was a youth of spirit. Little wonder that, in the words of the perceptive Charles de Brosses, President of the Parliament of Dijon, he felt 'deeply the oppressive character of his present position, and, should he not one day be relieved from that oppression, a want of enterprise will certainly not be the cause'. 'Had I soldiers,' the Prince declared, 'I would not be here now, but wherever I could serve my friends.'

The trouble was that he had no soldiers nor any real prospect of again displaying his military prowess. His father was as anxious as he was that he should gain more military experience. But no army would accept him. At the moment neither France nor Spain wanted trouble with the British, if they could avoid it. The Emperor likewise refused to let him join an expedition he was preparing against the Turks. No one outside Italy would employ him and the little Italian States had long since learnt how sensitive the London Government could be on this subject. So Charles was reduced to drawing plans of imaginary fortifications and covering long distances on horseback and on foot to harden himself for a future campaign, should he ever take part in one. A well-planned marriage could equally have furthered his cause, but the various promising matrimonial projects launched during these early years on his behalf came to nothing, including one with his pretty twelve-year-old cousin Louise de la Tour, daughter of his mother's sister Charlotte and of Louis XV's Grand Chamberlain, the Duc de Bouillon. At every step considerations of political expediency seemed to get in the way. It was not even possible for him to visit his mother's family in Poland.

So Charles stayed in Rome and went out shooting or riding in the Campagna, attended the usual round of receptions and balls and dinners, went to the theatre, played the violin (he loved music and had a certain talent for it) and, with his father, received any British visitors who called to pay their respects, while all the time Baron von Stosch kept watch and reported on their every move. The visitors were a mixed lot. There was Charles's illegitimate great-aunt, the aged and eccentric Duchess of Buckingham, who could only talk of plots. And Lord Elcho, the eldest son of Lord Wemyss, a loyal Jacobite, who, however, preferred to live in Paris and keep out of disturbances at home. Elcho, at this time on the Grand Tour, was a year younger than Charles and had been educated at Winchester 'with', we are told, 'a taste for pleasurable vice' (evidently considered a *sine qua non* for any well-bred youth). James made the two young men stand back-to-back to see who was the taller. To the Palazzo Muti at this time came likewise young John Murray of Broughton in Peebleshire, bright, ambitious, penniless and of sound Jacobite stock, who quickly became a close friend and confidant, and was later to be appointed Secretary for Scottish Affairs and serve as a link with leading Jacobites in Scotland.

President Charles de Brosses who, like Lord Blandford a score of years earlier, dined at James's table, which he found to be 'always laid for eleven', tells how the two Princes knelt to ask their father's blessing before taking their seats. 'The dinners', he writes, 'are not amusing. If they chance to become so, the King appears well pleased ... he speaks little.' He also describes James's 'sad and simple look' and calls him 'devout to excess', while the poet Thomas Gray, who was clearly no Jacobite, declares unkindly that he had 'extremely the looks and air of an idiot particularly when he laughs or prays ... the first he does not often, the latter continually'. Yet another Englishman describes the appearance of the two Princes at a masked ball at the Palazzo Bolognetti, 'two as fine youths as ever I saw, in their masquerade habits of two young Shepherds, very rich, white silk hats with Diamond Loops and Buttons, bankes of White Ribbands at their knees and shoes'. James, in his way, was proud of both his sons. 'My children', he declared, 'give me a great deal of comfort.'

In February 1741 Lady Mary Wortley Montague observed that both Princes were 'very richly adorned with jewels', while James's Secretary, James Edgar, has left us a description of Charles at a ball at the Palazzo Pamphili wearing a kilt that had been sent him from Scotland by the Duke of Perth – 'masked in a fine complete Highland Dress, which became him very well'. All of which the egregious Stosch busily reported to London, observing of Charles's Highland dress that, 'being a costume unknown in Italy, it attracted considerable attention', and adding that Charles, conscious of this, 'swaggered about the rooms, and chatted in terms of enthusiasm about Scotland and his people'.

But for the young Prince life in Rome had, with the years, become increasingly irksome. He does not seem to have possessed that 'polite taste for pleasurable vice' which the Duke of Wharton would have liked to see instilled in him and which might have provided some welcome distractions. Field sports were almost his only real pleasure. In a letter dated 1 October 1742 his father describes him as 'quite wearied of this country'. 'I don't wonder at it', he adds, 'for his sole amusement here is to go out shooting, to which he has gone every other day during all this season before daybreak, whether fair or foul, and has killed a great deal of game, such as this place affords.' And, in the same letter, he goes on to speak of his son's unflagging energy: 'I doubt if you could find many that would not tyre with the constant fatigue and exercise he takes.' 'No fatigue and no exercise', writes Edgar, 'does HRH any harm, on the contrary he is always ye better for it.' Clearly Charles was well fitted to withstand any hazards and hardships that the future might hold for him. 'What a pleasure it would be', wrote James Edgar in a letter to the Earl Marischal, 'to see better game than the shooting of quails.'

CHAPTER TWO

But now at long last events in Europe were beginning to move in a direction which offered more hope of the opportunity for action which the young Prince so fervently desired. In October 1740 the Emperor Charles VI of Austria had died, leaving as heiress to the Imperial Throne his daughter Maria Theresa. Despite all the Emperor's efforts to buttress his daughter's claim by means of the Pragmatic Sanction, his death immediately threw open the whole tormented question of the Austrian succession. In December Frederick II of Prussia, 'in order that he might rob a neighbour whom he had promised to defend', invaded Silesia. Following his example, Bavaria, Saxony, Spain and, needless to say, Naples all laid claim to different parts of the unfortunate young Empress's dominions, while in January 1742 the Elector Charles Albert of Bavaria boldly assumed the imperial title as Emperor Charles VII. Soon most of Europe was involved in the dispute.

It could by now only be a matter of time before France and Britain, between whom, thanks to the sustained efforts of Sir Robert Walpole and Cardinal Fleury, a sometimes uneasy peace had been maintained for the past twenty years, were drawn into the conflict on opposing sides. France, welcoming an opportunity to harm Austria, hastened to support Bavaria's claims against her. King George II, for his part, embraced the cause of Maria Theresa. Having in May 1742 sent a British force to the Netherlands, he proceeded in person to Germany and there assumed command of a joint Anglo-Hanoverian force to be known as the Pragmatic Army. In June 1743 this encountered and, despite George's somewhat inept generalship, defeated a French army at Dettingen; though Britain and France were still not officially at war, their respective armies had now actually met in battle.

For some time desultory exchanges had been taking place between the French Government and various representatives of the Jacobite interest. From 1739 a channel of communication between James in Rome, Louis xv's minister Cardinal Fleury and leading Jacobites in Britain and more particularly in Scotland had been provided by an odd assortment of Jacobite exiles in France, amongst them John Murray of Broughton, John Gordon of Glenbucket, popularly known as Old Glenbucket, Robert Sempill, the son of an officer in the French service, whom James had made a Lord, and the ruffianly William MacGregor (or, as he was forced to call himself, his own name being banned, Drummond) of Balhaldie, Chief, in so far as there was one, of Clan Gregor, 'a low-lifed fellow void of truth', who was reputed to have stolen the Earl Marischal's baggage after Sheriffmuir and to be 'master of as much bad French as to procure himself a whore and a dinner'. In Scotland, meanwhile, a Jacobite Association or Concert of Gentlemen had been formed which included the titular Duke of Perth (the title had been bestowed on his grandfather by James vii and ii, Perth's uncle Lord John Drummond, Cameron of Lochiel, Lord Lovat, the Earl of Traquair and others. But, though ready to talk to the Jacobites, the cautious and peace-loving Cardinal Fleury had in the event given them little actual support. 'The French Government', reported Baron von Stosch, with some justification, 'are using the Pretender and his followers like so many marionettes, making them dance to any tune which suits the interests of France.'

But now French interest was growing keener. In March 1741, after a visit to Scotland, Balhaldie had brought back with him a signed assurance from the Associators, as they were called, of their readiness to resort to arms, together with a not unimpressive list of potential supporters. As early as 1742 there had been talk of French landings in Scotland and England. The Associators had been instructed to hold themselves in readiness and for weeks George Keith, the Earl Marischal, whom James had hopefully appointed his Commander-in-Chief for Scotland, had sat patiently at Boulogne-sur-Mer, 'waiting', as he put it, 'for the Angel to stir the Pool'. In the event nothing had come of this particular project, but in January 1743, Cardinal Fleury who, when it came to the point, was still reluctant to go to war with Britain, had died and his place now seemed likely to be taken for a time by Cardinal Pierre de Tencin. Cardinal de Tencin largely owed his success in life to his sister, Claudine, rightly described as *'une des femmes les plus galantes, les plus intrigantes et les plus intelligentes de son temps'*, which, when it is recalled that we are talking of the eighteenth century, was saying a good deal. A defrocked nun who, realizing she had missed her true vocation, became mistress in turn to the Regent, to Cardinal

Dubois, to Argenson, to Fontenelle and to many others, she remained throughout devoted to her brother Pierre, loving him, some said, with a more than sisterly love, and doing everything in her power (which was considerable) to further his career in politics, in high finance and in the Church.

It was, however, to the titular King James, sitting quietly in the Palazzo Muti with his two teenage sons and attending to his never-ceasing correspondence, that Pierre de Tencin actually owed the Cardinal's hat bestowed on him in 1739. For James by now knew his way round the Vatican and was always on the lookout for useful friends at court and elsewhere. And for the newly-appointed Cardinal what better way could there be, when the time came, of showing his gratitude and indeed making his presence felt in politics and elsewhere than by promoting the restoration of the Catholic Stuarts to a throne that was rightfully theirs? Cardinal de Tencin's influence was in fact soon to wane. Louis xv, who now announced that he intended to be his own First Minister, had never liked the 'roués de la Régence', as he called them, and, as for Claudine de Tencin, she gave him, he declared, 'the gooseflesh'. But for the time being, Tencin was still there as a Minister without portfolio, a valuable ally and confidant for the end-lessly plotting Jacobite agents and exiles in Paris. To Louis and to Amelot, the Foreign Minister, he now proposed an invasion of Britain, which Charles would lead. 'If he landed in Scotland, with a reasonable escort of troops to regain his ancient patrimony', he wrote enthusi-astically, 'all Scotland would fly to arms and a large part of England would come under Scottish rule.' From the French point of view, the outbreak of actual hostilities between France and Great Britain had already made the Jacobites a considerably more interesting proposition. Accordingly the plans were revived for a French landing in Great Britain in support of a Jacobite rising. In the spring of 1743 Francis Sempill brought to the French Ministry of Foreign Affairs a formal request for armed intervention, this time from a number of leading English Jacobites, notably the Duke of Beaufort, Sir Watkin Williams Wynn, Sir John Hynde Cotton, Lord Orrery and Sir Robert Abdy. A French agent, sent to Britain to form an estimate of the strength of the Jacobite movement, reported favourably and in November 1743 firm orders were given to make ready the shipping required for an expeditionary force to be launched without any previous declaration of war.

Early in December, thirty-eight transports were assembled at Dunkirk ready to carry some 12,000 men under Marshal Saxe, while an escorting force of twenty-two ships of the line gathered at Brest under Admiral de Roquefeuil. At the same time an expeditionary force of 3,000 men was to be sent to Scotland under the command of the Earl Marischal. Half of these were to land at Inverness, where, it was hoped, they would be joined by Lovat and his Frasers, and the other half on the West coast, where the Macleans, MacDonalds and Mac-Leods would also rise and eventually join forces with the Frasers.

Meanwhile Amelot had informed Sempill of the project and on 17 December Balhaldie arrived in Rome with an invitation to Charles to come at once to France so as to be ready to accompany the expedition and thus lend legitimacy to what might have seemed an act of unprovoked aggression. The moment for which the young Prince had been waiting all his life seemed to have arrived.

Charles, who had jumped at the opportunity, left Rome before dawn on 9 January 1744, bearing a commission from his father to act as Regent on his behalf when he reached Britain. It was clearly of vital importance that his ultimate destination should remain a secret and a pretended shooting party at Cisterna provided a pretext for his early morning departure from the Palazzo Muti. Once outside the city, Charles, saying that it was too cold to drive, left his coach and, mounting a horse, galloped off in the direction of Albano, while his tutor, James Murray, obligingly caused a diversion by falling off his horse and into a ditch. Having thus shaken off the rest of the party, Charles changed his clothes and wig, and set out as fast as he could for Genoa, accompanied only by a couple of servants. At first he travelled under the guise of a Neapolitan courier and then of a Spanish officer, the necessary passports and post horses for the journey having been provided by the good offices of Cardinal Acquaviva. Meanwhile, in order to keep his departure secret, his brother Henry stayed on at Albano for the next week, sending presents of game to their friends in Rome in Charles's name.

Despite these elaborate precautions, it was not long before Baron von Stosch and Sir Horace Mann, the British Minister in Florence, got wind of Charles's departure and the latter despatched to the Duke of Newcastle in London what purported to be an accurate description of the Prince's physical appearance. 'The young man', he wrote, 'is above the middle height and very thin. He wears a light bag-wig, his face is rather long, the complexion clear, but borders on paleness; the forehead very broad, the eyes fairly large, blue, but without sparkle, the mouth large, with the lips slightly curled, and the chin more sharp than rounded.'

From Genoa, Charles travelled by sea, first to Savona, where, we are told, he was 'locked up and in a very ugly situation', and then, having somehow succeeded in extricating himself, by a Catalan felucca to Antibes, cleverly running unnoticed through the British Mediterranean fleet on the way. From Antibes he posted night and day to Paris, arriving there just eleven days after leaving Rome. His attendants were exhausted by the speed at which he travelled. 'If I had had to go much further', he wrote to his father, 'I should have been obliged to get them ty'd behind the chase with my Portmantle.' Once safely in Paris, Charles spent a fortnight lying low at the house of his father's agent Lord Sempill before continuing to Gravelines on the coast near Dunkirk to wait until the expedition was ready to sail.

It was now February 1744 and at Dunkirk Marshal Saxe, perhaps the greatest military commander of his age, had already begun to embark some 10,000 French troops. His instructions were to await the arrival of the escorting convoy and then sail up the Thames and take London. On 3 March a part of his escort under Admiral de Barailh arrived off Dunkirk. 'I hope in a few days', Charles wrote to his father on 6 March, 'to date my letters from a place which will show of itself that all is finished.'

Well before this, however, news of the intended invasion had reached London and a score of British ships of the line under Admiral Sir John Norris now appeared in the Downs, where they met and headed off another part of Saxe's escort under Admiral Roquefeuil. Then, on 6 March, before any real action could take place, a violent and prolonged storm dispersed the French warships and drove many of the troopships ashore. Most of the transports which had already put to sea were lost with all hands, though that containing Marshal Saxe and the Prince himself somehow survived. As a result, Saxe decided on 11 March that the enterprise must be abandoned. On learning the news, Charles was in despair. '*Ne me convient-il pas mieux*', he said to Saxe, '*d'aller périr, s'il le faut, à la tête de des braves gens, que de traîner une vie languissante dans l'exil et la dépendance?*' And to the Earl Marischal he proposed in vain that they should together charter a fishing smack and sail for Scotland alone.

By now Charles's presence in France and its purpose were common knowledge and a few days later the British Government made a formal protest through a Mr Thompson, whom, though in practice at war, they still retained as their diplomatic representative in Paris, pointing out that it was a clear contravention of the treaties which existed between their two countries and demanding that Prince Charles should at once be required to leave French territory. The French reply to this communication was so 'injurious and offensive' that Mr Thompson received instructions from London to leave France immediately without taking leave. After which, on 20 March, France formally declared war on Britain.

To Charles, still lingering disconsolately at the dreary little town of

Gravelines under the alias of Chevalier Douglas, this formal exchange of declarations of war brought but cold comfort. The French Government, who by April had already begun to make offers of peace to the British and were by now considerably less interested in the Jacobite cause, allowed him to remain in France on their own terms. But that was all. From the French court he received no further encouragement or indeed recognition and, though grudgingly prepared to pay for his keep, Louis xv refused even to see him. There seemed, for the time being at any rate, little prospect that the French would mount another expedition in support of the Jacobites, though the Prince still clung desperately to the hope that they might, while Balhaldie boldly declared that 20,000 Highlanders would rise once Charles gave the word.

Early in April Charles moved back from the coast to 'a pretty little house' with a garden in Montmartre, then on the outskirts of Paris, where he continued to live incognito. '*Le Prince Edouard arriva à Paris la nuit du 5 au 6 avril et s'y tient très caché,*' noted an official of the French Foreign Office. 'I have learned from you', he wrote to his father, 'to bear with disappointments.' And again, on 3 April:

> The situation I am in is very particular, for nobody nose where I am or what is become of me, so that I am entirely Burried as to the publick, and cant but say but that it is a very great constrent upon me, for I am obliged very often not to stur out of my room, for fier of some bodys noing my face. I very often think that you would laugh very hartily if you saw me going about with a single servant bying fish and other things and squabling for a peney more or less. I hope your Majesty will be thoroughly persuaded, that no constrent or trouble whatsoever either of minde or body, will ever stope me in going on with my duty, in doing anything that I think can tend to your service or your Glory....

And, a week later, on 10 April: 'Whether I am free from company or diversions, its all alike to me for I can think of nothing, or taste nothing but your service, which is my Duty...' To which James in due course replied, a trifle discouragingly, begging Charles to 'avoid precipitate and dangerous measures, some rash or ill-conceived project, which would end in your ruin, and that of all those who would join with you in it.'

At this difficult time the men round Charles were of little comfort to him, bickering and intriguing among themselves as exiles and secret emissaries will. Inclined to be negative in his approach, George Keith, the Earl Marischal, perhaps the most balanced and worldly-wise of the exiled Jacobites, soon fell out of favour with the Prince. Remembering his own experiences in 1715 and 1719, Keith had all along strongly

27

discouraged any project likely to involve loyal Highlanders in another hopeless venture without proper support from abroad and, to Charles's disgust, personally intervened to stop him from taking part in the French campaigns in Europe ('dose all that lise in his power to hinder it'), on the grounds that it would be impolitic to fight with the French against his own countrymen. 'He has don all this', wrote Charles angrily, 'without telling me anything of the matter or consulting me about it.'

But, whatever view the Earl Marischal might take, Charles, having reached France, was determined not to turn back without striking a blow for the cause. 'It is my first entry into the world,' he wrote. 'It will get known that I was near the place of embarcation and if I retire without attempting anything, after such fine appearances, the whole world will say that the misfortunes of my family are attached to all its generations.' If he knew he could be of service to England, he wrote to Sempill, he 'would venture thither in an open boat'. Charles was by now staying with Aeneas MacDonald, one of the twenty-three children of MacDonald of Kinlochmoidart, who had set up in Paris as a banker. To Murray of Broughton, who came to Paris from Scotland in July 1744 and whom he met at Aeneas's house situated somewhere behind the stables of the Louvre, he announced 'with great keenness' that he was determined to land in Scotland the following summer, 'if he brought only a single footman'.

Having warned Charles that, if he came alone, not more than 4,000 or 5,000 Jacobites would join him, John Murray returned to Scotland, where in November 1744 he apprised the seven members of the Jacobite Association of the Prince's intentions. The supposedly clandestine meetings of the Association, some of whose members had formed what they called the Buck Club, took place, for the most part, in Edinburgh 'in the tavern under the Piazzas of Parliament Close'. The news of Charles's intended arrival seems to have filled most, if not all, of the Jacobite leaders with dismay. 'Lochiel', we are told, 'thought it a desperate undertaking; Lord Perth thought otherwise.' MacLeod of MacLeod, the Member of Parliament for Inverness-shire, considered 'the Design . . . a very mad one', adding that no one would join Charles, but that he himself would do so if the Prince came over. As MacLeod had been drinking, Murray asked Lochiel to see him next morning when he was sober, in order to find out if he really meant what he said. And MacLeod, whom Murray found still in bed, again declared that, despite the rashness of the undertaking, he would join the Prince if he came, and even gave him a written undertaking to this effect.

Charles, meanwhile, lingered on in France, surrounded by intrigues, trying to sift the reliable information from the unreliable and the loyal

Jacobite agents from the less loyal, trying, finally, with less and less prospect of success to get help from the French. 'You may well imagine', he wrote to his father on 16 November 1744, 'how out of Youmer I am.' But his resolve never weakened. 'Whatever I may suffer', he wrote to James on 3 January 1745, 'I shall not regret in the least as long as I think it of service for our great object. I would put myself in a tub, like Diogenes, if necessary.'

By agreement with the French King and Government, Charles moved in February 1745 to Fitz-James in Picardy, the country seat of his cousin, the Duke of FitzJames, the Duke of Berwick's younger brother, where he could at least find relaxation in the field sports he so much enjoyed. 'It is now', he wrote to his father, with his usual disregard for orthography, 'two months I have not handeled a gun, because of the bad weather and cold, for which I would be called *cacciatore di panbianco* by the Duke (his brother Henry) if he new'it, in revenge for my calling him so formerly. As soon as I am arrived at Fitz-James, I intend to begin again to shute, but not whin it rens.' 'You see by this', he added reassuringly, 'that according as one advanced in years one gets reason.'

At Fitz-James, no more than fourteen leagues north of Paris, on the high road to Calais, Charles was within easy reach of the capital. On his not infrequent visits there, he was able during the months that followed to enjoy such pleasures as it offered, to keep in touch with his new-found friends and relations and above all pursue his plans for what he fervently hoped would prove to be the early future. On occasion, he reported, he would assume the identity of a German baron hastening 'between Balls and business'.

Already in January he had, with the King's permission, made contact with his uncle by marriage, Charles-Godefroy, Duc de Bouillon, Great Chamberlain of France and husband of his mother's sister, Marie Charlotte Sobieska, who had died five years earlier. Likewise with his own first cousins, Charles-Godefroy's young son and heir, Godefroy-Charles, Prince de Turenne and the latter's disturbingly pretty nineteen-year-old sister Louise, who had been married a couple of years earlier to the seventeen-year-old Duc de Montbazon, now serving in the French Army as a captain in the Royal Pologne Regiment. A contemporary and close crony of Louis XV as well as an enthusiast for the Jacobite cause, Charles-Godefroy de Bouillon, who had taken an immediate liking to his nephew, could be an invaluable ally in court and government circles as well as a congenial companion. Something of a rake, he had not long before caused a resounding scandal and greatly upset Marie Charlotte by having a passionate affair with his own attractive young stepmother.

For Charles, separated from his father and brother and dining constantly at the Hotel de Bouillon, his new-found uncle and cousins quickly became a second family. 'I have already seen the D. of Bullion, the P. of Turain and his sister', he informed his father, 'and last night I supt with all that family and after supper I went to the Opera Ball in mask.' 'I am mightely well pleased with the D. of Bullion and his family', he added, 'with their sivilitys and expressions to me.' And again: 'the more I am acquainted with him [the Duc de Bouillon], the more I like him, for he has the best hart in the world'.

In his cousins' congenial company, Charles attended, *'dans le plus grand incognito'*, says the Duc de Luynes somewhat unconvincingly, a whole series of *bals masqués* at the Opera, the Hotel de Ville and at Versailles where the Queen herself made discreet enquiries as to his thinly veiled identity. Meanwhile between Charles and his cousin Louise in particular a sympathy seems to have sprung up perhaps rather stronger than that which is usual between cousins – or so they fancied.

But, whatever counter-attractions there might be, Charles was as determined as ever to press on with the project that still lay nearest his heart, namely his plan to land in Britain when and where he could, with or without adequate support. 'It would be a great comfort to me', he wrote to his father in February, 'to have real business on my hands.'

By the English Jacobites Charles set but little store. 'Our friends in England', he wrote with some justification, 'are affred of their own shaddo, and think of little else than of diverting themselves.' His hopes centred instead on Scotland and in May he despatched Sir Hector Maclean of Duart from France to Edinburgh to announce his early arrival to John Murray of Broughton, the Duke of Perth and the other Associators. But, 'having appeared too publickly' in the city and lingered in Edinburgh longer than was advisable in order to have some new boots and shoes fitted, the notoriously Jacobite Duart was quickly arrested and imprisoned by the authorities. This was a disaster. 'I can safely say', wrote Murray of Broughton, who fully appreciated the importance of both chief and clan to the Jacobite cause, 'it was one of the greatest misfortunes that could have befallen the Prince at that time.'

The Prince's message, duly delivered by Duart shortly before his arrest, still further increased the alarm of those to whom it was addressed. Seriously disturbed, they now despatched to him through Murray of Broughton a letter urging him most strongly not to come – a letter, incidentally, which seems never to have reached its destination.

Many of Charles's companions at this time were Irish. Sir Thomas Sheridan, his former tutor and bastard cousin, now seventy, had come from Rome to join him in France. Another favourite with the Prince was Colonel John William O'Sullivan, a fat, well-fed former seminarist of about forty-five who, having decided he was better suited to be a soldier of fortune than an ecclesiastic, had served for a time in the French army, taking part, he claimed, as a staff officer in some operations in Corsica. 'The Prince', wrote his valet, Michel Vezzosi, 'was never easy but when this agreeable Irishman was with him.' Then there was the Rev George Kelly, an exiled non-juring Protestant clergyman, once secretary to the Jacobite Bishop Atterbury, who, before escaping to France, had spent fourteen years as a prisoner in the Tower of London ('Trick, falsehood, deceit and imposition, joined to the qualities that make up a sycophant are the rules of his policy,' wrote Balhaldie, who had no love for the Irish). And Father Kelly, parson George Kelly's Roman Catholic cousin, who acted on and off as Charles's confessor. The Irish, who had nothing to lose and who quarrelled intermittently with Sempill and Balhaldie and the other Scots round the Prince, were full of enthusiasm for the idea of an expedition. Indeed, in the words of Aeneas MacDonald, the banker, 'the expedition to Scotland was entirely an Irish project'.

Whatever the truth of this, Charles was now making serious plans for his departure. At the end of May 1745 he left Fitz-James for Navarre, near Evreux, the seat of his uncle the Duc de Bouillon, where at the beginning of June he received the news of Maurice de Saxe's great victory over the British and Hanoverian forces at Fontenoy, where the British army, commanded by George II's plump young son the Duke of Cumberland, had only been saved from a complete rout thanks to a stubborn rearguard action fought by the Black Watch, as the newly raised Highland companies were now known.*

Encouraged by the victory, Charles at once started to make active preparations for his own early departure. But first he made a final attempt to win French help. 'Monsieur Mon Oncle,' he wrote to Louis XV, 'Having in vain sought to gain access to Your Majesty in the hope of obtaining from your generosity the help I need to play a part worthy of my birth, I have now decided to make myself known for my own deeds and to undertake alone a course of action the success of which could be guaranteed by quite a small measure of assistance. I flatter myself that Your Majesty will not refuse me this.'

In the absence of effective French support, which clearly remained unlikely, nothing could be done without hard cash. From Mr Waters, his family's banker in Paris, and his son Charles now managed to

---

*'By two o'clock the whole retreated, and we were ordered to cover the retreat of the army, as the only regiment that could be kept to their duty,' wrote Capt. John Munro, of the Black Watch, to Lord President Forbes of Culloden.

borrow 180,000 livres, enough to pay his existing debts and buy the armaments he needed for the expedition: 1,500 muskets, 1,800 broadswords, twenty small field-pieces, as well as 'a good quantity of powder, ball, flints, dirks, brandy, etc.', leaving some 4,000 louis d'or for his privy purse. He likewise directed that his mother's jewels in Rome should be pawned. Antoine Walsh, a rich Franco-Irish merchant, shipowner and slave trader with Jacobite connections living in Nantes, declared himself ready to take the Prince to Scotland in his sixteen-gun trading brig or frigate, the *Du Teillay*, commanded by Captain Darbé. 'The most important service anyone could ever do me', Charles called it. At the same time, the Prince enlisted the services of another Irishman, Walter Ruttledge, who had been given letters of marque by the French to cruise off the coast of Scotland with an old man-of-war, originally British, the *Elisabeth*, carrying sixty-eight guns and a crew of 700, under the command of Captain Douaud. He persuaded Ruttledge to let the *Elisabeth* act as escort to the *Du Teillay* in case she were to be attacked by a British warship. The *Du Teillay* lay at Nantes and the *Elisabeth* at Belle Isle, where she was now loaded with the armament that Charles had been able to collect. Surprisingly, no word of these preparations seems to have reached the French Government, though it is hard to see how they could have failed to realize that something unusual was afoot.

When everything was ready, Charles returned to Paris and invited his friend Aeneas MacDonald to dinner. Aeneas, as it happened, was on the point of leaving for Scotland on legal business. 'I hear', said the Prince casually in the course of the conversation, 'that you are going to Scotland: I am going there too – we had better bear each other company.'

And so it fell out. It was agreed that Aeneas and the other bold spirits who were to join Charles in his desperate venture should precede him to Nantes and there await his arrival. 'After the Prince had settled everything for his subsequent undertaking', writes Aeneas,

> the gentlemen who were to accompany him in his voyage took different routes to Nantes, the place appointed to meet at, thereby the better to conceal their designs. During their residence there, they lodged in different parts of the town; and if they accidentally met in the street, or elsewhere, they took not the slightest notice of each other, nor seemed to be in any way acquainted, if there was any person near enough to observe them. During this time, and whilst everything was preparing to set sail, the Prince went to a seat of the Duke of Bouillon, and took some days' diversion in hunting, fishing, and shooting – amusements he always delighted

in, being at first obliged to it on account of his health. By this means he became inured to toil and labour, which enabled him to undergo the great fatigues and hardships he was afterwards exposed unto.

Charles's companions on what Cameron of Lochiel had called his 'rash and desperate undertaking', the Seven Men of Moidart, as they came to be known, were a strangely assorted little band. In addition to Aeneas MacDonald there was the titular Duke William of Atholl, usually known as Lord Tullibardine, who, having been out in 1715 and again in 1719, had been attainted and deprived of his title and estates in favour of his younger brother James, a staunch Hanoverian now firmly in possession of both. There was Sir Thomas Sheridan, Charles's seventy-year-old Irish tutor; the Rev George Kelly, once secretary to Bishop Atterbury; John William O'Sullivan, the seminarist turned soldier of fortune to whom the Prince was so attached; yet another Irishman, Sir John MacDonald, a lieutenant-colonel of cavalry in the Irish brigade which formed part of the French army; and an Englishman, Colonel Francis Strickland of Sizergh in Westmorland, whose father had followed James VII and II to France. Then there was Antoine Walsh, the Franco-Irish owner of the *Du Teillay*, and Aeneas MacDonald's ex-steward, Buchanan. With them went various attendants, including Duncan Cameron, a former servant of Cameron of Lochiel's, who came from the Isle of Barra and who it was thought would be able to help find guides and pilots when they reached their eventual destination.

Before setting out, Charles despatched from the Duc de Bouillon's château at Evreux a long letter dated 12 June, in which he broke the news of his departure to his father:

Sir,
    I believe your Majesty little expected a courier at this time, and much less from me; to tell you a thing that will be a great surprise to you. I have been, above six months ago, invited by our friends to go to Scotland, and to carry what money and arms I could conveniently get; this being, they are fully persuaded, the only way of restoring you to the Crown, and them to their liberties ... After such scandalous usage as I have received from the French Court, had I not given my word to do so, or got so many encouragements from time to time as I have had, I should have been obliged, in honour and for my own reputation, to have flung myself into the arms of my friends, and die with them, rather than live longer in such a miserable way here, or be obliged to return to Rome, which would be just giving up all hopes ... Your Majesty cannot disapprove a son's following the example of his father. You yourself

did the like in the year '15; but the circumstances now are indeed very different, by being much more encouraging, there being a certainty of succeeding with the least help; the particulars of which would be too long to explain, and even impossible to convince you of by writing, which has been the reason that I have presumed to take upon the managing all this, without even letting you suspect there was any such thing a brewing, for fear of my not being able to explain, and show you demonstratively how matters stood ... and had I failed to convince you, I was then afraid you might have thought what I had a mind to do, to be rash, and so have absolutely forbid my proceedings ... I have tried all possible means and stratagems to get access to the King of France, or his Minister, without the least effect ... Now I have been obliged to steal off, without letting the King of France so much as suspect it, for which I make a proper excuse in my letter to him; by saying it was a great mortification to me never to have been able to speak and open my heart to him. Let what will happen, the stroke is struck, and I have taken a firm resolution to conquer or to die and stand my ground as long as I shall have a man remaining with me.

Whatever happens unfortunate to me cannot but be the strongest engagements to the French Court to pursue your cause. Now if I were sure they were capable of any sensation of this kind, if I did not succeed, I would perish as Curtius did, to save my country and make it happy; it being an indispensable duty on me, as far as lies in my power. Your Majesty may now see my reason for pressing so much to pawn my jewels, which I should be glad to have done immediately; for I never intend to come back; and money, next to troops, will be of the greatest help to me. I owe to old Waters about 60,000 livres and to the young one above 12,000 livres ... I write this from Navarre, but it won't be sent off till I am on shipboard ...

I should think it proper (if Your Majesty pleases) to be put at His Holiness's feet, asking his blessing on this occasion; but what I chiefly ask is your own, which I hope will procure me that of Almighty God upon my endeavours to serve you, my family and country, which will ever be the only view of
Your Majesty's most dutiful son
Charles P.

To his father's Secretary, James Edgar, Charles wrote at the same time, giving further details of his financial transactions and of the arms he had bought and sending him a copy of a proclamation to be distributed after his landing. 'I have forgot also to mention', he added in a postcript, 'that I intend to land in or about the Isle of Mull.' In Mull, the *duthaic* or heartland of Clan Maclean though now in Campbell hands, Charles knew he could count on loyal support.

After which, having assumed the name of Douglas and the subfusc dress of a seminarist of the Scots College in Paris and having allowed his beard to grow, Charles left secretly for Nantes, where his friends were already assembled. At Nantes the weather was unfavourable, but on 22 June it improved and at seven o'clock in the evening the whole party went aboard the *Du Teillay*, lying off St Nazaire at the mouth of the Loire, whence they sailed to Belle Isle to await the arrival of their escort, the *Elisabeth*.

For more than a week the *Du Teillay* lay off Belle Isle and Charles, impatient at the delay, passed the time, as best he could, fishing. He also wrote once more to his father:

Sir,
    The contrary winds that have been blowing hitherto, have deferred my embarking, which will be this afternoon, at seven, for to go to the rendezvous of the man-of-war of 67 guns, and 700 men aboard, as also a company of sixty volunteers, all gentlemen, whom I shall probably get to land with me, I mean to stay; which, though few, will make a show, they having a pretty uniform. The number of arms are just as I mentioned in my last of the 12th, that goes with this, except the augmentation I was in hopes of is of a hundred or two less than I expected, which is no odds. I keep this open, and do not send it until I am fairly set off from Belle Isle – *id est* the rendezvous – so that I may add a note to it, if being sea-sick does not hinder; if it does, Sir Thomas will supply in mentioning what more may occur . . .

At the same time he despatched another letter to James Edgar:

    This being the last note I shall write this side of the seas, I would not fail to give you adieu in it, making my compliments to Lord Dunbar, and to as many of my friends as you shall think convenient and proper. I enclose herewith letters for the King and Duke. I hope in God we shall soon meet, which I am resolved shall not be but at home.
    P.S. Belle Isle à la Rade, the 12th July. After having waited a week here, not without a little anxiety, we have at last got the escort I expected, which is just now arrived, *id est*, a ship of 68 guns and 700 men aboard. I am, thank God, in perfect good health, but have been a little sea-sick, and expect to be more so;

but it does not keep me much a-bed, for I find the more I struggle against it the better.

'*Je ne pouvois qu'admirer*', was James's characteristic reaction to the news, '*ce que je n'aurois jamais conseile.*'

CHAPTER THREE

On 4 July 1745, the *Elisabeth*, under the command of Captain Douaud, finally made her appearance and at first light on the morning of 5 July Old Style (15 July New Style)* the two ships set sail for Scotland.

On the morning of 9 July what looked like a British man-of-war was sighted off the Lizard, bearing down on them. This was HMS *Lion*, a ship of the line of fifty-eight guns, commanded by Captain Brett RN, on his way from Spithead to join Admiral Martin's squadron in the Bay of Biscay. After a brief council of war on board the *Du Teillay*, it was decided that there was nothing for it but to stand and fight before any more British warships made their appearance.

It was now five in the afternoon. The French chaplain gave absolution and, as the *Lion* came on, the *Elisabeth* lay to, hoisted French colours and fired a gun. According to a report of the action later published in the *London Gazette*, the *Lion* now 'ran alongside the large ship and began to engage within pistol-shot and continued in that situation till 10; during which time they kept a continual fire at each other'.

By nightfall, after an engagement lasting five hours, both warships 'were so greatly disabled that they could hardly be kept afloat', and both ships' companies had suffered severe casualties. The *Lion* now sheered off 'like an old tub' and the *Elisabeth*, having suffered even greater damage, was too crippled to give chase. The Prince, 'who in his little frigate beheld this obstinate conflict' and who, according to one account, had vainly urged Antoine Walsh to go to the help of the *Elisabeth*, showed himself 'extremely uneasy as to the result'. He had good reason to be. The *Elisabeth*, severely damaged and having lost

*We shall be using Old Style dates with reference to events in Great Britain.

37

some 200 wounded and dead, including her captain, could now do no more than limp back to Brest under the command of her Flag Captain, Captain Bar, taking with her most of the arms and military stores which Charles had managed to assemble and leaving the little *Du Teillay* to go on her way alone.

At least two of the Prince's companions, Sir John MacDonald, the Irishman, and Aeneas MacDonald, the banker, now urged him to turn back to France, the former describing their onward journey as 'a desperate undertaking'. But this Charles would not do. 'You will see', he replied to all their objections, 'you will see.' 'Seeing this', concludes the log of the *Du Teillay*, 'as we did not want to put into port, we decided by the Prince's order to continue our course to Scotland, which we did after wishing *bon voyage* to Monsieur Bar.'

Henceforward every care was taken to avoid any further encounters with the Royal Navy, no lights being allowed at night except one, carefully shaded, for the compass. On 11 July, another vessel gave chase but was quickly outdistanced, and on 22 July, after some rough weather en route, land was finally sighted. 'At 4 in the morning', wrote Captain Darbé in his log, 'I saw land. It appeared to be a round hill, flat at the top, very high, like a platform, to the South. Other pointed hills, about 5 or 6, ssw, and others joined together forming also round hills, to the SE.' He was looking at the towering cliffs of Barra Head on the Isle of Berneray, the southernmost point of the Outer Hebrides.

Keeping a northerly course, the *Du Teillay* now made for the Isle of Barra, where Duncan Cameron, who was a native of the island, went ashore in the long boat to see if he could find a pilot for these perilous waters. Some hours later he came back with a friend of his, Callum MacNeil, piper to MacNeil of Barra, who on the afternoon of 23 July brought them in a high wind and what O'Sullivan calls 'a cruel rain' safely into harbour on the West side of the little Isle of Eriskay between Barra and South Uist. It was here, on Eriskay, in a sandy cove between two rocky promontories, that the Prince, after eighteen days at sea, first set foot on British soil, and to this day it is said that the big pink convolvulus which grows there and nowhere else in the Hebrides sprang from some seeds which Charles had brought in his pocket from France. As Charles and his companions came on deck after dinner, a golden eagle was seen circling above the ship. 'Sir,' said old Duke William of Atholl to the Prince, 'I hope this is an excellent omen, and promises good things to us. The King of Birds is come to welcome Your Royal Highness upon your arrival in Scotland.'

An unknown British ship, possibly a man-of-war, having been sighted at no great distance, the Prince's party decided to spend the night on shore, with the exception of the Duke of Atholl, who was suffering from a sharp attack of the gout and therefore stayed on board. It was still wet and stormy and the best shelter available on the island was the cottage of one Angus MacDonald, which was thatched with a peat fire in the centre of the room and a hole in the roof to let the smoke out. Nor was there much to eat. 'They could not find a grain of meal, or one inch of bread; but they catched some floundres, which they roasted upon the bare coals in a mean low hut they had gone into near the shore, and Duncan Cameron stood cook. The Prince sat at the cheek of a little ingle upon a fail sunk and laughed heartily at Duncan's cookery.' Soon the peat reek became too much for Charles who kept stepping outside to breathe the fresh air. 'What a plague is the matter with that fellow', said Angus MacDonald, who had no idea of his guest's identity, 'that he can neither sit or stand still and neither keep within nor without doors?' Nor was he best pleased when the tall young man in clerical garb started to examine the bed which old Sir Thomas Sheridan was to occupy, 'to see that the sheets were well aired'. 'A Prince', he declared irritably, 'need not be ashamed to lie in it.' But Charles for his own part announced that he was going to spend the night sitting up, as he was not very tired.*

The next step was to make contact with the nearest Jacobite chieftains from whom they could expect some measure of support. The Isle of Eriskay itself belonged to MacDonald of Clanranald, a scholarly Roman Catholic riddled with rheumatism who made his home at Nunton on the neighbouring island of Benbecula. A message announcing the Prince's arrival was sent to his half-brother, MacDonald of Boisdale, who lived only a mile or two away in South Uist across the Sound of Eriskay. 'Popish, but not so thievish as in Knoidart' is how these MacDonalds were described by the Rev Alexander Macbain, Church of Scotland minister in Inverness.

Boisdale, who was 'rechoned of good sense' and reputed to be 'one of the strongest men at a glass in all the Highlands', came hurrying over next morning in a state of some alarm, dismayed to find that Charles should have landed without the hoped-for foreign aid. His advice to the Prince was, to say the least of it, discouraging. 'Mr M'donald', according to Murray of Broughton, 'took the liberty to object to his undertaking and advised him very strenuously, tho' in a manner not over polite', to return home. But Charles's answer admitted

*Today, the nearest dwelling to *Coilleag a phrionnsa*, the Prince's Strand, as it is known, is a small house of indeterminate age. It stands empty and is likely to remain so, the last man who slept there (for a bet) having emerged shattered by the experience. Exactly what this was is hard to elicit, more especially as what he saw was a vision, not of anything that had happened there in the past, but of some horrendous event that is due to occur there at some unspecified time in the future.

of no further argument. 'I am come home, Sir,' he replied, 'and I will entertain no notion at all of returning to the place from whence I came; for I am persuaded my faithful Highlanders will stand by me.'

The Prince next questioned Boisdale as to the attitude of MacDonald of Sleat and MacLeod of MacLeod, both of whom had expressly committed themselves to his cause. And again Boisdale was discouraging, assuring the Prince that, far from supporting him, the two chiefs in question were very much more likely to be on the opposing side. 'Everybody', recalls O'Sullivan, 'was strock as with a thunderboult to hear that sentence.' In the end, however, Boisdale agreed to send an express to Sleat 'and let his return be the test of what he had advanced'.*

Next day, without waiting for an answer from Sleat or MacLeod, Charles set sail in the *Du Teillay* for the mainland, a distance of some sixty miles, dropping anchor in Lochnanuagh, a rocky inlet of the sea between Morar and Arisaig.

For his landfall, the Prince could scarcely have found a remoter, more isolated or more impenetrable region than this distant western seaboard of Arisaig, Morar and Moidart, lying to the south of the Isle of Skye and with nothing to seaward but the Outer Hebrides between him and North America. To the East he was protected by the massive redoubt of the Western Highlands, a formidable tangle of high mountains and steep rock-strewn ravines, sometimes rising directly from the shore and divided by a succession of deepcut sea-lochs often reaching far inland and possessing in those days no links but the sea with the rest of Scotland save for a few precipitous tracks through the mountains known only to those who used them, shepherds, fishers and hunters. Here, if anywhere, in *Oirer Ghaidheal*, the true coastland of the Gael, and in the fringe of islands beyond it, in this ultimate refuge of an ancient civilization, could Charles hope for a friendly welcome, from a Gaelic-speaking, in the main Catholic population, barely touched by the Reformation, still dwelling in the turf-roofed black houses their forefathers had inhabited before them and owing allegiance to various local MacDonald lairds and chieftains united by a long tradition of loyalty to the Stuart cause and a healthy distrust of the by now all-encompassing and strongly Presbyterian Campbells. For the Prince, fresh from a life spent in the stiff formality of an exiled court and amid the gilded splendours of papal palaces, it is hard to conceive of any greater contrast than this, or of one better calculated

---

*Events were to prove Boisdale's judgement right. MacLeod's reaction to the news of Prince Charles's landing was at once to inform the Government. 'It is certain', he wrote on 8 August to Lord President Forbes, 'that the pretended Prince of Wales is come into the coast of South Uist and Barra.' And Sleat likewise, when it came to the point, went over to the Hanoverians.

to catch the imagination of a young man of spirit now setting out after years of waiting on what promised to be the great adventure of his life.

From Eriskay Charles had sent Aeneas MacDonald on ahead by boat to summon his elder brother MacDonald of Kinlochmoidart, who, with other members of their clan, now came aboard the *Du Teillay* to pay his respects. One of them has left a first-hand account of the occasion:

We called for the ships boat and were immediately carryed on board, and our hearts were overjoyed to find ourselves so near our long wished for Prince. We found a large tent erected with poles on the ships decks covered and well furnished with variety of wines and spirits ... there entered the tent a tall youth of a most agreeable aspect in plain black coat with a plain shirt not very clean and a cambrick stock fixed with a plain silver buckle, a fair round wig out of the buckle, a plain hatt with a canvas string haveing one end fixed to one of his coat buttons; he had black stockins and brass buckles on his shoes; at his first appearance I found my heart swell to my very throat ... he saluted none of us, and we only made a low bow at a distance. I chanced to be one of those who were standing when he came in, and he took his seat near me but immediately started up again and caused me sitt down by him upon a chest. I at this time taking him to be only a passenger or some clergyman, presumed to speak to him with too much familiarity yet still retained some suspicion that he might be one of more note than he was said to be. He asked me if I was not cold in that habite [viz. the highland garb] I answered I was so habituated to it that I should rather be so if I was to change my dress for any other. At this he laughed heartily and next enquired how I lay with it at night, which I explained to him; he said that my wraping myself so closs in my plaid I would be unprepared for any sudden defence in the case of a surprise. I answered that in such times of danger or during a war we had a different method of using the plaid, that with one spring I could start to my feet with drawn sword and cock'd pistol in my hand without being in the least incumber'd with my bedcloaths. Severall such questions he put to me; then rising quickly from his seat he calls for a dram, when the same person whisper'd me a second time, to pledge the stranger but not to drink to him, by which seasonable hint I was confirm'd in my suspicion who he was. Having taken a glass of wine in his hand he drank to us all round, and soon after left us.

Charles was to spend the next two weeks either on board the *Du Teillay* or at Borrodale in Arisaig at the agreeable medium-sized house

41

of Clanranald's kinsman Angus MacDonald, lying snugly under the lea of the hill and sheltered then as now by plenty of well-grown timber. Soon after the Prince's arrival MacDonald of Kinlochmoidart had set out to inform the neighbouring Jacobite clans that he had landed. As he was crossing Loch Lochy, Kinlochmoidart met another boat. In it sat Bishop Hugh MacDonald, brother of MacDonald of Morar and Roman Catholic Vicar Apostolic of the Highlands, just returned from a visit to Edinburgh. 'What news?' shouted Kinlochmoidart as the two boats drew near to each other. 'No news at all have I,' replied Bishop Hugh. 'Then,' said Kinlochmoidart, 'I'll give you news. You'll see the Prince this night at my house.' 'What prince do you mean?' asked Hugh. 'Prince Charles,' came the answer. 'You are certainly joking,' said Hugh. 'I cannot believe you.' And, on being told that the Prince had indeed landed, 'Then, what number of men has he brought with him?' 'Only seven.' 'What stock of money and arms has be brought with him, then?' 'A very small stock of either.' 'What generals or officers fit for commanding are with him?' 'None at all.' At which the Bishop in dismay declared that he 'did not like the expedition at all'. 'I cannot help it,' was Kinlochmoidart's only reply. 'If the matter go wrong, then I'll certainly be hanged, for I am engaged already. I have no time to spare just now, as I am going with a message from the Prince to the Duke of Perth.'*

And so Kinlochmoidart, 'engaged already', went on his way and Bishop Hugh, full of misgivings, pushed on to Arisaig to add his voice to those already urging the Prince to go back to France. But Charles only retorted that

> he did not chuse to owe the restoration of his father to foreigners, but to his own friends to whom he was now come to put it in their power to have the glory of that event ... As to returning to France, foreigners should never have it to say that he had thrown himself upon his friends, that they turned their backs on him and that he had been forced to return from them to foreign parts. In a word, if he could get but six trusty fellows to join him, he would chose far rather to skulk with them in the mountains of Scotland than to return to France.

And in the end the Bishop could only advise him at least to keep quiet about his arrival as there was a regular garrison not far away at Inverlochy as well as any number of hostile Campbells in the neighbourhood. 'I have no fear about that at all,' replied the Prince.

So far Charles had met with little encouragement. And now young

---

*Kinlochmoidart's foreboding was justified. He was taken prisoner a few weeks later and hung, drawn and quartered at Carlisle on 18 October 1746.

Clanranald, who had gone to Skye to sound out Sleat and MacLeod, came back with the news that neither would move. Moreover a letter from MacLeod immediately reporting their conversation to Lord President Forbes of Culloden, indicates that Clanranald had himself declared that it was his intention to be 'prudent'. It began to look all too much as though, in the words of historian Home, 'the Prince was single in his resolution of landing'.

It was now, according to tradition, that Charles turned to Kinlochmoidart's other brother Ranald, 'whose colour came and went' as he heard his kinsmen refusing him their services, and asked him if he at any rate would not assist him. 'I will', was the reply, 'though no other man in the Highlands should draw his sword.' Things it is said, now took a turn for the better. At any rate among the MacDonalds there was less hanging back and following Ranald's example, young Clanranald likewise pledged himself to the Prince, while Charles lost no time in making clear his own total commitment to the Rising. Until this moment the *Du Teillay* had been lying at anchor off Arisaig. Charles now gave orders for her to return to France. Having first knighted Antoine Walsh on the spot and presented him with a handsome gold-handled sword, he handed him the following letter for his father:

Loughaylort
August 4. os 1745

I am, thank God, arrived here in perfect good health, but not with little trouble and danger, as you will hear by the bearer, who has been along with me all along, that it makes it useless for me to give any accounts and particulars on that head. I am joined here by brave people, as I expected. As I have not yet set up the Standard, I cannot tell the number, but that will be in a few days, as soon as the arms are distributed at which we are working with all speed. I have not as yet got the return of the message sent to the Lowlands, but expect it very soon. If they all join, or at least all those to whom I have sent commissions, everything will go on to a wish ... the commissions, along with the declaration, are arrived safe, and in a proper hand. The worst that can happen to me, if France does not succour me, is to die at the head of such brave people as I find here, if I should not be able to make my way; and that I have promised to them, as you know to have been my resolution, before parting. The French Court must now necessarily take off the mask, or have an eternal shame on them; for at present there is no medium, and we, whatever happens, shall gain an immortal honour by doing what we can to deliver our country, in restoring our master, or perish with sword in hand. Your Majesty may easily conceive the anxiety I am in to hear from you. Having nothing more particular at present to add (not being able to keep the ship longer, for fear of men-of-war stopping her passage entirely), I shall end, laying myself with all respect and duty at your Majesty's feet, most humbly asking a blessing.

Your most dutiful son
Charles P.

With the *Du Teillay* gone, the Prince established himself at Borrodale House, where it lay snugly sheltered between the hills and the shore of the loch. An eyewitness has described the gathering which now ensued. Clearly Charles's charm and personal magnetism were already beginning to win hearts.

We did our best to give him a most hearty welcome to our country, the P. and all his company with a guard of about 100 men being all entertained in the house of Angus McDonald of Borradel in Arisaig in as hospitable a manner as the place could afford. HRH being seated in a proper place had a full view of all our company, the whole neighbourhood without distinction of age or sex crouding in upon us to see the P. After we had all eaten plentifully and drunk chearfully, HRH drunk the grace drink in English which most of us understood; when it came to my turn I presumed to distinguish myself by saying audibly in Erse (or highland language) *Deoch slainte an Righ*; HRH understanding that I had drunk the King's health made me speak the words again in Erse and said that he could drink the King's health likewise in that language, repeating my words; and the company mentioning my skill in the highland language, HRH said I should be his master for that language.

But, despite his friendly reception by the Highlanders he had actually met, the fact still remained that time was passing and so far only a handful of MacDonalds had openly rallied to him. From Borrodale he accordingly despatched the following letter, calling on the chiefs of the loyal clans to rally to the Standard when he raised it at Glenfinnan:

Boradel, August ye 8th, 1745

Having been well inform'd of yr Principles and Loyalty, I cannot but express at this juncture, that I am come with a firm resolution to restore the King, my father, or perish in ye attempt. I know the interest you have among those of yr name, and depend upon you to exert it to ye utmost of yr Power ... I intend to set up the Royal Standard at Glanfinnen on Monday ye 19th instant, and shou'd be very glad to see you on that occasion. If time does not allow it, I still depend upon your joyning me with all convenient speed. In ye meantime, you may be assured of the particular esteem and friendship I have for you.

CHARLES P. R.

Of the neighbouring clans, besides the MacDonalds, the Camerons were as famous as any for their loyalty to the Stuart cause and able, it was estimated, to muster some 800 men. Old Cameron of Lochiel, their former chief, had been attainted after the 'Fifteen and was now living in exile in France, while his son Donald, Young Lochiel, ruled at Achnacarry in his stead. To him Charles had already written from Arisaig announcing his arrival and inviting him to join him. Like others, Donald was convinced that the venture was hopeless. As Chief, he felt responsible for the lives of his clansmen; and yet he obeyed the Prince's summons, hoping like the others to reason with Charles and, if possible, dissuade him from his purpose. On his way from Achnacarry to Borrodale, he stopped at Fassiefern on Loch Eil, the house of his younger brother John, an astute and reasonably prosperous West India merchant and burgess of Glasgow. Fassiefern's first question was what men, money and arms the Prince had brought with him. On being told none, he sought to strengthen his brother's resolve to have no part in a rising. He even urged him not to see the Prince. But to this Lochiel would not agree. 'No', he said, 'I ought at least to wait upon him and give my reasons for declining to join him ... which', he added hopefully, 'admit of no reply'. To which Fassiefern, foreseeing the result of such an interview, replied, 'Brother, I know you better than you know yourself. If this Prince once sets his eyes upon you, he will make you do whatever he wishes.' But, despite his brother's entreaties, Lochiel pressed on to Borrodale and there was received by the Prince.

The ensuing audience, which was private, appears to have followed the course Fassiefern had foreseen. To Lochiel's earnest suggestion that he should return to France, Charles made the usual reply. He then reminded his visitor of the solemn undertakings which he and other Highland chiefs had given to rise in his support. And when this did not at once produce the desired response, 'In a few days', he said, 'with the few friends that I have, I will erect the Royal Standard and proclaim to the people of Britain that Charles Stuart is come over to claim the crown of his ancestors, to win it, or perish in the attempt; Lochiel, who, my father has often told me, was our firmest friend, may stay at home, and learn from the newspapers the fate of his Prince.'

To this there could for Lochiel only be one answer. 'No,' he replied reluctantly, 'I'll share the fate of my Prince, and so shall every man over whom nature or fortune has given me any power.' And, having first, it is said, made it a condition that the Prince should give full security for the value of his estate and that MacDonald of Glengarry should likewise give an undertaking to raise his clan, he set out with a heavy heart for Achnacarry to fulfil the promise extracted from him.

Of the western chiefs Clanranald, Keppoch, Lochiel and Stewart of Ardsheil, who led the Stewarts of Appin, had by now also declared their readiness to join Prince Charles. The Macleans, who had played a leading part in the 'Fifteen and in whose territory Charles had originally planned to land, had been thrown into disarray by the arrest of Maclean of Duart. One of the sons of the aged Chief of Ardgour was later to join the Prince with a party of clansmen and in due course a Maclean Regiment, several hundred strong, was formed under the command of Maclean of Drimnin. The Mackenzies, after their experience in 1719, did not move. The Fraser Chief, Lord Lovat, who in 1715 had seized Inverness Castle on behalf of King George and at one time briefly commanded a company of the Black Watch for the Government but since had intermittent dealings with the Jacobites, did not reply directly to the letter which the Prince addressed to him, but 'answered in a squint way to Lochiel, complaining of his age and infirmities, with how well he wished ye family of Steuart in general and how unable he was to serve them'. At the very same time he wrote off in the following terms to General Guest, the aged English Commandant of Edinburgh Castle. 'We are daily alarmed here from the South and from the West about Invasions and the Chiefs of Clans, taken or being ordered to be taken upp. I wish I was as young as I was in the year 1715. I would engage to the Government for a moderate reward to Suppress any Disturbance that Highlanders will make this year.' After some references to his 'cousin McLeod' and the Duke of Argyll and some broad hints that he should be given 'an Equivalent' for his onetime company of the Black Watch, he added that it was his intention to go to London 'and kiss His Majesty's hands at St. James's'. 'I am,' he concluded, 'more than I can express, with Uncommon Esteem, Gratitude and Respect, My Dearest General, Your most obedient, most obliged and most Affectionate faithfull Humble Servant. – Lovatt.'

Another absentee at this stage, though through no lack of enthusiasm for the cause, was the Duke of Perth. Letters found on Sir Hector Maclean at the time of his arrest had, it appeared, focused the authorities' suspicion on the Duke and led to the issue of a warrant for his arrest. Having narrowly escaped capture at Drummond Castle at the end of July, he had taken to the hills and, after various adventures (including a drinking bout with his friend Robertson of Struan, which laid him low for some weeks), was eventually to join the Prince in September.

On 11 August, meanwhile, Charles had left Borrodale and rounding the dark wooded promontory of Arnish sailed across to Moidart, where he was enthusiastically received by the inhabitants with a wild reel danced on the shore. The next week he spent at Kinlochmoidart House at the head of Loch Moidart, assembling such supplies as he had and planning his next moves.

At Kinlochmoidart Charles was joined on 18 August by his old friend John Murray of Broughton, whom he now appointed his Secretary. While he was there, his supporters had their first encounter with an unsuspecting enemy. On 14 August a Captain Swetenham of Guise's Regiment, 'recon'd a very good ingeneer', was seized without a fight by a party of Kennedys from Glengarry at the top of Corryarrack Pass. Another encounter was to follow a couple of days later when two small parties of clansmen and a piper, commanded by MacDonald of Tiendrish and MacDonald of Keppoch, successfully ambushed two companies of Royal Scots on their way from Perth to Fort William by the inn at Highbridge on the River Spean, 'rushing out from behind the house with a loud huzza', while the piper played as loud as he could.

Captain John Scott, who was in command of the detachment, has left a lively account of the action. As he was about to cross the river, Captain Scott heard the sound of the pipes and 'saw some Highlanders on the other side of the bridge skipping and leaping about with swords and firelocks in their hands'. He accordingly sent a sergeant and his own servant to find out who they were. In the ensuing skirmish, in which the Highlanders suffered no casualties, a sergeant and three privates of the Royal Scots were killed and the remainder, numbering over sixty officers and men, taken prisoner. Captain Scott, who had himself been shot in the shoulder, was taken to Lochiel's house at Achnacarry with the other prisoners and there 'treated more like a friend and a brother than an enemy and a prisoner', his wound being dressed by Lady Lochiel herself. After the elderly Governor of Fort William had, when given the opportunity, refused to send a surgeon to Achnacarry to care for him, Lochiel, 'shocked with the old man's barbarity', directed that Captain Scott should be sent on to Fort William under parole. His horse Tiendrish was presented to Prince Charles.

The day appointed for the raising of the Standard at Glenfinnan was now approaching. On the previous day, Sunday 18 August, Charles, escorted by fifty of Clanranald's men, set out from Kinlochmoidart for Loch Shiel. Thence he took boat to Glenaladale and there spent the night, continuing next morning up the loch by boat to Glenfinnan, where the clans were to gather. Arriving in the middle of the morning, Charles, with the high hills looming above him, found no one there save two shepherds who wished him God-speed in Gaelic. He accordingly repaired to a nearby hut to await events. There, after a time, he was joined by 150 or so MacDonalds under MacDonald of Morar and by James Mor MacGregor, son of the notorious Rob Roy. James Mor, like his famous father a highly equivocal character and double agent, was acting at the time as a spy for the Lord Advocate, who had sent him over from Edinburgh to report on what was happening in the Western Highlands. This did not, however, prevent him in his capacity as a Jacobite from bringing Charles encouraging information about the intentions of his own clan, the MacGregors, and, more important still, the welcome news that the men of Clan Cameron were already on their way to join him. Not until four in the afternoon did the sound of the pipes playing a war-pibroch finally proclaim the arrival of some 700 or 800 of Lochiel's Camerons followed not long after by Keppoch with 300 more MacDonalds and Captain Scott's charger.

More than 1,200 loyal clansmen – Camerons and MacDonalds – were now assembled on the flat ground at the head of Loch Shiel. In the secret report he submitted a few days later to the Lord Advocate, James Mor MacGregor gave a detailed account of the Prince's force, noting in particular

> that most of them appeared to be good men, but some Young and Raw, and some Old that had been at Sheriffmuir. That he believed 600 or so of Lochiel's men were very good ... That most of Lochiel's men had no Arms, supposing that they were to have been provided when they came to the camp, and accordingly they went ... to Kenlochmoydart's house, or somewhere thereabouts and came back with Arms ... That he saw 22 Field Pieces about the size of one's leg, that were brought in a boat from Kenlochmoydart's house up Loch Shiell to Glenfinnan, with a number of Barrells of Powder and Ball and about 150 Pair of Pistolls ... That he observed many of the Guns that Lochiel's men got ... were in great Disorder, some of them with their Locks broken and others with Broken Stocks, and many of them wanted Ramrods, and the men were complaining that they were in great want of Smiths, Lochiel having but one ... That he did not see above 20 Saddle Horses in the Camp but there were a number of Country Horses for carrying Baggage.

By the time the clans had gathered, it was already late afternoon. All round them the dark hills sloped steeply down. The moment had arrived for the raising of the standard. The Prince, wearing a dun

coloured coat, scarlet-laced waistcoat and breeches and a yellow bob
on his hat, now took up his position outside the small hut where he
had spent the morning. Round him stood those who had come with
him from France and, with them, Lochiel, Keppoch, Murray of Broughton, old Gordon of Glenbucket, who had been out in the 1715 and
served in the interval as a double agent, and Father Colin Campbell,
a priest from the Scots College in Paris. Amongst other onlookers was
Miss Jenny Cameron of Glendessary, a buxom, middle-aged lady, later
widely rumoured, though for no good reason, to be the Prince's
mistress, and finally the English Captain Swetenham taken prisoner
at Corryarrack.

After being duly blessed by Bishop Hugh MacDonald, the Royal
Standard of 'white, blue and red silk' was now unfurled by the aged
and gout-ridden Duke William of Atholl, supported by an attendant
on either side. Whereupon there followed 'such loud huzzas and
schiming of bonnets up into the air, appearing like a cloud, was not
heard of, a long time'. Once the shouting had died down, Atholl read
out the commission from King James appointing Charles Regent and
then a manifesto which amounted to a declaration of war on the
Elector of Hanover. The Prince then made 'a short but very Pathetick
speech'. With the help of those who were certain to join him, he said,
'he did not doubt of bringing the affair to a happy issue'. Only a few
of the assembled clansmen can have had enough English to understand
what he was saying, but, being conscious of the solemnity of the
occasion and wishing to show their loyalty, they again tossed their
bonnets in the air and again emitted loud huzzas. From an eyewitness,
MacDonald of Tiendrish, we learn that he never saw the Prince more
cheerful than at this moment.

CHAPTER FOUR

For some weeks past rumours of an impending rising in the Highlands and of a possible landing by Prince Charles, with or without French support, had been circulating in Edinburgh and Whitehall. The letters seized from Maclean of Duart after his arrest in June had indicated that something of the kind might be afoot and towards the end of July reports began to reach London that Charles had actually set sail from France. On 1 August, a week after Charles had landed on Eriskay, the Duke of Newcastle, King George's principal Secretary of State, passed to the Duke of Argyll, as the Government's 'manager' for Scotland, a report that 'the Pretender's eldest son embarked on the 15th of July, NS, at Nantes, on board a ship of about sixty guns, attended by a frigate loaded with arms for a considerable number of men, and that it was universally believed that they were gone for Scotland'. And on the same day a proclamation was issued from Whitehall, 'ordering a reward of thirty thousand pounds to any person who shall seize and secure the eldest son of the Pretender, in case he shall land, or attempt to land, in any of his Majesty's dominions'.

From London, meanwhile, in a letter dated 30 July, the Marquess of Tweeddale, Secretary of State for Scotland, had written in the following terms to Andrew Fletcher, Lord Milton, the Lord Justice-Clerk:

My Lord,
    This day have been communicated to the Lords Justices several informations, importing, that the French Court was meditating an invasion of His Majesty's dominions, and that the Pretender's son had sailed on the 15th inst. NS from Nantes, on board a French

50

man-of-war; and by some accounts it was said that he was actually landed in Scotland; which last part I can hardly believe, not having had the least account of it from any of his Majesty's servants in Scotland.

Your Lordship will easily judge how necessary it is for all his Majesty's servants to keep a strict look out; and it has been recommended to me by the Lords Justice that I should give you an account of this intelligence, that you may consult with the rest of his Majesty's servants, and concert what is proper to be done, in case of such an attempt taking place. You will likewise give the necessary orders for making the strictest inquiry into the subject matter of this intelligence (copies of which I have sent to the Lord Advocate), and transmit to me some constant accounts of any discovery you shall make.

I was very glad to find by your Lordship's, of the 24th June, that you was persuaded the new Highland regiment, commanded by the Earl of Loudon, would be soon completed, and with good men, since it will be an additional strength to his Majesty's friends at this juncture. I have wrote to the Lord Advocate, and Sir John Cope on this subject.

I am, my Lord, Your Lordship's Most humble servant,

TWEEDDALE

To this Lord Milton replied on 4 August from Roseneath ('thus far in my way to Inverary') that he was 'glad to acquaint your Lordship, that I do not yet hear any surmise of the Pretender's son having landed', but added that 'if the intelligence about the Pretender's son landing in Scotland with arms proves true, I fear he will be joined with numbers enough to make it very difficult for the small number of troops here to dislodge him'. His colleague the Lord Advocate, William Grant, likewise discounted the rumours. 'I cannot believe', he announced to Tweeddale on 6 August, 'the intelligence you have of his actually being landed.' 'I consider the report as improbable', was the comment of Duncan Forbes of Culloden, the usually well-informed Lord President of the Court of Session two days later.

But on 7 and again on 10 August came further reports which seemed to show that Prince Charles had indeed landed. One of these originated with the Reverend Lauchlan Campbell, Church of Scotland Minister for Ardnamurchan, the parish in which the Prince now was. The Reverend Lauchlan reported that 'in the moneth of July, 1745, all the people living on the North coast of Ardnamurchan saw a ship put in to Lochnanna in Arisaig where no man alive saw ship drop anchor before that time'. Those who asked who was on board were, it appeared, first sworn to secrecy and then told that it was their wished-for Prince. On returning home they had duly explained that the ship carried a cargo of smuggled brandy, but the price had been too high. Later they strongly denied that there had ever been such a ship. Meanwhile Mr Campbell 'observed at that time that all my Jacobites were in high spirits'. He also observed that at the next Communion Service certain of his congregation were reluctant to 'gang forrard' although they had previously given in their names as wishing to receive Communion. On 'the Lord's Day following' (4 August) at Kilmory he accordingly thought it advisable to preach on the evils of rebellion, citing the fate of Absalom and expounding I Timothy ii, but his sermon was not well received. Indeed he was warned by one of the congregation 'not to preach in yon stile again, else beware of the consequence'. 'The people', he said afterwards, 'were like go mad. I can take my oath upon it that the Pretender is in my parish.' Finally, later that same Sunday, he had managed to extract from a certain Anna Cameron the admission that Charles 'with six men and himself' had landed from the ship and that word of his landing had been sent to 'all the Highland Chiefs about'.

Having obtained this information, the Reverend Lauchlan, as a Campbell, a good Presbyterian, and a good Whig, was desperate to transmit it to 'the Shirriff of the Shire', but 'alas I had not as much money as would bear the charges of an Express'. He accordingly communicated it verbally the same night to Campbell of Achindown, the Baillie of Ardnamurchan, who passed it on to Campbell of Airds, Factor to the Duke of Argyll, who on 5 August wrote to Campbell of Stonefield, the Duke's Chamberlain, at Inveraray, who hurriedly passed the intelligence to Lord Milton at Roseneath, who was thus able to incorporate it in a report of 7 August to Lord Tweeddale in London.

A second letter from Lord Milton ran as follows:

Roseneath, 10th August 1745

My Lord,

This morning I have information from one that lives in Glencoe, and has connexions both in Lochaber and Glengary, that the Pretender's eldest son landed in Uist the first of this month; that the disaffected Highlanders expect every day to hear of a landing in England; money is sent to this person, who lives in Glencoe, to enable him to travel northward, and get more sure intelligence of the designs, movements, and progress of these people. Since my last of the 7th, I have heard nothing further worth your Lordship's knowing.

I have the honour to be, with great respect, My Lord,
Your Lordship's Most obedient and Humble servant,
AND. FLETCHER

In his letter he enclosed his agent's secret report:

Prince Charles, the Chevalier's son, is landed in Uist, eight days
ago. General MacDonald is with him. I cannot give true account
of what company they have, but it is surely believed by this time
General Keith is in England, or on that coast. I must travel before
I can give you any account of their progress or resolution; only
what is narrated is truth. Let me understand if you want to keep
the correspondence, per bearer.

For the rest of August conflicting reports and rumours continued to
fly back and forth, while the tone of the correspondence between Lord
Tweeddale and Lord Milton, who had little liking for each other, grew
increasingly acrimonious. 'I own', wrote Tweeddale to Milton on 24
August, five days after the raising of the Prince's Standard, 'I am
surprised your Lordship is not more particular as to the Pretender
himself, since there are several letters in town, absolutely contradicting
the accounts sent to the government here from Scotland, of his ever
having landed there. I think it is incumbent on all his Majesty's
servants in that country, to use their utmost diligence to sift to the
bottom the truth of this particular.'

To which Lord Milton, who had by this time received James Mor
MacGregor's eyewitness account of the gathering at Glenfinnan, and
who, as it happened, knew the Highlands and their inhabitants rather
better than Lord Tweeddale, replied as follows:

Brunstane, 29th August, 1745

My Lord,
I had the honour to receive your Lordship's of the 24th,
yesterday, wherein your Lordship says you are surprised I am not
more particular as to the young Pretender himself, since there were
several letters in town absolutely contradicting the accounts of his
ever having landed in Scotland.
From whom the letters contradicting the accounts sent to the
Government at London came, I do not know; nor can I conceive
upon what foundation they proceeded; for my own part, I never
saw any cause to doubt the truth I sent by my letter of the 7th,
repeated in my letter of the 10th current, to your Lordship, that
the Pretender's son was on board the French ship; and by the after
letters [sic] I wrote, I took notice that my former intelligence was
confirmed. I know the Pretender's friends for some time

endeavoured to conceal his son's being in the Highlands and denied the fact. And I am willing to believe that such as sent intelligence, grafted on their evidence, were imposed upon. I dare say, from the accounts I know your Lordship has now received from the Advocate, and in the channel of Sir John Cope by R. Roy's son, and a gentleman who came from the Pretender's son's camp on the 21st, there remains not the least doubt that the repeated intelligence I sent was true; nor was it worth while to mention his dress, which was said to be a white coat and a brocade vest; that he had the Star and George, and a broad-brimmed hat with a white feather, and other minutiae, not worthy to be noticed...

Which, written more than a month after the Prince had landed on the mainland could, in Lord Milton's opinion at any rate, evidently be considered to clinch the matter.

The immediate responsibility for any military measures in the event of a landing or rising rested with General Sir John Cope, who had recently been appointed Commander-in-Chief, Scotland, with his head-quarters in Edinburgh. The forces under Cope's command amounted in all to barely 3,000 men, and consisted of two untried Dragoon regiments – Gardiner's and Hamilton's – scattered in squadrons with their horses out at grass, three infantry regiments (Guise's 6th, Murray's 57th, Lascelles' 58th), five companies of Lee's 55th, nine additional companies, mostly under strength, and a few weak companies from the newly raised Highland Regiment commanded by Lord Loudon. The Edinburgh Castle garrison was under the command of General Joshua Guest, a 'very alert' veteran of eighty-five.

Cope, who had distinguished himself as a cavalry commander at the battle of Dettingen and been given his present appointment 'without much consultation' and greatly to the indignation of 'Lord Mark Ker and others, who were very solicitous to have it', is described by one contemporary as 'what the world calls lucky in his profession' and by another as 'one of these ordinary men who are fitter for anything than the Chief Command in war, especially when opposed, as he was, to a new and uncommon enemy'. 'I pity poor him', wrote Horace Walpole, 'who with no shining abilities, and no experience, and no forces, was sent to fight for a crown.'

In fact Cope seems to have shown rather more foresight and common sense than the civil authorities. Already in early July, having been alerted by the astute and well-informed Forbes of Culloden (since 1737 Lord President of the Court of Session), he had reported to Lord Tweeddale that the clans were said to be stirring. He asked for artillery (he had only one trained artillery-man) and money, and suggested that certain precautions should be taken, notably the rearming of the Whig clans, in particular the Campbells, who had been required, along with the Jacobite clans, to disarm after 1715 and, unlike the latter, had complied with their orders. In this he had the wholehearted support of the Duke of Argyll, who did his best to manage Scottish affairs for the Government in London. 'It is a pity', wrote the latter sourly to Tweeddale on 11 August, forwarding fresh reports of Charles's landing,

> that we should be so much in danger from the Jacobites in the Highlands when the Government has certainly a great majority in that country on its side; the well affected are in despair, and some of them consider themselves as sacrificed to those who used to stand in awe of them. I am very glad there are Arms ordered for Scotland, though I fear it will be late before they come, and it is not yet lawful in the Highlands to defend the Government or his own house, family or goods, though attacked by Robbers or Rebells; in this condition I can do nothing but wish well to the Government.

But neither Cope nor Argyll received much encouragement from Tweeddale, who stoutly maintained that they were making a fuss about nothing, and continued to discount rumours that Prince Charles was about to land or had landed. Nevertheless Cope had of his own accord ridden to Aberdeen and thence despatched Guise's Regiment to help garrison the Government's three main strongholds in the Highlands, Fort George, Fort Augustus and Fort William, though it was not until 2 August that he was grudgingly and belatedly instructed by Tweeddale (who in his turn had received instructions from Newcastle) to dispose of his forces as he thought best, to secure the forts and garrisons in the Highlands and 'to take the dragoon horses from grass'.

On 8 August, having by now received from Lord Milton further reports indicating that the Prince had in fact landed and that a rising was imminent, Cope made a fresh appeal to Lord Tweeddale for more money, troops and weapons. 'I submit it to consideration', he wrote, 'if the few Troops in Scotland can be thought sufficient to defend this country in case the enemy is supported from abroad; all I can say is, I will march with what I can draw together, wherever we can be of most service.'

On the following morning Cope received a visit from Lord President Forbes of Culloden. By this time the invariably well-informed Lord President, who had hitherto been doubtful, had received what he at any rate regarded as conclusive evidence of the Prince's landing, 'from a gentleman of consequence in the Highlands', in other words MacLeod of MacLeod, not to mention his fellow renegade Sir Alexander Mac-

Donald of Sleat and was 'in his boots on his way northward' to Culloden to 'give some countenance to the friends of the Government and prevent the seduction of the unwary' – both tasks for which he was eminently well qualified.

In so far as anyone on the Government side can be said to have sought at this time to pursue a consistent or realistic policy in regard to the Highlands, it was Duncan Forbes. Indeed it is not too much to say that, despite or rather because of his moderation, he was the Jacobites' most dangerous enemy. By now a man of sixty, he had some ten years earlier succeeded his brother as fifth Laird of the sizeable estate of Culloden some five miles East of Inverness. Born and brought up there, he had long been on intimate terms with the chiefs of most of the Highland clans, whether Jacobite or Whig, and to a surprising extent enjoyed their confidence. A lawyer by profession, a man of charm, ability and, by the standards of his age, of principle, congenial by nature, a hard worker and an even harder drinker with a taste for good claret, of which he had an excellent cellar, he had for some years served as a Member of Parliament and before becoming Lord President had been Lord Advocate. Close to the Duke of Argyll, the Government's 'manager' for Scotland, he remained, like him, in these times of shifting loyalties, a staunch Whig. In Scotland his influence was considerable and he used it as far as he could in what he believed to be Scotland's best interests. In 1715, jointly with his friend and neighbour Simon Fraser of Lovat, he had helped retake Inverness for King George. Thereafter he had, with some measure of success, urged on the Government a policy of clemency, in the hope, as he put it, of 'weakening the strength of the rebels in future'. For thirty years after this he had made it his business to keep in as close touch as he could with what was happening in the Highlands and, in particular, to use his influence to encourage the chiefs he knew either to support the Government or at any rate not to side against it. He also did all he could to further the recruitment from the Whig clans of Independent Highland Companies, designed to serve if necessary in a counter-insurgency role in the Highlands. To his influence was very largely ascribed the negative attitude at this time of such traditional Jacobites as Macdonald of Sleat, MacLeod of MacLeod (on both of whom he seems to have had some kind of a hold), Lord Fortrose, the titular Earl of Seaforth, the Duke of Gordon, and others, not to mention his old friend Lord Lovat, who in any case believed in keeping his options open until the last possible moment. In short, it was largely thanks to him that the force now marching South with the Prince was not a very great deal stronger.

By this time a feeling that the situation called for some kind of action had finally begun to gain ground in Government circles. Cope himself had long been urging that the large numbers of officers absent on leave should be officially recalled – only to be told that this would frighten the country. On 12 August, however, an order was finally issued from the War Office instructing all officers 'to repair immediately to their respective posts', and on 13 August Lord Tweeddale, while still stubbornly maintaining that 'it is not certain that the Pretender's son is actually landed', grudgingly announced that 'credit has been sent down by the Lords of the Treasury to Sir John Cope, for receiving money to answer the exigencies of the Government in Scotland'.

Cope, for his part, had by now bought up all the biscuit in Edinburgh with which to feed his troops on the march, while more was being hurriedly baked in Stirling and Perth. 'The Ovens at Leith, Stirling and Perth were kept at Work Day and Night, Sunday not excepted.' A butcher was also provided 'with a drove of black cattle, without which', according to one of Cope's officers, 'we had starved upon the march'.

Following a meeting of the Council in Edinburgh, a number of other decisions were taken and dispositions made. The plan was that General Cope should assemble all the available infantry at Stirling and march thence along General Wade's military road, by way of Fort William in the direction of Fort Augustus, to meet any rebels they could find and crush the insurrection 'in the bud'. No regular artillery units were available, but, having decided that 'a Show only of some Artillery' might impress the Highlanders, Cope instructed Mr Eaglesfield Griffith, who for the past thirty years had been Master Gunner at Edinburgh Castle, to provide 'a light team of four $1\frac{1}{2}$-pounders and four coehorn mortars'. To man these, Mr Griffith produced an aged man who many years before had served as a gunner in the old 'Scots Train', and three invalids from the Castle garrison. A better qualified assistant 'in the Business of the Train' was an officer who happened to be serving as a volunteer, Lieutenant-Colonel Whitefoord of Cochrane's Marine Regiment.

Himself a Highlander, the Duke of Argyll was not convinced that the plan would succeed. 'Sir John Cope', he wrote to the Duke of Newcastle on 19 August, 'will march as he is ordered, though I am not sure *that such a march is practicable*; for if the rebels can come near with the numbers they say they were to have this day at the setting up their standard, the advantage those Highlanders will have in the mountains inaccessible to regular troops, *may produce a very bad effect*; and if they can actually defeat him in an action, I fear that very few of all the men he has with him can escape to the Low Country. In that case they will immediately have possession of all Scotland. On the other side, if he can arrive at Fort Augustus with the 1500 foot he has with him, it will cast a great damp on the rebellion, though, even in that case, he cannot pursue them through the mountains without Highlanders ... the raising of which', he continues acidly, 'is criminal till the militia is called out by royal authority, and arms must be delivered to them before they can act. As to all this the time is far spent'.

The Lord Justice Clerk also had doubts about the scheme. He, too, was concerned at the danger of leaving the Lowlands virtually unprotected. 'Sir John Cope', he wrote to Tweeddale, 'will have no small difficulty in getting at the rebels with regular troops in so inaccessible a country, or preventing them from getting betwixt him and the Low Country without the help of the friends of the Government, who remain still without arms, or power to make use of them.'

Nor was General Cope himself any less conscious of the threat to the Lowlands. He had expressly asked for reinforcements to be sent to Edinburgh, but these had failed to arrive and so, early on 19 August, the very day on which the Prince's standard was raised at Glenfinnan, he set out northwards with some 1,500 men, two regiments of dragoons and a vast quantity of baggage, leaving the aged General Guest in charge of the Castle and Colonel Gardiner of Gardiner's Dragoons in command of the remaining cavalry. Having reached Stirling on 20 August Cope at once set out for Crieff, leaving his two regiments of dragoons behind for the defence of the Lowlands. With him on his march northwards went Murray's regiment, five companies of Lee's and two additional companies of Lord John Murray's Highlanders, the Black Watch. At Crieff next day he was met by eight companies of Lascelles' with further supplies of bread.

At Crieff a number of Highland personalities came to pay their respects to King George's Commander-in-Chief. There was MacDonell of Glengarry, whose son Aeneas was even now waiting to welcome Prince Charles at Invergarry. And Duke William of Atholl's younger brother, Duke James, who had come over from Blair. And their brother, Lord George Murray, the newly appointed Sheriff-Depute, who had been out with the Jacobites in 1715 and 1719, but had since been pardoned. Hoping for support from the Athollmen and from the Breadalbane Campbells, General Cope had brought with him 1,000 stands of arms with which to equip the 'well-affected' Highlanders whom he expected to join him. But in this he was to be disappointed. The hoped-for volunteers simply did not materialize. Transport, too, presented a problem – there were not even enough horses to carry provisions. And so in the end most of the arms he had collected had to be sent back to Stirling.

Nor were these Cope's only difficulties. His troops were in poor shape. On 22 August he arrived at Amulree, where he was forced to spend the night. 'I did intend to go further', he wrote to Lord Tweeddale, 'but the difficulty of getting horses to march at daylight, and they, being weak, keep the men so long on the march that I must leave many behind (which I can't well afford) if I made long marches.' Large quantities of the bread, too, that he had so carefully provided, had either to be left behind or were spoilt by bad weather. Worst of all, his Black Watch companies 'mouldered away' by desertion and, what is more, having deserted, reported his movements to the enemy. The appearance at Taybridge (Aberfeldy) of another weak company of Lord Loudon's Highlanders did little to console him. He was coming to like the expedition less and less. Neither the Highlands nor the prospect of tangling with their uncouth inhabitants appealed to him in the least. 'Nothing', he confided to the aged General Guest, 'but the strongest orders received at Edinburgh, and since received at Crieff, would have prevailed with me to come further than Crieff.'

On 25 August Cope reached Dalnacardoch to the north of Blair Atholl. There he received his first eye-witness account of the forces opposing him from Captain Swetenham of Guise's Regiment, who, as a prisoner, had witnessed the raising of Prince Charles's standard in Glenfinnan and had subsequently been released on parole. From Swetenham Cope received the alarming news that the Highland army was now about 3,000 strong and that it was the Prince's intention to attack him on his way through the Corryarrack Pass between Dalwhinnie and Fort Augustus. The pass itself was, it appeared, by now commanded by the enemy's cannon. What is more, the very next day at Dalwhinnie, while Cope was digesting this information, he received a letter from Lord President Forbes, written from Culloden, confirming Captain Swetenham's report and warning him 'in the most decent manner his Lordship could think of', against attempting to force the pass.

General Cope did not need much persuading. At 2,500 feet above sea level in wild mountain country the Corryarrack Pass marked the highest point of General Wade's fine new military road linking Dalwhinnie with Fort Augustus, and was by any standards a remarkable feat of military engineering, on its eastern side possessing no less than seventeen carefully constructed and solidly buttressed traverses. To Highlanders, operating in their own country and possessing both the initiative and the advantage of surprise, a regular force making their way painfully across it would present a perfect target. To attempt to reach Fort Augustus by way of Corryarrack was, he wrote to his friend General Guest, to court the utter destruction of his troops. At a council of war held at Dalwhinnie on 27 August the idea of continuing the march to Fort Augustus was accordingly abandoned. After the alternatives of staying in the neighbourhood of Dalwhinnie or retreating to Stirling had in turn been rejected, the decision was taken to make at once for Inverness in the hope that this would give the 'well-affected' clans, if only he could find them and if, when it came to the point, they so desired it, a chance of rallying to King George. It was thus that, having continued along the Corryarrack road for a short distance in order to conceal his change of plan, Cope turned back just short of Garva Bridge and, after rejoining the Inverness road, spent the night of 27 August at Ruthven or Kingussie. There he added to his force a company of Guise's Regiment from the troops stationed in the Ruthven barracks, leaving behind Sergeant Terence Mulloy and twelve men to guard the barracks as best they could. Next day he pushed on through the narrow defile of Slochd to Inverness, arriving on the night of 29 August.

From Inverness Cope despatched a gloomy letter to Lord Tweeddale. 'From the first', he wrote, 'I treated this as a serious affair. I thought it so, I am sorry I was not mistaken. My fears were for the Publick and the Publick only, they still continue the same. I came to engage the Rebels, they would not let me but in Passes, as has been described. I'll still engage them if I can. I'll do my best for his Majesty's Service.'

While General Cope was thus floundering about in half-hearted pursuit, Prince Charles was preparing to meet his enemies. For two days, 20 and 21 August, he had remained in Glenfinnan. Thence, on 22 August, he made his way to Kinlochiel, where he wrote 'a great number of letters ... to the different friends of the Cause throughout Scotland', begging for help and money – 'money in particular'. He also did what he could to arm and equip his supporters. Such swords and muskets as there were were distributed to those who lacked them and 150 stand of arms ('a Gun and a Bayonet, and a Broad Sword with a Brass Handle like a small Sword') despatched across Suinart to Appin for the Stewarts under Stewart of Ardsheil and the MacDonalds of Glencoe, who had assembled in Duror ready to join the Prince when he reached Lochaber. The clansmen, another informant reported to the Government a few days later, did not much like the swords, but greatly appreciated the muskets. Unfortunately twelve out of twenty of the 'large swivel guns' he had brought with him from France had to be buried in a bog for want of pack-horses.

While Charles was at Kinlochiel, a copy of the London Government's proclamation was brought to him, offering £30,000 for his person, dead or alive. This he found distressing, as being 'unusual among Christian Princes' and revealing a shocking lack of manners on the part of his Hanoverian 'kinsman', and he was only with difficulty prevailed upon by his followers to put the same price on his kinsman's head 'representing ... that I did not see how my cousin's having set me the example would justify me in imitating that which I blame so much in him'.

While still at Kinlochiel, Charles received definite information that Cope was marching in the direction of Fort Augustus by way of Dalwhinnie. This made the prospect of an encounter with the Government troops much more immediate. On 23 August the Prince 'lodged at Fassafern', the house of Lochiel's unenthusiastic brother John, and next day marched to Moy in Lochaber, making a detour through the hills in order to avoid an English warship which had been sighted lying off Fort William. Meanwhile at Corran Ferry a party of eighty men from Appin, Ardgour and Glencoe were standing by to prevent any of the enemy's boats from getting through to Fort William.

On 26 August Charles set out by way of Letterfinlay and Laggan, where MacDonell of Lochgarry 'had al the Glengarry men conveen'd', for Invergarry, the stronghold of the MacDonells of Glengarry. Here he was made welcome by Old Glengarry's son, Young Angus or Aeneas MacDonell, 'a modest, brave and advisable lad', whose father, as we have seen, had only a few days before gone to Crieff to pay his respects to Cope. That night the Highlanders, having reached Invergarry, seized the Corryarrack Pass, thus, as it seemed to them, successfully blocking Cope's line of advance to Inverness.

At Invergarry Charles received further reinforcements, being joined by Stewart of Ardsheil and 260 Appin Stewarts, whose chief, 'a bashfull man, of few words and but ordinary parts', had seemed unready to bring them out, and by further contingents of MacDonalds from Knoydart and Morar, 'who made a very handsome appearance before the Prince, being completely armed, and most of them had targes'. He also received a visit from Fraser of Gortleg, Lord Lovat's 'Chief Doer'. Not long after landing the Prince had sent a message to Lovat, as a leading member of the Jacobite Association, informing him of his arrival and telling him 'how much he depended on his function, interest and advice'. To this Lovat, being anxious to keep his options open, had, as we have seen, replied 'in a squint way' through Lochiel, dwelling on his advanced age and infirmities, and adding that, although he wished the Prince well, he was unable to serve him in person. Meanwhile he had continued in friendly correspondence with his nearby neighbour, Forbes of Culloden, to whom he described Charles as 'a mad and unaccountable Gentleman'.

Lovat's purpose in sending Fraser of Gortleg to visit the Prince, it now transpired, was to 'offer his humble duty to the Chevalier, with apologys for his mens not being in readiness', and at the same time to ask on his behalf for two commissions from King James, one making him Duke of Fraser or indeed Beaufort and the other appointing him Lord-Lieutenant of Inverness-shire. Lovat also asked for the Prince's authority to arrange the murder of his friend and neighbour Lord President Forbes and urged him to march northwards through Stratherrick to Inverness, where he claimed that not only the Frasers but the MacLeods, Sir Alexander MacDonald of Sleat, the Mackenzies, Grants and Mackintoshes would very probably rally to him.

To these requests Charles responded by issuing a fresh commission, appointing Lovat Lieutenant-General. This he despatched to him under cover of a letter of compliment and apology drawn up by Murray of Broughton, at the same time promising to send him as soon as possible two original commissions which had been left behind with the baggage. He also sent him a warrant for the arrest (though not the elimination) of Lord President Forbes. To Lovat's proposal that he should march North through Inverness-shire, Charles, after some consultation, preferred a suggestion from Duke William of Atholl that he should march southwards through Perthshire, 'before his brother could make any party in that country'. At the same time an agreement was drawn up and signed by all the chiefs present, binding them not to make peace or lay down their arms except by general agreement.

On 27 August Charles, having received 'sure accounts' that Cope was at Dalwhinnie and preparing to cross Corryarrack, set out from Invergarry for Aberchalder. On the march he wore Highland dress for the first time since landing – much to the delight of his followers, whom Lovat's envoy, Fraser of Gortleg, described in a report to Forbes of Culloden as being 'in top spirits'. 'The young forward leader', Gortleg informed the Lord President, 'called for his Highland cloaths; and at tying the latchets of his shoes, he solemnly declared that he would be up with Mr Cope before they were unloosed.' On reaching Aberchalder, the Prince was joined by 400 more MacDonalds from Glengarry, 120 MacDonalds of Glencoe, and some Grants of Glenmoriston. Unfortunately a number of Keppoch's MacDonalds, who had been granted a day's leave of absence, chose this moment to desert, not, we are told, 'from any reluctancy they had to the undertaking', but simply on account of a temporary difference of opinion with their chief.

Having reached Corryarrack next day, Charles at once sent Murray of Broughton and Lochgarry forward to reconnoitre. But, when they got to the top of the pass, 'where they expected to discrey the Enemy', there was no one to be seen. Half expecting to be ambushed, they cautiously made their way back to the foot of the hill, where they came on a number of Cope's soldiers who had deserted and who now told them of their General's sudden change of plan and abrupt departure in the direction of Inverness.

This was in one way a disappointment to the Highlanders, who had been keenly looking forward to their first real encounter with the enemy. But Charles, on catching up with the advance party at Garviemore, pointed out that Cope's withdrawal was a good omen and gave orders that a guinea should be given to all forty of the deserters and some cattle killed for his troops' dinner. The deserters, meanwhile, no doubt encouraged by the guineas and the dinner, regaled their listeners with stories of Cope's troops being 'very much fatigued and freightened' and having with them large number of horses and enormous quantities of baggage, news which so aroused the Highlanders' predatory instincts that soon 'there was nothing to be heard but a continued Cry to be march'd against the enemy'. Delaying his own dinner, Charles now summoned the chiefs to a council of war, at which it was suggested that Cope should immediately be pursued or intercepted and brought to action before he reached Inverness. But in the end it was agreed that the distance was too great and, much to the disappointment of the Highlanders, 'who were quite intoxicated with the scheme proposed by their officers', the project was abandoned. All idea of pursuing Cope northwards having thus been discarded, the decision was taken to start next morning at full speed for the Lowlands, which Cope's withdrawal had left entirely unprotected.

Finding it 'very grateing' to abandon the idea of an early battle and wishing to console his frustrated followers, Charles, somewhat against his better judgment, now agreed to a proposal that a hundred Camerons, led by Lochiel's brother, Dr Archibald Cameron, and John William O'Sullivan, should attack the barracks at Ruthven, now held only by the solitary Sergeant Mulloy and his twelve men. The attack was, however, a failure, the attackers being beaten off with one man killed and three 'very ill wounded' while trying to blow-in the door. Colonel O'Sullivan, according to one rather unkind account of the action, spent most of his time hiding in a barn. The defenders lost only one man, 'shot through the head', as Sergeant Mulloy reported to the Commander-in-Chief, 'by foolishly holding his head too high over the Parrapets, contrary to orders'. 'I expect another visit this night', he continued, 'with their Pattaravoes, but I shall give them the Warmest Reception my weak party can afford. I shall hold out as long as possible.' But the Highlanders did not come back.

Another raid, undertaken that same night by a party of Camerons, was, though, entirely successful. Its purpose was to capture Ewan Macpherson of Cluny, whom Murray of Broughton had visited on the Prince's behalf while in the Western Highlands earlier that year, though with exactly what result is not clear. Cluny, who was Lochiel's first cousin, Lovat's son-in-law and chief of what was 'looked upon as one of the most civilized Clans in the Highlands', held a commission in Lord Loudon's Regiment and had in fact reported to Cope and Loudon for duty at Dalwhinnie just two days earlier. But Cope who, as an Englishman, possibly did not fully appreciate his importance, had in his view not treated him with the respect due to a chief and he had gone back to Cluny in a rage. His capture there by the Prince's men, if not actually pre-arranged, does not seem to have been unwelcome. Next morning Cluny, 'of a low Stature, very square, and a dark brown complection', was brought before Charles who was by now on his way to Dalwhinnie. Like others, Cluny quickly yielded to the Prince's charm. 'An angel', he wrote later, 'could not resist the soothing close applications of the rebels.' In a letter to Duncan Forbes, on the other hand, he put it more pithily, explaining that for him the choice in fact was to 'be burnt or join'. Before many days were out, he and his clan had thrown in their lot with the Jacobites. Meanwhile his wife, who was not Lord Lovat's daughter for nothing, had duly reported his removal to the Lord President, thus establishing for future reference that he had been taken prisoner and not joined the Prince of his own accord.

After sleeping the night of 29 August in the heather at Dalwhinnie, Charles marched the twelve miles along Wade's road to Dalnarcardoch in the forest of Atholl, where he stayed the night at an inn. His early training had fitted him for the rigours of war, and his men found it hard to keep up with him. 'So speedily he marched', writes an eyewitness, 'he was like to fatigue them all.' And when he lost the heel of one of his boots, the Highlanders were 'unco' glad to hear of it, for they hoped the want of a heel would make him march more at leisure.

CHAPTER FIVE

Following Duke William of Atholl's suggestion, Prince Charles now made for Blair Atholl, for centuries the seat of the Earls and Dukes of Atholl and occupying a position of considerable strategic importance. For Duke William, after thirty years of exile, this was a notable home-coming. From Dalnacardoch, which is no more than six miles from Blair, he sent a messenger on ahead to his widowed cousin, Mrs Robertson of Lude, announcing the Prince's arrival and asking her to make arrangements for his reception at the castle, which his younger brother James, the substantive Duke, had hurriedly vacated ten days earlier. At the same time he wrote to all his principal tenants, telling them to come to Blair, armed and with as many men as possible, on Sunday 1 September.

Charles reached Blair on the afternoon of Saturday 31 August, escorted by Duke William, who was greeted by 'men, women, and children who came running from their houses kissing and caressing their master'. Two or three miles before reaching Blair they were met, with much less enthusiasm, by Mr Thomas Bissat, Commissary or Factor to Duke James, whom the latter had left in charge of the castle and who had come to receive their instructions. That evening Mr Bissat despatched by safe hand a lively account of their arrival to his master in Edinburgh, where the latter had briefly paused on his way to London. 'The Young Pretender, your Brother, and the Highlanders', he wrote, 'came here about three o'clock in the afternoon. They all as yet behave verry civilly and I expect they'll continue so dureing their stay here, which will be till Munday morning ... The Highlanders doe not yet exceed in number 2000, and they'l scarce be so much, two thirds of which are the poorest naked like creatures imaginable and very indifferently armed; I doe not think the one half of their guns will fire. Some of them have guns without swords, and some have swords without guns.' 'The Young Gentleman himself', Bissat continued, 'seems to be good natured, but I doe not think that he hath verry much in him.' And of Duke William: 'Your brother is still the old man as he was; he looks as if he were of greater age by ten years than he is.' (Duke William's age was fifty-six.) The rest of Charles's entourage, the Seven Men of Moidart, Bissat dismissed in a single sentence: 'There are with them five or six gentlemen that came over in the ship with them, old aligrogue like fellows as ever I saw.' His irritation at the behaviour of Mrs Robertson of Lude he vented in a postscript. 'Lady Lude', he wrote, 'is here with them and behaves like a light Giglet, and hath taken upon her to be sole mistress of the house.' And he went on to report that she had given the Prince pineapples to eat – a gastronomic detail which in due course reached the receptive ears of Horace Walpole in London. 'He stayed sometime', the latter wrote to a friend, 'at the Duke of Athols; whither old Marquis Tullibardine sent to bespeak dinner; and since sent his brother word that he likes the alterations made there. The Prince found pineapples there, the first he ever tasted.'

Much to the disgust of Commissary Bissat, Charles and his army spent several days at Blair. 'I thought the Highlanders', he wrote in a second letter to Duke James, 'would leave this place tomorrow. But I hear your brother is to keep them for four or five days, that he may raise and press the Atholl men; meantime I see all this poor country will be eat up and ruined. They have parties out on every corner, that it's scarce possible any letters can escape them.' Meanwhile, the Prince's troops were 'very commodiously quartered' and for the first time since they had left Glenfinnan tasted bread, 'having eaten nothing but beef roasted on the hearth, without even bread or salt during their march thither'.

Duke William's efforts to 'raise and press the Atholl men', though accompanied where necessary by threats of violence, seem to have met with only moderate success. On 1 September, however, a number of local lairds and tenant farmers made their appearance and announced their willingness to join the Prince. Among these were the Duke's cousin Lord Nairne and his brother Mercer of Aldie. Another arrival at Blair was the Gaelic poet and soldier of fortune Colonel John Roy Stewart from Strathspey, once Quartermaster of the Scots Greys, who after a scandal of some kind and a spell in a British jail had fled abroad and joined the French service. This picturesque officer who, we are told, 'always went very gay', had arrived from France in a Dutch ship, carrying letters for Charles, said to hold out hopes of

French and Spanish help, though Bissat, as sour as ever, claimed that this was 'only contrived to encourage those already joynd to stand by him and others to joyn'. However this may have been, Charles, who had met John Roy in France and formed, rightly or wrongly, a high opinion of his military attainments, now sent him North with despatches for Lord Lovat and instructions to enlist as many recruits as he could among the Grants in his native Strathspey with or without the consent of their Chief, Sir Ludovic.

On 2 September Charles visited Mrs Robertson at Lude, where 'he was very cheerful and took his share in several dances, such as minuets and Highland reels'. 'She was so elevate when about the Young Pretender', wrote an eyewitness, 'that she looked like a person whose head had gone wrong.' Next day he set out with his main force for Dunkeld by way of Killiecrankie. Meanwhile, Lochiel, accompanied by Lord Nairne, had gone on ahead with 400 of his clansmen and, having formally proclaimed King James in Dunkeld, did not wait for the Prince but pressed on to Perth and with his 400 Camerons took possession of the city in King James's name. At Dunkeld, Charles established himself at another residence of the Dukes of Atholl, Dunkeld House, from which Duke James had made a hurried departure only a few days before.

On 4 September the Prince set out for Perth, stopping on the way to dine at Lord Nairne's house near Auchtergarven, a magnificent new mansion built thirty or forty years earlier to the designs of Sir William Bruce. During dinner one of the company spoke of the anxiety which the Prince's father must be feeling at his being engaged on so dangerous a mission. To which Charles, according to Duncan Cameron, who was presumably waiting at table, replied that he did not pity his father so much as his brother. 'For the King has been inured to disappointments and distresses, and has learnt to bear up easily under the misfortunes of life. But poor Hary! his young and tender years make him much to be pitied, for few brothers love as we do.'

On the evening of 4 September Charles, dressed in a tartan suit trimmed with gold lace, entered the ancient city of Perth, of which Lochiel had taken possession the day before. The Prince rode at the head of his troops on the horse taken from Captain Scott at Loch Lochy and carried in his pocket a single gold piece which was all that remained of the 4,000 louis d'or he had brought with him from France. As he showed the coin to George Kelly, he remarked with a cheerful smile that it would not be long before he got more. The crowds of onlookers who lined the streets gave him a reasonably enthusiastic welcome. 'I have got their hearts,' he wrote in a letter to his father despatched from Perth, 'to a degree not to be easily conceived by those who do not see it.'

In Perth, Charles made his headquarters at an inn kept by a vintner of the name of John Hickson, which is today the Salutation Hotel and where he is said to have pulled his newly appointed Quartermaster General, John William O'Sullivan, unceremoniously out of his bed at an early hour in the morning. He may also have stayed for part of his visit at Lord Stormont's town house in the High Street, where, in its owner's absence, his sisters are believed to have entertained him. On Sunday 8 September he attended a service conducted by a Minister of the Scottish Episcopal Church. During the week Charles spent in Perth he was joined by a number of local notabilities: James Drummond, titular Duke of Perth, young and educated in France, who had made his way there after narrowly escaping arrest and who, it was hoped, would be able to add as many as 1,000 men to the Prince's force; the latter's kinsman, Lord Strathallan; the Earl of Airlie's son, the twenty-year-old Lord Ogilvy, with the promise of 600 men; Oliphant of Gask and his son; and, finally, Lord George Murray, the younger brother of the two rival Dukes of Atholl, whom we last saw paying his respects to General Cope at Crieff.

Of these new recruits none was destined to play a more important part in the Rising than Lord George Murray. At fifty-one Lord George, unlike the greater part of the Prince's officers, was a trained soldier and possessed some actual military experience. This Charles immediately recognized by giving him the rank of Lieutenant-General. As a young man, after holding a regular commission in the British army, he had taken part in the Jacobite risings of 1715 and 1719. Subsequently exiled, he had served for a time in the Sardinian army, after which, having been pardoned by the London Government, he had returned to Scotland and there married and settled down to live quietly on his estates at Tullibardine. His son he had sent to be educated at Eton.

Right up to the time of Prince Charles's arrival in Perth, Lord George had shown every sign of having forgotten his Jacobite past and of having, like his brother James, become a loyal adherent of the House of Hanover. Writing to the Lord Advocate barely two weeks earlier, he had referred to Charles as 'the Young Pretender' and had also accepted from his brother James the appointment of Deputy Sheriff for Perthshire with the special task of providing transport horses and food for Sir John Cope's army. Indeed it was in this capacity that he had recently visited Cope's camp at Crieff.

Now, to all appearances, he was making a sudden and complete *volte-face*. And though there can be no real doubt that Lord George was always Jacobite in his sympathies, for him as for so many others the step he was now taking was not an easy one. His much loved wife Amelia, in poor health at the time, viewed his decision with dismay, but would not stand in his way. 'She is much against my rashness (as she calls it), yet, when she found me determined, she did not dispute with me upon it,' he wrote to his brother James, adding:

> Her acquiessing to my will makes so deep an impression upon me, that nothing but so strong an attachment as I have to the cause I am to imbark in, could make me do what in all appearance must disturb her future quiet and happiness... After what I have said you may believe that I have weighted what I am going about with all the deliberation I am capable off, and suppose I were sure of dieing in the attempt it would neither deter or prevent me... My Life, my Fortune, my expectations, the Happiness of my wife and children, are all at stake (and the chances are against me) and yet a principle of (what seems to me) Honour and my Duty to King and Country outweighs everything.

The Chevalier de Johnstone, who was to serve as Lord George's aide-de-camp, has left a convincing account of him, describing him as 'tall, robust and brave, vigilant, active and diligent' but also 'fierce, haughty, blunt and proud'. Possessing, he tells us, 'a natural genius for war', he had 'charge of the whole detail of our army' and 'conducted it entirely'. 'He desired', Johnstone continues, 'always to dictate everything by himself and knowing none his equal, he did not wish to receive his advice.'

It is easy to see how Charles might have found him hard to get on with. Though the Prince entrusted him with what were in fact the duties of Deputy Commander or Chief of Staff, Lord George seems never to have enjoyed his entire confidence. One reason was without doubt incompatibility of temperament between the two men. Lord George had a quick temper and a blunt, arrogant, uncompromising manner which some found hard to take. But it was equally due to the constant insinuations and doubts cast on Lord George's loyalty by the Prince's Secretary, the ambitious John Murray of Broughton, who, we are reliably informed, 'assured the Prince that Lord George had joined on purpose to have the opportunity of delivering him up to the Government'. Nor were some other members of Charles's entourage – the Irish in particular – any better pleased at the addition of a newcomer to their own inner circle.

Rather more surprisingly, Prince Charles likewise awarded the rank of Lieutenant-General to the tall, slender, affable Duke of Perth, who, after narrowly escaping capture, had joined his forces at about the same time. Of delicate constitution, a Roman Catholic (though no bigot) and brought up in France until the age of nineteen, the Duke, at thirty-two, still possessed an imperfect knowledge of the English language, which, to make up for this, he spoke with an exaggeratedly broad Scots accent. 'Although brave even to intrepidity, a perfectly upright man, endowed with a great deal of sweetness of character', he was, the Chevalier de Johnstone tells us, 'of a feeble genius and intermeddled with nothing', while Horace Walpole dismissed him as 'a silly race-horsing boy' – clearly, in short, a very different character indeed from his fellow Lieutenant-General. Meanwhile, on the strength of his real or imaginary exploits in the Irish brigade of the French army, that bibulous and quarrelsome Irishman, Sir John MacDonald, had been appointed the Prince's Master of the Horse.

Charles used his stay in Perth to collect men and money and, with the help of Lord George Murray to give the irregular force he had assembled, which now numbered 2,400 men, something of the character of an army. The sum of £500 was readily paid by the Provost and Bailies of Perth out of the Fund for the Town Common Good on the understanding that neither the citizens nor their property would be molested. At the same time, representatives of the Prince were despatched to Dundee, Fife and Angus on similar missions, while the Duke of Perth, Duke William of Atholl, Lord Ogilvy, Oliphant of Gask and the rest of them had set out for their estates in order to bring out by one method or another as many of their tenants and clansmen as they could persuade to follow them. In this they seem to have been only moderately successful, the Duke of Perth in particular returning with no more than 150 men instead of the 1,000 he had hoped for. In anticipation of their first encounter with the enemy a serious start with training was now made, at Lord George's instance, arming and equipping the Prince's small force and organizing its supply system and commissariat. This led almost immediately to friction between Lord George and the Prince's other officers, in particular Colonel John William O'Sullivan who, as Quartermaster General, resented any interference in what he chose to regard as his province.

As for the Prince, he was well enough satisfied with what had been achieved. His good looks and agreeable manners won the hearts of all with whom he came into contact. He enjoyed drilling his troops and even found time to attend the balls and other social gatherings given in his honour by the local notabilities. 'Since my landing', he wrote to his father, 'everything has succeeded to my wishes. It has pleased God to prosper me hitherto even beyond my expectations... I keep my health better in these wild mountains than I used to do in the Campagna Felice, and sleep sounder lying on the ground than I used to do in the Palaces of Rome'. From the literary flavour of this long letter (dated 10 September) and its careful grammar and spelling, it seems likely that Sir Thomas Sheridan or some other member of the Prince's suite had a hand in its composition.

After a few days in Perth Charles received the news that General Cope, who had remained in Inverness from 29 August until 4 September, was now making as fast as he could for Aberdeen, where he intended to put his force on board a number of vessels sent there from Leith and sail with them to one or other of the ports on the Firth of Forth with the object of helping defend Edinburgh. At once Charles called a council of war, which decided that the right course was to march South immediately in the hope of reaching Edinburgh before Cope. Accordingly on 11 September the Prince's army, numbering over 2,000 men, marched out of Perth by the Stirling road in the direction of Edinburgh. On the first day's march there was an unfortunate scene when the Prince's newly appointed Master of the Horse, Sir John MacDonald, blamed Lord George Murray, in the most unrestrained language, for giving him a bad horse and for being generally incompetent. Still worse trouble was only avoided when Keppoch tactfully explained that Sir John was either drunk or mad. Later the same day there was another unpleasant incident when Lord George found, much to his indignation, that Colonel O'Sullivan had for no good reason arrested the Provost of Perth and one of the Bailies, and the Prince was obliged to intervene personally before they were released.

On 12 September, according to the report of a Government informer, a review of the Jacobite army was held at Auchterarder. Although accurate in most other respects, this report put the numbers of the Highlanders at about 4,000 and gave their immediate destination as Glasgow – which, as it happened, was the impression which the Prince had intended to convey. From Auchterarder Charles made for Dunblane, where he spent the nights of 11 and 12 September at the house of MacGregor (or Drummond) of Balhaldie waiting for the whole of his force to gather before crossing the Forth. By the evening of 12 September his army had duly assembled and bivouacked for the night in the grounds of the house of a sound local Jacobite, James Stirling of Keir, or rather of his son, for he himself had by now been forfeited.

It had seemed possible that the Prince's passage of the Forth might be opposed by the garrison at Stirling, where Gardiner's Dragoons were now quartered. But next morning, thanks to a skilful diversion, there were no enemy troops to be seen in the area chosen for the crossing and, having reached the ford of Frew near Kippen at ten o'clock in the morning, the Prince's army crossed without difficulty

71

with Charles and Lord George at their head, claymore in hand and both wearing Highland dress.

Once across the Forth, the Highlanders halted for refreshment at the house of Moir of Leckie, another known sympathizer, only to find that, in anticipation of the Prince's arrival, Leckie himself had been carried off the night before by Government troops, who, however, had fortunately not touched the food and drink he had thoughtfully provided. From Leckie Charles now addressed to the Provost of Glasgow a letter demanding £1,500 'which put the Town in great confusion', but which the Provost and Council, on finding that the Highlanders were in fact bound for Edinburgh, felt that they could safely ignore.

On 14 September the Prince's army pressed on in the direction of Edinburgh, skirting round Stirling Castle, whose garrison fired a shot or two in their direction, which did no one any harm, 'tho the balls fell very nigh the Prince', and halting briefly on the historic field of Bannockburn. Here Charles received the news that Gardiner's Dragoons had withdrawn from Stirling to Linlithgow and were encamped between the town and the bridge across the river. The Highlanders accordingly marched on to Falkirk and camped in a field to the East of Callendar House, where Charles himself spent the night. Here he found that his host, Lord Kilmarnock, whose wife was an enthusiastic Jacobite, had made a point of dining that very day with the officers of Gardiner's Dragoons and was therefore able to regale him at dinner with much interesting information. On the strength of this Charles decided to attempt a surprise attack on the Dragoons' camp that night, only to find that they had left Linlithgow the night before and made off in the direction of Edinburgh as fast as they could, not halting until they reached Coltbridge, a mile or two West of the city.

After receiving a reasonably enthusiastic reception from the population of Linlithgow, Charles next day resumed his march on Edinburgh, arriving on the afternoon of 16 September at Corstorphine, 'three miles from the Capital, where were numbers of people mett him from thence, chiefly from curiosity'. Here his army 'filed off to the right' and encamped at Slateford, while the Prince took up his quarters nearby at Gray's Mill, whence he addressed to the Lord Provost and magistrates of Edinburgh a summons to surrender the city.

The fact of the Prince's landing had been known in Edinburgh for more than a month and as long ago as 27 August a meeting of the town council had been held to discuss the desirability of putting the city into a better state of defence. At this meeting resolutions had been passed recommending that steps should be taken to repair the crumbling city walls and that, in addition to the existing Town Guard, a body of 1,000 men should be raised for the defence of the city, to be paid and armed by public subscription. At the same time the celebrated Professor MacLaurin, who held the Chair of Mathematics at the university, was invited to see what he could do to strengthen the fortifications. But, though news of Cope's withdrawal to Inverness and of the Prince's advance into Perthshire had been brought to the city on 31 August by the fugitive Duke James of Atholl, in practice little or nothing had been done, quite possibly, some said, because Archibald Stewart, the Lord Provost, was at heart a secret Jacobite.

Although practically impregnable, Edinburgh Castle could give no effective protection to the city below. Its obsolete cannon, if fired (and there was some doubt as to whether they could be fired), would almost certainly do more damage to the city itself than to an invading army. The castle's actual Governor was General Preston, a veteran of eighty-six, while the Commander of the Edinburgh District and senior officer in point of rank, now also residing in the castle, was General Guest, the 'very alert' officer of eighty-five who had been left in charge by General Cope before he marched North. The garrison itself consisted at this time of two companies of Lascelles' (47th) Regiment, a few artillerymen hastily imported from London to work the guns, and a number of invalided and veteran soldiers. In addition to these, Hamilton's Dragoons were encamped to the North of Edinburgh on Leith Links, while Gardiner's Dragoons were falling back on the city from Linlithgow as fast as they could. On the latter's arrival, both regiments, together with a few hundred men of the Town Guard and some newly raised volunteers, encamped in a field near Coltbridge. Of General Cope's transports, which had set sail from Aberdeen on 15 September, there was no sign.

Such was the position when news reached the city that the Highlanders had crossed the Forth, had reached Linlithgow and were rapidly approaching the capital. Clearly action of some kind was called for. By this time an energetic officer called Brigadier Fowke had arrived from London to take command of the two regiments of cavalry, of a Dutch regiment, believed to be on its way to Scotland, and of a few hundred volunteers recruited from among the citizens and the students of the university. In the end, after much anxious discussion with the city authorities and General Guest in the castle, the decision was taken that the two regiments of dragoons, with the support of such volunteers as there were and of the Town Guard, should march out to meet the advancing Highlanders.

Both regiments of dragoons were now at Coltbridge and on Monday 16 September Brigadier Fowke, accompanied by the Town Guard and volunteers, set out to meet them. He found Gardiner's troops in a bad way. Colonel Gardiner himself was already a sick man 'muffled in a rude blue surcoat, with a handkerchief drawn round his hat, and tied under his chin', while his troopers and their horses were utterly fatigued after their forced march from Stirling, for which, after months at grass, they had been quite unprepared. They were also short of food and forage – 'in need', as Brigadier Fowke put it, 'of everything'.

While discussions were proceeding as to what the next move should be and whether it might still not be better for the dragoons to withdraw eastwards pending the much hoped for arrival of General Cope's transports, Brigadier Fowke, on his own initiative, sent out a party of scouts to try to discover what they could of the enemy's movements. Colonel Gardiner, a deeply religious man, much prone to premonitions, was by this time feeling worse than ever. 'The Brigadier', he declared gloomily, 'might do as he pleased; for his part he had not long to live.' The discussions were still proceeding and opinion beginning to harden in favour of a withdrawal, when, at three o'clock in the afternoon, the scouting party came galloping back into camp in a state of high excitement with the news that the Highlanders were already at Corstorphine and had actually fired on them as they approached.

This was too much for the dragoons, who had no intention of staying there to be shot at. Fowke succeeded in marching off the front squadrons in some sort of order, but soon those in the rear were completely out of control. Stricken with panic at the rumoured approach of the enemy, they broke into a gallop. Immediately their fears communicated themselves to those in front; the panic became general; and soon the whole regiment was in headlong flight between the Lang Dykes, as the present site of Prince's Street was then known, in the general direction of Leith Links, anxiously watched from the castle heights by large numbers of nervous citizens.

In the words of a contemporary, 'this precipitant flight occasioned a general consternation in the city'. News of the 'Canter of Coltbrigg', as it came to be called, spread rapidly through the town, quickly giving rise to rumours that the Highlanders had actually defeated the dragoons in battle. Before long indignant crowds had gathered in the streets, loudly demanding that in no circumstances should any attempt be made to resist the Prince's army and Lord Provost Stewart, feigning dismay at their lack of spirit, was mobbed by the crowd on his way to Parliament Close. While the dragoons continued their precipitate withdrawal in the direction of Musselburgh, messages and messengers were flying back and forth. With some difficulty, General Guest had been persuaded to allow a hundred dragoons to be detached from the main body for the defence of the city. But by the time the Lord Advocate, who was the bearer of the order, had caught up with the dragoons, news had been received from the Provost of Dunbar that

Sir John Cope's transports had now at long last been sighted off May Island and could reasonably be expected to reach Leith that night. At the suggestion of Colonel Gardiner, by this time seriously ill, the two regiments of dragoons were halted near Preston, not far from his own house of Bankton, where he could receive medical treatment and where his dragoons would have the city of Edinburgh between them and the enemy. At the same time a message was sent by boat to General Cope, inviting him to land, not at Leith, but rather at North Berwick or Prestonpans, where it was hoped he might be able to join forces with the fugitive dragoons.

In Edinburgh itself, meanwhile, a crowded meeting of townspeople had been convened by the Lord Provost in the New Church to decide whether or not an attempt should be made to defend the city. The flight of the dragoons had done nothing whatever to strengthen the citizens' resolve. To make matters worse, a Writer to the Signet, a Mr Alves, was broadcasting the story that, while out riding near the Prince's camp, he had encountered the Duke of Perth, who had told him that, whether the city was defended or not, the Prince intended to pay it a visit. 'If', the Duke had said to him, 'they will ... allow us peaceably into the town, they will be civilly dealt with; if not, they must lay their account with military execution.' At this Mr Alves himself was promptly locked up on a charge of high treason, but even so the words 'military execution' stuck unpleasantly in people's minds and still further lowered morale.

Meanwhile, the newly raised volunteers had to all intents and purposes been disbanded, or rather had disbanded themselves. An unknown man on a grey horse, it was said, had suddenly appeared in the Lawnmarket, where the volunteers were drilling, and announced that he had seen the Highland army and that it was 16,000 strong. Whereupon the four companies who were drilling had immediately marched to the castle and handed in their arms – greatly to the relief of their anxious families.

And so when at the meeting in the New Church the question was put: 'Defend or not defend?', only three or four of all those present could be persuaded to vote in the affirmative and, when it was suggested that some dragoons might be brought in to defend the city, there were loud shouts of, 'No dragoons!' As for the Lord Provost, having bravely announced that, in case of danger, he himself 'would be the first man to mount the walls', he next put the question: 'Shall we send any to treat with them?' By now the tone of the meeting had still further deteriorated, a number of rowdies and pickpockets having joined the crowd, and it became harder than ever to keep any sort of order. Then all at once a man was seen trying to force his way through the crowd carrying a letter for the Lord Provost, which, on closer inspection, was found to bear the signature 'Charles PR'. Amid shouts and counter-shouts, the decision was taken, first, to read it out and then not to read it. On its being read out notwithstanding, its terms were found to be as follows:

> From Our Camp
> 16th September, 1745
>
> Being now in a condition to make our way into the capital of his Majesty's ancient kingdom of Scotland, we hereby summon you to receive us, as you are in duty bound to do; and in order to it, we hereby require you, on receipt of this, to summon the Town Council, and to take proper measures for securing the peace of the city, which we are very desirous to protect. But if you suffer any of the Usurper's troops to enter the town, or any of the cannon, arms, or ammunition now in it (whether belonging to the public or to private persons) to be carried off, we shall take it as a breach of your duty, and a heinous offence against the king and us, and shall resent it accordingly. We promise to preserve all the rights and liberties of the city, and the particular property of every one of his Majesty's subjects. But if any opposition be made to us, we cannot answer for the consequences, being firmly resolved, at any rate, to enter the city; and in that case, if any of the inhabitants are found in arms against us, they must not be expected to be treated as prisoners of war.
>
> CHARLES P.R.

Skilfully drafted by John Murray of Broughton, the Prince's letter produced an immediate effect. With scarcely a dissentient voice, the meeting decided to send four of the city bailies to the Prince to beg him not to attack them until the matter had been further deliberated, in other words, to take a first step towards capitulation. No sooner had the bailies set out, however, than news arrived that Cope's troopships were now in the Firth of Forth. This led to second thoughts and further discussion, and eventually to the decision to send yet another bailie after the four to stop them and bring them back. But the bailie in question, who, like the Lord Provost himself, was suspected of Jacobite sympathies, somehow failed to overtake his colleagues before they reached the Prince's camp with the result that in the end it was finally decided to let the original resolution stand.

By this time the four bailies were in any case already on their way back with the Prince's answer. This ran as follows:

His Royal Highness the Prince Regent thinks his Manifesto, and the King his father's Declaration, already published, a sufficient capitulation for all his Majesty's subjects to accept with joy. His present demands are to be received into the city as the son and representative of the King his father, and obeyed as such there. His Royal Highness supposes that since the receipt of his letter to the provost, no arms or ammunition have been suffered to be carried off or concealed, and will expect a particular account of all things of that nature. Lastly, he expects a positive answer before two o'clock in the morning, otherwise he will think himself obliged to take measures conform. At Gray's Mill, 16th September 1745. By His Highness's command.

[Signed] J. Murray.

This uncompromising communication was at once submitted to yet another meeting of the town council, who, after further prolonged and inconclusive discussion, suddenly awoke to the fact that the time limit set by the Prince had already expired. Whereupon, shortly after two in the morning of 17 September, a fresh deputation of five was despatched by coach to beg for a further delay of seven hours, to allow for further consultations with the citizens of Edinburgh.

Charles had by this time come to the conclusion that he was being trifled with. The message brought by the town council's first deputation had struck him as unconvincing and on their departure he had given orders that Lochiel and his men should prepare to force an entry into the city as soon as the time limit expired. By midnight a force of about 1,000 Camerons and MacDonalds was standing by to attack the town. On the arrival of the council's second deputation, its members were sent away again with the answer that it was already well after two and that the time limit had therefore expired. Shortly after three the assault force set out, making their way by Merchiston and Hope's Park to the South of the city in order to keep out of range of the castle guns. Having reached the head of the Canongate near the Netherbow Port without attracting attention, they hid themselves among the narrow closes and tall houses and waited for a chance to force their way in.

By this time it was beginning to get light. An attempt to induce the sentry to open the gate by means of a ruse was unsuccessful and the Highlanders, having failed to force an entry, were just about to withdraw to St Leonard's and the shelter of Salisbury Crags and there seek further instructions, when suddenly the Netherbow Port opened and a coach came out. This was the coach that had carried the second deputation to Slateford, had brought them back to Edinburgh and now, having deposited them at the tavern of a certain Mrs Clark, where they were anxiously awaited by the Lord Provost and other members of the council, was making its way back to its stables in the Canongate, outside the city wall.

This afforded Lochiel and his party an unhoped for opportunity. Hardly had the coach emerged from the gate when the Highlanders, led by Lochiel himself, burst through it, seized the guard and then rushed on into the High Street sword in hand, with a piper blowing for all he was worth. After which, having re-formed their ranks, they marched in an orderly fashion up the High Street to Parliament Close, where, having taken up their position, they were quickly surrounded by a crowd of curious onlookers. These events occupied so little time that all was over before the citizens of Edinburgh realized that their city had changed hands. Indeed the story is told of one worthy citizen who, taking a stroll on the ramparts later that morning, found a Highlander sitting astride one of the cannon. 'You do not belong', he enquired, 'to yesterday's guard?' 'Ach, no', came the answer in polite but halting English. 'She pe relieved.'

Charles, meanwhile, having received news of Lochiel's successful assault, was preparing to make his entry into Edinburgh with the main body of his troops. The Castle was still in enemy hands and, not wishing to expose themselves unnecessarily to the fire of its guns, the Highlanders followed a route which led them by way of Morningside and the King's Park to a glen known as the Hunter's Bog, situated between Arthur's Seat and Salisbury Crags. Here, at about midday on 17 September 1745, the Prince mounted his horse and, accompanied by his commanders and personal staff, set out along the bridle path to St Anthony's Well, where, dismounting briefly, he took his first view of the Palace of Holyroodhouse, which, from its first foundation, had played so important a part in the history of his family.

By now, news of his arrival had spread and a growing crowd flocked out to greet him or at any rate to stare at him. At St Ann's Yards, in order to be better seen by the crowd, he again mounted his horse and, 'smiling all the time', rode on towards Holyrood with the Duke of Perth on his right hand, young Lord Elcho, who had joined him only the night before, on his left, and the remainder of his staff and regimental commanders following. Huge crowds had assembled and were cheering wildly. 'The populace of a great city who huzza for anything that brings them together, huzzaed', wrote one rather sceptical eyewitness, 'and a number of ladies in the windows strained their voices with acclamation, and their arms with waving white handkerchiefs in honour of the day ... many shewed their dislike by a stubborn silence.'

'He was', wrote another witness, 'a tall slender young Man, about five Feet ten Inches high, of a ruddy Complexion, high nosed, large rolling brown Eyes, long visaged, red-haired, but at that Time wore a pale Periwig. He was in Highland Habit, had a blue Sash, wrought with Gold, that came over his Shoulder; red Velvet Breeches, a green Velvet Bonnet, with a white Cockade, and a Gold Lace about it. He had a Silver-hilted broad Sword, and was shown great Respect by his Forces.'

On reaching the gate of the Palace, the Prince dismounted and was escorted to his apartments by Hepburn of Keith, an ardent Jacobite and strong opponent of the union with England, who, since being out of the 'Fifteen, had 'kept himself for thirty years in constant readiness to take arms'. That same day, 17 September, at the Mercat Cross in the High Street near Parliament Close, in the presence of the Duke of Perth, Lord Elcho, and 'an immense multitude' of onlookers, James VIII and III was duly proclaimed king 'of Scotland, England, France and Ireland' and Charles Prince Regent by a somewhat reluctant City Herald and his Pursuivants, who had been routed out for this purpose by some of Lochiel's detachment. Particularly prominent on this occasion was the handsome Mrs John Murray of Broughton, who, on horseback, with her habit freely adorned with white rosettes and a drawn sword in her hand, took up her position as near to the Cross as she could. After the relevant proclamations, declarations and manifestos had been read out, the trumpeter blew a blast on his trumpet, the pipers gave a skirl on their pipes, Lochiel's Camerons brandished their broadswords and fired their muskets in the air, the crowd cheered yet again and the ceremony was over.

CHAPTER SIX

While King James VIII and III was being proclaimed in Edinburgh, Sir John Cope's much travelled troops were at long last disembarking some twenty miles away at Dunbar, where they were greeted with the news that the Prince had already occupied the capital and where in due course they were joined by Gardiner's and Hamilton's dragoons, whose morale was by now not of the highest. For both sides the chief preoccupation was when and where the inevitable encounter between them would take place.

'Is he, by God?' was the Prince's terse comment on being told later that day that General Cope was disembarking. Whereupon he immediately turned his attention to the very necessary task of arming and equipping his troops for the forthcoming battle. As a first step, a proclamation was issued calling on the city fathers to surrender all available arms and ammunition. This brought in about 1,200 muskets as well as some powder and ball. A certain amount of food, shoes, clothing and other equipment was also either bought or requisitioned. On Thursday 19 September the Highlanders, who, with the exception of a few guards in the city itself, had hitherto been encamped in the King's Park, moved to a new camp near Duddingston, and at a council of war that evening the decision was taken to advance and attack the Government forces at the first opportunity.

Cope, for his part, was no less anxious to engage the enemy without delay but, after disembarking his troops on 18 September, he was told that the dragoons, who had now joined him, were 'so fatigued they could not march'. Accordingly, it was not until the following morning that he finally set out in the direction of Edinburgh. Lord Loudon's and Lord John Murray's Highlanders in their dark Government tartan led the way. After them came the rest of the infantry, six guns manned by six seaman-gunners borrowed from the Navy and, finally, the two regiments of tired dragoons. Accompanied by large numbers of curious onlookers, the column with its artillery and baggage wagons, 'extended for several miles along the road'. On the march Cope himself did what he could to improve morale by 'riding through the ranks and encouraging the Men', until 'even the Dragoons breath'd nothing but Revenge, and threatened the Rebels with nothing but Destruction'. Reaching Haddington in the early afternoon, Cope's troops camped for the night in a field to the west of the town, some fifteen miles from the Prince's encampment at Duddingston. The seaman-gunners, who came from HM ships *Fox* and *Hazard*, did not in the event prove a success. They were, we are told, 'generally drunk upon the March, and upon the Day of Action, ran away before the Action began'.

Cope, whose force, with the dragoons, now amounted to some 2,200 men, still had no very clear idea of the numbers or nature of the Jacobite army. During his march from Inverness to Aberdeen he had received reports that led him to believe that he would have to face as many as 4,000 Highlanders and on his arrival at Dunbar a similar figure had been quoted to him by Colonel Gardiner. Other sources put the enemy's strength as high as 5,000. A more accurate account of the Prince's army, which does not seem to have received the attention it deserved, came from John Home*, a young Divinity student, who, having first shown his zeal for the Hanoverian cause by joining the volunteers, had, after the Prince's arrival, managed to make a careful round of the points held by his troops in the city and also visited their camp in the King's Park. There he found the Highlanders 'sitting in ranks upon the ground, extremely intent upon their food' and taking advantage of this had counted them 'man by man', arriving at the conclusion that there were no more than 2,000 of them altogether. This he reported to Cope on the latter's arrival at Dunbar, adding that

> most of them seemed to be strong, active and hardy men; that many of them were of a very ordinary size, and if clothed like Lowcountrymen, would (in his opinion) appear inferior to the king's troops; but the Highland garb favoured them much, as it showed their naked limbs, which were very strong and muscular; that their stern countenances and bushy, uncombed hair gave them a fierce, barbarous, and imposing aspect. As to their arms ... they had no cannon or artillery of any sort, but one small iron gun

---

*John Home was later the author of *Douglas*, an historical tragedy of such excellence as to enable his excited compatriots to exclaim with natural pride, 'Whaur's yer Wullie Shakespeare noo?' and, perhaps more significantly the author of an admirable *History of the Rebellion*.

which he had seen without a carriage, lying upon a cart, drawn by a little Highland horse; that about fourteen hundred or fifteen hundred of them were armed with firelocks and broadswords; that their firelocks were not similar nor uniform, but of all sorts and sizes, muskets, fusees, and fowling-pieces; that some of the rest had firelocks without swords, and some of them swords without firelocks; that many of the swords were not Highland broadswords, but French; that a company or two (about a hundred men) had each of them in his hand the shaft of a pitchfork, with the blade of a scythe fastened to it, somewhat like the weapon called the Lochaber axe, which the town-guard soldiers carry; but all of them would soon be provided with firelocks, as the arms of Trained Bands of Edinburgh had fallen into their hands.

Two other enterprising student-volunteers who attempted a reconnaissance in depth were less fortunate than John Home. These were Robert Cunningham and Francis Garden (later Lord Gardenstone), who, with other parties of scouts, had been sent out by Cope to reconnoitre the approaches to the Prince's camp at Duddingston. Having reached Musselburgh on the Firth of Forth at the mouth of the River Esk, they caught sight of a little tavern on the far side of the Esk, well known for its oysters and white wine. This, after a night in the open air, was a temptation they could not resist. Fording the river, they entered the tavern. In the best room, already doing ample justice to the oysters and wine, they found two other officers in uniform, with whom, assuming that they too were Hanoverians, they not unnaturally entered into conversation. The talk had turned to the strength and position of the Jacobite forces, when all at once one of the officers charged them with being rebels. This they not unnaturally indignantly denied, producing the passes they had been given by General Cope and explaining the nature and purpose of their mission. Whereupon the two officers, who were in fact Colonel John Roy Stewart and Captain George Hamilton of the Prince's army, also on a reconnaissance, at once laid hold of them, disarmed them and carried them off in triumph to Duddingston, where they were told they would be hanged as spies. Fortunately for them, a Jacobite fellow student intervened on their behalf and in the end they were allowed to go, Cunningham in particular being so terrified that he did not let his horse out of a gallop until he reached Jedburgh.

General Cope, whose intention had been to concentrate his forces at Musselburgh and thence mount his attack on the Highlanders wherever they chose to make a stand, left Haddington on the morning of Friday 20 September. But he had scarcely reached Seton when Lord

THE SON'S OF THE OLD CHEVALIER.

Princes Charles Edward and Henry Stuart

Prince James Edward Stuart, titular King James VIII and III, father of Prince Charles, circa 1712

Princess Clementina Sobieska, mother of Prince Charles

Prince Charles and the Irish Jacobite Antoine Walsh on the shore of Lochnanuagh, July 174

Duncan Forbes, Lord President of Scotland

The entry of Prince Charles and his troops into Edinburgh after the battle of Prestonpans

William, Duke of Cumberland by Morier

Loudon, his Adjutant-General and several of his other officers, who had ridden on in advance of the main body, came galloping back with the news that the Prince's army had already crossed the Esk at Musselburgh and was now advancing rapidly on Preston, barely a mile or two away.

Prince Charles had started from Duddingston at approximately the same time as Cope had left Haddington. Before setting out he 'putt himself att the head' and 'drawing his sword, said with a very determined countenance: "Gentlemen, I have flung away the Scabbard, with Gods assistance I dont doubt of making you a free and happy people. Mr Cope shall not escape us as he did in the Highlands".'

Having crossed the Esk and arrived at a point a little to the South of Pinkie House on the outskirts of Musselburgh, Lord George Murray, who was commanding the advance troops of the Jacobite army, including Lochiel's Camerons, had by this time received from his patrols a first report of the enemy's movements. It suggested that Cope might well try to seize Falside Hill, which was situated to the West of the village of Tranent, a couple of miles South-East of Preston. This was something that Lord George, knowing the Highlanders' preference for a commanding position, was determined to prevent. He accordingly at once took his men at a rapid pace across country and by noon was in possession of the high ground at Birsley Brae, West of Tranent. Here the Highlanders came into full view of the enemy, drawn up beneath them on the low ground to the North-West of Tranent less than a mile away, and on that fine, sunny September afternoon the two armies greeted each other with defiant cheers.

Cope now changed his army's disposition, wheeling to the left, so as to face the Highlanders on Birsley Brae. The position he had chosen at such short notice was well protected. To the North, at his rear, was the sea and the villages of Preston, Cockenzie and Port Seton. To the South and to his front, between him and the enemy, was a deep ditch and a stretch of boggy marshland known as Tranent Meadows. To the West, on his right flank, was the ten-foot wall of Preston House and, immediately adjoining it, Colonel Gardiner's estate of Bankton. Only to the East was Cope's position relatively exposed save for a few walls and other enclosures, and, further away, the cottages of Seton village. 'There is not', he wrote later, 'in the whole of the Ground between Edinburgh and Dunbar a better Spot for both Horse and Foot to act upon.'

Certainly it was difficult to see how a force without artillery support, as were the Highlanders, could easily take the offensive against so well placed an enemy. Cope showed no sign of budging from the position he had so judiciously occupied and clearly the open, boggy, broken ground which lay between them did not favour the headlong downhill charge, which was the Highlanders' usual tactic. A reconnaissance by Colonel Ker of Graden, who, mounted on 'a little white pony' and under heavy fire from the enemy, coolly examined the ground between the two forces, only served to confirm this impression. It would, he reported to Lord George Murray, be impossible to cross the morass and attack the enemy 'without risking the loss of the whole army'. 'We spent the afternoon reconnoitring his position', wrote Lord George's aide-de-camp, the Chevalier de Johnstone, 'and the more we examined it, the more our uneasiness and chagrin increased, as we saw no possibility of attacking it without exposing ourselves to be cut to pieces in a disgraceful manner.' Nor, for that matter, could they fail to feel some uneasiness when they contemplated Cope's troops, 'which made a most gallant appearance both horse and foot with the sun shining upon their arms', and then looked at their own line, all 'broken into clumps and clusters'.

That afternoon was unfortunately marked by a number of incidents which illustrated all too well the mutual lack of confidence of the Jacobite leaders and a failure to co-ordinate their plans, which boded ill for the future. Concerned lest Cope might slip away in the night and make for Edinburgh, the Prince, in concert with John William O'Sullivan, but without consulting Lord George Murray, had given orders that the latter's Athollmen, who formed part of the reserve under Lord Nairne, were to be sent to guard the roads leading to Musselburgh. This enraged Lord George, who asked the Prince 'in a very high tone what was become of the Athol Brigade; the Prince told him, upon which Ld George threw his gun on the Ground and Swore God he'd never draw his sword for the cause if the Bregade was not brought back', and was only 'brought to himself' after this outburst by the tactful intervention of Lochiel. Meanwhile O'Sullivan, 'for what reason', writes Lord George, 'I could not understand', had ordered fifty of Lochiel's regiment to occupy Tranent churchyard, where they soon came under fire from Cope's $1\frac{1}{2}$-pounders and whence Lochiel subsequently withdrew them on Lord George's authority and without bothering to inform O'Sullivan.

By now Lord George had come to the conclusion that, if Cope was to be attacked, it must be from the East. For one thing, the enemy position was more open on that side and, for another, knowing the Highland mind, he realized that Highlanders 'had a freit [superstition] not to turn their backs upon the first sight of the enemy'. And so, neglecting in his turn to consult his fellow commanders, he ordered Lochiel's Camerons, including the fifty he had withdrawn from the churchyard, to march through Tranent and take up a position in the fields to the East of the village. At the same time he sent an officer to the Prince to explain what he had in mind and ask him to follow with the rest of the front-line troops.

As the Camerons were about to enter Tranent a hare got up in front of them and was greeted with a regular fusillade, much to the alarm of a passing villager who thought the firing was directed at him. The reason, in fact, was the deep-rooted Highland belief that any animal crossing the path of an army going into battle must at once be killed, as to let it escape would be to risk defeat. Not long after, in Tranent itself, a large sow was imprudent enough to cross the Camerons' line of march, and, 'in a moment there were twenty dirks in the beast, who fell down dead, makeing such squeks as may be imagined'.

Surprised to see the Highland right in motion and having failed to get Lord George to change his mind, O'Sullivan was by now giving free vent to his indignation at Lord George's sudden initiative. Needless to say, he received a thoroughly sympathetic hearing from his fellow Irishman Sir John MacDonald, who found him 'in great distress because Lord George would do nothing that he advised'. Finally, as darkness began to fall, the Athollmen, whom O'Sullivan had just finished posting in accordance with his own and the Prince's plan but without Lord George's consent, were ordered briskly back to their former position on the ridge above Bankton.

Observing these movements on the part of the Jacobite forces, but being understandably not quite clear as to their exact significance, Cope now changed front from South to South-West, taking up a position slightly to the West of his original one. His artillery he kept where it was, on the left, while shifting his baggage to the East of Cockenzie. At nightfall he ordered his troops to take up their positions for the night on a line running parallel to the large ditch to their South and slightly to the East of that occupied earlier in the afternoon. Still believing himself to be heavily outnumbered by the Highlanders and wishing to make quite sure that he was not taken by surprise, he also detailed no fewer than 200 dragoons and 300 infantry as outguards, thus covering all possible approaches to his already strong defensive position.

At about eight o'clock that evening, while the Highlanders' reserve remained to the West of Tranent, their front line began moving eastwards to join Lochiel's regiment on the other side of the village. When this movement had been completed, the Prince held a council of war at which Lord George Murray explained his plan for attacking the enemy at dawn. Briefly it was to march round the East end of the morass and fall on Cope's open left flank. 'I told them', writes Lord George, 'I knew the ground myself and had a gentleman or two with me who knew every part thereabouts; there was, indeed, a small defile at the east end of the ditches; but once that was past, there would be no stop, and though we should be long on our march, yet when the whole line was past the defile, they had nothing to do but face left, and in a moment the whole was formed, and then to attack.'

With this bold but simple plan the Prince and his officers, with the exception of O'Sullivan, who was not present, were, it appears, 'highly pleased'. That night, when they sat down to their supper, the differences of the afternoon were forgotten and the Prince, once more in high spirits, was 'great at Cup and Can' with his Lieutenant-General. After which, sentries having been posted, the army settled down for the night in the open fields, officers and men using the sheaves of freshly cut corn for bedding and lying down in rank and file, so as to be ready to move at short notice.

Lord George had not been asleep for long when he was woken by Robert Anderson, the son of a local laird, with news of the very greatest import. There was, it appeared, a much more direct way to the enemy's position across the morass, which he himself habitually used when shooting snipe. Quickly grasping the significance of this information, Lord George at once sent urgent orders to Lord Nairne and his men to rejoin the main force; the other officers were roused; and at 4 a.m. on Saturday 21 September, the Highland army moved off. The narrow path along which Anderson led them would just allow three men to march abreast, while here and there it was so boggy that they found themselves sinking up to their knees. First came the MacDonalds with Clanranald's leading; then Glengarry's and Keppoch's Regiments, including the MacDonalds of Glencoe. At Perth the Prince had decided that the clans should draw lots for their places in the line of battle and this time the Camerons and Stewarts had drawn the right, but, characteristically, the MacDonalds had protested, claiming that by right they had held the place of honour since Bannockburn, and in the end Lochiel had generously waived his claim. Next came the Duke of Perth's men and the MacGregors, followed by the Stewarts of Appin and Lochiel's Camerons. As senior Lieutenant-General, the Duke of Perth commanded the van, or right of the line, and Lord George the rear, or left. After the front-line troops came the reserve under the Prince and Lord Nairne, consisting of the Athollmen, the followers of Menzies of Shian and finally young Maclachlan of Maclachan, newly arrived from distant Cowal with a hundred of his clansmen. In order to maintain silence, Lord Strathallan's fifty cavalrymen were kept in the rear and all officers required to leave their horses behind and fight on foot. A light mist rising from the bog gave useful cover during the approach march and by first light the Highlanders, having successfully traversed the morass with Robert Anderson to guide them, were drawn up in line facing the enemy.

Warned by his patrols that the Prince's army was on the move, Cope had caused an alarm-gun to be fired soon after four o'clock and by dawn his troops, too, were in position. His infantry, three deep, were now facing East, the direction from which he expected the enemy attack to come. Their left was towards Cockenzie and their right was protected by the ditch which ran along the side of the morass. From left to right, there were nine companies of Murray's Regiment, eight of Lascelles', two of Guise's and five of Lee's. The artillery, with the guns on the left and the mortars on the right, was dressed in line with the infantry and separated from Lee's companies by a sufficient gap to leave room for two squadrons of cavalry. To the right of the mortars was an artillery guard of a hundred men. Once the infantry were drawn up, the cavalry moved into position. They consisted of two squadrons of Gardiner's Dragoons and two of Hamilton's, formed two deep, with one squadron of each regiment in reserve. 'My lads', cried Brigadier Fowke hopefully, riding up to the front of Gardiner's, 'this is the Day in which I doubt not your Behaviour will do us Honour.' And General Cope, too, rode along the line, 'encouraging the Men, begging them to keep up their Fire, & keep their Ranks, & they would easily beat the Rebels'.

The Highlanders began their attack soon after sunrise. Their left and right wings were at some distance from each other, and speed was of the essence. Without waiting to hear from the Duke of Perth on the right of the line, Lord George accordingly ordered the left wing to advance, simply sending his ADC to inform Perth of this and invite him to do likewise. Though the right now followed suit, the left had gained a considerable lead. Fearing that the Camerons might be outflanked by Cope's right, Lord George advised Lochiel to incline inwards to the left as he advanced and it was from this direction that the Camerons' attack went in. Casting away their plaids and pulling their bonnets down over their brows, the Highlanders came on fast with 'a hideous shout'. 'The stubble of the cornfield', wrote John Home, the theology student, observant as ever, 'rustled under the feet of the Highlanders as they ran on, speaking and muttering in a manner that expressed and heightened their fierceness and rage.'

At this the veteran gunner and the three invalids who had taken over Cope's artillery from the six seaman-gunners, who had by now already deserted, likewise turned and fled, leaving Lieutenant-Colonel Whitefoord of the Marines and Mr Eaglesfield Griffith, for the past thirty years Master-Gunner of Edinburgh Castle, to handle the guns as best they could. Whitefoord, for his part, managed to discharge five

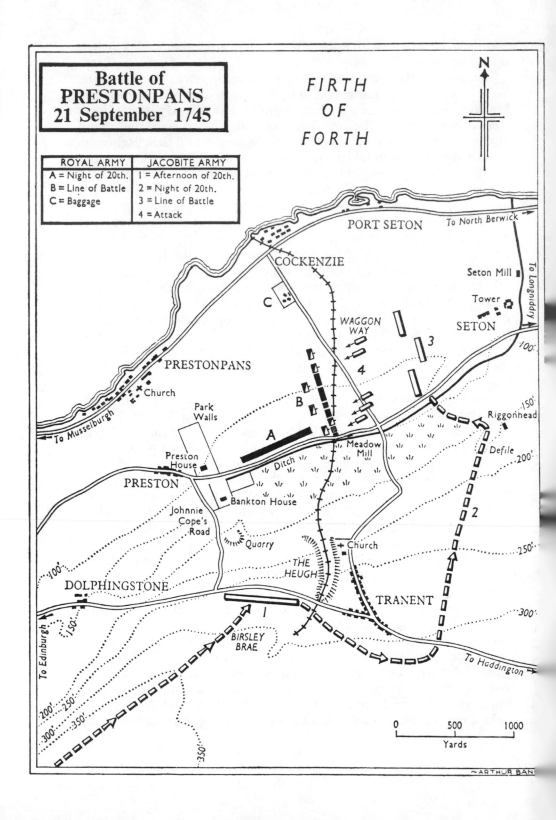

Battle of PRESTONPANS
21 September 1745

ROYAL ARMY	JACOBITE ARMY
A = Night of 20th.	1 = Afternoon of 20th.
B = Line of Battle	2 = Night of 20th.
C = Baggage	3 = Line of Battle
	4 = Attack

FIRTH
OF
FORTH

N

PORT SETON

To North Berwick

COCKENZIE

Seton Mill

Tower

SETON

To Longniddry

WAGGON WAY

C

3

4

PRESTONPANS

Church

B

Riggonhead

Park Walls

A

Meadow Mill

Defile

To Musselburgh

Preston House

Ditch

PRESTON

Bankton House

2

Johnnie Cope's Road

Quarry

Church

THE HEUGH

TRANENT

DOLPHINGSTONE

100'

150'

1

BIRSLEY BRAE

To Edinburgh

To Haddington

150'

200'

250'

300'

350'

100'

150'

200'

250'

300'

0   500   1000
Yards

~ARTHUR BAN

of his $1\frac{1}{2}$-pounders and old Mr Griffith all six of his mortars. This, we are told, caused the Jacobite line to give 'a great Shake' and the Government troops 'huzza'd'. Whereupon the Highlanders, returning the cheer, broke up into several columns, of which the three on their left wing came on 'with a swiftness not to be conceived', firing as they came.

One of the Highlanders engaged, MacDonald of Morar, gives a vivid account of what ensued:

> We then marched chearfully on and engaged the enemy; ... the enemys artillary plaid furiously upon our left, especially on Lochiel's battalions; their cannon also racked our right wing but did little execution. Their great guns were followed by a very regular fire of the dragoons on and left, and this again by closs platoons of all their infantry, which our men received with intrepidity and an huzza ... Our march up to the enemy hill we came near was without pipe or drum, in the most profound silence till the attack was begun, when all our instruments tongues and hands were at work ... The P. left his guard on the march to the attack, talking earnestly to the Duke of Perth and Clanronald and giveing his last orders and injunctions; but returning to his guard, as I happened to pass near by him, he with a smile said to me in Erse, 'Greas ort, greas ort', that is, 'make haste, make haste'. ... At this time the enemys guard first perceived us, for we heard them call out 'Who is there? Who is there? Cannons, cannons, get ready the cannons, cannoneers'; but our quick march and sudden and intrepid attack soon brought us into the midst of our enemy.

The strongest of the Highland columns, consisting of Camerons, 'at least 20 in Front and 30 in Depth', now made straight for the guns. Seeing this, Colonel Whitefoord called out to Colonel Shugbrough Whitney of Gardiner's Dragoons that now was his time to attack and Lord Loudon also urged him to charge the Highland flank. But, though Whitney himself pressed forward, he could not induce his Dragoons to follow him. 'And immediately the Rear Rank began to run away, and the rest followed in Tens and Twenties.'

The infantry, too, had by this time begun to waver and, when ordered by Colonel Lascelles to wheel in support of Colonel Whitney's demoralized dragoons, some of the platoons on the right of the line were seen to be 'crouching and creeping gently backwards, with their arms recovered', while the artillery-guard likewise abandoned their position and huddled together behind the guns and mortars. Seeing the artillery-guard fall back in disorder, Colonel Gardiner's squadron also 'began to be a little shy', despite the angry exhortations of Brigadier

Fowke, as keen as ever to instil a more martial spirit into his troops. 'What do you mean, Gentlemen, by reining back your horses?' he yelled. 'Advance up to your Ground; have you anything to fear? We shall cut them to Pieces in a Moment.' But when Lord Loudon ordered the Squadron to charge, the dragoons, who had momentarily come under fire, simply turned tail and fled.

At the other end of the line, where the Jacobite right had now also joined battle, things were going equally well for the Highlanders. Of this sector we have a vivid account from Lord Drummore, a middle-aged judge who had accompanied the Government forces as a spectator, 'resolved to see the Fate of a Battle in which I was most sensibly interested'. From where he sat quietly watching on his horse, about 150 yards to the left of Hamilton's Dragoons, he could see the MacDonalds advancing in two 'Columns, Clews or Clumps ... and upon the Right of those Columns a long Line which far outflank'd our Line'. What is more, their advance was so well ordered that he 'could see thro' from Front to Rear, yet to my Astonishment, every Front Man cover'd his Followers, there was no Man to be seen in the Open ... in short, tho' their Motion was very quick, it was uniform and orderly, and I confess I was surprised at it'.

Like the Camerons on the other wing, the MacDonalds, outflanking the Government left, attacked obliquely, swinging inwards towards the enemy and at the same time firing some 'dropping Shot' at long range, which killed or wounded several of Hamilton's Dragoons. This was more than the latter's comrades could stand. In panic both of Hamilton's squadrons now turned tail and galloped off the field, 'not in a Body, but quite broke in twos or so', though not fast enough to catch up with their reserve squadron, already well on its way out of the battle. Abandoned by the cavalry, the infantry now faced the charging Highlanders alone. Most of the Camerons had gone off in pursuit of Cope's cavalry 'Sword in hand, as fast as they could run', but about 150, waiting for the other two columns to come up with them, now fell on the Government right. In vain Colonel Lascelles tried to form a flank against them; his men refused to stand their ground and turned tail like their comrades.

At the start of the battle, General Cope had ridden over to the right of his line but, by the time he reached it, the dragoons were already in full flight. Returning to the left, he did his best, with his officers, to rally the infantry. But here again he was unsuccessful and soon the whole Hanoverian line was broken by wave after wave of charging Highlanders, who, throwing away their muskets, hacked their way through the fleeing rabble with broadsword and dirk. 'For shame, Gentlemen, behave like Britons,' cried Cope despairingly. 'Don't let us be beat by such a set of Banditti.' But there was no stopping them. As Charles wrote to his father afterwards, 'they eskaped like rabets'.

Before the battle, Prince Charles had announced that he would himself lead his army and charge at their head, but in the end had allowed himself to be dissuaded and had agreed to march with the reserve. During the actual engagement he placed himself well in front of the reserves, not more than fifty yards behind the front line, but even so saw relatively little fighting, mainly because of the speed of the Highland advance. In not more than a quarter of an hour the battle was over and barely five minutes elapsed between the first Highland onslaught and the total disruption of the enemy's front line.

It was probably the speed of the Highland attack as much as any other single factor that decided the outcome. 'The manner in which the Enemy came on', Cope wrote afterwards, 'was quicker than can be described.' This was something quite different from the slow, formal movements of traditional warfare which were the accepted convention of the age, and better troops than Cope's could have been thrown off balance by it. Once his blood is up, the Highlander is not easily stopped and, having once gained an advantage, the Prince's troops were quick to make good use of it. In the ensuing rout Cope's foot soldiers threw away their arms and equipment and, though the great majority ran away or were made prisoners, some were literally hacked to pieces by their pursuers as they sought to escape. Cleverly wielded, the broadsword is a formidable weapon and soon the battlefield 'presented a spectacle of horror, being covered with heads, legs, arms and mutilated bodies'. Scarcely less effective were the scythe blades employed by the company of MacGregors belonging to the Duke of Perth's Regiment, which 'cut the legs of the horses in two; and their riders through the middle'. Despite their early withdrawal, Hamilton's Dragoons lost eighty seven horses and Lord Elcho speaks of the 'notion the Highlanders had that the horses fought as well as the men, which made them kill a great many of them after their riders were dismounted'.

For all this, the casualties suffered by the Government forces seem to have amounted to no more than 300 killed and 400 or 500 wounded as against 1,500 or more made prisoner, including eighty officers. Among the Hanoverian officers killed was, as he had foreseen, Colonel James Gardiner of Gardiner's Dragoons, who by a series of strange chances died in the manse at Tranent, less than a mile from his own house, after being twice shot and then finished off by blows from a scythe and a Lochaber axe. He lies buried in Tranent churchyard. All war is cruel, but the Prince's officers did their best to discourage unnecessary slaughter and it was Lord George Murray's proud claim that 'never was quarter given with more humanity than by the Highlander'. Certainly he and the Duke of Perth did all they could to save lives and to see that the wounded on both sides were properly cared for.

The Jacobites gave their own losses as thirty killed and seventy or eighty wounded. One of the Jacobite officers wounded was Rob Roy's son, the same James Mor MacGregor who barely a month earlier had been acting as a spy for the Government and who is described by the Chevalier de Johnstone as 'brave and intrepid, but, at the same time, altogether whimsical and singular'. 'My lads,' he cried menacingly to his clansmen after he had been hit by no less than five bullets, '*I am not dead*, and, by God, I shall see if any of you does not do his duty.' He was in fact to survive not only this engagement, but the campaign, later reverting characteristically to a no less equivocal role.

Of Prince Charles's own conduct and frame of mind on the field of battle, the Whig historian Andrew Henderson, who was present, has left a vivid, if biased, account. 'I went', he writes,

to the Road-Side where the Chevalier, who by Advice of Perth &c. had sent to Edinburgh for Surgeons, was standing. He was clad as an ordinary Captain, in a coarse Plaid and blue Bonnet, his Boots and Knees were much dirtied; he seemed to have fallen into a Ditch, which I was told by one of his Lifeguards he had. He was exceeding merry; Speaking of his Army, he said twice, 'My Highlandmen have lost their Plaids.' At which he laughed very heartily. When talking of the Wounded, he seemed no Way affected. There were seven Standards taken, which when he saw, he said in French, a Language he frequently spoke in, 'We have missed some of them.' Then he refreshed himself upon the Field and with the utmost Composure eat a Piece of cold Beef, and drank a Glass of Wine, amidst the deep and piercing Groans of the wounded and dying, who had fallen a Sacrifice to his Ambition.

A rather different version comes from the pen of John Murray of Broughton, who writes that Prince Charles 'breakfasted on the field, but not amongst the dead and within hearing of the wounded, as has been falsely asserted by a little ignorant Schoolmaster, who has pretended to write the history of an affair of which he could be no judge'.

Among the last of the Government troops to surrender were those guarding Cope's baggage at Cockenzie. This proved a rich prize, for in addition to the baggage it included Cope's papers and his military chest containing between £2,000 and £3,000, found under a stairway at Cockenzie House. On the battlefield itself the Highlanders also found plenty of booty – arms, ammunition, clothing, money and other valuables – all most acceptable to an army that lacked for everything.

Leaving his infantry to their fate, General Cope himself had by now made good his escape from the stricken field and, with what was left of his two regiments of dragoons, headed South as fast as he could go, reaching Coldstream on the night of the battle and Berwick the following afternoon. At Berwick he encountered Lord Mark Ker, his former rival for the post of Commander-in-Chief, Scotland, who had recently been appointed Governor of Edinburgh Castle and who, it is said, greeted him with the uncharitable observation that he must be the first general in history to outstrip the news of his own defeat.* Whatever the truth of this, there was certainly a difference of opinion between the two generals, who were in any case not the best of friends, as to whether Cope's troops were still under his command now that they were on English soil. Nor were Lord Mark's farewell words overkind. 'God bless you, Gentlemen', he said, 'I go tomorrow; things have not been conducted very well hitherto. I wish you may henceforward conduct matters as they ought to be for his Majestie's Service.'

In due course, Sir John Cope was 'examined' by a board of general officers. Asked 'from what Cause he imagined, or conceived, the shameful and scandalous Behaviour of the Soldiers proceeded', he replied that he knew of no other reason than that they were seized by 'a sudden Pannick'. Having considered the evidence, the board found that 'he did his Duty as an Officer, both before, at, and after the Action: and that his personal Behaviour was without Reproach'. Today perhaps the most enduring memory of this unfortunate officer is the pipe tune which is still played at reveille to rouse the soldiers of our surviving Highland regiments from their slumbers:

> Hey Johnie Cope are ye wauking yet?
> Or are ye sleeping, I would wit
> O haste yet get up for the drums do beat,
> O fye Cope rise in the morning.

In London, meanwhile, Horace Walpole was forced to admit that the Highlanders were 'not such raw ragamuffins as they were represented'.

Prince Charles's victory at Prestonpans convinced him once and for all that his Highlanders were invincible, and to a meeting of his commanders held that day on the battlefield he characteristically proposed that they should at once march on Berwick as a preliminary to invading England. His proposal was however rejected by the others on the grounds of their inadequate numbers. Instead it was decided to

---

*In fact, Brigadier Fowke, travelling by a more direct route, had reached Berwick the night before.

remain in Edinburgh and there try to build up the strength of their forces.

On the day after the battle, Sunday 22 September, the Prince's victorious army re-entered the capital, marching in one long column through the lower gate of the city and along the main streets with pipes playing, drums beating and colours flying. At the same time the captured cannon, colours and standards of the enemy were proudly displayed and several hundred prisoners marched through the city in the rear of the column.

After spending the night after the battle at Pinkie House, Charles returned next day to Holyrood. On hearing that bonfires were to be lit and rejoicings held in honour of the victory, he 'gave positive orders against it, saying that he was far from rejoicing att the death of any of his father's Subjects, tho' never so much his Enemys, yt he pittied their unhappy way of thinking, which had drawn so many misfortunes upon the Country, and ended in their own fall'. As was his custom, he sent word to the ministers of the city, inviting them to hold their services that Sunday as usual. Some refused to take advantage of this and one of those who did, being 'sheltered under the Castle guns', is said to have prayed in the following terms: 'Bless the King – Thou knowest what King I mean; may the crown sit long and easy on his head. And for this man that is come amongst us to seek an earthly crown, we beseech Thee in mercy to take him to Thyself and give him a crown of glory.'

All this time the castle had remained in Government hands and for more than a week after the battle communications between the city and the garrison had continued uninterrupted. But, hearing that the garrison were beginning to run short of provisions, Charles decided to 'streten' them still further by cutting off their daily supplies. Old General Guest's immediate reply was to open fire with the castle guns, at the same time sending out raiding parties to attack, demolish and set on fire such neighbouring houses as they could reach. This did little harm to the Highlanders but caused a number of civilian casualties, and in the end Charles, not wishing to be held responsible, put an end to his blockade.

Having once more taken up residence at Holyrood, the Prince now divided his time between Edinburgh and Duddingston, where the bulk of his army was encamped safely out of range of General Guest's guns. The weather was fine and for the first time for many years there was a court again at Holyrood – 'a very brilliant court'. Occasionally balls and receptions would be held in the great picture gallery of the palace at which the Prince himself would appear. A Government spy who attended one of these functions reported on him as follows:

The young Chevalier is about five feet eleven inches high, very proportionably made: wears his own hair, has a full forehead, a small but lively eye, a round brown-complexioned face; nose and mouth pretty small; full under the chin; not a long neck; under his jaw a pretty many pimples. He is always in Highland habit, as are all about him. When I saw him, he had a short Highland plaid waistcoat; breeches of the same; a blue garter on, and a St Andrew's cross hanging by a green ribbon at his button-hole, but no star. He had his boots on, *as he always has.*

From another observer, we learn that 'their came a Great many Ladies of Fashion, to Kiss his hand, but his behaviour to them was very Cool: he had not been much used to Womens Company and was always embarrassed, while he was with them'. 'The Prince,' wrote O'Sullivan afterwards, 'went to see the Lady's dance, made them complyments on their dance and good grace, and retired; some gents. followed him and told him, yt they knew he loved dancing, and yt the Ball was designed for him to amuse him; "its very true", says the Prince, "I like dancing, and am very glad to see the Lady's and you divert yr selfs, but I have now another Air to dance and until that be finished I'l dance no other".' Yet another observer 'beheld his countenance thoughtful and melancholy ... he seemed to have no confidence in anybody, not even in the ladies who were much his friends...'

Doubtless the Prince felt more at his ease with his troops at Duddingston. 'I went', wrote a Mrs Hepburn to a Miss Pringle on 12 October 1745,

to ye camp at Duddington and saw ye Prince review his men. He was sitting in his Tent when I came first to ye Field, the Ladies made a circle round ye Tent and after we had gaz'd our fill at him he came out of the Tent with a grace and majesty that is unexpressible he saluted ye Circle with an air of Grandeur and Affability capable of charming ye most obstinate Whig, and mounting his Horse which was in ye middle of ye Circle he Rode off to view ye men. As ye circle was narrow and ye Horse very gentle we were all extremely near to him when he mounted and in all my life I never saw so noble nor so gracefull an appearance as his Highness made, he was in great spirits and very cheerful which I have never seen him before: he was dressed in a blue Grogram coat trimm'd with Gold Lace and a lac'd Red Wastcoat and Breeches: on his left Shoulder and Side were the Star and Garter and over his Right Shoulder a very rich Broadsword Belt, his sword had ye finest wrought Basket hilt ever I beheld all silver:

His Hat had a white feather in't and a White Cockade and was trim'd with open gold Lace: his Horse furniture was green velvet and gold, ye Horse was black and finely Bred (it had been poor Gardner's) his Highness rides finely and indeed in all his appearance seems to be cut out for enchanting his beholders and carrying People to consent to their own slavery in spite of themselves, I don't believe Cesar was more engagingly form'd nor more dangerous to ye Liberties of his Country than this Chap may be if he sets about it. I follow'd him through ye Field and saw him often Riding about attended by some of his Lifeguards they were clothed in Blue faced with red: just when he was on ye Field Lord Pitsligo's men arriv'd from ye North a good many Gentlemen well mounted and a great many servants with them: and some Foot, not many: Pitsligo himself made a very odd figure, he's like an auld carrier, ye Prince lighted and went into his Tent a second time to receive a' newcomers and we all circled the Tent door, he mounted again as gracefully and in ye same manner as the first time and rode to Town where we all follow'd not a little pleas'd with the show ... I assure you I would not have wanted ye Sight I got of ye Prince for a great deal as he will make a great noise and be much spoke of weather he win or lose. I'm glad I have so thorough a knowledge of his looks and manner; he looks much better in Lowland than in Highland dress Poor Man! I wish he may escape with his life. I've no notion he'll succeed.

In their new situation the Jacobites were confronted with a number of more or less urgent administrative and other problems. To deal with these, Charles now set up a properly constituted Council, which met regularly every morning in his drawing-room at Holyrood and consisted of the Duke of Perth, Lord George Murray, Lord Elcho, John William O'Sullivan, Sir Thomas Sheridan, Lochiel, John Murray of Broughton and his other principal commanders. Of its meetings Lord Elcho later gave a clearly somewhat prejudiced account. 'The Prince', he wrote, 'used Always first to declare what he was for, and then he Ask'd Every bodys opinion in their turn ... The Prince would not bear to hear any body differ in Sentiment from him, and took a dislike to Every body who did.'

The first and most important problem to be tackled was that of manpower. The Prince's victory at Prestonpans had presented the Highlanders, whose predatory instincts were keenly developed, with unprecedented opportunities for plunder, and after the battle many of them had simply made off with all the booty they could carry. One good example of this at a high level is furnished by the aged Robertson of Struan, who, immediately after the battle, left for home in General Cope's personal travelling carriage, wearing his chain and fur-lined nightgown. The story is also told of the Highlander who readily parted with a looted watch which had stopped ticking, explaining that 'he was glad to be rid of the creature, for she lived no time after he caught her'.

Such was the falling off in numbers from desertion and from other causes that within a few days of the battle the total strength of the Prince's army was found by Patullo, the muster-master, to have fallen to barely fourteen hundred, which, considering that Jacobite casualties had numbered less than a hundred, pointed to at least a thousand desertions. Fourteen hundred men were not enough to hold Scotland, let alone invade England, and the Prince and his advisers now turned their attention urgently to the problem of finding and bringing in more recruits.

The English Jacobites remained an unknown quantity, though the Prince still seems to have had hopes of them. As a first step, John Hickson, a vintner and proprietor of the inn at which Charles had stayed in Perth, was despatched to England immediately after the battle to inform them of 'the wonderful success with which it has hitherto pleased God to favour my endeavours for their deliverance' and to 'let them know that it is my full intention, in a few days to move towards them, and that they will be inexcusable before God and man if they do not all in their power to assist me in such an undertaking'. Hickson was also to ask for 'provisions and money'. But the unfortunate man got no further than Newcastle, where he was arrested by the English authorities and the Prince's letter found hidden in his glove and taken from him. Which provided the English Jacobites with yet another pretext for inaction.

In Atholl meanwhile Duke William was not finding it easy to raise more recruits. His tenants showed but little inclination to follow their Chief or, indeed, anybody else. 'For God's sake', wrote the normally kindly Lord George to his brother, 'cause some effectual method to be taken about the deserters; I would have their houses and crop destroyed for an example to others, and themselves punished in the most rigorous manner.' 'The men are turn'd intirely obstreperous,' wrote Commissary Bissatt gleefully to Duke James, 'and ... verry Fue will rise for him.'

Hoping his recent successes might help to bring in some of the waverers on his side, Charles now sent out fresh emissaries to the Highlands to reason with those of the clans who had not yet finally committed themselves. On 24 September Alexander MacLeod, Younger of Muiravonside was despatched to Skye to visit MacDonald of Sleat, MacLeod of MacLeod, MacKinnon of MacKinnon and some lesser neighbouring chieftains, while MacDonald of Kinlochmoidart, MacDonell of Barisdale and Hugh Fraser of Dalcraig were sent on a similar mission to Lord Lovat.

The Prince's envoys met with varying success. Neither MacLeod of MacLeod nor MacDonald of Sleat allowed themselves to be shaken in their new-found allegiance to the House of Hanover. It was clear that both had gone back without compunction on the formal undertakings they had given the Jacobites the year before. Indeed, MacLeod was actually raising a body of men for the service of the Government. Thanks very largely to the influence of Duncan Forbes, the loyalties of the Mackenzies, Mackintoshes, Gordons and Grants were divided, while most of the northern clans, Mackays, Munros and Sutherlands were, as always, solidly against the Stuarts. Lord Lovat, for his part, continued to play a waiting game, at one and the same time assuring the Jacobites of his loyalty to the Prince and likewise the Government, through Lord President Forbes, of his loyalty to King George. Since Prestonpans, however, there were indications that he was now inclining more to the Jacobite side. Indeed, in the course of October he went so far as to send his son, the Master of Lovat, with a body of clansmen to join the Jacobites and, as he put it, 'venture the last drop of his blood in the glorious Prince's service'. At the same time he took good care to write to the Lord President denying 'several villainous malicious and ridiculous reports' about himself, assuring him that 'nothing ever vexed my soul so much as my son's resolution to go and join the Prince', and talking in reply to the Lord President's somewhat sceptical response of 'the mad foolish actings of an unnatural son, who prefers his own extravagant fancies to the solid advice of an affectionate old father'.

In all this manoeuvring a most important part was played throughout by Forbes of Culloden, who made use of his considerable standing and influence in the Highlands to bring in as many of the chiefs as he could on the side of the Government or at any rate dissuade them from committing themselves to the Prince. This did not escape the Jacobites. 'He has rendered himself a scandal to all Scotsmen, and a nuisance to all society,' was Lochiel's angry comment. In the end the indignant Jacobites decided to revive a proposal to kidnap him, which had been put forward on behalf of Lovat by Fraser of Gortleg when he met Charles at Invergarry in August, and a formal warrant for his arrest was issued to Lovat in the Prince's name. An attempt to put this project into execution was made by a party of Frasers on 15 October. But Forbes, who knew his neighbour, was ready for them and they were driven off with only a few head of cattle to show for their pains. Next day, needless to say, a long letter of condolence and apology arrived at Culloden House from Lovat, explaining that he had 'cursed for two hours' when he heard what had happened, at once offering 'a hundred fat wedders' as reparation and 'solemnly swearing' that 'if any villain or rascal of my country durst presume to hurt or disturb any of your lordships tenants, I would go personally, though carried in a litter, and see them seized and hanged'. And so Duncan Forbes, who had now been given authority to raise twenty Independent Companies of Highlanders for the Government, continued to do what he could to prevent the chiefs from joining the Prince, using the offer of a company as a bait to bring waverers over to the Hanoverian side. Which, we are told, 'intirely putt a Stop to most of these Gentlemens balancing, as a Great Many that the Prince counted on accepted them'.

But, despite the efforts of the Lord President, the indecision or reluctance of many of the chiefs, and the continuing prevalence of desertion especially among the Athollmen, the numbers of the Prince's army were nevertheless gradually increasing. In addition to Lovat's Frasers (who in fact had not yet arrived), Lord Ogilvy had brought 600 men from Angus and Old Gordon of Glenbucket, riding crouched on a 'little grey Highland beast', 400 from Aberdeenshire. From Strathbogie and Enzie David Tulloch and John Hamilton brought a force of 480 men while Gordon of Aberlour and Stewart of Tinntinnar contributed two companies of foot. From the West came a further contingent of Camerons and MacDonalds of Keppoch and a hundred more MacGregors from Balquhidder, while before the end of October the Prince was rejoined by Duke William of Atholl with 600 more Athollmen and Cluny Macpherson brought in another 400 of his clan. From Skye came MacKinnon of MacKinnon with 120 clansmen. Lovat's son in law, Macpherson of Cluny, who, having been taken prisoner at Ruthven, was now wholeheartedly on the Jacobite side, led 300 of his followers to join the Prince. Lord Lewis Gordon, a younger brother of the Duke of Gordon, who continued to support the Government, was raising recruits from among his brother's tenants. Besides these, there were various smaller groups, while new drafts joined the existing clan regiments. There were also further accessions of strength to the Prince's small force of cavalry. Lord Elcho and Lord Balmerino were each given a troop of Life Guards to command, all 'gentlemen of familly and fortune ... their uniform blew and reed and all extremely well mounted'. From Banffshire and Aberdeen came Alexander Forbes, Lord Pitsligo, 'a little thinn fair man' of sixty-six, 'being a great Schollar', bringing 130 horse and 250 foot. Though his son was serving on the Government side, Lord Kilmarnock likewise commanded a newly raised body of horse, while Murray of Broughton had a troop of Hussars, dressed in tartan waistcoats and fur caps, a costume now also adopted by his good-looking wife. 'The Secretary Murray's Lady', wrote one onlooker, 'equipped herself in this dress with pistols at her syde sadle.' Altogether, by the end of October the Prince could muster some 5,000 foot and 500 horse.

Not all of his new adherents stayed the course. On 18 October he entertained to dinner Lords Kilmarnock, Kenmure and Nithsdale. But next day Lord Kenmure sent Murray of Broughton a letter from his wife, excusing him. Lord Nithsdale, for his part, 'after he retired home from the palace was Struck with such panick and Sincere repentance of his rashness that he was confined to bed for some days ... where nothing but the most dreadful scene of Axes, Gibbets and halters presented themselves to his waking thoughts'. As a result he too declined to join, though without the approval of his wife. And so in the end, of the three, only Lord Kilmarnock, no doubt egged on by his wife (the former Anne Livingstone, a dedicated Jacobite), finally took the plunge.

Money was almost as important as men. £5,000 in cash and £500 more in goods were, with the help of some MacGregors and a detachment of horse, extracted from the Provost and magistrates of Glasgow, and the Provosts of the other principal towns were ordered by Murray of Broughton to report to him at Holyrood, where they would be told how much was required of them. At the same time, the Customs officials and collectors of taxes were told to hand over any public monies in their possession while all impounded goods in the Customs House were confiscated and sold on the Prince's behalf.

Finally, in response to Charles's repeated appeals, came the first signs of actual support from France. Since learning that Charles had landed at Arisaig, the French court had been waiting to see what success he achieved. It was only on learning of his victory at Prestonpans that they belatedly took action. During October three French ships arrived at Montrose and Stonehaven bringing a certain amount of arms and equipment including six Swedish 4-pounder field guns, which were now added to the artillery captured from Cope. With these came ten French artillerymen and Lieutenant-Colonel James Grant, 'an able mathematician, in the French service', who now took command of the Prince's artillery. At the same time the Prince was joined by a more or less official emissary of the French court, the Marquis d'Eguilles, an adventurous Southerner from Provence, primarily despatched to find out how effective the Jacobites were, but on whom Charles at once bestowed the title of French Ambassador. With him came the personal greetings of the French King and a welcome present of 4,000 guineas. Having managed to avoid the Government warships that were patrolling the coast, the Marquis, with the thirty-man crew of the French ship that had brought him, promptly took possession of the town of Montrose. '*Arrivé par le plus grand des hasards à la rade de Montrose à cinq heures du soir*', he wrote delightedly, '*je me suis emparé de la ville avec trente hommes de l'équipage, qui on été joints sur le champ à la moitié du peuple.*'

In November the Duke of Perth's more robust brother Lord John Drummond, 'a tall jolly man of dark brown complexion, neither fat nor lean', landed in his turn from France with 800 men, consisting of his own regiment, the Ecossais Royaux, elements of the Irish Brigade, two squadrons of FitzJames's cavalry regiment and an artillery company with two 16-pounders, two 12-pounders and two 8-pounder guns. With him he brought letters from Louis xv promising further early support.

Nor was this all. Not surprisingly the news of Charles's victory at Prestonpans had been greeted in Paris with enthusiasm. Continuing British troop withdrawals from Flanders had already convinced the French that it was in their own interest to keep the Rising alive. But now, in early October, the French King directed that plans should be put in hand for a full scale invasion. By the middle of the month these were well advanced and on 24 October a secret treaty was signed at Fontainebleau by the Marquis d'Argenson and a Jacobite represen- tative, specifically committing France to give Charles all practicable military assistance against their common enemy, the Elector of Hanover. What is more, on the very same day that the Treaty of Fontainebleau was signed, Charles's brother Henry arrived at Fon- tainebleau from Rome and was at once granted an audience by Louis xv, on whom he urged the absolute need to give early and effective military assistance to the embattled Jacobites.

Not long after this it became known that the planned invasion would take place before the end of the year and be under the command of the Duc de Richelieu and that Prince Henry would himself accompany it, taking as his aides-de-camp his cousin the Prince de Turenne and the latter's brother-in-law, Louise's husband Jules de Montbazon, by now just nineteen. Soon Prince Henry was himself on his way to Dunkirk, where the invasion fleet was beginning to assemble, with his two aides-de-camp and, it was reported to Rome, 'victory in his face'. 'All our advices agree', wrote the Duke of Newcastle gloomily to old General, now Marshal Wade on 19 November, 'that the Court of France intend now to support the Pretender in earnest.'

In the Highlands, meanwhile, the Whig clans were by now also beginning to gather their strength, first and foremost the Campbells. Their chief, Archibald 3rd Duke of Argyll, had succeeded his father in

101

1743, two years before the Rising, the suppression of which quickly became his principal preoccupation. As was to be expected, the Duke gave the London Government his total support, placing all his very considerable human and material resources at their disposal. To his influence and power Prince Charles himself bore significant witness. 'There is one man in this country whom I could wish to have my friend', he had written to his father from Perth in September, 'and that is the Duke of Argyll, who I find is in great credit amongst them, on account of his great abilities and quality, and has many dependents by his great fortune; but I am told I can hardly flatter myself by the hope of it.'

Though a lawyer by profession, Argyll now actively concerned himself with military matters. From the first his largely Campbell-manned Argyll Militia took a leading part in the campaign. Since 1730 he and his friend Forbes of Culloden had been busy raising from clans known to be loyal to the House of Hanover the six Independent Highland Companies of loyal militia, known as the Black Watch. By this time some of these had already been formed into a regular infantry regiment, the 42nd Foot, which in April of that year had been used to good effect at Fontenoy.

A no-less important part in marshalling the resources and directing the military operations of Clan Campbell fell to the Duke's cousin and heir, General John Campbell of Mamore and his son John. While making it their business to raise fresh levies and gather supplies throughout the Western Highlands, neither showed quite the same vindictive spirit as the London Government's other Scottish supporters.

Once the news of the Prince's landing had been received, the chiefs of the Whig clans and other leading adherents of the House of Hanover had started calling out their clans and assembling their forces with varying degrees of enthusiasm. By the middle of September 1745 John Campbell, 4th Earl of Loudon, was seeking to recruit as many as twenty companies for service with the regiment which bore his name. In this task he enjoyed the active support of the Mackays, Munros, MacLeod of MacLeod, MacDonald of Sleat, the Earl of Sutherland, and curiously enough of Lord Seaforth's son and successor, known since the attainder as Lord Fortrose, who under Forbes's influence had actually joined the Government forces under Lord Loudon. '*Hé, Mon Dieu!*' the Prince had exclaimed sadly on hearing this, '*et Seaforth est aussi contre moi.*' Lady Fortrose, on the other hand, had displayed her independence by bringing out a number of Mackenzie clansmen for the Prince, while Lord Cromartie, after some hesitation, had finally joined the Prince's army with 500 more Mackenzies.

Despite his clan's Whig traditions and the urgings of Forbes of

Culloden, Sir James Grant of Grant seems to have evinced no great enthusiasm for either side, advising Ludovick, his son and heir, 'to stay at home and take care of his country and join no party'. While staying at home as his father had suggested, Ludovick made every effort to prevent his clansmen, some of whom had strong Jacobite sympathies, from joining the Prince. Even so a number of Grants, including once again the Grants of Glenmoriston, had managed to do so, after which Ludovick made it his business to hunt down as many of them as possible and hand them over to the Government.

PART II

PATHS OF GLORY

'Il ne manquait à l'entreprise que la possibilité'

Voltaire,
*Précis du Siècle
de Louis* XV

CHAPTER SEVEN

To the Government in London, who had expected Cope to win an easy victory and 'nip the rebellion in the bud', the news of his humiliating defeat at Prestonpans came as a severe shock. In the space of a few minutes a well-equipped regular force had been utterly routed by a 'ragged, hungry rabble of Yahoos of Scotch Highlanders' and Scotland, with the exception of the castles of Edinburgh, Stirling and Dumbarton and a few forts and barracks in the Highlands, was now in Jacobite hands. In the words of the Chevalier de Johnstone, Charles was now 'entirely master of the Kingdom of Scotland'.

Not for the first or indeed the last time, the Duke of Newcastle showed signs of losing his nerve. He derived, it is true, some slight reassurance from the timely arrival in England, under the terms of an old treaty with Holland, of the first of some 6,000 Dutch troops. Had these, he wrote, in a revealing letter to King George's second son, the Duke of Cumberland, not landed 'providentially the day before the news of Cope's defeat, the confusion in the city of London would not have been to be described and the King's crown, I will venture to say, in the utmost danger'. Three days later the Dutch contingent was followed by ten British battalions from Flanders and soon still more troops were being recalled, while in different parts of England, despite widespread apathy, Loyal Associations were beginning to be set up to raise funds and, as far as possible, enthusiasm for the established regime. This, so far as one can judge, was most necessary, for in a letter written to a friend at this time, Horace Walpole, who in his way kept his finger on the pulse of public opinion, gave it as his view that, if Marshal Saxe with 10,000 men appeared within a day's march of the metropolis, people would 'be hiring windows at Charing Cross and

Cheapside to see them pass by'. For his own part, he was inclined to take a gloomy view of the situation. 'I look upon Scotland as gone', he wrote. And again, 'I think of what King William said to the Duke of Hamilton when he was extolling Scotland: "My Lord, I only wish it was a hundred thousand miles off, and that you was King of it!"'

Meanwhile Parliament had been recalled; King George brought back from his native Hanover; and, in addition to the 6,000 Dutch auxiliaries, altogether three battalions of Guards, eighteen line regiments, nine squadrons of cavalry and four companies of artillery were rushed over from Flanders. With such regular forces as were already in England, the new arrivals had been formed into three army groups, all now moving into position. The first, commanded by old Marshal Wade and with a strength, including the Dutch, of 14,000 men, was on its way to Newcastle, which it reached on 29 October. The second, under Lieutenant-General Sir John Ligonier, was on the march to Lancashire. The third, in anticipation of a French landing, was dispersed along the South-East coast. In addition to these regular forces, there were also the County Militia and a number of volunteer regiments, newly raised for the emergency by enthusiastic supporters of the House of Hanover, such as the Duke of Kingston's Light Horse. In London two new verses had been added to the National Anthem and were sung nightly at Covent Garden and elsewhere amid scenes of patriotic enthusiasm:

> God grant that Marshal Wade
> May by thy mighty aid
> > Victory bring.
> May he sedition hush
> And like a torrent rush
> Rebellious Scots to crush.
> > God save the King.

> From France and Pretender
> Great Britain defend her,
> > Foes let them fall;
> From foreign slavery,
> Priests and their knavery,
> And Popish reverie,
> > God save us all.

Clearly the balance of military strength between the opposing forces was most uneven and the success or failure of the Prince's venture likely to depend on two factors: firstly the scale of French assistance, and secondly the amount of active support afforded, when it came to the point, by the English Jacobites. Charles himself had few doubts on either score. D'Eguilles had assured him that a French landing might be expected any day and similar information had also reached him from perennially optimistic Jacobite agents in Paris. The English Jacobites, despite the Prince's successes, were, it is true, still lying remarkably low, but Charles had nevertheless persuaded himself that 'a great body ... would join him upon his entring their Country'. Indeed, he had already written to them in the most rousing terms: 'There is no more time for Deliberations. Now or Never is the Word. I am resolved to conquer or perish. If this last should happen, let them judge what they and their Posteriety are to expect.' He also believed with good reason that he could not afford to wait. Time, clearly was of the essence. 'What is sed is very short,' he wrote to his father on 15 October, 'pressing to have succor with all haste by a landing in England, for that as matters stand I must either conquer or perish in a little while.' In these circumstances his proposal was that they should at once march on Newcastle and attack Marshal Wade, 'for he was sure he would run away'.

On consulting his Council, however, Charles found to his dismay that as a body his Scottish advisers were against leaving Scotland. At a meeting on 30 October the chiefs told him 'that they had taken arms and risked their fortunes and lives, merely to set him on the throne of Scotland; but that they wished to have nothing to do with England'. 'Our men,' wrote one of the sons of MacDonald of Leek in a letter to his father from Musselburgh dated 31 October, 'are terribly afraid to march to England.' To the chiefs it seemed sensible that Charles, who, in a proclamation dated 17 October, had declared 'the pretended Union now at end', should simply establish himself as Regent in Scotland, annul the union and defy any force his cousin George might send against him. What might have been the outcome, had such a plan been put into execution, is an interesting matter for speculation. But Charles, having promised his father to win three crowns for him, was determined to invade England and in the end the chiefs agreed to his proposal, on the assumption that both French support and active help from the English Jacobites would, as he assured them, be forthcoming. But even now the Council did not like the Prince's suggestion that they should march by way of Newcastle and at once attack Field Marshal Wade. As an alternative, Lord George Murray put forward the proposal that they should enter England by way of Cumberland, 'where,' he said, 'he knew the Country, That the Army would be well Situated to receive reinforcements from Scotland to join the French when they landed, or the English if they rose, and that it was a Good Country to fight Wade in, because of the Mountanious Ground'.

To this Charles objected that he was reluctant to give the impression that he was deliberately avoiding a battle with Wade and that this would be disheartening for his troops, who, once they had advanced, would feel in danger of being cut off. On the other hand, if Wade were once defeated and the North of England cleared of the enemy, the way South would be wide open, the effect on the morale of their own troops would be prodigious and the consternation of the enemy would know no limits. Whatever the merits of the argument, Charles failed to win over a majority of the Council and so adjourned the meeting. Next morning, on 31 October, having in the interval thought things over and realized the danger of antagonizing all his principal advisers at this early stage, he reconvened the Council and 'told them in a very obliging manner that he had seriously considered of their arguments of the night before, and was now, upon reflection, given to think they were in the right, and that he was ready to follow their advice, and then proposed yt the rout might be agreed upon, and proper orders conserted for their speedy march'.

The better to confuse Field Marshal Wade, Charles now proposed that the army should be divided into two columns. One he would lead himself, with Lord George Murray as second in command. This column would march by Lauder and Kelso, as though making for Newcastle, before turning South-West at Jedburgh in the direction of Carlisle. The other, led by Duke William of Atholl and the Duke of Perth, would march directly South by Peebles, Moffat and Lockerbie and join the first at Newton of Rockcliff in Cumberland. This plan was agreed and the Duke of Perth and Lord George Murray instructed to make all necessary arrangements forthwith. Meanwhile the city of Perth, where further reinforcements would in due course arrive, was left under the command of Lord Strathallan, who in the absence of the Duke of Atholl, was appointed Commander-in-Chief North of the Firth, with subordinate commanders at Dundee, Aberdeen and Montrose, and Robertson of Drumachine as Governor of Atholl.

By nightfall on 31 October the outlying units of the Prince's army had already been brought in from Duddingston, Musselburgh and their other cantonments and assembled at Dalkeith, where Charles in due course joined them. Next day, Edinburgh, too, was evacuated by the Highlanders, who once more marched through the streets of the capital with colours flying and pipes playing. Lord George Murray brought up the rear. 'We march today,' he wrote to his wife. Only a few wounded men, who could not be moved, were left to the tender mercies of the castle garrison, who, once the Jacobite army was safely gone, 'broke out like a parcel of hungry dogs' to vent their rage on the Highland wounded.

While his troops were assembling, Charles spent two days at Dalkeith Palace in the absence of its noble owner, a loyal supporter of King

George. His army was by now better armed, clad and equipped, and much of the time spent in or near Edinburgh had been devoted to more badly needed training and drill. The column commanded by the Prince and Lord George Murray was made up mainly of Highlanders, MacDonalds, Camerons, Stewarts of Appin and approximately half the cavalry, including Lord Kilmarnock's and Lord Pitsligo's newly raised regiments. The second column, led by the Dukes of Atholl and Perth, consisted of the three battalions of the Atholl Brigade; the foot regiments of the Duke of Perth, Lord Ogilvy, Gordon of Glenbucket, Roy Stuart and Cluny Macpherson, the cavalry commanded by Lord Elcho and Lord Balmerino, the artillery under James Grant, and the baggage train.

On Sunday 3 November both columns marched out of Dalkeith on their way to the border, each taking the route decided on three days earlier. The Prince's stratagem, as it turned out, was completely successful and old Marshal Wade, thinking the enemy was heading for Northumberland (although he had received reports to the contrary), remained inactive at Newcastle, while the Prince's two columns converged on Carlisle.

Marching with his column by way of Kelso and Jedburgh and then along Liddesdale, Charles crossed the Esk into Cumberland near Canonbie on 8 November. 'This being the first time they entered England', writes Murray of Broughton, 'the Highlanders, without any orders being given, all drew their swords with one Consent upon entering the River, and every man as he landed on t'other Side wheeled about to the Left and faced Scotland again.' While unsheathing his broadsword, Lochiel was on this occasion unlucky enough to cut his hand, an accident which was taken by those who witnessed it as a bad omen for the success of the campaign. Next day the Prince, having duly joined forces with the Duke of Atholl's column at Rockliff, crossed the River Eden and encamped for the night two or three miles ouside Carlisle.

Four or five hundred years earlier Carlisle had been one of the most strongly fortified towns in England. By 1745, however, its ancient citadel built by William Rufus and its massive red sandstone walls strengthened by Richard III and Henry VII had fallen into disrepair, while the battlements had recently largely been demolished. The regular garrison consisted of eighty 'invalids', mostly 'very old and infirm', under a Captain Gilpin. The castle's artillery, consisting of twenty 6-pounders, was in charge of Master-Gunner Stevenson and three gunners, two half-trained civilians and one very decrepit old man. The civic control of the city rested, for the time being, with the Deputy-Mayor, Alderman Thomas Pattinson, a local tradesman.

111

As soon as it became clear that Carlisle lay in the probable line of march of the Prince's army, Dr Waugh, the distinguished Chancellor of the Diocese of Carlisle, had with considerable presence of mind drawn the attention of the Government to the dangers of leaving the city so inadequately defended. Their answer had been to send a single Guards officer, Lieutenant-Colonel Durand of the Coldstream, post haste, to see what could be done. The first request made by Colonel Durand, only recently recovered from a sharp attack of the gout, was for 500 regular infantry to reinforce the garrison. On being told that this was impossible, he managed to arrange for a roughly equivalent number of men of the Cumberland and Westmorland Militia, then undergoing their annual training, to be brought over from Whitehaven and mounted on the walls; for large numbers of sandbags to replace the newly dismantled battlements; and for a hundred or so townspeople to be enrolled as volunteers and part-time artillerymen. Finally he posted on the Cathedral tower a couple of Dr Waugh's clergy armed with 'a very large spying-glass' which he had brought with him from London, giving them strict instructions to keep a sharp look-out for any signs of the approaching enemy.

The two clergymen got their first sight of the enemy at about noon on 9 November, when a party of the Prince's cavalry appeared to the north of the town. Not long after, a local farmer's son rode in with a letter from one of the Prince's Quartermasters demanding quarters for 13,000 foot and 3,000 horse. Whereupon Mr Stevenson and his men discharged their guns and the Highlanders withdrew, while Colonel Durand at once despatched an express to Marshal Wade in Newcastle, informing him of the enemy's approach and repeating his request for help.

Next morning, when the mist lifted, three Highland columns were seen approaching the town. These withdrew when the castle guns again opened fire, but not long after another countryman arrived with a letter from Prince Charles, calling upon the inhabitants to open the gates so as to 'avoid the effusion of English blood' and pointing out that otherwise 'it will not perhaps be in our Power to prevent the dreadful Consequences which usually attend a Town being taken by Assault'. To this it was decided to return no reply, but simply to open fire on the enemy whenever they showed themselves.

It was at this stage that Prince Charles received a report that Marshal Wade was marching to the relief of Carlisle. Welcoming the prospect of an early encounter with the aged Marshal, Charles at once decided to move eastwards with his whole force in the hope of meeting him in the hilly country round Brampton, seven miles or so north-east of

Carlisle. By 12 November not a Highlander was left in sight of the town.

This was Alderman Pattinson's finest hour. On the first appearance of the Highlanders he had at once issued a proclamation declaring that he was not Paterson a Scotchman, but Pattinson a true-born Englishman and that he would never surrender. Delighted at the latest turn of events, he now sat down to pen a despatch to Lord Lonsdale, the Lord Lieutenant of the county. 'Last Saturday night,' he wrote, 'our city was surrounded with about nine thousand Highlanders. At three o'clock that afternoon I received a message from them for billets for thirteen thousand men to be ready that night. I refused. On Sunday, at three in the afternoon, I received the enclosed message [the summons of the Prince]. The answer returned was only by firing our cannon. Then Charles and the Duke of Perth, with several other gentlemen, lay within a mile or two of us, but have now all marched for Brampton, seven miles on the high road for Newcastle.' 'I told your Lordship,' he continues proudly, 'that we would defend this city; its proving true gives me pleasure, and more so since we have outdone Edinburgh, nay, all Scotland. We are bringing in men, and arms, and covered wagons frequently. I shall in a little time fully set forth everything to your Lordship. If you think proper I would have you mention our success to the Duke of Newcastle and to General Wade.'

Lord Lonsdale did so and in due course the Deputy-Mayor received a personal acknowledgement of his report from the Duke of Newcastle. 'Immediately,' wrote the Duke, 'I laid it before the King, and his Majesty was so sensible of the loyalty and courage which the magistrates and officers at that place have showed on this important occasion, that his Majesty commanded me to take the first opportunity of returning his thanks to them, with which I am to desire you would be pleased to acquaint them. I most heartily congratulate you upon the great honour the town of Carlisle has gained by setting this example of firmness and resolution, which it is to be hoped will be followed in other places should the rebels attempt to advance further.'

On the afternoon of 13 November Colonel Durand received from Marshal Wade a reply to his express of 9 November. This made it clear that there could be no question of any help from that quarter. The roads between Newcastle and Carlisle, wrote the Marshal, were impassable to artillery; the depredations of the Highlanders would mean that there would be insufficient provisions for his men; he did not in any case believe that it was really the intention of the rebels to besiege Carlisle; and he concluded by wishing the garrison 'all imaginable success'.

In the meanwhile, Prince Charles had on 12 November received fresh intelligence showing that his earlier information concerning

113

Wade's movements had been unfounded and that the latter had in fact never left Newcastle. On the strength of this, he decided to resume the siege of Carlisle without delay. The Duke of Perth was to conduct the siege with his own regiment, while Lord George Murray with six battalions blockaded the approaches to the city and the Prince himself remained at Brampton with the rest of his force in case of any change of plans on the part of Marshal Wade. It was thus that on the afternoon of 13 November, while Colonel Durand and the garrison were digesting the terms of Marshal Wade's reply, the Highlanders again appeared in strength before Carlisle and at once began to throw up earthworks about 300 yards East of the citadel between the Scots and English Gates, the tall, willowy Duke of Perth and the aged, gouty Duke of Atholl taking their coats off and helping dig the trenches alongside their men. At the same time, Lord George Murray threw a cordon of troops right round the city.

The arrival of Marshal Wade's letter and the simultaneous reappearance of the Prince's army had a bad effect on the morale of the garrison. On learning the position, the local militia officers who had never fully accepted Durand's authority and who, like their men, resented the fact that they were being kept under arms without proper authority after they had completed their one month's annual training, now presented the unfortunate Colonel with a round-robin, announcing that it was their intention to surrender the town and demanding that they and their men should be allowed to leave the city by the English Gate. Having refused this request out of hand and ordered his gunners to maintain their bombardment of the enemy's entrenching-party, Colonel Durand repaired to a meeting of the militia officers at the King's Arms. Here he did his best to reason with them, talking of 'the dishonour of treating with the rebels', dismissing the Duke of Perth's earthworks as 'of no great consequence' and assuring them that, if they would stand by him, it should be possible for them to hold out for a considerable time. But to no avail. 'They had,' said the militia officers in their stubborn North-country way, 'shaken hands upon it and would do it.' Soon the militiamen's mood spread to the townspeople, who, after passing a variety of resolutions and counter-resolutions, finally decided at a meeting in the town hall to join the militia in surrendering the town. At this Colonel Durand, old Captain Gilpin and the eight invalids, after spiking their guns on the ramparts, laying in provisions for a siege and buying up all the gunpowder in the town, bravely withdrew to the castle, determined to defend it to the last.

While the militiamen deserted by dropping as best they could from the crumbling walls and general confusion prevailed, a formal deputation of townspeople left the city under a white flag to offer its surrender to the Prince. To this the Prince, no doubt remembering Edinburgh, replied on the morning of 15 November that 'he would grant no terms to the Town nor treat about it at all unless the Castle was surrendered'. As soon as the terms of the Prince's reply became generally known, there was fresh panic in the city and widespread fear that at any moment a bombardment might begin. Accordingly a party of militia officers and leading citizens was sent without delay to beg Colonel Durand 'for God's sake' to agree to surrender the castle.

Colonel Durand, as was recognized at his subsequent court martial, had done what he could. After first calling a council of war, he and Captain Gilpin were now prevailed upon to put their signatures to a declaration which, having emphasized the deplorable behaviour of the militia and citizens and the weakness of the regular garrison, expressed the view that 'the Castle being not teneable, it is for his Majesty's service that it be abandoned'.

On the afternoon of 15 November, after the terms of surrender had been agreed (though not by Colonel Durand, who would have no part in the capitulation), the Duke of Perth and his regiment entered the town by the English Gate and next morning, attended by the Mayor and civic officials, proclaimed King James from the Market Cross. The siege had cost the Highlanders one man killed and one wounded. On 16 November the Mayor and corporation rode out to Brampton in their robes and, kneeling as a sign of submission, presented the keys of the city to Prince Charles, who on the following day entered Carlisle at the head of his troops, mounted on a white horse and preceded by a hundred pipers.

Much to the relief of the population the Highlanders proved less ferocious than they had been led to believe. When some of the Prince's officers came on a little girl of five or six hidden under a bed in the house in which they had been quartered, the child's mother, Murray of Broughton tells us, at once 'called out for God's sake to Spare her Child for She was the only remaining one of Seven she had bore'. And, on being asked what she meant, 'answered that indeed She had been assured from Creditable people that the highlanders were a Savage Sett of people and eat all the young Children'. 'You never saw a woman in yt condition,' recalls O'Sullivan. 'She thought the child wou'd be set upon the Spit, as there was not much to eat in the house, but Sr Thomas, who spoak their language very well, appaissed her and rassured her.'

Meanwhile, sixty miles away to the East, Marshal Wade had at long last set out from Newcastle with the intention of coming to the relief of Carlisle. After struggling through deep snow for two days he reached Hexham, where he learned that he was too late. He then struggled back to Newcastle with 1,000 sick soldiers on his hands.

The ease with which the Prince had captured Carlisle might have seemed to bode well for the future success of his arms. But at this very moment another of those disturbing incidents occurred which were to become ever more frequent as the campaign proceeded. For some time Lord George Murray had felt that he did not enjoy Prince Charles's full confidence. Incensed by the action of the Duke of Perth in reporting directly to Prince Charles on the conduct of the siege and by the fact that the Prince had subsequently entrusted the negotiations for the surrender of the city to the Duke of Perth and to Murray of Broughton rather than to him as Lieutenant-General, he had on the night of 14 November, before the final surrender of the city, written a short note to the Prince resigning his commission as Lieutenant-General and announcing his intention of serving as a volunteer in the trenches. To this the Prince had replied the same night in an even shorter note, accepting both his resignation and his offer to serve as a volunteer. A subsequent interview between them, arranged with the best intentions by old Duke William of Atholl, had done nothing to improve matters. 'I told his Royal Highness', wrote Lord George to his brother, 'that you had acquainted me he desired to see me. He said, No, he had nothing particular to say to me.'

And there things might have rested, had it not been for the High-landers' strong and openly declared preference for Lord George as a leader. A petition was now quickly sent to the Prince, begging 'that Lord George be desired to take back his Commission'; the Prince yielded to the pressure of opinion; the Duke of Perth resigned as joint Lieutenant-General; and Lord George emerged from the dispute as sole commander under the Prince. This, in the rather jaundiced view of Murray of Broughton, was what he had been aiming for all along. Even so, the episode left an unpleasant taste in everyone's mouth and further increased the tension between the Prince and his General.

On the day after Charles's entry to Carlisle, a council of war was held there to discuss the next move. At this a variety of views were advanced. Some of the Prince's advisers held that the best course would be to return to Scotland and go over to the defensive until the arrival of further reinforcements. Others were in favour of staying in Carlisle until it was seen what support was forthcoming from the English Jacobites. Yet others wanted to march on Newcastle and attack Marshal Wade. But the Prince himself, with his eyes firmly fixed on London, was strongly in favour of at once marching southwards through Lancashire, where there was generally believed to be strong support for his cause. On being asked for his opinion by the Prince, Lord George, by now again Lieutenant-General, but speaking 'with the more caution' in view of recent events, replied that he could not advise Charles to advance much further into England without more encouragement than he had received hitherto, but that if he resolved to march South his army, small as it was, would follow him. 'Upon this', we are told, 'he immediately said he would venture it', and the rest of the council acquiesced in his wish.

Leaving a garrison of around 150 to defend Carlisle, the first division of the Prince's army started their march south on 20 November, the Prince himself following next day with the remainder. In the absence of any firm promise of help from the French Government or of any valid undertaking to rise on the part of the English Jacobites, with whom there seems to have been a surprising absence of liaison, the enterprise on which they were embarking was clearly a precarious one. Meanwhile, the tidings from Scotland were mixed. A number of fresh Jacobite recruits, it appeared, were assembling at Perth. There was news that 700 Frasers were drilling in front of Castle Downie, 'with White Cockades and springs of yew in their bonnets'. And there were also, strangely enough, assurances of good will from MacLeod of MacLeod, although that chief was in fact raising four companies of his clansmen for the Government. On the other hand, the citizens of Edinburgh, Glasgow, Dundee, Dumfries, Paisley and Perth (where there had been a brush with the Jacobite garrison), had by this time all in one way or another declared for the House of Hanover, while in Inverness the Lord President and Lord Loudon were busy rallying the Whig clans for King George.

There could be no doubt that numerically the Jacobites were still at a great disadvantage. Though they had suffered practically no casualties, they had lost at least 1,000 men by desertion since leaving Edinburgh and now numbered less than 5,000 men in all. Meanwhile beyond the Pennines, Marshal Wade, having abandoned any idea of relieving Carlisle, was lumbering slowly southwards into Lancashire with a force of over 9,000 regular troops. 'The Marshal knows best what he is about,' wrote his second-in-command surreptitiously in a letter to the Duke of Newcastle. 'For my own part I don't pretend to it.' And again, in a thumb-nail sketch of his superior officer: 'He is infirm both in mind and body, forgetful, irresolute, perplexed, snappish....'

But Wade's army was only one of three forces opposing the Highlanders. Alarmed by the news from Carlisle, the Government were now assembling a further force some 10,000 strong in Staffordshire under Sir John Ligonier, a distinguished veteran of Marlborough's wars, their task being to cut the Jacobites off should they make for Chester or Derby. When a few days later Sir John fell seriously ill, the command of his army was taken over by George II's corpulent younger son, William, Duke of Cumberland. Cumberland had been brought back from Flanders where, appointed Commander-in-Chief at twenty-four, he had shared responsibility for the British defeat at Fontenoy. On being told by an English prisoner that they had narrowly missed capturing the British Commander-in-Chief, 'We took good care not to', said some French officers. 'He does us better service at the head of your army.' Now, leading an army which included large numbers of seasoned troops who had served with him in Flanders and liked him for his physical courage, the plump (eighteen-stone) young Duke was full of confidence and longing to come to grips with the rebels threatening his father's throne. 'In which case,' he wrote to the Secretary of State on the day after his arrival, 'I flatter myself the affair would be certain in my favour.' Finally a third rather mixed force of several thousand men based on Finchley and charged with the defence of the capital was gathering in and around London, bringing the enemy's combined strength to at least 30,000 men against less than 5,000 Jacobites.

From Carlisle Prince Charles's line of march took his army through Penrith, Shap, Kendal and Lancaster to Preston, where his vanguard arrived on 27 November, the very day, as it happened, of his kinsman Cumberland's arrival in Staffordshire. The Highland army marched in two divisions, usually separated by half a day's march, the first commanded by Lord George Murray and the second by the Prince himself. Throughout the march Charles marched at the head of his division. 'He never', we are told, 'dinn'd nor threw of his cloaths at night, eat much at Supper, used to throw himself on a bed at Eleven o clock & was up by four in the morning. As he had a prodigious strong constitution, he bore fatigue most surprisingly well.' In each town they reached King James was duly proclaimed, but usually without arousing much enthusiasm. At Kendal, 'the people were civiler than in Cumberland'; at Lancaster, where the Prince stayed at a handsome house in Church Street belonging to a Mrs Livesay, they 'testify'd no joy'; only at Preston were there 'for the first time in England several huzzas'.

Recalling that the advance of the Scottish armies had been disastrously checked at Preston in 1648 and 1715 and wishing to avoid anything his troops might consider a bad omen, Lord George Murray, 'than whom nobody knew the humours and disposition of the Highlanders better', did not halt in the town itself but, pressing on, crossed the River Ribble and quartered his troops in the villages on the southern side, 'to convince them that the Town Should not be their *ne plus ultra* for a third time, which seemed to give them a good deal of Satisfaction'.

It is recorded that over dinner that night at the Joiner's Arms, Lord Elcho, asked by Counsellor David Morgan, a Monmouthshire Jacobite who had just joined them, what were the Prince's religious beliefs, replied simply that they were 'yet to seek'.

As Lancashire was generally believed to be strongly Jacobite in sympathy, it was hoped that large numbers of volunteers would now flock to join the Prince's army. But these hopes were to be sadly disappointed. 'If arms were offer'd to them and they were desir'd to Go along with the army', the Lancastrians 'all declined and Said they did not Understand fighting.' Despite the several huzzas that had greeted the Jacobites' arrival in Preston, in the end only 'a few common people' showed themselves ready to take up arms, as did three persons of greater consequence: Mr Francis Townley of Townley Hall, a member of an old Lancashire Catholic family, who had seen service in the French army, and two Welshmen from Monmouthshire, Counsellor Morgan and Mr William Vaughan, who held out hopes of more recruits in due course from North Wales. They were followed a few days later by an emissary from Lord Barrymore and Sir Watkin Williams Wynne bringing promises of help from London and from Wales. But only promises. The fact was that in England there was no longer any martial tradition of the kind that existed in the Highlands. With the exception of serving soldiers, men were now simply not trained in the use of arms.

From Preston Charles marched South along roads that were lined with curious and not unfriendly onlookers by way of Wigan to Manchester. Here he had been preceded by one of his sergeants, a young Scotsman by the name of Dickson, who had been taken prisoner by his troops at Prestonpans and had subsequently joined them, acting as servant to the Chevalier de Johnstone. Sergeant Dickson had on his own initiative set out from Preston on the evening of 27 November, accompanied only by his mistress and a drummer, and, after riding all night, had reached Manchester the following afternoon. Having dined in style at the Bull's Head Inn, the three of them at once set about enlisting volunteers for 'the yellow haired laddie'. At first the inhabitants, believing that the Highland army was close at hand, made no attempt to interfere. As time went by, however, and there were no signs of any army, Highland or otherwise, some of the bolder spirits decided to try and capture the Sergeant. But at this Dickson simply announced that he would blow out the brains of anyone who laid hands on him and, by turning round continually to face his assailants with his blunderbuss at the ready, kept them at bay until a party of some 500 or 600 local Jacobites eventually came to his help. Placing himself at the head of these, he then marched freely round the town for the rest of the day, offering five guineas to any who would join the Prince. By the time the Prince arrived he had already collected 180 volunteers for him, which led to the widely repeated saying that Manchester was taken by a Sergeant, a Drummer and a Whore.

Charles made his own entry into Manchester on the afternoon of 29 November on foot, surrounded by his bodyguard of Highlanders. 'The Mob Huzza'd him to his Lodgings, the town was mostly illuminated and the Bells rung', and over supper that night at a house in Market Street Lane, where 'substantial people came and kis'd his hand' and 'a vast number of people of all sorts came to see him supp', Charles, in the best possible spirits, discussed 'in what manner he should enter London, on horseback or a foot, and in what dress'.

But to some of the Prince's companions his prospects of ever reaching London seemed a good deal less promising than they did to him. The Jacobites had expected a substantial accession of strength in Manchester. 'We expected yt at least one thousand five hundred men wou'd have joyned us here,' wrote O'Sullivan. But in fact only another hundred or so fresh recruits had been added to those brought in by Sergeant Dickson, and many of these made it clear that they were simply out of work and would as soon have joined King George's army had it reached Manchester first. Nor had the great Lancashire families, the Stanleys, Molyneux, Listers and others shown the active enthusiasm for the cause that had been expected of them, despite the fact that many of them were believed to have Jacobite portraits and keepsakes tucked away in secret drawers and to drink privately to the King over the water. Indeed, in the words of John Murray of Broughton, 'during the whole time of their being in England, they received no application or message from any persons in England, which surprised and disappointed them extremely'.

In the end a Manchester Regiment of some 250 or 300 men was formed and Francis Townley appointed to command it with a tartan sash across his chest to show his rank. On the day after his arrival Charles inspected his new regiment and also 'rode through the Town to view it by way of amusement, attended by the principal officers of his Army, when he was followed by vast Croweds of people with loud huzzas and all demonstrations possible of their zeal for his success'. But for all their zeal, the good people of Manchester did not volunteer and amongst the Prince's advisers there were by now those who began to talk of turning back. But Charles himself was determined to go on and in the end Lord George and the chiefs reluctantly agreed to 'make a further trial and go the length of Derby'.

On 1 December the Prince left Manchester for Macclesfield. He had first given orders to repair a bridge which the county authorities had

had destroyed on his approach. 'His Royal Highness', he wrote in a proclamation to the people of Manchester, 'does not propose to make use of it for his own army, but believes it will be of service to the country; and if any forces that were with General Wade be coming this road they may have the benefit of it'. Charles marched at the head of two regiments of foot wearing, an onlooker tells us, a light plaid, belted about with a blue sash, a grey wig and a blue bonnet with a white cockade in it. The Mersey he forded above Stockport, the water reaching to his waist. On the Cheshire bank a very old lady was presented to him, a Mrs Skyring, who as a small child had seen Charles II land at Dover in 1660; for years she had contributed half her income to the Jacobite cause and now, having sold all her plate and jewellery, she handed to the Prince a further substantial sum, remarking as she did so: 'Lord, now lettest thou thy servant depart in peace.'*

That night at Macclesfield Charles received news which demanded immediate and decisive action. Having duly taken command in Staffordshire a few days before, the Duke of Cumberland was now advancing to meet the Highland army; his forward troops, it appeared, were no more than seventeen miles away at Newcastle-under-Lyme.

At once a council of war was called. At this, writes Hay of Restalrig, 'it was unanimously agreed to make some forced marches, so as to get between the Duke's army and London, and then march on as fast as they could to London. One of the keenest for that measure was Lord George Murray'. 'We resolved', writes Lord George himself, 'to march for Derby, and, to cover our intentions, I offered to go with a column of the army to Congleton, which was the straight road to Litchfield, so that the enemy would have reason to think we intended to come on them, which would make them gather in a body, and readily advance on that road, so that we could get before them to Derby'.

Lord George's manoeuvre was completely successful. Leaving the Prince's division at Macclesfield, he turned off south-westwards to Congleton as planned and there engaged Cumberland's advance guard, the Duke of Kingston's Light Horse, commanded by that nobleman in person, who at once withdrew hastily in the direction of Newcastle-under-Lyme, leaving his dinner for the enemy to eat. 'The Duke of Kingston with his regiment of horse left that place in pretty much of a hurry,' wrote Lord George after chasing them some miles along the Newcastle road. That night, as it happened, a Jacobite patrol, sent out to collect intelligence under Ker of Graden, managed to bring back several prisoners, including a certain Captain Weir or Vere, said to be the chief Government spy, who forthwith communicated to his captors

---

*Her prayer was not granted. She was to die from disappointment and disgust at the subsequent course of events.

Cumberland's complete order of battle, showing a total strength of 2,200 horse and 8,250 foot. He also seems to have given them a good idea of the Duke's immediate intentions. There was some debate among the Jacobites whether or not to shoot Vere, who was alleged, rather improbably, to have managed to keep within ten miles of the Prince since the day he landed and to have spied on him in France before that. In the end the question was settled by the Prince himself, who pointed out that he had not been 'found in disguise' and refused to let him be executed.*

So far everything had gone according to plan. Next day, believing, as it was intended he should, that the Highland army was making for Wales, Cumberland withdrew his forward troops to Stone, where they were joined by the rest of his army, advancing northwards from Stafford. This effectively blocked any move westwards by the Highlanders, but left wide open to them the road to Derby and the South. Seeing that his stratagem had succeeded, Lord George now moved as fast as he could in a south-easterly direction through Leek to Ashbourne, leaving the rest of the army to follow, and on the morning of 4 December the first Highland troops reached Derby.

The unexpected approach of the Highland army had caused considerable alarm in Derby, always a Whig stronghold. For the past fortnight the Duke of Devonshire, greatest of all the Whig magnates, and his son Lord Hartington had been busily collecting a force of some 600 men for the protection of the district and on 3 December had himself come over from Chatsworth especially to review them. But the review was scarcely over and the newly raised force still under arms in the market place when they received the unwelcome news that the Highlanders were already in nearby Ashbourne and now apparently heading for Derby. This gave the unfortunate Duke barely time to take himself and his men hurriedly off that same night by torchlight in the direction of Nottingham before their arrival. Whereupon many other leading citizens, prudently following his example, likewise packed their belongings, gathered their families together and left with equal promptitude.

By now the Prince's forward troops were already entering Derby. 'On Wednesday the 4th of December, about eleven o'clock', wrote an eyewitness,

> two of the rebel vanguard entered this town, inquired for the magistrates, and demanded billets for 9,000 men or more. A short while after, the vanguard rode into town, consisting of about thirty

*Weir or Vere, for his part, later did not hesitate to send a lot of Jacobite prisoners to their death by the evidence he gave against them.

122

men, clothed in blue faced with red, and scarlet waistcoats with gold lace; and, being likely men, made a good appearance. They were drawn up in the market place, and sat on horseback two or three hours. At the same time the bells were rung, and several bonfires made, to prevent any resentment from them that might ensue on our showing a dislike of their coming among us. About three after noon, Lord Elcho, with the lifeguards, and many of their chiefs, arrived on horseback, to the number of 150, clothed as above. These made a fine shew, being the flower of their army. Soon after, their main body marched into town, in tolerable order, six or eight abreast, with about eight standards, most of them white flags and a red cross; their bag-pipers playing as they marched along. While they were in the market-place they ordered their Prince to be publickly proclaimed before he arrived; which was accordingly done by the common cryer. They then insisted upon the magistrates appearing in their gowns; but being told they had sent them out of town, were content to have that ceremony excused. Their Prince did not arrive till the dusk of the evening. He walked on foot, attended by a great body of his men, who conducted him to his lodgings, the Lord Exeter's; where he had guards placed all round the house. Every house almost by this time was pretty well filled; but they continued driving in till ten or eleven at night, and we thought we should never have seen the last of them. The Dukes of Athol and Perth, the Lords Pitsligo, Nairn, Elcho, and George Murray, old Gordon of Glenbucket, and their other chiefs and great officers, Lady Ogilvie and Mrs Murray, were lodged at the best Gentlemens houses. Many common ordinary houses, both publick and private, had forty or fifty men each, and some Gentlemen near one hundred. At their coming in, they were generally treated with bread, cheese, beer, and ale, whilst all hands were aloft getting their suppers ready. After supper, being weary with their long march, they went to rest, most upon straw, and others in beds.

That night the Prince, who had marched the twenty-six miles from Leek on foot with his troops, himself went to bed in Lord Exeter's fine mansion tired but in good spirits. He was now only about 125 miles from London. Thus far his army had not suffered a single defeat and once again his conversation turned to whether it would be better for him to make his entry into the capital on horseback and in Highland costume, as he had done at Holyrood, or on foot and in plain English dress.

Best of all, there now seemed every prospect of early help from France. At Manchester the Prince had received a letter from his brother

Henry, dated 26 November from Bagneux, informing him that Louis xv's Foreign Minister, the Marquis d'Argenson, had told him only a few days before 'that the King of France was absolutely resolved upon the expedition into England, *qu'il y avait mis le bon*, and that you might count upon it being ready towards the 20 December'. And now, on reaching Derby, he heard for the first time that already on the last day of November six French transports from Dunkirk had successfully landed some 800 men of the Royal Scots and Irish Regiments of the French army, commanded by the Duke of Perth's brother, Lord John Drummond, at Montrose and Peterhead, and that this fresh accession of strength had done much to improve Jacobite morale in Scotland. There were also some encouraging letters from Parson George Kelly, whom Charles had sent back some time before to negotiate with the French on his behalf. 'We are flattered here', Kelly had written a few days earlier to Colonel Strickland, 'with the hopes of making you all easy very soon, which I long for extremely, and everybody believes it will be done in fifteen days or three weeks. I wish you may be able to stand your ground, since a retreat must be fatal...'

In France in the meantime preparations for an invasion had been going ahead as planned. Early in November Antoine Walsh, the wealthy Irish shipowner cum privateer who had brought Charles safely to Arisaig in July, had been put in charge of procuring the necessary shipping and throughout November and the early part of December the Duke of Newcastle had to his dismay been receiving alarming and all too accurate reports of the large numbers of vessels gathering in the Channel ports in readiness to embark a force of 10,000 or 20,000 troops now actually assembling at Dunkirk.

In Derby Charles's good spirits had communicated themselves to his men who swarmed through the streets, chattering to each other in Gaelic. To a 'Gentleman of Derby', who had some of them quartered on him, and later wrote to the press about it, the unfamiliar inflexions of the Gaelic tongue in which they conversed among themselves made them sound like 'a herd of Hottentots, wild monkies in a desert, or vagrant gipsies'. And now with, as they believed, a battle in prospect, they were flocking into the various churches in the town to receive the Sacrament and crowding into the cutlers' shops 'quarrelling about who should be the first to sharpen and give a proper edge to their swords'. 'I hear', wrote one Highlander to his wife, 'that General Wade is behind us, and the Duke of Cumberland and General Ligonier upon one hand of us, but we are nearer London than any of them, and it is thought we are designed to march straight there, being only 90 miles from it. But though both these forces should unite and attack us, we do not fear them, for our whole army is in top spirits and we trust in

God to make a good account of them.'

In London, meanwhile, the news that the Highland army had reached Derby was, together with rumours of an early French invasion, causing utter panic. 'When the Highlanders', wrote Fielding in *The True Patriot*, 'by a most incredible march got between the Duke's army and the metropolis, they struck a terror into it scarce to be credited.' Business came to a standstill. The shopkeepers shut their shops. Jacobite posters suddenly appeared on the walls as the Jacobites of the capital openly prepared to welcome the Prince and quickly collected £10,000 for him. There was a run on the Bank of England, which, to gain precious time, paid in sixpences that, according to Fielding, were deliberately heated to such a pitch as to be too hot to handle. The Government ordered a search to be made of all the livery-stables in the capital. The Archbishop of Canterbury composed a special prayer imploring divine deliverance from 'the dangers and calamities of foreign war ... rebellions insurrections at home and ... powerful invasions from abroad'. The Duke of Cumberland was urged by an anxious government personally to supervise the somewhat haphazard arrangements which were being made for the defence of the capital. Soldiers were posted in the main squares. Volunteers were called for. Companies of the trained bands patrolled the streets. The Guards, after their own fashion, encamped on Finchley Common in a manner to be immortalized by Hogarth. Another camp, scarcely less disorderly, was marked out near Highgate. Some cavalry were stationed at Barnet. King George, it was said, had given orders for his yachts, laden with his more precious personal belongings, to be kept anchored off Tower Quay, ready to sail at a moment's notice for the Continent. As for his chief minister, the Duke of Newcastle, that statesman had at the height of the crisis shut himself up in his own apartments for a whole day, inaccessible to any who wished to see him and debating even at this late hour whether perhaps the time had perhaps not arrived to transfer his allegiance to the House of Stuart – or so people were saying, which in the panic prevailing came to very much the same thing. In short, England, as old Marshal Wade very appositely observed, was for the first comer.

Such, though he was only partly informed of it, was the encouraging background against which Prince Charles awoke in his comfortable quarters at Exeter House on the morning of Thursday 5 December. He had just put on his bonnet and was about to go out when, an eye-witness tells us, 'Lord George Murray came in and said to him that it was high time to think what they were to do; Charles asked him what he meant, as he thought it was resolved to march on. Lord George said that most of the chiefs were of a different opinion, and thought they should march back to Ashbourne and join the army in Scotland, which was believed to be following them fast'. A council of war was at once called and for the rest of that day, from eight in the morning till late at night, sat in acrimonious discussion or, as Hay of Restalrig puts it, 'in brigue and cabal'.

To the Prince himself the mere idea of retreat was intolerable. 'Rather than go back', he said, 'I would wish to be twenty feet under ground.' The line of argument taken by the chiefs was easy enough to foresee. The case for withdrawal was put clearly and cogently on their behalf by Lord George Murray. That same night, he said, Cumberland, with over 12,000 men, would be at Stafford, as close to London as they themseles were. Wade, with only slightly fewer men, was pushing south by forced marches. A third force of several thousands was forming for the defence of London. Together, these three armies numbered over 30,000 regular troops against their own force of under 5,000, of whom not one man, not even the Prince, would have a chance of escape or survival in the event of defeat. The Scots, no one would deny, had up to now played their full part. They had marched deep into England to support an English rising or a French landing. Neither had materialized. The time had therefore come for them to return to Scotland, an added reason being the recent arrival there of Lord John Drummond's expeditionary force. Those who spoke after Lord George took the same line; only the Dukes of Perth and Atholl showed the slightest inclination to support the Prince.

Charles, as can be imagined, listened without much attempt to conceal his impatience and despair. Indeed, according to Lord Elcho, he 'fell into a passion and gave most of the Gentlemen that Spoke very Abusive Language and said that they had a mind to betray him'. The argument that he would be risking his own life carried no weight with him whatever. 'His Royal Highness', Lord George tells us, 'had no regard for his own danger, but pressed with all the force of argument to go forward. He did not doubt but the justness of his cause would prevail, and he could not think of retreating after coming so far; and he was hopeful there might be a defection in the enemy's army and that severals might declare for him.'

But nothing the Prince could say or do would make the council change their minds. Nor would they consider the alternative suggestion of a march into Wales, where strong support was believed to exist. After the morning's meeting had been adjourned, Charles did what he could to win over individuals to his point of view, but again unavailingly, and, at a second meeting that evening, finding the council's opinion unaltered, he reluctantly and with the worst possible grace accepted what proved to be the council's unanimous view. 'In future', were his concluding words, 'I shall summon no more Councils, since I am accountable to nobody for my actions but to God and my father, and therefore I shall no longer either ask or accept advice.'

The Irish had been excluded from the discussions. But it was not long before old Sir John MacDonald, who had as usual dined too well, discovered what had been decided and began to make the most of it. 'What', he said to Keppoch, 'a Macdonald turn his back!' And to Lochiel, 'For shame, a Cameron run away from the enemy! Go forward and I'll lead you!' By now there were, of course, others who in retrospect were not entirely happy about the council's decision. Old Duke William of Atholl for one 'seemed much for going forwards'. But by now the die was cast.

Early on Friday 6 December the drums beat 'To Arms'; the pipers played through the town; the Prince's army had begun their retreat. In order to maintain morale, it was given out that they were marching to attack Marshal Wade or to join up with a French force from Scotland. But no one believed these stories and the men were 'sullen and silent that whole day'.

So, by all accounts, was the Prince, who mounted upon a black horse, (said to be the unfortunate Colonel Gardiner's) left his lodgings about nine o'clock. 'He was obliged to get on horseback', writes Home, 'for he could not walk, and hardly stand (as was always the case with him when he was cruelly used).' And Lord George Murray observes that 'His Royal Highness, in marching forwards, had always been the first up in the morning, and had the men in motion before the break of day, and commonly marched himself afoot; but in the retreat he was much longer of leaving his quarters, so that though the rest of the army were all on their march, the rear could not move till he went, and then he rode straight on and got to the quarters with the van.' 'If we had been beat', writes the Chevalier de Johnstone, 'the grief could not have been greater.' At his own request, Lord George now took command of the rearguard, rightly foreseeing that this would be the most difficult task. He asked, however, 'that the cannon and carriages with the ammunition, should march in the van ... which was promised me'.

Two days after the Prince had left Derby an emissary arrived there from the English and Welsh Jacobites, a certain Dr Barry from London. 'He had been sent', the Prince wrote to his father, 'by Sir Watkin Wynn and Lord Barrymore to assure me in the name of my friends that they were ready to join me in what manner I pleased, either in the capital, or every one to rise in his own country'.

In France, meanwhile, the decision had been taken to postpone the invasion, originally fixed for 15 December. But French troops continued to reach the coast in large numbers and on 17 December the Duc de Richelieu himself arrived at Dunkirk, only to receive a day or two later news of the retreat from Derby. In spite of this, the build-up for the invasion continued as planned. As was to be expected the Royal Navy under Admiral Vernon were watching these proceedings closely, with the result that in a very few days a score of French ships were captured or sunk. Just before Christmas Richelieu called a council of war to discuss the proposal that the expedition should sail on the afternoon of 26 December and land at Dungeness. But after full discussion of the latest developments and the undoubted problems involved (not least the continued presence of the Royal Navy) the project was for the time being abandoned and Richelieu returned to Paris.

Of few moments in history can it more justly be said that there is a tide in the affairs of men than of the Jacobite decision to turn back from Derby. The decision which Lord George Murray and the chiefs took in the teeth of Prince Charles's despairing opposition was, it could be argued, based on plain common sense. For an irregular force of some 5,000 men in hostile country hundreds of miles from their base to try conclusions with regular forces some six times their strength would by the ordinary rules of warfare (of which Lord George had a more than adequate grasp) clearly have been madness. But this, it is at least arguable, was not an occasion for plain common sense, less still for application of the ordinary rules of warfare or indeed for rational behaviour of any kind; an occasion, rather, for what T. E. Lawrence calls 'the irrational tenth ... like the Kingfisher flashing across the pool'.

Ever since he had of his own initiative set sail from Nantes less than six months before, Charles had been taking a whole succession of quite unacceptable risks, and for one reason or another (and life is often like that) they had paid off. Logically, landing as he had, alone and without support, the Prince should never have been able to raise a force of 5,000 men in a matter of weeks. Logically, they should never have reached, let alone taken, Edinburgh. Without any doubt they should have been annihilated by Sir John Cope. With three armies and three reasonably experienced generals trying to prevent them, they should quite certainly never have reached Derby.

But, now that they had done so much and come within 120 miles of London unscathed, true logic, if there is such a thing, surely demanded that they should take yet another unacceptable risk and march on the capital. If ever there was one, it was a time to take the tide of Jacobite success at the flood.

Hypothetical history is a fruitless if entertaining pursuit. But in this instance it is hard to resist the temptation to consider what might have been the consequences of such action.

Of the three armies ultimately confronting them, old Marshal Wade's was immensely slow-moving and still a long way away. Cumberland, who, judging by his performance against the Comte de Saxe at Fontenoy, was no great strategist, had, thanks to Lord George, already been neatly out-manoeuvred and left behind. There remained the hastily assembled and ill-assorted force at Finchley, largely consisting of the so-called trained bands. Judging by the morale and actual performance of the Hanoverian forces they had encountered so far, it seems more than possible that the Prince's army might either have scared them off, defeated them or, by making skilful use of country (as Finchley then was), avoided them altogether. Indeed, even Lord George at his gloomiest had admitted they might reach London, only to add that, once they had done so, 'if the Mob was against the affair, 4,500 men would not make a great figure in London'.

This of course begs several important questions. Could it for instance be taken for granted that the London mob would in fact be against them? Mobs, as they had found in the other cities they had taken, have a way of being on the winning side, so long as it seems to be winning. And not only mobs. Undoubtedly there were Jacobites in England. Might they not, with the Prince actually in London, have finally shown their faces? Had they done so, what kind of support might they have enjoyed and what sort of opposition would they have encountered? To catch people's imagination is what matters at such times and Charles's amazing exploit, if carried in so short a time and to such a spectacular conclusion, might well have done just that. Nothing, it must be remembered, succeeds like success. As John Home, a loyal Whig, was to write so appositely in the opening passage of his admirable *History of the Rebellion*: 'There were moments when nothing seemed impossible; and, to say truth, it was not easy to forecast, or to imagine, anything more unlikely than what had already happened.'

With the Prince installed at St James's, what course would the three Hanoverian armies have taken? Whether King George had returned to his native Hanover, as it was rumoured he was preparing to do, or fallen gallantly in battle at Finchley, the likelihood surely was that, when it came to the point, someone would have been found to play the role of a General Monk. Nor can there be much doubt either that, whether or not the English Jacobites had risen, had Charles in fact reached London, any council of war held by the Duc de Richelieu that same month at Dunkirk would have approached the question of a French invasion in a quite different spirit. With Charles at St James's, however precarious his position there, some way would without doubt have been found of transporting those thousands of waiting French troops across the Channel and up the Thames estuary in the shortest possible time.

Which takes us back to the drawing-room of Exeter House in Derby and raises the question why the day-long discussion there took the turn it did and, after a long unseemly wrangle, reached such a conclusion. That the answer lies largely in the Prince's own character and personality and more particularly in his relationship with Lord George Murray seems clear enough.

In addition to personal charm, Charles possessed courage, charisma and a certain aura of kingship. He also possessed in a high degree a manifest will to win which, springing from his utter and single-minded determination to regain the throne for his father, had given the rising its initial impetus and carried it as far as Derby. What he lacked, in contrast to Lord George, who was without doubt an able commander and at times an inspired tactician and a strategist of genius, was any kind of military knowledge or experience (save that acquired in a few weeks at Gaeta). Nor did he possess, when it came to the point, the requisite authority, the gift essential in a leader of being able to carry utter conviction, inspire total confidence and impose his will no matter how unpromising the circumstances. As Maxwell of Kirkconnell observed with irrefutable wisdom: 'One general officer of reputation in the world would have been of infinite service.'

At Derby two other things badly impaired his credibility: the continued failure of the French to land and of the English Jacobites to join the rising. Nor, when it came to discussing the courses of action open to them, were things made any easier by the differences of age, rank, experience and temperament which separated the Prince and his Lieutenant-General, himself no easy man to get on with. This, as was by now already apparent, was apt to become an obstacle to rational discussion between them. It was thus that at Exeter House, despite a number of convincing arguments for going on, the decision was taken to turn back.

Once that decision had been taken, the character of the Rising inevitably suffered a sea-change. 'No one', wrote Horace Walpole, with his irritating gift for hitting the nail on the head, 'is afraid of a rebellion that runs away.'

CHAPTER EIGHT

Following the route they had taken on their way South, the retreating Highlanders found the population along their line of march a great deal less friendly. Stragglers were set upon by the country people and either knocked on the head or dragged to the nearest gaol. In Manchester, where they had been welcomed only a few days before with bonfires and pealing bells, stones were thrown and the advance-guard threatened by an angry mob.

Nor did the Highlanders, now that they were retreating, behave as well as they had on the march South. 'The army', wrote one of them, 'irritated by such frequent instances of the enemy's malice, began to behave with less forbearance, and now few there were who would go on foot if they could ride; and mighty taking, stealing and pressing of horses there was amongst us! Diverting it was to see the Highlanders mounted, without either breeches, saddle or anything else but the bare back of the horses to ride on, and for their bridle only a straw rope! In this manner did we march out of England.' Lord George, too, had problems with the rearguard. 'My great difficulty', he writes, 'was to bring up stragglers, who could not be kept from going into houses and committing abuses.'

Charles was above all anxious that his army's withdrawal should not take on the appearance of a headlong flight, and urged that more frequent halts should be made. To this Lord George, conscious of the need for haste, agreed only with reluctance. As it was, a day's halt was made at Manchester and another at Preston. From Preston the Duke of Perth was sent on ahead of the army with a cavalry escort and Lady Ogilvy and Mrs Murray of Broughton in a travelling carriage, in order to make contact with the reinforcements. These, it was hoped, were standing by in Perthshire or were possibly by now already on their way South, for the Prince had sent back Maclachlan of Maclachlan with instructions to Lord Strathallan to follow on into England with as many men as he could muster.

On the night of 13 December the army reached Lancaster. There Lord George found on arrival that Charles had ordered another day's halt, 'to show the world the Prince was retiring and not flying, and if the enemy came up he would give them battle'. Next morning, when he called at the Prince's lodging, Charles told him that he had decided to stand and fight and wanted him and O'Sullivan to pick a good place for a battle. Taking Lochiel and a strong escort with them, Lord George and O'Sullivan accordingly made a reconnaissance of the area immediately to the South of the town, beyond Scotforth, 'where we found a very fine field, upon a rising ground that could contain our whole army' and also, incidentally, took prisoner several enemy soldiers out on a reconnaissance ahead of Cumberland's main force, by now hard on their heels. But, when Lord George, who had a good eye for country, returned to Lancaster and reported to the Prince 'that, if our number would answer, I could not find a better field for Highlanders', it was only to find that Charles had changed his mind and now wished to march on next day.

By this time the enemy were in hot pursuit and from the prisoners taken on his reconnaissance Lord George learned that their forward troops were only now eight miles away, at Garstang, and that 'a great body of dragoons were come to Preston'. On first learning that the Prince's army was retreating, Cumberland, who up to then had been moving as fast as he could in the direction of Coventry and Lichfield in a desperate attempt to intercept his adversary's march on London, had at once sent an express to Marshal Wade, by this time at Doncaster. 'We', he wrote, 'are here at Coventry, the rebels at Ashbourne, and you at Doncaster. It seems to me much to be feared that if you can't move westward into Lancashire, these villains may escape back unpunished into the Highlands to our eternal shame.' In response Wade detached from his army a body of cavalry under General Oglethorpe and sent them off across country in advance of his main force, while he himself followed more slowly. Cumberland, meanwhile, leaving Sir John Ligonier, by now recovered from his illness, to remain behind with the infantry, had left his camp near Coventry on 8 December with all his cavalry and a thousand mounted infantry and volunteers and set out in pursuit of his cousin. 'But I fear', he wrote to the Duke of Newcastle, 'it will be fruitless, for they march at such a rate that I can't flatter myself with the hopes of overtaking them.' Nor, knowing Wade, was he more hopeful of his fellow commander's chances. 'There is little hope', he wrote, 'of that army being able to intercept them or prevent their retreat to Scotland.' And indeed, having learned on his arrival at Wakefield that Charles was already in Manchester, the old Marshal, after calling a council of war, decided to fall back on Newcastle with his main force, leaving the pursuit, as far as he was concerned, to General Oglethorpe and his cavalry.

After a series of forced marches Oglethorpe reached Preston on 13 December, only a few hours behind the Prince. Cumberland, meanwhile, had arrived at Macclesfield on 10 December and Manchester the next day, his men much fatigued by their rapid march from Lichfield 'over the most dreadful country'. He had, it seemed, 'flattered himself' that the Highlanders would have waited for him in Manchester. 'And if they had halted there all yesterday', he wrote to the Duke of Newcastle on 11 December, 'I should have been in reach of them with my whole cavalry and volunteers.' As it was, he pushed on to Preston and there, on the evening of 13 December, joined forces with Oglethorpe with a view to continuing his pursuit next day – the very day, incidentally, on which Charles was debating whether or not to stand and fight on the ground which Lord George had selected for him South of Lancaster.

It was at this juncture that Cumberland received by courier from London an agitated letter from 'his dutiful slave', the Duke of Newcastle, informing him that the King had heard from Admiral Vernon that a large number of French vessels now really were assembled at Dunkirk and there was every reason to believe that an early attempt would be made to land troops on the South and East coasts. In the circumstances the Duke begged him to send some of his troops to join Marshal Wade and to return to London himself with the rest of his cavalry and infantry. At the same time Newcastle had written direct to Sir John Ligonier, requesting him to start at once for London with the regiments under his command. 'We are under the greatest alarm', he wrote,

> of an immediate embarkation from Dunkirk, and perhaps some other ports ... we shall be but very ill-prepared to receive them till you come to our assistance, not having, according to our last account, 6,000 men in all. I therefore hope you will make all possible haste to us by waggons, horses, etc. ... I hope His Royal Highness will not dislike coming home with his troops. I am sure if he knew the real apprehensions people here are under of an invasion from France, and how much the King desires to have him with him in times of action and danger, His Royal Highness would fly faster and more cheerfully hither than he ever did to meet the rebels. I must beg your good offices to make my peace

with His Royal Highness – I doubt he is angry with me, but I am his most dutiful slave.

Scarcely had these dispatches been received, however, than fresh orders arrived from London, cancelling them and instructing Cumberland to resume his pursuit of the rebels. The story of an impending French invasion had, it now seemed, been unfounded or at any rate greatly exaggerated.

Thanks to this false alarm Charles had gained twenty-four hours on his pursuers. Arriving in Kendal on the evening of 15 December, he found that the Duke of Perth, whom he had sent on from Preston to bring back reinforcements from Scotland, had run into serious trouble and been obliged to turn back. Shortly before his party's arrival, news had reached Kendal that the Prince had suffered a major defeat and, when Perth arrived in the town, riding hard with an escort of a hundred or so hussars and a travelling carriage containing his two female companions, this was not unnaturally taken as confirmation of the news, and rumours at once began to circulate that one of the ladies was Prince Charles in disguise or else his alleged mistress, the famous Jenny Cameron. On reaching Finkle Street, Perth's party, it appeared, had been attacked by a hostile mob and in the ensuing scrimmage had fired several shots, killing four people and thoroughly enraging the crowd. After a further attempt at a stand and losing four of their men, they had managed to extricate themselves and reach Shap, where they spent the night. At Shap, 'perceiving Penrith beacon on fire', they had inquired the reason and learned to their dismay that its purpose was to raise the country against them. They had accordingly tried to make a detour and had spent the whole of the next day riding across the moors pursued by angry peasantry and members of the County Militia. Eventually, on the following day, 15 December, they had found their way back to Kendal and there joined up again with the rest of the Prince's army, without having fulfilled their mission. Their experience did not bode well for the future.

On the evening of 17 December Charles and his force, after successfully negotiating Shap Fell, reached Penrith. Although Lord George Murray had expressly asked that the rearguard should not be burdened with the artillery, ammunition and baggage, these had in fact been left to his care. An attempt to reason with the Prince before leaving Kendal had been unsuccessful. He and O'Sullivan had found a bottle of 'mountain Malaga' and were making the most of it and all Lord George had been able to get out of them had been 'a glass or two of it' and, next morning, instructions to leave 'not the least thing, not so much as a cannon-ball behind'. It was 'a very bad, rainy day'. As

Lord George had feared, the lumbering gun carriages and ammunition wagons greatly delayed his progress. The wagons stuck fast in a sea of mud and one entire load of cannon-shot fell into a stream so that, in order to comply with the letter of the Prince's instructions, more than 200 shot had to be carried over the pass by hand, for which Lord George paid the men sixpence apiece.

During their painful progress Glengarry's MacDonalds brought up the rear – 'not the most patient', wrote Lord George, 'but I never was more pleased with men in my life'. Even so, it soon became impossible for them to keep up with the forward troops and in the end Lord George decided to halt for the night in Shap village, a dozen miles short of Penrith. The enemy were now hard on their heels. As they were setting out early next morning – 18 December – small parties of enemy cavalry began to appear on the high ground to their rear, 'but so soon as the Glengarry men threw their plaids and ran forward to attack them, they made off at the top gallop'.

Assuming that an enemy force was quartered in the vicinity of Lowther Hall, the seat of Lord Lonsdale, a staunch Whig, Lord George, on reaching the village of Clifton, sent forward the artillery and ammunition carts in the direction of Penrith, while he himself and the Glengarry men scoured Lord Lonsdale's policies. The enemy continued to take avoiding action, but in spite of this Lord George managed to take two prisoners, a militia officer and one of the Duke of Cumberland's footmen, who had been sent on ahead to prepare suitable quarters for the Duke and who, on the Prince's instructions was, after due interrogation, courteously returned to his royal master. Learning that Cumberland, with a strong force of cavalry, was barely a mile behind, Lord George sent the prisoners on to the Prince at Penrith in the charge of John Roy Stewart, at the same time seeking urgent instructions. With Glengarry's regiment he then returned to Clifton, where he found the Duke of Perth, who had been sent back from Penrith to join him with Cluny's and Ardshiel's regiments, giving him a total strength of about 1,000.

That afternoon a formidable-looking force of enemy cavalry came into sight to the south of Clifton village and drew up in two lines, 'upon an open muir, not above cannon-shot from us'. The Highlanders were by now occupying a number of hedges and walled fields and enclosures in and around the village: the MacDonalds to the west of the main road, with John Roy Stewart's men, the Stewarts of Appin and Cluny's Macphersons on the other side. In order to confuse the enemy and make them think his strength was greater than it was, Lord George 'caused roll up what colours we had, and made them pass half open to different places'.

135

The sun was now setting, but Cumberland seemed in no hurry to attack, his troops contenting themselves at first with 'shooting popping shots' at the Highlanders. Only later did he give orders for detachments from his three dragoon regiments, Bland's, Cobham's amd Mark Ker's, numbering about 500 men in all, to dismount and advance on the positions held by the Highlanders.

It was at this point that John Roy Stewart returned from Penrith with a message from Prince Charles. The Prince, he reported, had decided to press on to Carlisle immediately. His orders to Lord George were to continue his withdrawal as fast as he could. This sudden reluctance on the Prince's part to stand and fight was greeted with derision by Lord Elcho. 'As', he wrote, 'their was formerly a Contradiction to make the army halt when it was necessary to march, so now their was one to march and shun fighting when their Could never be a better opportunity gott for it.' As for Lord George, the Prince's instructions filled him with dismay. The perils of retreating down a narrow lane and then a walled road in the darkness pursued by a well-mounted, more mobile and numerically superior enemy, were obvious, 'whereas', he writes, 'I was confident I could dislodge them from where they were by a Irish attack'. After a quick consultation with John Roy Stewart and Cluny, the decision was in the end taken to ignore the Prince's orders and say nothing about them to anyone else. This, it was agreed, 'was the only prudent and sure way'.

'It was now', writes Lord George, 'about an hour after sunsett, pretty cloudie, but the moon, which was in its second quarter, from time to time broke out and gave good light but this did not continue above two minutes at a time. We had the advantage of seeing their disposition, but they could not see ours.' It was in one of these brief periods of moonlight that Lord George caught a glimpse of a party of Bland's Dragoons creeping along a low stone wall towards the enclosures on the East side of Clifton village. 'We only', writes MacDonell of Lochgarry, who was also keeping a sharp look out, 'heard the noise of their boots and could plainly discern their yellow belts.'

At this Lord George gave the Macphersons, who were nearest to the enemy, the order to clear the first hedge and take up a position behind the second. In so doing they were more than likely to encounter the dragoons. 'If such will happen', he said to Cluny, 'I'll attack on the right of your regiment and doe you the same on the left of it, and we'll advance soe if you approve of it.' To which Cluny replied that 'he was very well satisfied to attack when his Lordship pleased' and the Macphersons started to scramble through the hedge. 'Through the hedge we made our way', writes Macpherson of Strathmashie, 'with the help of our durks, the prictes being very uneasy, I assure you, to

136

our loose tail'd Lads.' At this moment the English opened fire and, as the Macphersons reached the second hedge, they received a volley 'full in the teeth'. 'What the Divle is this?' exclaimed Cluny and then, at a shout of 'Claymore!' from Lord George, charged at the head of his clan.

The sudden impact of the Macphersons' charge knocked the dragoons off balance, sweeping them back into the ditch at the bottom of the field, where many were killed and wounded, while the remainder fled across the moor under heavy fire from Lochgarry's MacDonalds. 'The poor swords', writes Strathmashie, 'suffered much, as there were no less than fourteen broke on the dragoons skull caps ... before it seems the better way was found of doing their business' – presumably with the point. With difficulty Cluny managed to halt his men at the ditch. Only one gigantic clansman, Angus of Knappach, who happened to be deaf, charged on alone, sword in hand, after the fleeing English. Then, finding, when he looked back, that his comrades had halted, 'Why the devil', he shouted, 'do you turn back? I see a great many more a little farther on.' And it was only with great reluctance that he abandoned their pursuit. The skirmish had lasted no more than half an hour, in the main between Bland's Dragoons and the Macphersons. Cumberland's losses were given as forty killed and wounded. Five Highlanders were killed and a few, who in their enthusiasm charged too far across the moor, were taken prisoner.

Having thus beaten off the enemy and secured the Prince's rear, Lord George felt able to continue his march North. 'We had now', he writes, 'done what we propos'd, and being sure of no more trouble from the enemy, I order'd the retreat.' Cumberland gave rather a different account of the action. 'Our men', he wrote in a despatch to the Duke of Newcastle, 'drove them out of Clifton in an hour's time, with very small loss.' He 'dared not follow them', he added, 'because it was so dark; besides, his troops, both horse and men, were so fatigued with these forced marches'. 'The English', is Strathmashie's dry comment, 'have their own way of telling stories.' For having failed to prevent the rearguard's withdrawal General Oglethorpe was later courtmartialled, but acquitted.

On reaching Penrith, Lord George found that the Prince had already sent the artillery on to Carlisle and was himself preparing to follow with the rest of the army. His Steward had managed to buy him three bottles of cherry brandy and he was in a good enough mood. 'He seem'd', writes Lord George, 'very well pleas'd with what had hapn'd'. As well he might be.

At about eight o'clock that night, 18 December, the Highland army left Penrith, entering Carlisle at about nine the next morning. Once more Charles, now in a better frame of mind, marched with his troops.

'This', writes one of them, 'was one of the darkest nights I ever saw, yet did his R.H. walk it on foot, and the most part of the way without a lanthorn, yet never stumbled, which many of us Highlanders did often.' As for the rearguard, by the time they reached Carlisle, they had 'marched two days without resting from Kendal to Penrith, which is along 20 miles, and, without halt, 16 more on to Carlisle, all without sleep and very little provision'. At Carlisle, the Prince found letters from Lord Strathallan, giving a reasonably encouraging account of the army at Perth, and from Lord John Drummond, telling him that he had brought over enough men and artillery to reduce the Scottish fortresses and that a strong French expeditionary force would be following before long.

At dawn on 20 December the Prince's army marched out of Carlisle, leaving behind them a garrison of some 400 officers and men and all their artillery except for three Swedish field-guns. The decision to leave a garrison at Carlisle was taken at Charles's instance. He was convinced that the castle could be held and he wished at all costs to keep a foothold in England for when he marched South again. His advisers were strongly opposed to the idea. 'This was done against the opinion almost of Everybody but the Prince said he would have a town in England and he was sure the Duke could gett no Cannon to take it with.' Lord George was to point out later that 'had a council of war been consulted as to leaving a Garrison at Carlisle, it would never have been agreed to, the place not being teneable'. 'But', he writes, 'I found he was determined in the thing.' Thus a couple of hundred dejected Highlanders, together with Colonel Francis Townley and his Manchester Regiment, who had no great desire to cross the border, were, on a whim of the Prince's, fecklessly left to their fate.

From Carlisle the Highland army marched the ten miles or so to Longtown, where they crossed the Esk, swollen by the winter rains and with a strong current flowing. 'The foot marched in, six in a brest, in as good order, as if they were marching in a field, holding one another by the collars, every body and every thing past, without any losses but two women, yt belonged only to the publick, yt were drownded.' 'I was', writes Lord George, 'this day in my Pheilybeg, that is to say without Britches ... and nothing encourag'd the men more than seeing their Officers dress'd like themselves and ready to shear their feat.' When they had crossed the river, the pipers played a reel and the Highlanders, glad to be back in Scotland, lit fires and danced to dry themselves.

At Lord George's suggestion the army was now once again divided into two columns. One, made up of six battalions, with himself in command, marched by Ecclefechan and Lockerbie to Moffat, whence, after making a feint along the Edinburgh road, it continued its march through Hamilton to Glasgow. The other, commanded by the Prince and comprising the clan regiments and most of the cavalry, followed by way of Annan, Dumfries, Thornhill, Douglas and Hamilton.

At Dumfries, where the Prince stayed at a fine old house in the High Street, now the County Hotel, the retreating Highlanders are reported to have 'behaved very rudely, strip'd everybody almost of their shoes, obliged the town to give them £1,000 and a considerable quantity of shoes, and carried away Provost Crosbie and Mr Walter Riddell, merchants, as hostages for £1,000 more which was yesterday sent them to relieve these gentlemen'. Reaching Thornhill on 23 December, the Prince and most of his troops spent the night at Drumlanrig as uninvited guests of the Duke of Queensberry, whose predecessor fifty-five years earlier had so successfully promoted the cause of William of Orange and seventeen years after that had played a leading part in bringing about the union with England. 'When they came here', wrote the Duke's Commissioner, Mr James Fergusson (Annie Laurie's eldest son) some days later,

> they laid straw the whole rooms for the private men to lye on, except your Grace's bed-chamber (where their Prince lay), and a few rooms more. They killed about 40 sheep, part of your Grace's, and part of mine, most of them in the vestibule next the low dining-room and the foot of the principal stair, which they left in a sad pickle, as they did indeed the whole house. Under the gallery they keep'd several of their horses which they made a shift to get up the front stair. They have destroyed all the spirits and most of the wine in your Grace's cellars ... a good deal of hay and what corn they could get, all my ale and spirits and other provisions. They have broken several chairs and tables, melted down a good deal of pewter by setting it upon the fire with their victuals, carried away a good deal of linen and several other things, which I have not time to know particularly ... They would have done much more mischief, as the servants tell me – at least plundered the whole house – had not the Duke of Perth stayed till most of them were gone. He took sheets and blankets from several who were carrying them off, and returned them to the servants ... May God grant there may never again be any such guests here.

In addition to whatever other damage they did at Drumlanrig, the Highlanders also took good care to deface with their claymores the Duke's handsome portrait of his predecessor's patron, King William of Orange.

Letting Lord Elcho and Lord George Murray go on ahead to take possession of Glasgow, Charles spent Christmas night at Hamilton Palace and there enjoyed a morning's shooting on the Duke of Hamilton's estate. Next afternoon at the head of his troops, he himself entered the pretty, prosperous little city and took up his quarters at Shawfield House in the Trongate, 'the great and stately lodging, orchyard and garden belonging to Colonel William M'Dowall of Castle Semple'. Here he was to spend the next ten days.

At no stage of the rising had the citizens of Glasgow shown any enthusiasm for the Jacobite cause. The previous September the magistrates had strongly resisted the Prince's demand for a contribution of £15,000 and it was only under the threat of military execution that £5,500 had finally been extracted from them. Since then they had raised some 500 volunteers to fight for King George, but at the Prince's approach these had prudently withdrawn to Edinburgh, leaving the city completely undefended though still anything but friendly to the Highland intruders. Tradition says that many of the Highlanders would gladly have shown their resentment by putting the rich, peaceful, hostile town to the sack and that they were only restrained from their purpose by Lochiel's personal intervention, in gratitude for which the bells of Glasgow to this day traditionally ring out to welcome the Chief of Clan Cameron. In any case a peremptory order was now addressed to the Provost, instructing him to arrange for the immediate supply of a good many thousand pairs of shoes and hose, shirts, coats, waistcoats, bonnets and other articles of clothing at a total cost to the city of several thousand pounds. Nor did the magistrates, though doubtless seething with resentment, make any attempt to resist this demand.

The Prince, meanwhile, continued to reside at Shawfield House, holding informal receptions for those who were loyal or curious enough to attend them and dining and supping each day in public at a table laid in the small drawing-room, where a number of devoted Jacobite ladies ministered to his needs. He dressed 'more elegantly when in Glasgow than he did in any other place whatsomever', wearing silk tartans and court dress in place of his usual campaigning attire.

Morale had to some extent been restored. During the Prince's stay parades were held in different parts of the city for the purpose of proclaiming King James and on most days a detachment of Highlanders marched through the city streets. By 2 January 1746 the army had been re-equipped and was ready to move off, and on that day Charles held a general review of the whole force on Glasgow Green. 'We marched out', writes Captain Daniel, a volunteer from Lancashire, 'with drums beating, colours flying, bagpipes playing, and all the marks of a triumphant army, to the appointed ground, attended by multitudes of people who had come from all parts to see us, and especially the ladies, who, though formerly much against us, were now charmed by the sight of the Prince into the most enthusiastic loyalty.'

It was not long after reaching Glasgow, however, that Charles received sobering news of the surrender of Carlisle to the Duke of Cumberland. Cumberland had reached Carlisle on 21 December and had at once closely invested the town, cursorily dismissing its fortifications as 'an old hen-coop which he would speedily bring down about their ears when he should have got artillery'. The necessary artillery, six 18-pounders, arrived from Whitehaven a week later. The garrison had done their best to strengthen the town's defences, but even so it was clear that they could not hope to hold out for more than a few days. All supplies of food had been cut off; the besieging troops were becoming daily more numerous; and in the end the fortifications began literally to crumble under the incessant bombardment.

Faced with a well-nigh desperate situation, Francis Townley, commanding the Manchester Regiment, gave it as his view that 'it was better to die by the sword than fall into the hands of those damned Hanoverians'. But Colonel John Hamilton, whom the Prince had left in command, was nevertheless in the end prevailed upon to capitulate and sent a messenger with a letter to Cumberland, offering to surrender the town on condition that the garrison were allowed the usual privileges of prisoners of war. To this communication no reply was returned, the bearer being simply made prisoner. At the same time a new battery was installed and the bombardment continued with more devastating effect than ever. Finally on the morning of 30 December, a white flag was hung out on the walls and a letter sent to Cumberland to ask what terms he was prepared to grant the garrison if the town and castle surrendered. The Duke's reply to this was as follows: 'All the terms his R. Highness will or can grant to the rebel garrison of Carlisle, are – That they shall not be put to the sword, but be reserved for the King's pleasure.'

It was on these terms that the surrender was finally agreed. That afternoon Brigadier Bligh entered the town with 1,000 foot and 120 horse and, after taking over their arms and military stores, placed the whole garrison under lock and key, the officers in the castle and the men in the Cathedral. He was followed after an appropriate interval by the Duke of Cumberland and his staff.

Cumberland would personally have preferred to massacre the whole garrison without further ado and only refrained for fear of reprisals. 'I wish', he wrote to the Duke of Newcastle that same day, 'I cold have blooded the soldiers with these Villains, but it would have cost us many a brave man, and it comes to the same thing in the end, as they have no sort of claim to the King's mercy, and I sincerely hope will meet with none.' He was not to be disappointed. A few days later the Jacobite prisoners set out from Carlisle, herded and driven like cattle, along the high roads and through the villages and towns of England to new places of confinement, whence, in due course, they were taken out to stand their trial, a process that ended for many of them in the elaborate and barbarous sentence of hanging, drawing and quartering then imposed on those found guilty of high treason.

Cumberland now hurried back to London to make a full report to Newcastle and to his father, while in the English Channel the ships of the Royal Navy kept watch for any signs of a French invasion (though this now seemed no more than a remote possibility). Meanwhile, yet another verse had been added to the National Anthem;

> George is magnanimous,
> Subjects unanimous;
> > Peace to us bring:
> His fame is glorious,
> Reign meritorious,
> > God save the King!

On 3 January 1746 Prince Charles and his army marched out of Glasgow, their immediate objective being Stirling. Now that he was back in Scotland, it was easier for him to take stock of his position. The news that greeted him was not discouraging. As he already knew, Lord John Drummond had arrived at Montrose from France on 25 November with 800 men and the promise of more to come. 'The Prince', Lord John had written on 6 December to his friend Lord Fortrose who, despite his Jacobite antecedents, was still withholding his support, 'will be shortly joined by the Duke of York and the Earl Marischall with a further force of 10,000 men.' Moreover Lord John's arrival, following the news of the Prince's early successes and of his unchecked progress through England, had by this time brought in a number of new Scottish recruits to the Jacobite cause.

In the Gordon country, while the Duke of Gordon himself, though possibly in sympathy with the Jacobites, prudently remained aloof, his brother, Lord Lewis Gordon, had since his return from Edinburgh at the end of October been conducting a vigorous if not very successful recruiting campaign. 'I have found', he wrote to the Duke of Perth, 'both ye Gentlemen and the Commonalite more Remiss than I expected, and I am credibly informed ... yt there slowness is chiefly owing to Vile Presbeterian Ministers who abuse ye Prince's goodness towards them by inculcating a Parcell of infamous Lyes into ye people's heads.'

142

This particular obstacle to recruiting he had dealt with by giving a written order 'to declare publickly to all ye ministers in my Jurisdiction yt if after ye day of my arrival they should dare to say anything in ye least disrespectful of his Royal Highness or any of his friends, I would punish them severely'. 'And', he added confidently, 'I am assured it will have ye desired effect.' Certainly, having issued his order to the clergy, he succeeded in raising two well-equipped battalions in Banff and Aberdeenshire and also helped his neighbours, Farquharson of Monaltrie amd Farquharson of Balmoral, to raise a battalion of their clansmen some three hundred strong. This despite the 'backwardness' of their chief, old Farquharson of Invercauld, who chose to regard himself as still bound by a promise of good behaviour which he had given to the Government after being out thirty years before in the rising of 1715.

In Inverness-shire, the Mackintoshes, though for the most part Jacobite in sympathy, had hitherto lacked a leader owing to the decision of their chief Angus to accept a commission in one of the new companies of the Black Watch, recently raised by the Government at 'half a guinea a day and half a guinea the morn'. Their need was, however, now more than adequately supplied by Angus's handsome and lively young wife Anne, daughter of the 'backward' chief of Invercauld. Wearing a habit of Mackintosh tartan trimmed with lace and with a blue bonnet on her head and a pair of pistols at her saddle-bow, 'Colonel Anne' now rode far and wide through the countryside, winning herself lasting fame and bringing in enough recruits for the Prince to make up a battalion, which at the end of December marched South to Perth in company with the force commanded by Lord Lewis Gordon.

Indeed, Anne's only weakness seems to have been her spelling, as is amply demonstrated by the following letter, written by her to Duke William of Atholl:

> My Lord Douke,
>
> The Beraer of this is a veray Pretay fellew, Brother to Mcenzie of Killooway. He had a Compannay resed for the Prince's servace, but was handred by Lord Silforth to keray them of, which meks me geve this trobal to beg your Grace to geve hem en ordar for rasing hes men & thene he can wous a lettel forse. My God preaserf your Grace, and all that will searve ther Prince and contray, which is the ernast woush of Your Grace Most Affnett. & Obd. Sarvant,
>
> A. McIntosh

Further North the Mackenzie chieftain, Lord Cromartie, though a Jacobite at heart, had, like his kinsman Fortrose, at first waited on events, keeping in touch with both sides and committing himself to

143

neither. In September, however, the news of the Prince's victory at Prestonpans had so excited and encouraged him that he had at once started recruiting, and before the end of November had, in contrast to his nominal chief Lord Fortrose, sent a Mackenzie battalion over 200 strong under his son Lord MacLeod to join the Jacobite force assembling at Perth.

Finally, of the 700 Frasers reputed to be drilling before Castle Downie, 500 had by now completed their training and, commanded by the reluctant nineteen-year-old Master of Lovat, were moving South by way of Fort Augustus, in the hope of surprising the Hanoverian garrison there on the way. From Castle Downie, meanwhile, their commander's father continued to assure his old friend Forbes of Culloden that he himself was opposed to the whole venture, assuring him of his 'zeal and attachment to His Majesty's person and Government' and referring to Charles as 'that mad and unaccountable gentleman'. 'I could not', he wrote of his son, 'have done more to save my own life, and the lives of my clan, as well as the estate of Lovat, than I have done by smooth and rough usage to detain him at home.'

But by now the Lord President's patience with the Frasers and their chief was beginning to wear thin. Since mid-October the Earl of Loudon had been in Inverness trying to raise the twenty Independent Companies authorized by the Government. By the beginning of December he had managed to assemble eleven, seven recruited from the Munros, Mackays, Gunns, Grants and other Whig clans of the North and from the townspeople of Inverness, and four of MacLeods recruited by the renegade MacLeod of MacLeod, who had made his task easier by putting it about that he was really recruiting for the Prince and even providing the more fanatical Jacobites among his clansmen with white cockades to wear on the way across from Skye. With part of this hastily assembled force Lord Loudon left Inverness on 3 December for the purpose of relieving Fort Augustus and intercepting the Master of Lovat on his way South. But by the time he and his men reached Fort Augustus, the Frasers, learning of his approach, had already raised the siege and were on their way to Perth.

Lord Loudon accordingly now returned to Inverness and on 11 December appeared with a force of some 800 men before Castle Downie. Here he and his officers were affably received by Lord Lovat, who at once pledged himself to answer for the good behaviour of the rest of his clan and hand over any remaining weapons they might have to the Government, while himself readily agreeing to accompany Lord Loudon to Inverness as a token of good faith. His offer being accepted, he spent the next week or so at his town house in Inverness. But when, at the end of this period, there was still no sign of any arms being surrendered and Lord Loudon, growing suspicious, placed a guard on the house, it was discovered next morning that during the night a party of Frasers had surreptitiously entered the house from the back and carried the old man off to safety on their shoulders. And now from Perth, adding insult to injury, came the news that two well-armed Fraser contingents, one commanded by Charles Fraser of Inverallachy and the other by the young Master of Lovat, had arrived there safely together with a small party of Chisholms from neighbouring Strathglass.

All through November and December more groups of Jacobite recruits had been arriving in Perth from different quarters and by the beginning of January there were, including the 800 men Lord John Drummond had brought with him from France, some 4,000 more troops ready to join the Prince, numbering roughly as many again as the force with which he had marched South. Moreover, at the end of December Lord Lewis Gordon had managed to inflict a decisive defeat on MacLeod of MacLeod at Inverurie near Aberdeen and driven him right back across the Spey.

Leaving Glasgow on 3 January, Charles himself now marched by way of Kilsyth to Bannockburn, some three miles from Stirling, where, while his troops were assembling, he stayed at Bannockburn House as the guest of Sir Hugh Paterson, a loyal local Jacobite. There he met Sir Hugh's niece, Clementina Walkinshaw, a handsome girl of twenty-two or -three, called Clementina after his own mother, whose god-daughter she seems to have been.

Charles's immediate military objective was to take the town and castle of Stirling, both still in Government hands. At his disposal was a force of some 9,000 men, a larger number than at any time since his arrival. In order to conceal his true intentions, he again divided his army into two main columns, one, consisting of six battalions of Highlanders under Lord George Murray, and the other under his own command. From Glasgow Lord George marched on 3 January to Falkirk, as though to threaten Edinburgh, long since in Government hands. Thence he returned on 5 January to Bannockburn to join the Prince, leaving a force of cavalry under Lord Elcho to patrol the Edinburgh road and thus confirm the impression that this was Charles's true objective. In addition to his 800 men, Lord John Drummond had also brought with him from France a train of artillery, consisting of two 16-pounders, two 12-pounders and two 8-pounders. In anticipation of the forthcoming siege of Stirling these were now ferried across the Forth from Perth 'with great labour' and 'in the teeth of a squadron of frigates' of the Royal Navy, which sought, though unsuccessfully, to intercept them while seaborne.

On the evening of 5 January, soon after Lord George's return to Bannockburn, a drummer was sent to Stirling to demand the surrender of the town, now almost completely surrounded by the Jacobites. At this the garrison, consisting of some 500 part-trained and confused militiamen, opened fire and the drummer, after trying vainly to make himself understood, dropped his drum and ran away. Next morning, however, a battery of guns was set up 'within musket shot' of the town. Soon after this the town council thought it wiser to open negotiations and, after much discussion, the surrender of the town was finally signed on 8 January. But not of the castle, on its precipitous rock high above the surrounding plain. There a small garrison of regulars and militia, indifferent to the presence of the Highland army only a few hundred yards away, continued to hold out under Major-General William Blakeney. Whether worth the effort involved or not, the siege of the castle was accordingly now begun, the conduct of operations being entrusted by the Prince to a certain Monsieur Mirabel de Gordon, also known as the Marquis de Mirabelle, who had come over with Lord John Drummond. A French engineer officer of Scottish descent, he had been decorated with the Order of St Louis and was said to be one of the first engineers in France. 'It was supposed,' writes the Chevalier de Johnstone, 'that a French engineer of a certain age and decorated with an order must necessarily be a person of experience, talents and capacity; but it was unfortunately discovered, when too late, that ... he was totally destitute of judgment, discernment, and common sense. His figure being as whimsical as his mind, the Highlanders, instead of M Mirabelle, called him always Mr Admirable.' Other judgments were hardly less critical. 'He was so volatile', writes Lord George, 'that he could not be depended upon', while Lord MacLeod describes him as 'always drunk'.

Whatever the reason, Monsieur Mirabelle proved singularly unsuccessful both in the siting of his batteries and the conduct of the siege. Nor did he get much help from the Prince's army, the Highlanders considering the spadework involved beneath their dignity and the Lowlanders being too lazy for it, with the result that it was left in the end to the French regulars. And so, during the weeks that followed, General Blakeney stayed where he was, politely informing the Prince when invited to surrender, that 'his Royal Highness would assuredly have a very bad opinion of him were he capable of surrendering the castle in such a cowardly manner.'

Nor was Charles's failure to take Stirling Castle his only cause for concern. Desertion was by now rife among his troops, particularly among the Athollmen. 'We are quite affronted', wrote Lord George Murray to his brother Duke William, 'with the scandalus desertion of

Prince Charles by Blanchet

English Footguards saying farewell at Tottenham Court Road turnpike before marching
to Finchley to meet Prince Charles's forces

The Battle of Culloden, 15 April 1746, by Morier

The Battle of Culloden as depicted by Holford

Henry, Cardinal York

your men.' Not that the morale of their leaders was very much better. The chiefs deeply resented the Prince's decision to hold no more councils as well as his increasing reliance on the advice of such intimates as Murray of Broughton and old Sir Thomas Sheridan. In the end on 6 January, just a month after the last fateful council at Derby, Lord George Murray handed to him on their behalf a memorandum in the following terms:

6th January 1746

It is proposed that His Royal Highness should from time to time call a councile of War, to consist of all those who command Battalions or Squadrons: but, as severalls of those may be on party, and often absent, a Committee should be chosen, to consist of Five or Seven, and that all operations for the carrying on of the War should be agre'd on by the Majority of those, in his Royal Highness' presence; and, once that a measure is taken, it is not to be changed except by the advice of those, or most of them, who were present when it was agre'd on.

That upon any sudden emergancy, such as in a Battle, Scirmish, or in a Sege, a Discrationary power must be allowed to those who command. This is the method of all armys, much (more) so should it be of this, which consists of Volunteers, and where so many gentlemen of fortune, not only venture their own and their family's all, But, if any misfortune happen, are sure of ending their Lives on a Scaffold, should they escape in the field.

If this plan is not followed, the most Dismall consequences cannot but ensue. Had not a Councill Determined the Retreat from Derby, what a catastrophy must have followed in tow or three days!

Had a Council of War been held the evening the army came to Lancaster on their return, a day (which at that time was so precious) had not been lost. Had a Council of War been consulted as to leaving a Garison at Carlisle, it would never have been agreed to, the place not being teneable, and so many brave men wou'd not have been sacrifized, besides the reputation of His Royal Highness's arms.

It is to be considered that this army is an army of Volunteers, and not mercinarrys, many of them being resolved not to continue in the army were affars once settled.

GEORGE MURRAY

To this the Prince, in high indignation and egged, no doubt, by his intimates, at once replied as follows:

147

When I came to Scotland, I knew well enough what I was to expect from my Ennemies, but I Little foresaw what I meet with from my Friends. I came vested with all the Authority the King could give me, one chief part of which is the Command of his Armies, and now I am required to give this up to fifteen persons, who may afterwards depute five or seven of their own number to exercise it, for fear, if they were six or eight, that I might myself pretend to ye casting vote.

By the majority of those things are to be determined, and nothing left to me but the honour of being present at their debates. This, I am told, is the method of all Armies, and this I flatly deny, nor do I believe it to be the method of any one Army in the world.

I am often hit in the teeth that this is an Army of Volontiers, consisting of Gentlemen of Rank and fortune, and who came into it meerly upon motives of Duty and Honours; what one wou'd expect from such an Army is more zeal, more resolution, and more good manners than in those that fight merely for pay: but it can be no Army at all where there is no General, nor, which is the same thing, no obedience or deference paid to him.

Everyone knew before he engaged in the cause what he was to expect in case it miscarried, and shou'd have staid at home if he cou'd not face death in any shape. But can I myself hope for better usage? at least I am the only person upon whose head a price has been already set, and therefore I cannot indeed threaten at every other word to throw down my arms and make Peace with the Government.

I think I shew every day that I do not pretend to act without asking advice, and yours oftner than any body's else, which I shall still continue to do. You know that upon more occasions than one I have given up my own opinion to that of others.

I staid, indeed, a day at Lancaster, without calling a Councile, yet yrself proposed to stay another. But I wonder much to see myself reproched with the loss of Carlile. Was there a possibility of carrying off the Cannon and Baggage, or was there time to destroy them? and wou'd not the doing it have been a greater dishonour to our Arms? After all, did not yrself, instead of proposing to abandon it, offer to stay with the Athol Brigade to defend it?

I have insensibly made this answer much longer than I intended, and might yet add much more, but I chose to cut it short, and shall only tell you that my Authority may be taken from me by violence, but I shall never resign it like an Ideot.

CHARLES, P.R.

In these angrily worded communications the pent up frustrations and antagonism which ever since Derby had been building up between the Prince and his advisers found all too clear expression. Faced with the Prince's sharp reaction, Lord George and the chiefs seem in the end to have decided to drop the matter for the time being. But their resentment did not diminish and it could only be a question of time before it again declared itself.

CHAPTER NINE

While the Highlanders were thus bickering ineffectually among themselves and wasting their time besieging Stirling Castle, a considerable reorganization and redeployment of the Government's forces had taken place. From Carlisle the Duke of Cumberland had returned to London, where he had been put in charge of such measures as were still being taken to meet the threat of a French landing. Old Marshal Wade had at long last retired and had, on Cumberland's recommendation, been replaced by Lieutenant-General Henry Hawley, reputedly a bastard son of George I and renowned above all for his brutality. ('Frequent and sudden executions', wrote Horace Walpole, 'are his rare passion.') His own brigade-major, James Wolfe, wrote of him, 'The troops dread his severity, hate the man and hold his military knowledge in contempt.' General Hawley's army was said to be 'composed of the best troops of the armies of the Duke of Cumberland and Marshal Wade'. On paper its strength must have been in the region of 8,000 men or more, though its commander, in a letter to the Duke of Newcastle, put the figure at 'but 6,600 men Rank and file fitt to march', while describing his infantry as 'quite *délabrée*'.

As it was considered likely that Charles would again make for Edinburgh, Hawley at once began moving his army north from Newcastle. Edinburgh had by this time been in Government hands for a good many weeks, having been re-occupied on the Prince's departure by Cope's successor, Lieutenant-General Roger Handasyde, with a couple of infantry battalions and the remains of Gardiner's (now Ligonier's) and Hamilton's Dragoons, last seen, it will be recalled, in full flight from Prestonpans. Of the two latter units General Handasyde reported that they were 'cowed' and had 'a damned Rebellious Spirit and a disposition to Rob Everywhere'. They were shortly to be joined by Cobham's Dragoons, who had taken part in the skirmish at Clifton, making a total of three regiments of cavalry.

At the end of December ten regular battalions of infantry, nine of them recently returned from Flanders, had begun marching north from Newcastle in pairs, the first two reaching Edinburgh on 2 January and the rest following at short intervals, until by 10 January a total of twelve battalions were assembled there. In addition to regular troops there were also three militia units, the Edinburgh Volunteers, the Yorkshire Blues, and the Earl of Home's 'Glasgow Regiment of Enthusiasts'. As for General Hawley's artillery, it left much to be desired. The officer he had picked to command it had pleaded sickness ('The Major's sickness', wrote Hawley, 'I suspect to be only a young Wife he wants to be withe'). It accordingly became the responsibility of Captain Archibald Cunningham – 'ane old Trooper of the Duke of Argille's', wrote Hawley, 'who is suche a Sott, and so ignorant that I believe he and I shan't agree long'. Under his command Captain Cunningham had 'a boy of eighteen', Fireworker Baillie Bryden, '2 Bombardeers and 14 Unexperienced Matrosses and 12 Country People' to man a train of artillery consisting of some ten assorted pieces, ranging from $1\frac{1}{2}$- to 6-pounders.

General Hawley himself reached Edinburgh on 6 January and, putting first things first, immediately caused two pairs of gallows to be erected, one in the Grassmarket and the other between Edinburgh and Leith. He next took stock of the troops under his command and after a week was gloomier about them than ever. 'Nobody', he wrote, 'can worke without Tooles, and as to that point my situation is as bad as ever any bodyes was.' 'I only beg of youre Grace', he wrote to the Duke of Newcastle, 'not to call this yeat a considerable force in the Condition they are in.' Nor had he any great opinion of Highlanders, whom he had encountered thirty years earlier as a young officer at Sherriffmuir ('I do and allwayes shall despise these Rascalls') and, though 'resolved to do nothinge rashly', was anxious to come to grips with the Prince as soon as possible and in particular to relieve Stirling Castle. For his predecessor, the unfortunate General Cope, he felt nothing but contempt which he expressed in a number of singularly coarse jokes.

A week after Hawley's arrival his second-in-command, Major-General John Huske, set out westwards from Edinburgh with a force composed of five regular battalions of foot, the Glasgow Militia, and Hamilton's and Ligonier's Dragoons. Of these, the Militia were left at Queensferry and a regular battalion at Bo'ness, while the remainder under General Huske marched on to Linlithgow, where they were joined next day by three more battalions of regulars.

Of the Highland army, part, under the Prince's own command, were now in the neighbourhood of Bannockburn. The remainder, comprising five clan regiments and part of the cavalry under Lord George Murray, lay nine miles further East at Falkirk. Learning that supplies for the Government forces were being collected at Linlithgow, Lord George set out from Falkirk early on 13 January with the object of getting there before the enemy and seizing or destroying the supplies. At the same time the Prince's cavalry under Lord Elcho were sent forward to patrol the roads leading to Edinburgh.

At noon Lord Elcho reported that he had encountered a small party of enemy cavalry which had then fallen back to join a larger body of horse and foot, and a couple of hours later came the news that 'their was a very large body of horse and foot advancing as fast as they could'. Waiting till the enemy had reached the outskirts of Linlithgow, Lord George crossed the bridge over the Avon, half a mile to the West of Linlithgow, and waited there, with the object of attacking them 'when a half should pass the bridge'. In fact 'none of them passed it, the Hanoverians preferring to remain drawn up immediately on the other side. 'And very abusive language pass'd betwixt both sides.' Not wishing to become involved in a minor skirmish when a major engagement seemed imminent, Lord George fell back on Falkirk, where next day he received orders to join the Prince at Bannockburn.

By this time most of the Jacobite reinforcements had come in from the North and were quartered with the rest of the Prince's forces over a wide area round Stirling. With the arrival of their new recruits, the MacDonalds, Camerons and Stewarts had almost doubled their strength. Lord Ogilvy had been joined by a second battalion which was much stronger than his first and the recently arrived Frasers, Mackintoshes and Farquharsons numbered some 300 men each. The Irish picquets and part of Lord John Drummond's regiment had by now also reached Stirling, while the rest of the regiment and Lord Lewis Gordon's men were a day's march or so away. Lord Cromartie's Mackenzies were at Alloa. 'All', writes Maxwell of Kirkconnel, 'were in high spirits and expressed the greatest ardour upon the prospect of a battle.'

Meanwhile General Hawley's departure from Edinburgh had been held up by the difficulty of getting his artillery on the road. His chief purpose remained the relief of Stirling Castle and he quite reasonably felt that 'to go to Sterling without some Canon would be silly'. To move the guns from Edinburgh Castle down to Holyroodhouse took three days, but by 15 January they were ready and that same day the Government train of artillery set out from Edinburgh with most of the remaining Government forces, Hawley himself following next day with Cobham's Dragoons. That evening they encamped in a field a little to the West of Falkirk, where they were joined next morning, the 17th, by the Duke of Argyll's cousin and heir, Major General John Campbell of Mamore, who had arrived from Glasgow with three companies of Lord Loudon's Regiment, one of Lord John Murray's (The Black Watch) and twelve of the Argyll Militia. With these, the strength of the forces under General Hawley's command added up to some 8,000 men.

The distance separating the armies was now only a few miles and there was clearly a risk that General Hawley, whose forces could be quickly concentrated, might take advantage of this and of the wide dispersal of the Highlanders to attack them suddenly and defeat them in detail. Accordingly on the morning of 15 and again on 16 January the Prince's army had been drawn up in order of battle on Plean Muir, two miles to the South-East of Bannockburn, to await developments. But nothing had happened and on the 17th the same procedure was repeated. News was now received of Hawley's arrival with his main body the night before and, having once more reviewed his troops, who were beginning to grow restive, the Prince called a council of war at which Lord George Murray suggested that, rather than wait to be attacked, the Highland army should themselves take the offensive.

Lord George's proposal being at once approved, plans were promptly drawn up for putting it into execution. The Highlanders' first objective, it was decided, should be the Hill of Falkirk, a steep ridge or moorland to the South-West of the town. This lay not more than a mile from Hawley's camp, but it was hoped that, by using secondary roads and making a wide detour through the fields, the Prince's main body would be able to remain unnoticed, at any rate until they reached the ford across the River Carron some two miles from Falkirk. Meanwhile, to confuse the enemy and create a diversion, the Prince's standard was left flying on Plean Muir and Lord John Drummond was despatched with part of his own regiment, the Irish picquets and all the cavalry along the main road from Bannockburn to Falkirk, which at this point passed to the North of the Torwood and was in full view of the enemy's camp. Rather more than 1,000 men under the Duke of Perth having foolishly been left to cover the siege of Stirling Castle, the strength of the Prince's army was roughly the same as that of the enemy, namely around 8,000.

The Highland army began their advance soon after midday, marching in two parallel columns, the left-hand column commanded by Lord George Murray and the right-hand by the Prince. Lord George's column was led by the three regiments of Clan Donald and the Prince's by the Atholl Brigade. They had barely gone half a mile when the

153

egregious John William O'Sullivan came riding over to Lord George to say that 'he had been talking with the Prince and that it was not thought advisable to pass the water in sight of the enemy, and therefore it was best delaying it till night, and then we could do it unperceived'. 'This', writes Lord George with great restraint, 'surprised me; I told him that we could be all past the water in less than a quarter of an hour, and the place we were to pass was two full miles from the enemy.' 'I did not halt', he adds, 'and he went back to His Royal Highness, who was riding betwixt the two lines.'

The Prince now rode over himself, accompanied by O'Sullivan, some other officers and Brigadier Stapleton, the commander of the Irish picquets. Continuing to advance as they conversed, Lord George objected that the men could not lie out at night in mid-winter and that, if what O'Sullivan proposed were attempted, they would merely disperse and seek shelter. They should therefore either continue to advance or return to their quarters. Stapleton now agreed that, unless the enemy were near enough to dispute the crossing, there could be no danger. To this Lord George, still riding forward as they talked, replied that 'so far from disputing our passing ... we were now within half a mile of the water, which then was very small, and that the enemy were two full miles off, and could not see us till we were very near it'. This neatly settled the argument and the two Highland columns continued their advance, which, though Lord George did not realize it, had already been observed by the enemy.

On reaching Falkirk the night before, General Hawley had established himself just outside the town to the South-East, at Callendar House, the seat of Lord Kilmarnock, who, as we have seen, was commanding a troop of the Prince's cavalry and whose attractive and ardently Jacobite Countess was now compelled to entertain the enemy General, which, however, for reasons of her own, she did with reasonably good grace.

Early next morning Hawley rode over to the camp to visit his troops and at the same time make a personal reconnaissance of the ground lying between his own troops and the Torwood. During the General's reconnaissance a certain William Corse of the Glasgow Militia heard some officers say that they saw the enemy moving 'on this side the Torwood Southwards', 'though', he adds, 'I saw nothing, neither did Mr Hawley'. The General, having evidently concluded that there was no major movement on the part of the enemy, and considering any further reconnaissance unnecessary, had by now returned to Callendar House, convinced that an attack was unlikely.

At about eleven, however, some of Hawley's troops noticed a body of the Prince's horse and foot moving about to the North of the

Torwood. At this the Hanoverian army stood to arms. But the Prince's men soon withdrew again to Plean, at which the Government troops stood down and, like General Hawley, went in search of their mid-day meal. This, according to Militiaman William Corse, 'was not easy to be found', and for one reason or another took them the best part of two hours to prepare and eat, with the result that they had barely finished, when just before one o'clock an excited yokel rushed into their camp, shouting, 'Gentlemen, what are you about? The High-landers will be immediately upon you!' Whereupon two officers of the Old Buffs quickly climbed a tree and, with the help of a telescope, were able to confirm that what the yokel said was perfectly true. The main Highland army could now be seen rapidly approaching to the South of the Torwood.

At this Lieutenant-Colonel Howard, commanding the Old Buffs, at once galloped off to Callendar House to convey the disturbing information to General Hawley, only to find the latter quite unwilling or unable to grasp its significance and still convinced, in spite of what Colonel Howard told him, that there was no likelihood of an enemy attack. Clearly not wishing to be disturbed at the lavish repast with which the charming Lady Kilmarnock was entertaining him, he simply sent instructions for his troops to put on their equipment, without, however, standing to arms, while he himself continued to enjoy his midday meal and his hostess's agreeable company.

So things remained until between one and two o'clock when a party of volunteers rode into the Government camp 'upon the spur' with the news that the Highlanders were about to ford the River Carron at Dunipace Steps, evidently bound for the high ground beyond it. There was now quite clearly no time to lose. Ordering the drums to beat 'To Arms', General Huske, an experienced and competent officer, at once sent a second messenger to General Hawley at Callendar House.

By now the Government's regular troops were drawn up in two lines on the left of the camp facing South, with the dragoons on the flanks. 'I never was used to these things', wrote Militiaman Corse, 'but I was surpriz'd to see in how little time ye regular troops were form'd.' But despite the speed with which the regulars managed to form line, there was a good deal of confusion in the Government camp. General Hawley had still not arrived and, says an eyewitness, 'one might hear the officers saying to one another, "Where is the General? What shall be done? We have no orders." '

One of the more bewildered officers was Captain Archibald Cun-ningham, the 'Ignorant Sott' in charge of Hawley's artillery. Earlier that morning Captain Cunningham had gone into Falkirk 'to Shave & Shift himself, for he had no Tent in ye Camp, haveing been obliged to

155

leve that at Newcastle'. After completing his toilet, he now took up his position with his train of artillery on the left of the line. Being without orders, he first tried to find General Hawley then, learning that the latter had still not arrived, rode over to General Huske and, finally discovering that Huske could do no more than refer him back to Hawley, returned to his guns on the left of the line and simply stood in front of them.

As so often happens in war, a chance incident now came to distract attention and relieve the strain. While the Government troops stood waiting for something to happen, a hare got up in full sight of them, 'upon which,' says one of them, 'the soldiers raised a loud *view-hollo* and one, more ready-witted than the rest exclaimed, "Halloo, the Duke of Perth's mother!", it being a general belief that that zealous old Catholic lady was a witch and therefore able to assume the disguise of a hare . . .'.

It was only at this stage that the Hanoverians were finally joined in the field by their Commander-in-Chief, General Hawley, who arrived on the scene at the gallop with no hat and 'the appearance of one who has abruptly left a hospitable table'. His subordinates could now make more detailed dispositions for the battle that was about to begin.

The Hill of Falkirk rises steeply from its lower slopes to the South-West of the town to Falkirk Muir, then a flat moorland plateau scattered with occasional farms and patches of cultivated land. To the North the face of the hill is broken by a deep gully or ravine, running half-way up the hillside. The Government cavalry were the first to advance. Led by Ligonier's (late Gardiner's), the three dragoon regiments now moved off southwards from their encampment, crossed the Falkirk-Stirling road and, following a lane to the East of Bantaskin House, known as Maggie Wood's Loan, started to climb the hill. They were under the command of Colonel Francis Ligonier, a brother of General Sir John Ligonier. Following the cavalry in column of route came the front-line infantry: Wolfe's, Cholmondeley's, Pulteney's, The Royals, Price's and Ligonier's Regiments. The second line, forming the rear column, consisted of Blakeney's, Munro's, Fleming's, Barrel's, Battereau's and Howard's Old Buffs.

On reaching the River Carron, the Prince's army had found a strong wind blowing from the South-West and, in order that the Highlanders should have it at their backs, the two Jacobite columns had, on forming line, made a wide circuit after crossing the river and then marched 'very quick' up the hillside. From the other side the English dragoons were advancing up the hill as fast as they could and it was not until both had almost reached the top that they came in sight of each other. At first the Highlanders thought that the Government troops were only a reconnaissance party. Then more and more cavalry came into view and they realized that this was the enemy's main force.

The dragoons now made several moves towards Lord George Murray's column and tried to draw the Highlanders' fire, their object being to rush them before they had time to re-load. But to no purpose. The Highland column simply marched on until they came to a bog, when the whole force wheeled sharply to the left.

During the next quarter of an hour the three MacDonald regiments advanced slowly in line, so as to give the other regiments time to come up on their left. Lord George, meanwhile, on foot with broadsword and targe, walked down the line, telling the men to keep their ranks and not to fire until he gave the order. At the same time he sent his two mounted ADCs, Ker of Graden and young Anderson of Whitburgh, to make a reconnaissance. From this they returned with the news that the dragoons appeared to be unsupported by infantry (the latter having, in fact, been left behind during the climb).

Forming line as they climbed the hill, the Highland centre and left-wing regiments now extended right down the hillside from the level ground near the summit, which was occupied by the right. On the far left, near the mouth of the gully, were the Stewarts of Appin. On the right were the three MacDonald regiments and between them the Camerons, Frasers, Macphersons, Mackintoshes, Mackenzies and Farquharsons. The second line regiments were those of Lord Lewis Gordon and Lord Ogilvy, each comprising two battalions, and the three battalions of the Atholl Brigade. The reserve troops, having taken part in Lord John Drummond's diversion, arrived later and formed in rear of the second line under Prince Charles himself. In the centre were stationed the French regulars with the cavalry on either side. The Highland front line was more than double the length of the other two, with the result that there were large gaps between the centre and wings of the second and third lines.

Though Lord George Murray had twice urged 'that His Royal Highness would appoint the officers that were to command and where', the all-important question of command in the Highland army had not received due attention. Even Lord George himself had been given 'no particular charge' beyond that of leading the front-line troops, from which he had assumed that he was to command the right wing. The result was that in practice the left remained without a commander for, though some accounts of the engagement suggest that Lord John Drummond commanded it, he had, according to Lord George, 'no directions to do it and was not there when the Batle began'. Lord George had also to put up with the advice of John William O'Sullivan, who had been sent by the Prince 'to arrange' the front line for him.

157

Some of O'Sullivan's suggestions he long-sufferingly accepted; others he rejected out of hand.

During their advance up the hill, the Government dragoons had, as we have seen, considerably outdistanced their supporting infantry, while the unfortunate Captain Archibald Cunningham and his train of artillery had been left still further behind. When the battle began, two of his biggest guns were 'hopelessly stuck in a Bog' and he was still struggling to bring up some of the others. The Prince's artillery, for its part, was never to reach the battlefield at all.

The left wing of the Highland army was protected by the ravine at the top of the hill and the right by the patch of marshy ground at its foot. This made it impossible for the English cavalry to outflank them. Further attempts 'to draw the fire and ride in and break the High-landers' were frustrated, the MacDonalds remembering Lord George's instructions to stay where they were and not be tempted. Accordingly the three regiments of dragoons now simply drew up facing the Jacobite front line with wide intervals between their squadrons. Meanwhile the Government infantry were still toiling up the hill, the rear regiments 'running & quite out of breath wh the fatigue'. To make things worse, a violent storm had broken and the rain was coming down in torrents, blowing into their faces and drenching their cartridges. Hurriedly forming line on reaching the top, Wolfe's, the leading regiment, took up position to the right of Hamilton's Dragoons, while the remainder fell in on Wolfe's right as they came up. Following the front-line troops, the second-line regiments, led by Blakeney's, drew up in the rear, Howard's Old Buffs, the rearmost regiment, falling back in reserve, with the result the second line consisted of only five regiments. Though Lord Home's Glasgow Enthusiasts 'march'd up the Hill very stoutly', they were considered to be insufficiently trained to take their place in the line and so were stationed near some cottages, well to the rear of the dragoons. As for the Argyll Militia, they 'were posted or posted themselves' on the far right, near the bottom of the hill.

As they were now positioned, the Government infantry on the left found themselves outflanked by half the Jacobite front-line regiments, while on the Government right, the roles were reversed. Moreover the three Government right-wing regiments, Price's and Ligonier's in the front-line and Battereau's in the rear, were drawn up facing the ravine, which made it impossible for them to work round the Jacobite left. To the Camerons and Stewarts of Appin on the Jacobite left their presence was, however, distinctly disturbing and, when O'Sullivan came over with orders, 'one Daniel Cameron answer'd yt all he said shou'd be executed, if he'd answer yt they shou'd not be outwinged' – a reflection that O'Sullivan 'did not like'. Further to the left O'Sullivan was dis-

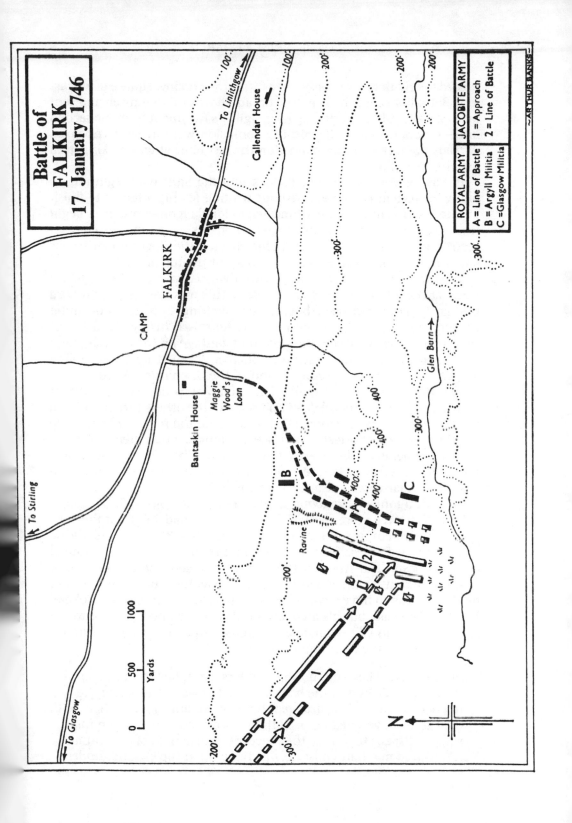

Battle of FALKIRK 17 January 1746

ROYAL ARMY	JACOBITE ARMY
A = Line of Battle	1 = Approach
B = Argyll Militia	2 = Line of Battle
C = Glasgow Militia	

~ARTHUR BANKS~

To Linlithgow

Callendar House

FALKIRK

CAMP

Bantaskin House

Maggie Wood's Loan

To Stirling

To Glasgow

Glen Burn

Ravine

B

C

N

Yards

0   500   1000

turbed to find that the enemy were forming 'a hollow square of at least four Battaillons'. But he kept 'the dread he was in' to himself and sent an ADC with orders to bring up Lord Ogilvy's Regiment from the second line – orders which in the ensuing confusion were never carried out. Already the lack of a commander on the Jacobite left was making itself felt.

It was by now nearly four o'clock and the light was beginning to fail, when General Hawley, without waiting for his infantry to finish forming, suddenly sent the astonished Colonel Ligonier orders to begin the attack, and a group of interested onlookers, watching the engagement from the steeple of Falkirk church, saw the Government troops 'enter the misty and storm-covered moor at the top of the hill'.

The three regiments of cavalry now advanced towards the Highland right 'at the full trot in very good order'. This was precisely what Lord George Murray had been hoping for. Waiting until the oncoming dragoons were barely ten yards away, he raised his own musket as the signal to fire, and from their point of vantage on the church tower the onlookers 'saw the dull atmosphere thickened by a fast-rolling smoke, and heard the peeling sound of the discharge'. At so short a range, the effect of the Highlanders' volley was devastating. About eighty enemy troopers fell dead and most of the others turned tail and fled. From his unit's position some distance to the rear, William Corse of the Glasgow Enthusiasts could 'see daylight through them in several places', while, from the steeple, the spectators 'beheld the discomfited troops burst wildly from the cloud in which they had been involved and rush in far-spread disorder over the hill'.

A few of Ligonier's Dragoons, led by Lieutenant-Colonel Shugbrough Whitney, showed more spirit. Colonel Whitney had fought at Prestonpans and, catching sight of Colonel John Roy Stewart, the Gaelic poet, who had himself once served in the British cavalry, shouted across to him, 'Ha! Are you there? We shall soon be up with you.' 'You shall be welcome when you come', was John Roy's reply, 'and, by God, you shall have a warm reception.' A few minutes later Colonel Whitney fell dead, but his men, continuing to advance, broke into the ranks of Clanranald's regiment. 'The most singular and extraordinary combat', writes the Chevalier de Johnstone,

> immediately followed. The Highlanders, stretched on the ground, thrust their dirks into the bellies of the horses. Some seized the riders by their clothes, dragged them down, and stabbed them with their dirks; several again used their pistols; but few of them had sufficient space to handle their swords. Macdonald of Clanranald ... assured me that whilst he was lying upon the ground, under

160

a dead horse, which had fallen upon him, without the power of extricating himself, he saw a dismounted horseman struggling with a Highlander: fortunately for him, the Highlander, being the strongest, threw his antagonist, and having killed him with his dirk, he came to his assistance, and drew him with difficulty from under his horse.

After thus successfully repulsing the enemy's cavalry, Lord George now ordered the three MacDonald regiments to stand their ground. But Glengarry's and Clanranald's could not be stopped from pursuing the fleeing dragoons. In their panic flight to the rear Hamilton's Dragoons galloped right through Lord Home's Glasgow Enthusiasts, '& carry'd off about a Company of our people; amongst whom I was', writes Militiaman Corse. 'I would then have given my life for a shilling. Some of us they rode over and some of us ran and rode so well that we got quit of them in about 5 or 600 yards, with the utmost difficulty.' Meanwhile Ligonier's and the rest of Hamilton's had broken away down the hillside, plunging into their own right wing and scattering the infantry in every direction, while Cobham's, choosing a course between the opposing armies, came under fire from the Jacobite centre and left.

For the Jacobites, 'it was', wrote Kirkconnel, 'a fine beginning; but the first success had like to have cost very dear'. On the right, the two MacDonald regiments were now almost completely out of control. 'Some pursued the dragoons, others fell a-plundering the dead; a considerable body that kept a just direction in their march fell in with the Glasgow Militia and were employed in dispersing them.' Further along the Prince's line the situation was equally confused. Having discharged their muskets at Cobham's, the Highlanders, who did not use cartridges and in the heavy rain could not re-load, found themselves unable to return the fire of the Government foot. They accordingly flung down their muskets and charged with their broadswords, the second line following hard on the heels of the first. Attacked on two sides and blinded by the rain, the Government's left flank, who had already been ridden down by their own cavalry, made little attempt at a stand. After firing one weak and ineffectual volley, four of the six front-line regiments simply turned and ran, followed almost immediately by most of the second line.

It was at this juncture that that keen observer of events, John Home, the young Divinity student and historian now serving with the Edinburgh Volunteers, caught sight of General Hawley 'involved in a crowd of horse and foot', and decided that this would be a good moment to ask his Commanding General a few questions: 'If there were any regiments standing? Where they were?' and so on. But he was to be disappointed. 'The General', he tells us, 'made no answer, but, pointing to a fold for cattle which was close by, called to him to get in there with his men.' After which, 'the disorder and confusion increased, and General Hawley rode down the hill'.

It is tempting at this stage to recall that General Hawley's orders for 12 January had contained the following passage:

> The manner of the Highlanders way of fighting, which there is nothing so easy to resist if Officers & men are not prepossess'd with the Lyes & Accounts which are told of them. They Commonly form their Front rank of what they call their best men, or True Highlanders, the number of which being allways but few, when they form in Battallions they commonly form four deep, & these Highlanders form the front of the four, the rest being lowlanders & arrant scum.

> When these Battallions come within a large Musket shot, or three score yards, this front Rank gives their fire, & Immediately thro' down their firelocks & Come down in a Cluster with their Swords and Targets making a Noise and Endeavouring to pearce the Body, or Battallions before them becoming 12 or 14 deep by the time they come up to the people they attack.

> The sure way to demolish them is at 3 deep to fire by ranks diagonaly to the Centre where they come, the rear rank first, and even that rank not to fire till they are within 10 or 12 paces but If the fire is given at a distance you probably will be broke for you never get time to load a second Cartridge, & if you give way you may give your foot for dead, for they being without a firelock or any load, no man with his arms, accoutrements &c. can escape them, and they give no Quarters, but if you will but observe the above directions, they are the most despicable Enimy that are.

While the Government's left wing was falling back in disorder, Major-General Huske kept his head. On their right Ligonier's, commanded by Lieutenant-Colonel Stanhope and protected by the mouth of the ravine, and Price's were still standing their ground. Of the second line Barrel's had also stood firm and, with the two front-line regiments, now moved up the hill towards the left. There, under orders from General Huske and Brigadier Cholmondeley, they took up position and directed their fire at the flank of the pursuing Highlanders, throwing them 'into great disorder'. To add to the confusion, Colonel John Roy Stewart, 'afraid lest this might be an ambuscade ... called out to the Highlanders to stop their pursuit; and the cry of stop flew immediately from rank to rank'. At this, some of the men stood still; others went back to the point where they had been drawn up, while many left the field and hurried back to Stirling and Bannockburn with the news that the Prince's army had been defeated.

Meanwhile Lord George Murray, out of sight on the ridge above, had rallied what remained of Keppoch's regiment and the Atholl Brigade, whose three battalions, alone of the Jacobite second line, had kept their ranks, and, advancing down the hill with them 'in perfect good order', set out to harry the enemy who by now were 'running off by forties and fifties to the right and left to get into Falkirk'. At the same time Lord George sent off Ker of Graden 'to entreat that the reserve might advance on the left'. By now the need for a senior officer to command the Highland left was becoming more urgent than ever. Indeed, as Lord George himself put it, 'had there been men brought up, either from the second line on the left, or the *corps de réserve*, to have faced these regiments that outlined the Highlanders, the battle would not have lasted ten minutes'.

As it was, Cobham's Dragoons, having rallied, rode up the hill again, apparently with the intention of outflanking the Highlanders and attacking them from the rear in the hope of capturing Prince Charles himself. At this moment, however, either on the Prince's own initiative or in response to an order from Lord George, the Irish picquets moved forward from the reserve, at which Cobham's Dragoons fell back on the three right wing regiments and, forming a rearguard, retired with them in reasonably good order down the hill in the direction of Falkirk.

At the foot of the hill, they came on what was left of the artillery, most of whose civilian drivers had made off on the gun horses when they saw what was happening higher up. Having harnessed themselves to one of the guns, some of Barrel's grenadiers finally succeeded in dragging it away, for which, wrote one of them, 'Brigadier was pleased to express his Satisfaction in our Behaviour, by kissing our Men, and making us a Present of ten Guineas'. Two more guns were later brought in by horse teams from Falkirk. But it had scarcely been a gunner's battle.

Lord George Murray now had with him 'not above six or seven hundred men ... the rest being all scattered on the face of the hill'. It was almost dark and pouring with rain and he thought it better not to pursue the enemy's rearguard any further. Instead he halted at the bottom of the hill, where he was joined by Lord John Drummond with the Jacobite reserve.

The next question to be decided was where the Prince's army should spend the night. No one was sure where the enemy were, though fires burning in their camp outside the town seemed to suggest that they were still there. Lord George was strongly in favour of pushing on into

163

Falkirk, whether the enemy were there or not. The Prince agreed to this and, after some discussion, the decision was taken to march into the town. Meanwhile Lord Kilmarnock, using his local knowledge, had made a reconnaissance through his own fields and grounds from which he came back with the news that he had seen the Hanoverians in full retreat along the high road to Linlithgow. Lord George with his Athollmen and Lord John Drummond with the French contingent now marched into Falkirk from either end, taking prisoner a few stragglers who had been left behind in the confusion. Among these was John Home, the Divinity student and historian, who, on comparing notes with his captors, came to the conclusion that the whole action had lasted only twenty minutes. Not long after this the Prince himself made his entry into Falkirk and 'profited of General Hally's supper wch he wanted very much'. From plump, well-fed John William O'Sullivan, who had a nose for such things, we learn that 'a great many hampers of good wines and liquors & other provisions were found in the Town'. Of even more importance was the capture of most of the enemy's tents, all their ammunition, and a large number of wagons, as well as 'three standards, two stand of colours, a kettledrum, many small arms, their baggage, clothing and generally every thing they had not burnt or destroyed'.

The Jacobite casualties in the battle had been small, not more than fifty killed, seven or eight of whom were junior officers. Hawley's losses were much heavier, a score or more officers killed and several hundred other ranks. Among the Hanoverian officers killed was Sir Robert Munro of Foulis, chief of the staunchly Whig Munros and a popular figure in the Highlands, who the year before had greatly distinguished himself in command of the newly raised Black Watch at the Battle of Fontenoy. During the next day or two the Jacobites took several hundred more prisoners, including some of General Hawley's hangmen, whom they released on parole, 'as it was Supposed they would keep them as well as the officers did'.

The Hanoverians took only one prisoner, Major MacDonald of Tiendrish, who, mistaking in his excitement Barrel's regiment for Lord John Drummond's, had rushed up to them, shouting, 'Why dont ye follow after the dogs and pursue them?' only realizing his mistake when it was too late. General Huske at once ordered him to be shot. He was saved for the time being by the kindly intervention of Lord Robert Ker, but later sent to Edinburgh and thence to Carlisle, where in the end he was hanged.

By the time darkness fell, the Prince's army was scattered all over the surrounding countryside. According to Lord George, barely 1,500 men found their way into Falkirk that night, making scarcely enough for guard duty. Of the remainder some were busy looting the dead or pillaging the enemy's camp, while others, including some of the regimental commanders, had returned to their quarters quite ignorant of the outcome of the battle, until they were informed of it by MacDonell of Lochgarry later that night. Indeed the Chevalier de Johnstone tells us that at Dunipace House, barely five miles from the field of battle, he found Lord Lewis Gordon, the Master of Lovat and others sitting round the fire with no idea of what had happened to their regiments or whether the battle had been lost or won. Meanwhile, under the pouring rain, the naked corpses of the dead looked, says an eyewitness, like so many white sheep upon the hillside.

On reaching Linlithgow that same evening, General Hawley, whose immediate reactions are said to have been 'rage and vexation', sat down to announce his defeat, in his own rather incoherent way, to his patron, the Duke of Cumberland:

> Sir,
> My heart is broke. I can't say We are quite beat today, But our Left is beat and Their Left is beat. We had enough to beat them for we had Two Thousand Men more than They. But suche scandalous Cowardice I never saw before. The whole second line of foot ran away without firing a Shot.
> Pardon me, Sir, that you have no more this time from
> The most unhappy, but most faithfull and most
> dutifull Your RH has,
> H. Hawley

Next morning an early visitor reported that the Commander-in-Chief 'looked most wretchedly; even worse than Cope did a few hours after his scuffle. . . .' But before long General Hawley had recovered his spirits. From Linlithgow his army returned later that day to Edinburgh (where, according to William Corse of the Glasgow Militia, they were 'much insulted by the Jacobites'), and two days later we find him reporting to the Duke of Newcastle that 'every wheele is at worke to gett the Engine in motion again'. 'The Foot', he goes on, 'recover theyr spiritts, they owne to theyr Officers they all deserve to be hanged.' Meanwhile he himself did what he could for their morale by hanging thirty-one of Hamilton's Dragoons for desertion and shooting thirty-two foot soldiers for cowardice.

As for Captain Archibald Cunningham of the Royal Artillery, he was arrested and, having tried unsuccessfully to take his own life by opening his arteries, was court martialled and sentenced to be cash-iered with infamy, a painful proceeding which involved having his sword broken over his head, his sash cut in pieces and thrown in his

165

face and finally 'a kick on the posteriors' administered to him by the Provost-Martial's servant.

In the English capital the defeat caused consternation, dispelling the optimism generated by the Highland army's retreat from Derby. On the day the news was received a Drawing-Room was being held at St James's Palace and it was remarked that the faces of those present displayed the deepest gloom, save only that of General Sir John Cope, who, it is said, looked remarkably cheerful.

Hawley did not remain Commander-in-Chief for much longer. Though his responsibility for the defeat seems somehow to have been overlooked and he was not actually removed from his post, it was nevertheless felt in London that the only man now likely to restore the army's morale was the Duke of Cumberland. It was thus that early on 30 January His Royal Highness arrived in Edinburgh to assume overall command. The Government forces had, meanwhile, received substantial reinforcements: a fresh artillery train with a complement of regular gunners; Campbell's Royal Scots Fusiliers; Sempill's 25th Regiment and three squadrons of Lord Mark Ker's Dragoons. At the same time the officers and men of the Glasgow Militia had been 'honourably dismissed' and the services of Hamilton's and Ligonier's Dragoons had also been dispensed with.

CHAPTER TEN

The Jacobites could well have claimed Falkirk as a victory. Instead, they chose to regard it as a semi-failure and characteristically at once set about blaming each other because things had not gone better. There was also a sharp difference of opinion as to what to do next. Some wished to set off immediately in pursuit of Hawley's demoralized army or even march once more on London. Others wanted to resume the siege of Stirling Castle, being encouraged in this by the fatuous Monsieur Mirabelle, who stoutly maintained that the castle could not possibly hold out for more than a very few days. In the end M. Mirabelle's view prevailed and it was decided, according to the Chevalier de Johnstone by Charles himself, to continue the siege.

It was to prove, for more reasons than one, a disastrous decision. Indeed Johnstone was later to argue, not unconvincingly, that from the Prince's point of view it was actually better that 'this petty fort ... should remain in the hands of the enemy', if only as a deterrent to Highland desertion. What is certain is that, in the situation then prevailing, the Jacobites' right course would have been to follow up Hawley immediately and hit him again hard before he had time to recover. In Johnstone's words, 'we ought to have pursued the English with the rapidity of a torrent, in order to prevent them from recovering from their fright; we should have kept continuously at their heels, and never relaxed till they were no longer in a condition to rally'. Not to have done so was, in the opinion of at least one eminent authority, 'as critical a mistake as the failure to press on to London from Derby'.

As it was, the Prince, leaving Lord George and the clan regiments at Falkirk, moved back to Bannockburn on 19 January with the rest of his army, again taking up his residence with Sir Hugh Paterson at

Bannockburn House, once more in the agreeable company of Sir Hugh's niece Clementina. By now a second summons to surrender had been delivered to old General Blakeney, the commander of the Stirling Castle garrison. But the latter, realizing no doubt that the more time the Jacobites wasted on the siege, the better for the Government, replied blandly 'that he had always been looked upon as a man of honour and that the rebels should find that he would die so'.

At the end of ten days, M. Mirabelle had managed to mount one 16-pounder and two 12-pounders in three of his battery's six emplacements and now gave the assurance that within eighteen hours of his opening fire the castle would surrender. Unmasked on 29 January, the battery opened fire. 'But,' writes the Chevalier de Johnstone, 'it was of short duration and produced very little effect on the batteries of the Castle, which being more elevated than ours, the enemy cold see even the buckles on the shoes of our artillerymen. As their fire commanded ours, our guns were immediately dismounted, and in less than half an hour we were obliged to abandon our battery altogether....' In this foolish fashion another ten precious days were wasted and a not unpromising opportunity missed of restoring the Prince's fortunes.

At Bannockburn House, meanwhile, Charles had been kept indoors by a feverish cold, from which, the story goes, he was nursed back to health by pretty Clementina who, according to Lord Elcho, had by now become his mistress. What seems more probable is that Clementina, like any other starry-eyed Jacobite maiden, was dazzled by having the Prince under her care and that he for his part flirted mildly with his pretty hostess. He may even have been sufficiently taken with her to show some neglect of his immediate military duties. 'I was just ready to get on hourseback in order to make you a visit', he wrote, perhaps a trifle guiltily, to Lord George on 23 January, 'but have been over-persuaded to let it alone by people who are continuously teasing me with my cold.' From Bannockburn the Prince also despatched an optimistic letter to the French King telling him of his victory at Falkirk and begging him yet again to send an expeditionary force: '*Si le Debarquement que j'attens depuis si longtems*', he wrote '*se fait a present on peut regarder l'Affaire comme finie.*'

But plans for a French landing were no further advanced than they had been a month earlier and, despite Charles's encouraging tone, the news of his withdrawal from Derby, whether tactical or not, had done nothing to make the French any keener on the project. Nor had the Royal Navy relaxed their watch on the Channel, nor indeed had the winter storms abated. Charles's brother Henry, like Charles himself the year before, continued to hang miserably about the Channel ports, waiting for a chance to embark, complaining that Boulogne was '*un vilain trou'* and irritating the Duc de Richelieu (insofar as they ever met) by his never ending genuflexions and what the latter regarded as incipient religious mania. Nor did the young Prince strike the Duke, who himself was famous for his innumerable mistresses, as being quite as manly as he might. Meanwhile both Henry's ADCs, his cousins Turenne and Montbazon, had gone off to join their regiments at the front, an opportunity of showing his own mettle sternly denied the young Prince by his French sponsors.

It was at this juncture, on 29 January, that Lord George and the commanders of the principal clan regiments presented to the Prince yet another memorandum which he was to find even more infuriating than its predecessor. 'We think it', they wrote, 'our duty in this critical juncture to lay our opinions in the most respectful manner before yr. R:H:.' And they went on to express the view that, as a result of widespread desertion ('a vast number of the soldiers of yr R:H:'s army are gone home'), the Highland army was not in a fit state to meet the enemy. 'If yr R:H: should risque a battle and Stirling Castle not in your hands, we can foresee nothing but utter destruction to the few that will remain.' They therefore recommended an immediate withdrawal to the Highlands, 'where we can be usefully employed the remainder of the winter, by taking and mastering the Forts in the North ... and in the spring we doubt not but an army of ten thousand effective Highlanders can be brought together, and follow yr. R:H: wherever you think proper'. The disposal of the artillery, they admitted, presented a difficulty; 'but better some of these were thrown in the River Forth as that yr. R:H: besides the danger to your own person, should risque the flower of your army'. There followed an expression of undying loyalty to the Prince 'and the Glorious Cause we have espoused' and the signatures of Lord George himself, Lochiel, Keppoch, Cluny Macpherson, Clanranald, Lochgarry, Ardshiel, Glengyle and the Master of Lovat.

It was certainly true that desertion and indiscipline were rife. With nothing better to do, the Highlanders 'sauntered about all the villages in the neighbourhood of their quarters, and abundance of them had been several days absent from their colours'. 'Our men', wrote Lord George to his wife, 'are Impatient to be home, and numbers have left us.' It could moreover be argued that withdrawal to the Highlands was in fact the logical alternative to an immediate attack on Hawley's demoralized Hanoverians, offering the Highlanders the possibility of continuing the war on their own terms, in their own territory and in country far better suited to their style of fighting.

But Charles, who had been looking forward to an early encounter with Cumberland, possibly on the historic field of Bannockburn, which he felt would 'decide the fate of Scotland', and for which he had until that very day been working out a plan jointly with Lord George, was utterly dismayed by the chiefs' letter. On receiving it, says Hay of Restalrig, who delivered it to him, he 'struck his head against the wall till he staggered and exclaimed most violently against Lord George Murray'. 'Is it possible', he asked in the long, reasoned reply which he now sat down to write,

> that a Victory and a Defeat shou'd produce the same effects and that the Conquerors should flie from an engagement, whilst the Conquer'd are seeking it? Shou'd we make the retreat you propose, how much more will that raise the spirits of our Ennemys and sink those of our own People? ... What Opinion will the French and Spaniards then have of us, or what encouragement will it be to the former to make the descent for which they have been so long preparing, or the latter to send us any more succours? ... What will become of our Lowland friends? Shall we persuade them to retire with us to the Mountains? Or shall we abandon them to the fury of our Merciless Ennemies? What an Encouragement will this be to them or others to rise in our favour? For my own Part, [he concluded in a more moderate tone] I must say that it is with the greatest reluctance that I can bring myself to consent to such a step, but, having told you my thoughts upon it, I am too sensible of what you have already ventured and done for me, not to yield to yr. unanimous resolution if you persist in it.

But, despite further argument, Charles could not convince the chiefs and, having again recorded his objections in a second letter in which he disclaimed all responsibility for the withdrawal, yielded once more to the majority. 'I can't see nothing', he wrote, 'but ruin and destruction to us all in case we should think of a retreat ... why shoud we be so much afraid now of an Ennemy that we attacked and beat a fortnight ago when they were much more numerous I cannot conceive. Has the loss of so many officers and men killed and wounded and the Shame of their flight made them more formidable? ... If you are all resolved upon it, I must yield; but I take God to witness that it is with the greatest reluctance, and that I wash my hands of the fatal consequences wch I foresee but cannot help.'

In the end it was decided that the retreat of the Highland army should begin on the morning of 1 February. But now came the news that the Duke of Cumberland and most of his army had already reached Linlithgow and on the evening of 31 January Lord George and the clan regiments fell back on Bannockburn, leaving a small force of cavalry at Falkirk to watch the enemy. Later that night it was agreed that the Prince's army, except for the troops remaining at Stirling under the Duke of Perth and Lord John Drummond, should rendezvous in 'a field to the east of St Ninian's and the houre nine in the morning', and that a rear guard should be formed under Lord George's command.

But when Lord George reached the rendezvous next morning he was dismayed to find no sign of any troops. At this moment, for reasons which have never been ascertained, the village church of St Ninian's, which had been used as a powder magazine, blew up with an explosion so violent as to throw Lochiel and the beautiful Mrs Murray of Broughton out of a post-chaise in which they happened to be passing.

The orders issued the night before had, it now appeared, either been altered or disregarded and since before daybreak that morning the Highlanders, including those left at Stirling, had simply been streaming Westwards as fast as their legs would carry them in the general direction of the Fords of Frew. 'Never', writes one eyewitness, 'was their a retreat resembled so much a flight, for their was no where 1,000 men together, and the whole army pass'd the river in Small bodies and in great Confusion, leaving Carts & Cannon upon the road behind them.' An account by Lord George, who no doubt rightly blamed O'Sullivan for what had happened, was even more bitter. 'It was,' he wrote, 'by no means a retreat, but a flight & the men were going off like so many sheep scatred upon the side of the Hill, or like a broken and flying armie after a defeat and hott pursuit.' And, bursting in on the Prince at dinner, he declared, according to O'Sullivan, 'after the most disrespectfull & impertinent manner', that 'it was a most shamefull & cowrdly flight. Yt they were a persel of Villans yt advis'd him to it'.

After thus crossing the Forth in total disorder, the Prince's army spent the night at Doune and Dunblane. On 2 February the Highland regiments made their way to Crieff, while the rest of the army marched on to Perth. That night a council of war was held in Crieff in a room at the Drummond Arms. The atmosphere was explosive in the extreme. Having reviewed his troops earlier in the day, Prince Charles had been able to establish that the total number of deserters could not have been more than 1,000 all told. As the scale of the desertions had been one of the main pretexts for the retreat, this discovery still further enraged him, while Lord George was no less enraged by the total disruption of his plans for an orderly withdrawal. 'It was', he said, 'worth the Government at London's while to have given a hundred thousand pounds to anyone who would have given such advice and got it followed.' Mutual recrimination followed in which all present joined vigorously, and treachery was openly hinted at. 'There never had been', we are told, 'such heats and animosities as at this meeting;

171

however, after a great deal of wrangling and altercation, it was determined that the horse and low-country regiments should march towards Inverness, along the coast, while the Prince, with the clans, took the Highland road thither.' No doubt glad to be on his own, Lord George 'offered to go the coast road, after others refused it', and on 4 February the two divisions set out for Inverness, each following its own route. Before the Jacobites left Perth thirteen pieces of cannon, 8- and 12-pounders, were nailed up and abandoned and fourteen swivel guns from the captured Government sloop *Hazard* thrown in the Tay, 'but', we are told, 'the guns were taken out again next morning'.

Leaving Crieff on 4 February and crossing the Tay at Aberfeldy, Prince Charles spent two nights at Castle Menzies, while Lord Lewis Gordon followed on with the baggage and what was left of the artillery – eight light guns. On 6 February Charles reached Blair Atholl and stayed there until 10 February as the guest of Duke William, 'hunting and hawking' – or so Cumberland was informed. From Blair he continued his march to Dalnacardoch, where he spent two more nights, leaving his main force to march on to Ruthven.

As the Prince's army began their withdrawal, Cumberland, having reached Holyroodhouse on 30 January at three in the morning and slept for a couple of hours in the bed occupied not many months previously by Prince Charles, immediately summoned General Hawley and his officers to a council of war. At this the decision was taken to march against the rebels the very next morning.

The troops now under Cumberland's command comprised all the regular regiments which had fought at Falkirk together with the Argyllshire Militia. To these had been added Lord Semple's 25th Foot, the Scots Fusiliers (21st Foot), Lord Mark Ker's Dragoons (11th Dragoons), the Duke of Kingston's Horse and a train of artillery. Further reinforcements were expected, notably Bligh's Regiment of Foot and 4,000 or 5,000 German mercenaries from Hesse.

Cumberland's army left Edinburgh on the morning of 31 January, the Duke himself setting out in a state coach, drawn by twelve horses and generously provided for the purpose by the Earl of Hopetoun, always glad of an opportunity to show his loyalty to the House of Hanover. At Linlithgow, where they spent the night, they managed, whether by accident or design, to set fire to the ancient palace of the Stuart kings, which was quickly reduced to a shell.

Leaving its smouldering ruins behind him, Cumberland, anxious, as he put it, for 'an opportunity of finishing this affair at once', pressed on next day to Falkirk, only to find that the Jacobites had already evacuated the town and started their withdrawal northwards. ('Their precipatate flight', he wrote, 'is not to be described.') His next stop was at Stirling, whence he wrote to the Duke of Newcastle on 2 February:

> As soon as I can get the Bridge here mended I shall follow to Perth, & so on whilst they remain in a body, but when once they are got into their Holes and Hiding-places it will be impossible to follow them in a Body, but whatever number of troops may be thought proper to be left must be for to keep the mouths of the Defiles. Little parties only can be sent in to burn and destroy that nest of Robbers, and orders should be given to kill all that have arms in their houses, as that will now be the only trace of Treason left on their getting back, and indeed I shan't be surprised to hear it affirmed that there never was a Rebellion. . . .

Continuing his pursuit, Cumberland left Stirling on 4 February, reached Crieff next day and Perth the day after, barely twenty-four hours behind Charles. On the way he made the best of his opportunities. 'This day', he wrote to Newcastle from Crieff on 5 February,

> we began marching through some of the Drummond's Strathallan's and other disaffected persons' estates; I thought it fit to let the soldiers a little loose, with proper precautions, that they might have some sweets with all their fatigues. The old Lady Perth and her daughter are left at Drummond Castle, and I have let them know they had best write to my Lord Perth to release all our officers and soldiers who are prisoners, and who at present, thank God, are but few, else I shall burn and destroy the castle immediately – and I have ordered a subaltern and twenty Dragoons to remain with her till an answer comes to her letter. I hope his Majesty wil approve this proceeding of mine, but I thought it pitty to let this troublesome old woman escape without making some use of her.

Having by now given up the idea of an immediate encounter with the Jacobite army, Cumberland spent the next two weeks at Perth, collecting stores and rations, sending out parties of troops to harass Jacobite supporters in the neighbourhood and in general preparing at his leisure for the next phase of his campaign. On 8 February, his brother-in-law, Prince Frederick of Hesse, accompanied by the Earl of Crawford, an amiable nonentity, landed at Leith with a force of between 4,000 and 5,000 Germans. 'His Serene Highness', we learn, 'was saluted on his arrival by the ships and the castle of Edinburgh; persons of distinction paid him their compliments; and he was entertained during his stay with balls, concerts of musick, assemblies, etc.' The Germans ('both men and horses looked well') took three or four days to land, after which they remained for the time being in Edinburgh to guard the southern counties.

At about the same time a further contingent of Argyllshire Militia had reached Perth under the command of Major-General John Campbell of Mamore. These were despatched to the Western Highlands to support Lord Glenorchy, son of the once Jacobite Lord Breadalbane, now commanding yet another force of Campbell Militia. Cumberland's dislike of the Scots in general and Highlanders in particular seems to have extended even to General Campbell, good Whig though he was. 'Yesterday', he wrote to the Duke of Newcastle on 10 February, 'General Campbell came hither to meet me, and has brought with him four companys of Western Highlanders. He assures me that they will show no favour or partiality to the other Highlanders; as he knows them best, he must answer for this; for my own part, I suspect them greatly, for those who were with us here before these came, absolutely refused to plunder any of the Rebels' houses, which is the only way we have to punish them, or bring them back.' Even Lord Milton, the Lord Justice-Clerk, did not entirely escape censure. 'The Justice-Clerk,' Cumberland wrote to Newcastle a couple of weeks later, 'is as able and as willing a man as there exists, but too much an Argyle man to be trusted with all that will be necessary after this affair.' 'I am sorry to say', he went on, 'that the bottom here is bad and that the greatest part of this kingdom are either openly or privately aiding the rebels and how it may be changed I don't know, at least immediately.'

The people of Perthshire pleased him but little better. 'I am sorry', he wrote in another letter to Newcastle, 'I don't find the same zeal for totally suppressing the Rebellion as there seemed to be for driving the Rebels northward.' Nor did Duke James of Atholl, whose chief preoccupation was not unnaturally the fate of his own castle and estates to which he had just returned, and whom Cumberland had sent off to try to raise his long-suffering tenantry in the Hanoverian cause, show much enthusiasm for the task assigned to him. 'I have *at last*', wrote Cumberland in the same letter, 'prevailed on the Duke of Athol to publish a Declaration to his Vassals.'

But it seems unlikely that by this stage many potential recruits to either cause were left in Atholl. Duke William had met with little response of late, even when he had resorted to *crois-tarra*, the fiery cross, and many of the Athollmen the Jacobites had recruited earlier had taken the first opportunity to desert. Meanwhile Lieutenant-Colonel Sir Andrew Agnew of the Scots Fusiliers had with five hundred men taken possession of Blair Atholl, lately evacuated by Duke William and the Prince, and another four hundred soldiers under a Captain Webster had been stationed at Castle Menzies, strategically situated near Taybridge. As for Duke James, he was only marginally happier to have Hanoverian troops occupying his castle than Jacobites.

174

'I was at Blair last week', he wrote to Lord Milton,

> Sir Andrew Agnew and his 500 men continue there, which has
> made that house in a most deplorable condition, but, as your Lop.
> sayes, patience is the only remedy; what can't be cured must be
> endured... By the by, how am I to be reimbursed of the expences
> of sending out parties, apprehending prisoners, procuring
> intelligence, sending expresses, &c, which is too much to bear after
> being plundered of everything, both here and at Blair, and not a
> shiling of rent to be expected. The Tennants here about being all
> ruined by money being exacted from them &c. . . .

On 15 February Cumberland returned briefly to Edinburgh for a
council of war at the house of the Lord Justice-Clerk. At this 'all the
Generals gave it as their opinion, that the war was at an end; and that
his Royal Highness had nothing to do but to give his orders to the
officers under him to march into the Highlands as soon as the season
would permit and ferret the rebels out of there strongholds and fastness-
es'. On being consulted, Lord Milton himself was at first reluctant as
a civilian to give his view, but on being pressed by the Duke said that
he only hoped he might be mistaken, but that, from his knowledge of
the Highlands and Highlanders, the rebellion was by no means at an
end.

Whatever the truth of the matter, Cumberland was determined to
end the campaign as soon as possible and in such a way as to prevent
any further outbreaks. The necessary stores were assembled and on
20 February, having despatched three battalions of foot to Coupar-
Angus and a regiment of dragoons to Dundee and left the Scots
Fusiliers under Colonel Colville to protect Perth, he set out with his
main force by way of Montrose for Aberdeen, where he arrived shortly
before the end of the month. On the day he left Perth, he sent a
despatch to Whitehall, calling for a short Act which would make it
easier for him to deal with the rebels in the manner they deserved. 'As
yet', he wrote, 'I have only taken up Gentlemen and yet all the jails
are full, whilst the common people, whom I pick up every day must
remain unpunished for want of being able to try such a number, so
that they will rebel again when anyone comes to lead them.'

In the meantime the two Jacobite columns had been making their
way each by its own route through heavy snow towards Inverness,
described by one English soldier as being in those days 'a small, dirty,
poor place', and now held for the Government by Lord Loudon and
MacLeod of MacLeod with a force of some 2,000 men. While Prince
Charles lingered briefly at Blair and Dalnacardoch, his main force had
marched on to Ruthven, where they found the tiny garrison still in

charge of the same Sergeant (now Lieutenant) Terence Mulloy, who had held out against O'Sullivan so successfully the previous September. This time Mulloy, finding himself hopelessly outnumbered, was in the end induced to surrender in return for a free pass home for all his men. The barracks were then blown up. At Ruthven Charles rejoined his main force, continuing his march northwards on 15 February. Charles's forward troops were by now within eight miles of Inverness, while his main force were quartered in and around the villages of Aviemore and Moy. On the evening of 16 February he arrived at Moy Hall, where he was enthusiastically made welcome by the now famous Colonel Anne Mackintosh, who, in her husband's absence on duty with the Government forces, rose splendidly to the occasion, providing 'a plentiful and genteel' supper for all seventy-five of her guests 'to compliment the Prince'.

It was not long before news of the Prince's arrival at Moy reached Lord Loudon, who at once saw it as an opportunity to win at one blow not only lasting fame but a reward of £30,000. Accordingly, that very night, having thrown a cordon of troops round Inverness and strengthened the castle garrison, he marched quietly out of the town, taking with him his own regiment and as many as he could muster of the Independent Companies, making some 1,500 men in all, his purpose being to take the Prince by surprise.

News of his intention had, however, reached the Dowager Lady Mackintosh, who lived in Inverness and did not share her son's Hanoverian sympathies. Summoning a fifteen-year-old Mackintosh clansman named Lauchlan, she instructed him 'to try if he could get past Lord Loudon's men, and to make all the haste he could to Moy, to warn the Prince of what was intended against him'. Successfully dodging Lord Loudon's patrols, young Lauchlan Mackintosh immediately set out for Moy, arriving there in time to get the Prince out of bed and warn him of the enemy's approach. Leaving the house 'with his bonnet above his nightcap and his shoes down in the heels', Charles now made his way down to the side of the loch with some of his men, while Colonel Anne was observed 'in her smock-petticoat, running through the close, speaking loudly and expressing her anxiety about the Prince's safety' – 'running about like a madwoman in her shift', O'Sullivan called it.

Meanwhile, madwoman or not, she had, with great presence of mind, sent the blacksmith of Moy, one Donald Fraser, and four others to take up a position 'upon a muir, at some distance from Moy, towards Inverness, and their await the approach of Lord Loudon's men'. On the appearance of the enemy's advance guard, who seem to have been led by the renegade MacLeod of MacLeod, 'the Blacksmith', we learn, 'fired his piece, and the other four followed his example', at the same time shouting at the top of their voices the war cries of the Camerons, MacDonalds, Mackintoshes and a number of other clans, 'which so far imposed on Lord Loudon and his command, (a pretty considerable one) and struck them with such panic that instantly they beat a retreat, and made their way back to Inverness, imagining the Prince's whole army to be at their heels'. This ingenious stratagem, which won for Colonel Anne the additional title of The Heroine, came to be known, appropriately enough, as the Rout of Moy. The only casualty was MacLeod's hereditary piper Macrimmon ('reputed the best of his business in all Scotland' and almost certainly Jacobite in sympathy), who fell mortally wounded at the blacksmith's first discharge. Before leaving Skye, Macrimmon, who possessed the second sight, had composed a prophetic lament, *Cha til me tuille* (I'll return no more):

> MacLeod shall come back,
> But Macrimmon shall
> never.

Earlier that evening in Inverness, a friend, who likewise possessed the second sight, had remarked on meeting Macrimmon that his body seemed suddenly to shrink to the stature of a small child.

Lord Loudon's own account of the engagement at Moy throws an interesting light on that nobleman's character and military capability.

We marched on to the heights above the watter of Nairn, when to my infinite mortification I saw and heard, about a mile to my left, a running fire from the whole detachment. They saw, or imagined they saw, five Men on which they had made the Fire. But the Consequence on the Main Body was very bad, for it threw us into the greatest confusion. I got my own Regiment, at the head of which I was, in the Front, saved from falling out of the Road. All faced to where they saw the Fire. They were ten men deep and all presented, and a good many droping shots, one of which killed a Piper at my Foot whilst I was forming them. The rest fell all back out of the Road to the Right a considerable way, in the utmost confusion, and it was a great while before I could get them brought up and formed, and the Panick still so great that it was with the greatest difficulty when the Party came in, which they did in twos and threes, that I could, standing before the Muzzles of their pieces, prevent them firing on them, and when I came to count the corps (if I may call Independent Companies by that name) I found I had lost the Five Companys in the Rear, of whom, after all the search I could make, I could hear nothing. After remaining an Hour on the ground and finding that I had lost one third of my Men in a

Body, besides those who had left the Companys that remained with me, and finding then the whole country was alarmed, I thought it improper, especially in the condition the men were, to march on to a superior Force, who must be prepared to receive me, and concluded that the best thing left for me to do, was to march back to town, which I accordingly did.

Their experiences at the hands of the blacksmith of Moy had sadly demoralized Lord Loudon's men. Next morning two hundred of them deserted and, after consultation with MacLeod and Lord President Forbes, their noble commander decided that his wisest course would be to withdraw with his men across the ferry at Kessock to Ross and Cromarty and there, in relatively friendly territory, await the arrival of Cumberland's great army. His withdrawal was further accelerated by the appearance before Inverness on the morning of 18 February of the Prince's advance guard. At this he and his force left headlong for the Kessock ferry, where they were cannonaded by the Jacobites and still more of his men deserted. A Jacobite force of Frasers and others was immediately sent over the ferry after them. Meanwhile Charles, 'having got up betwixt two and three thousand men', had taken possession of Inverness without a shot being fired. On 20 February the small Hanoverian garrison of the castle also capitulated and the castle itself was demolished.

Cumberland's reaction on learning of these events was one of exasperation and bewildered incomprehension.

I am really quite at a loss to explain all the contradictions I meet here from morning to night, for I am assured by people who should know the hills the best, that there are no places between the Blair of Athol and Inverness where 500 men can subsist in a body, yet Lord Loudoun has been driven across the Firth with 2,000 men which he said he had, and expecting a junction of 1,500 more, by that party of the rebels alone which marched from Blair with the Pretender's son, and which I could never make, by the best account I had, above 600 men ... But I am now in a country so much our enemy that there is hardly any intelligence to be got, and, whenever we do procure any, it is the business of the country to have it contradicted to me that I may be always kept in an uncertainty what I am to believe.

On 19 February Charles had established himself some five miles outside Inverness at Culloden House, the home of the Lord President, Duncan Forbes, who had left hurriedly the day before with Lord Loudon. He was joined two days later by Lord George Murray and Duke William of Atholl. Lord George's march North from Perth by way of Montrose and Aberdeen had not been an easy one. 'I gave the Prince,' he writes, 'an account of our march, and indeed it is inconceivable the fatigue and trouble we had undergone.' His column, 'consisting of about 100 Gentlemen, 50 of the life-guards, 20 huzzars and above 50 private men', had left Montrose on 8 February after spiking most of their guns. On setting out from Aberdeen, they had encountered 'a vast storm of snow' which made any progress difficult, especially for the cavalry. After leaving parties behind at Elgin, under Lord Pitsligo, and at Nairn, with the object of holding up Cumberland's advance and preventing him from joining forces with Lord Loudon, it was not until 21 February that they finally reached Inverness.

Having thus assembled the bulk of his forces at Inverness, Prince Charles, writes Maxwell of Kirkconnel, 'had three things principally in view; to reduce Fort Augustus and Fort William on one side; on the other to disperse Lord Loudon's army; and to keep possession, as much as possible, of the coast towards Aberdeen'. Accordingly, after taking possession of both town and castle, the Jacobites next turned their attention to the other Government-held strongpoints in the Highlands. A couple of days after the surrender of the castle garrison a small force commanded by Brigadier Stapleton and consisting of Lochiel's Camerons, Keppoch's MacDonalds and a detachment of Lord John Drummond's regiment, laid siege to Fort Augustus, situated on Loch Ness, some twenty miles South-West of Inverness, and held for the Government by three companies of Guise's Regiment. For ten days the garrison held out, but on 1 March, after a well-aimed shell had landed in the powder magazine, their commander decided to capitulate. He and his men were made prisoners and their provisions and armament – sixteen 4-pounders, two 6-pounders and six mortars – seized.

Brigadier Stapleton next turned his attention to Fort William, strategically sited at the head of Loch Linnhe as a standing menace to the traditionally Jacobite clans of Lochaber, Camerons, Stewarts, Mac-Donalds and Macleans, and garrisoned by some 500 men – three companies of Guises and three of the Argyll Militia under the command of the Deputy-Governor, Lieutenant-General Alexander Campbell. Appreciating the Fort's strategic importance ('from thence the Lowlands would be open to the enemy') and having doubts as to the competence of its commander ('Lieut.-Gen. Alex. Campbell is by all accounts no way fit for a thing of that importance') Cumberland now despatched Captain Caroline Scott, a competent and savagely anti-Jacobite Lowlander, to serve as the Governor's military assistant.

The fort's armament consisted of eight 12-pounders, twelve 6-pounders, and a dozen mortars together with plenty of powder and shot. Though in poor repair, the fortifications were substantial. To keep open communications with the Campbell strongholds of Inveraray and Dunstaffnage, a smaller detachment of Militia was stationed at Castle Stalker twenty miles away off the coast of Appin, while several sloops of war were kept at anchor close at hand to provide supplies. But the narrows at Corran commanding the entrance to Loch Linnhe were held on both sides by Jacobite forces based on the western side on Ardgour, for centuries the territory of the strongly Jacobite Macleans of that Ilk.

During the first week in March there was some skirmishing in the neighbourhood of Corran. The Jacobites having succeeded in capturing a boat and crew belonging to the Government sloop *Baltimore*, the Hanoverians retaliated by landing a party which killed and wounded some Highlanders, destroyed the ferry-houses and burned down a village on the Ardgour side. Meanwhile further contingents of Camerons and MacDonalds had joined Brigadier Stapleton's force. These were now encamped with their fellow clansmen in Glen Nevis, a couple of miles to the South of Fort William, under the command of Keppoch and Lochiel, while a further party of Highlanders established themselves in a stone building at Corpach on the northern shore of Loch Eil, from which a sharp bombardment by the *Baltimore* failed to dislodge them.

By now the artillery from Fort Augustus had arrived and on 20 March Stapleton, siting some mortars on nearby Sugar-Loaf Hill, began his bombardment of Fort William from a range of about half a mile. For the next two weeks the Highlanders continued to bombard the fort, while the garrison accurately returned their fire and resolutely refused all demands for surrender. Meanwhile, under the guns of the warships, parties of Government troops sallied forth into the surrounding country, burning houses, harassing the civilian population, and carrying off sheep and cattle.

Quite naturally Lochiel and Keppoch blamed everything on their hereditary enemies the Campbells, and gave vent to their indignation in a long letter despatched from Glen Nevis House on 20 March, expressing their horror that

> In spite of all the clemency that a prince could show or promise,
> the Campbells have openly appeared, with their unwonted zeal for
> rebellion and usurpation, in the most oppressive manner. Nor could
> we form a thought to ourselves that any men endowed with reason
> or commonsense could use their fellow-creatures with such
> inhumanity and barbarity as they do; of which we have daily
> proofs, by their burning houses, stripping of women and children,
> and exposing them in the open field to the severity of the weather,

houghing of cattle, and killing of horses; to enumerate the whole would be too tedious at this time.

'As God', the two chiefs concluded with undisguised relish, 'was pleased to put so many of their people into our custody, we hope to prevail upon his Highness to hang a Campbell for every house that will hereafter be burned by them.' But their advice, for better or for worse, was neglected.

By the end of March it had become clear to Brigadier Stapleton that he had little hope of attaining his objective. The besieged garrison, impervious even to the red hot shot with which he bombarded them, showed no signs of yielding. Enemy warships came and went at will, bringing supplies and reinforcements and giving covering fire with their guns; several of the Highlanders' own guns had been put out of action and their powder magazine with all their ammunition in it blown up and destroyed. And so, on the night of 2 April, after spiking his guns, Brigadier Stapleton abandoned the siege and withdrew with the whole of his force.

Further North, the Prince's troops had been seeking to overtake the scattered remnants of Lord Loudon's Independent Companies, which still numbered almost 2,000 men. Immediately after the capture of Inverness, Lord Cromartie had set out in pursuit of Lord Loudon with his own regiment of Mackenzies and some Mackintoshes and MacKinnons, later receiving substantial reinforcements from other clans, which brought the strength of his force up to almost 1,500. But Loudon had carefully destroyed every boat he could find on the Beauly, Cromarty and Dornoch firths and, by continually taking evasive action, succeeded in avoiding all contact with his pursuers, though numerically greatly superior to them.

Eventually, 'as it was found Lord Cromarty was doing no good, and the men had not much confidence in him', Lord George Murray was sent North by the Prince to see what could be done. On his recommendation Lord Cromartie was superseded by the Duke of Perth and a number of boats collected at Findhorn and sent North for the latter's use. With these the Duke's force managed on the night of 18 or 19 March to cross the firth and land near Dornoch, where Loudon had his headquarters. 'Upon our landing', writes MacDonell of Lochgarry, who had joined Cromartie some time before, 'to our great surprize we found no opposition; Loudon and the President were quarter'd very near the place where we landed, and had discovered us in time eneough to make their escape.' But though Lord Loudon and the Lord President again managed to escape, there were others who, for one reason or another, did not. 'The Laird of McIntosh', we

181

are told, 'capt in Loudon's regmt, and Major McKenzie of the same, with several other officers, came and surrendered themselves prisoners, with all the men under their command, among which were a good number of Loudon's own regiment.' The 'Laird of McIntosh' was, of course, none other than Aeneas or Angus, the husband of Colonel Anne. On the Prince's instructions he was now handed over to his wife at Moy, on the grounds that 'he could not be in better security or more honourably treated'. On being greeted by Anne with the words 'Your servant, Captain', the story goes that the Mackintosh replied, no less succinctly, 'Your servant, Colonel'.

Next day Perth resumed his pursuit of Lord Loudon and the Lord President, but having failed to catch up with them, turned back to Inverness after handing over the command to Lord Cromartie. Loudon and Duncan Forbes, meanwhile, accompanied by MacLeod of MacLeod, and taking with them the MacLeod and MacDonald Independent Companies, had continued their flight westwards, reaching Loch Alsh on 26 March. Thence they were ferried across to Skye, where they were to remain for the best part of a month as MacLeod's guests. The rest of Loudon's force, left to their own devices, took refuge in various parts of Sutherland, Ross and Caithness, where they could hope to enjoy the protection of Lord Reay, chief of Clan MacKay, and the Earl of Sutherland, both dedicated supporters of the Government.

But for the moment the northern counties were a less secure refuge for Government supporters than they had been. Lord Cromartie had by now returned home, handing over the conduct of operations to his son and to the huge Coll Ban, 'Fair haired Coll MacDonell', the notorious laird of Barisdale widely known as the Hercules of the Highlands. Coll Ban, 'a man of polished behaviour, fine address and a fine person', who brought to the Jacobite cause the same energy and enthusiasm which he normally devoted to raiding his neighbours and stealing their cattle, was during the next few weeks happily employed harassing the local Whigs and looting or burning their property.

Nor did Coll and his clansmen confine their attention to the smaller fry. On 20 March a party of some 200 MacDonalds actually managed to seize Lord Sutherland's great castle of Dunrobin, hastily evacuated by its owner, who eventually found refuge at the Duke of Cumberland's headquarters. His Countess, however, a handsome young woman of twenty-eight, who happened to be Lord Elcho's aunt and was accordingly inclined to be Jacobite in sympathy, preferred to stay behind and entertain the Prince's officers. 'They went the next day', writes O'Sullivan, 'to Dine at Donrobin, where they were parfectly well recd by the Lady, who made all the protestations imaginable of Zelle and attachemt to the cause.'

182

This provided Coll of the Fair Hair with yet another opportunity, of which he took full advantage. At the taking of the castle one of the MacDonald clansmen had treated the Countess with less courtesy than she liked and a few days later we find her persuading 'her acquaintance' Barisdale to write a letter of complaint to the Prince at her dictation. 'Least my letter be too tediouse', it ran, 'I will only give one Instance of my usadge, a man holding a drawn durk to my brest gave a scrach of a wound which merk itt will beare.' As for Coll, in a further letter addressed by him to his 'faire prisoner', he promises to inform the Prince of her zeal for the cause; says that he will endeavour to restore her favourite horses to her and concludes by declaring himself 'Nott onlie your Lady's prisoner in the strictest Confinement, but your Ladyship's most obd^{tt} and most humble ser^{tt}'. Which, for all concerned, must have provided a pleasant distraction from the more serious business of war. Meanwhile, further North, the Sinclairs, encouraged by Lord Sutherland's flight and the disintegration of Lord Loudon's army, were at last free to show their own long-felt sympathy for the Prince's cause.

But the Jacobites in the North were reckoning without Lord Reay, chief of Clan MacKay and like his forebears a sound Whig. Towards the end of March the *Prince Charles*, formerly HMS *Hazard*, a Government sloop which had fallen into the hands of the Jacobites, was returning from France with a number of expatriate Jacobite officers, £12,500 in cash and large quantities of stores and ammunition for the Prince's use, when she was sighted off the Banffshire coast by the Captain of HMS *Sheerness*, who at once gave chase and after a short engagement succeeded in driving the *Prince Charles* aground in the Kyle of Tongue. As the *Sheerness* could not follow her in, the officers and crew were able to land safely and bring the stores and money ashore near Melness. But next day they had only gone a short distance when they fell into an ambush laid for them by Lord Reay and after a short fight were overpowered. As a result the ship, money and stores, not to mention the new recruits, were lost to the Prince, who badly needed all of them. Worse still, Lord Cromartie now despatched the whole of his 1,500 men with his son and Coll Ban to Melness to try to recover the treasure (which in fact had already been sent to Aberdeen by sea). The result was that they later failed to come to the Prince's help when he most needed them and, after some confused skirmishing with the MacKays, were eventually all taken prisoner.

Lord George Murray, meanwhile, having returned from Ross-shire, had obtained the Prince's permission to try to recapture his brother's strategically situated castle of Blair, still in the hands of Sir Andrew Agnew, and at the same time to mop up a number of other enemy strongpoints in Perthshire. Setting out from Inverness on 12 March with 600 or 700 of the Atholl Brigade and two small cannon, he first marched to Strathspey and two days later took possession of Castle Grant, which, at the sight of his two 4-pounders, in their master's absence, the Laird of Grant's servants meekly surrendered to him. Leaving behind a detachment under Lord Nairne to protect his rear and cover his line of retreat, Lord George then continued his march southwards, being joined near Ruthven by Menzies of Shian and Macpherson of Cluny with 300 Macphersons. Thence, passing through Badenoch, he marched on 16 March by way of Dalwhinnie to Dalnacardoch, where he halted to make the necessary dispositions for a series of attacks on neighbouring enemy outposts, held in the main by contingents of Campbell militia. From a total of about thirty he picked the seven most important of these, sending out attacking parties under cover of darkness while he and Cluny went on to the Bridge of Bruar with the rest of the force to await the outcome. These operations were entirely successful. All seven posts were surrounded and seized, 300 prisoners taken and a number of enemy killed or wounded without any Jacobite casualties. After sending his prisoners back to Ruthven under escort and securing the strategically important Pass of Killiecrankie, Lord George now began preparations for his assault on Blair.

Entering Blair village on the morning of 17 March and setting up his headquarters at the inn, kept by a certain McGlashan and hurriedly evacuated by the enemy not long before, Lord George next wrote out a message to Colonel Sir Andrew Agnew, the formidable garrison commander, inviting him to surrender. The difficulty was to find a messenger, for 'no Highlanders, from the impression they had received of the outrageous temper of Sir Andrew Agnew, could be prevailed upon to carry that summons'. In the end one Molly, 'a maid-servant from the Inn at Blair ... being rather handsome and very obliging, conceived herself to be on so good a footing with some of the young officers that she need not be afraid of being shot and undertook the mission – taking care, however, when she came near the castle, to wave the paper containing the summons over her head as a token of her Embassy'.

On Molly's arrival at the castle, a 'window was opened and her speech heard'. In this she strongly advised surrender, warning the young officers who had come to the window that 'as the Highlanders were a thousand strong and had cannon, they would batter down, or burn the castle and destroy the whole garrison', and 'promising very good treatment by Lord George Murray and the other Highland Gentlemen'. This, according to one of the young officers in question, Ensign (later General) Robert Melville, 'was received from Molly with juvenile mirth by the officers, who told her that those Gentlemen would soon be driven away and the garrison again become visitors at McGlashan's as before'. But Molly persisted and in the end persuaded a young officer to carry the message to Sir Andrew. The latter, however, having cast his eye over it, threw himself on the unfortunate youth and drove him from the room, cursing Lord George Murray for a traitor and threatening to shoot any other messenger he sent. Hearing all this through the open window, Molly hurriedly retreated to the inn, where, as the officers of the garrison could see for themselves, Lord George and the members of his Staff were much amused by her account of what had happened.

That same evening the Jacobites' two little 4-pounders arrived. These were now placed in position behind a dyke, below the church, about 300 yards from the castle, and next morning the first shot was fired by Lady Lude, evidently still behaving 'like a light Giglet', in order, a trifle illogically, to demonstrate her indignation at the damage done to the castle by Sir Andrew Agnew and his men during their occupation of it. However, as the castle walls were seven feet thick, the effect produced by the Highlanders' cannon-balls was negligible and it soon became clear to Lord George that his best hope of inducing the already hungry garrison to surrender was to starve them out by a long siege. In order to deny the castle to the enemy, he even considered pulling it down. 'I hope', he wrote to his brother William, 'you will excuse our demolishing it.' His brother James he does not appear to have consulted.

But in fact the castle remained standing. By the end of March some 3,000 competent German mercenaries and about 300 English cavalry under Prince Frederick of Hesse and Lord Crawford had reached Dunkeld, where, though separated from Lord George by the Pass of Killiecrankie, which he still held, they clearly presented an unacceptable threat to his little force. By now, too, he had received several expresses from Prince Charles, urging him to return to Inverness, 'for it was believed the Duke of Cumberland would march in a day or two'. And so very early on 2 April the Jacobites raised the siege and set out once more for Inverness and next morning Molly from the inn was able to announce to her young friends at the castle 'that Lord George and all his men ... had gone off in the night'. 'The relief of Blair', was Cumberland's conclusion, 'is more owing to the cowardice of the rebels than to the Hessians putting my orders into execution.'

Sir Andrew Agnew, for his part, refused to take Molly's word for it and kept all his men inside the walls until later that day a messenger from Lord Crawford arrived at the castle announcing the arrival of the

English cavalry. That night Lord Crawford entertained the hungry officers of the garrison to dinner in the summerhouse at Blair. Amongst his guests was Duke James of Atholl, doubtless much relieved at the news of his brother's withdrawal, but complaining, as usual, of the damage done to his property by all concerned.

From Blair Lord George, after withdrawing his outlying pickets, marched along the valley of the Spey to Elchies. Here he joined forces with Lord John Drummond, who had been occupying Gordon Castle, and, leaving Cluny and his Macphersons to guard the passes of Badenoch 'from the Athol side, as they had done before this expedition', fell back on Inverness, arriving there on 3 April.

CHAPTER ELEVEN

Apart from occasional visits to his troops in the field, Prince Charles had during the past weeks been spending most of his time in Inverness, where, after leaving Culloden, he had found lodgings with the Dowager Lady Mackintosh in Church Street and also at Thunderton House in Batchen Lane, once the town house of the Earls of Moray. Towards the middle of March he fell ill of what O'Sullivan, relapsing into his native brogue, describes as 'a spotted favor' and, according to Lord Elcho, was 'sick ten days'. He seems, however, to have made a good recovery and, says Elcho, 'very often went shooting, and sometimes gave bals at night, where he danced himself, and Endeavour'd to keep up the peoples Spirits that approach'd him'. Amongst the local ladies who attended the Prince's balls was, of course, Colonel Anne Mackintosh, 'dressed,' it was reported to Cumberland, 'as nearly as she could in Highlandmen's cloathes'.

More serious in its consequences than the Prince's own illness was that contracted at this time by his capable Secretary, John Murray of Broughton, whose place was now inadequately filled by Broughton's brother-in-law John Hay of Restalrig, a middle-aged Writer to the Signet. John Murray had hitherto been largely responsible for the commissariat arrangements of the Prince's army and even Lord George Murray, who was no friend of his, admitted that he 'had always been extremely active in whatsoever regarded the providing of the army'. His successor, on the other hand, 'was Generally Esteem'd a man of neither parts nor capacity', and, according to Lord Elcho, 'governed the Prince entirely'.

Certainly the Prince's troops seem by this time to have been short of almost everything, and, according to Lord Elcho, 'their was great discontent in his Army at this time both amongst the Officers and the Soldiers'. For one thing, the Jacobites' financial resources were at a low ebb and it now seemed clearer than ever that there was very little hope of getting either men or money from France. The loss of £12,500 from the ill-fated *Prince Charles* had been a serious blow and the Prince, with only 500 louis d'or left to him, found himself reduced to paying his troops in meal, 'which the men being obliged to sell out and convert into money, it went but a short way for their other needs, at which the poor creatures grumbled exceedingly'. Few things are worse for morale than short or bad rations. In this crisis Hay of Restalrig, according to Lord George Murray, was 'the gentleman the army blamed for the distress they were in for want of provisions, he having had the superintendency of all those things from the time of Mr Murray's illness'. Discipline meanwhile was deteriorating. The hungry ragged Highlanders took to helping themselves to what they needed. Desertion was rife and more and more men who had gone home to see their families or sow their land somehow failed to return.

And yet, fresh reinforcements were still coming in. The Macleans, who had played a leading part in the rising of 1715, had suffered a serious setback through the arrest and imprisonment of their chief the previous year, as had the Prince's cause. 'Had he gone to the Highlands and joined His Royal Highness', wrote Murray of Broughton afterwards, 'his army would have been much more numerous than it ever was.' By this time, however, Charles Maclean of Drimnin and James, a son of the aged chief of Ardgour, had arrived from Argyll with 150 clansmen to join the Prince and another fifty soon followed. At the same time a number of other Highlanders, who had been serving in the Independent Companies under Lord Loudon and had deserted or been taken prisoner at Dornoch by the Duke of Perth, now also joined the Prince.

After spending rather more than a month in Aberdeen, which he used, among other things, to improve his infantry's proficiency with the bayonet for use against the Highlander's broadsword and targe, the Duke of Cumberland was by this time preparing to move North. Leaving Aberdeen on 8 April, he marched by way of Old Meldrum and Turriff to Banff. Here he caught and executed two Jacobite spies, hanging one from a convenient branch and the other from the roof-beam of a house. From Banff he continued on 11 April to Cullen, where he was joined by Lord Albemarle with the advance guard. He was now in command of a well-trained, well-equipped and well-fed force of some 9,000 men, with the warships, transports and supply ships of the Royal Navy following close inshore along the coast.

At Cullen, Cumberland was only twelve miles from a Jacobite force of 2,500 men known as the Army of the Spey, commanded by the Duke of Perth and his brother Lord John Drummond and occupying a position on the far side of the River Spey, much swollen by the rain and snow of recent weeks. Here, on the banks of the Spey, Cumberland not unnaturally expected the Jacobites to make a stand. Forming his army into three divisions and following the coast road, closely escorted by his fleet of warships and transports, he accordingly set out on the morning of 12 April for the town of Fochabers, his last march East of the Spey.

From Fochabers, which Cumberland reached at midday, his troops could see the whole of the Duke of Perth's force drawn up as though for battle on the other side of the river. But, just as the Hanoverians were preparing to ford the river and attack them, they were amazed to see their opponents start to withdraw without making any attempt to dispute their passage of the river. 'On which', wrote Cumberland to Newcastle next day, 'the Duke of Kingston's Horse immediately forded over, sustained by the Grenadiers and the Highlanders. But the Rebells were already got out of their Reach before they could pass. The foot waded over as fast as they arrived, and, though the water came up to their Middle, they went on with great Chearfulness.' 'It is a very lucky thing', he concluded, 'we had to deal with such an Enemy, for it would be most difficult undertaking to pass this River before an enemy who should Know how to take advantage of the situation.'

There can be no doubt that, by retreating as they did from the Spey and thus throwing away the natural advantage it offered, the Duke of Perth and his brother lost a precious opportunity of holding up Cumberland's advance and, with any luck, of inflicting heavy casualties on him. The time for a tactical withdrawal could have come later. Their orders seem, however, to have been to withdraw unless supported by the rest of the Prince's army, and the rest of the army was thirty miles or more away at Inverness. 'Had the rest of our Army been come up', writes Lord George Murray, 'we would have march'd there; Clanronald's and the MacKintoches were sent to strengthen them, & they had orders to retyre as the Duke of Cumberland advanced.'

Once Cumberland's troops had crossed the Spey, the road to Inverness lay open to them. The night of 13 April they spent at Alves, four miles west of Elgin and on 14 April reached Nairn, no more than ten miles from Inverness. As the Duke of Kingston's Horse and the Campbells entered the little town from one side, the Duke of Perth's rearguard were leaving it from the other and a running fight ensued in which the Jacobites suffered some casualties.

The news that Cumberland had crossed the Spey reached Inverness on 13 April and next day Prince Charles rode out of the city at the head of his troops with pipes playing and colours flying to set up his headquarters at nearby Culloden, leaving Lord George Murray to follow with the detachments quartered outside the town. That night Lochiel and his Camerons arrived at Culloden from Achnacarry as did some of Glengarry's men from Sutherland. The Duke of Perth and his force having meanwhile fallen back on Culloden from the Spey, that night the Prince's army bivouacked in strength in the grounds of Culloden House or on Culloden Moor nearby.

With Cumberland only ten miles away at Nairn, an early encounter was now probable and next morning, Tuesday 15 April, the Prince's whole force was drawn up, facing eastwards on Culloden Moor, which Charles himself had in his wisdom chosen as the best site for the impending battle – a battle for which Charles himself was longing and which he confidently believed he would win. But now the jealousy and mutual distrust never far below the surface among the Prince's officers broke out once more. After being unfairly accused of keeping his brigade out of harm's way in earlier engagements, this time Lord George Murray made a point of insisting that his Athollmen should be placed on the right wing. Predictably this outraged the MacDonalds, who since the time of Robert the Bruce had regarded the right of the line as theirs by right. At once Clanranald, Keppoch and Lochgarry protested to the Prince, but the latter, who knew that Lord George was already resentful at not having been consulted about the choice of ground, rejected their request. 'Clanranald, Keppoch and I', wrote Lochgarry, 'begged he would give us our former right, but he intreated us for his sake we would not dispute it as he had already agreed to give it to Lord George and his Atholl men.'

Meanwhile the Prince's choice of ground continued to rankle. Culloden and Drummossie Moor together form a large area of relatively flat, undulating moorland bounded on the east by the River Nairn with the hills of central Inverness-shire rising beyond the river. To Lord George it was at once apparent that for regular troops, supported by cavalry and artillery, the level, open moor would be the ideal site for a battle, while the poorly equipped, if more mobile, Highlanders would inevitably be at a disadvantage. He accordingly now despatched Brigadier Stapleton and Colonel Ker of Graden to make a reconnaissance of the higher ground beyond the river.

In the early afternoon Stapleton and Ker returned to report that the ground beyond the river was indeed more suitable for the Highlanders' type of warfare and that its hilly and boggy character would make it difficult for cavalry or artillery. In fact, as Lord George Murray pointed out in advocating an immediate move, there was a good chance that,

190

if they could manage to lure the enemy into the hills, the Highlanders might well be able to get them at a disadvantage and inflict heavy casualties on them. It was, he wrote afterwards, 'very strong ground ... such as the Highlanders would have liked very well'. But to this it was objected, probably by O'Sullivan, that, were this plan to be adopted, Cumberland might slip past, take Inverness, seize the Jacobite army's provisions and then, after leaving them to starve for a while, attack them when it suited him best. In the event Lord George was over-ridden and the decision taken in principle to await the arrival of the enemy on Culloden Moor itself, the strip of open moorland a mile to the South-East of the Lord President's house. 'There never could', wrote Lord George later, 'be more improper ground for Highlanders ... Not one single soldier but would have been against such a ffeeld had their advice been askt ... a plain moor where regular troups had ... full use of their Cannon so as to annoy the Highlanders prodigiously before they could possibly make an attack.' O'Sullivan he dismissed in a single pregnant sentence. He had, he said, 'forty-eight hours to display his skill and did it accordingly'.

Information was now received that Cumberland was not after all proposing to attack that day, but intended instead to stay where he was in order the better to celebrate his twenty-fifth birthday, which, as it happened, fell on 15 April. Around midday Charles accordingly rode over to lunch with Rose of Kilravock at his handsome castle some four or five miles from Cumberland's camp at Balblair on the outskirts of Nairn. As they were making a tour of the gardens before dinner the Prince noticed some men planting trees. 'How happy, Sir, you must feel', he said to his host, with a hint of irony and perhaps also of melancholy, 'to be thus peaceably employed in adorning your mansion, whilst all the country around is in such commotion.'

From Kilravock Charles rode back that afternoon to Culloden, where he and his officers then sat down to discuss plans. The suggestion was advanced that, instead of waiting to be attacked, they should that very night march on Nairn and try to surprise Cumberland before he and his troops had had time to recover from the Duke's birthday celebrations. For once the Prince and Lord George Murray were in agreement: both favoured the idea, though not for the same reasons. 'HRH and most others', writes Lord George, 'were for venturing it, amongst whom I was, for I thought we had a better chanse by doing it then by fighting in so plain a feeld; besides, those who had charge of providing for the Army were so unaccountably negligent, that there was nothing to give the men nixt day, & they had gott very litle that day.'

Clearly the plan had serious drawbacks. Most of the regiments were under strength. Lord Cromartie, with part of the Prince's army, was still, as far as anyone knew, in Sutherlandshire. Cluny and the Master of Lovat and their clansmen, though expected, had not yet arrived. Finally, what would happen if for one reason or another the plan miscarried did not bear thinking about. But Charles brushed all objections aside. He was, it appears from a letter attributed to Lord George Murray, 'vastly bent for the night attack, and said he had men enow to bear the enemy, whom he believed utterly dispirited and would never stand a brisk attack'. Finally at four in the afternoon, while the discussion was still in progress, MacDonald of Keppoch marched into the camp with 200 of his clansmen. Their arrival clinched the argument and it was now agreed that, provided the attack could be made before two or at the latest three in the morning, the attempt should be made.

In order that no word of what was planned should reach the enemy, nothing was said about the proposed attack to the junior officers or to the rank and file, and at nightfall the usual preparations were made for a bivouac. Some of the troops now wrapped themselves in their plaids and settled down for a night in the heather. Others, too hungry to sleep, set out on their own in search of food. It was thus that at seven that evening, when they were due to move off, no less than 2,000 men were missing. Nor could those who were eventually found be readily induced to return. The men, whose daily ration had been reduced to a biscuit apiece, were literally starving and told the officers sent out to fetch them that 'they might shoot them if they pleassd, but they could not go back till they got meat'.

The Prince was now strongly urged to abandon the idea of a night attack, as being something for which good morale and alertness were essential. But nothing would move him. The men, he said obstinately, would all be hearty as soon as the march began and those who had gone off would return and follow. The order to march was accordingly given as planned and a little after eight Lord George Murray moved off at the head of the leading column, which consisted largely of the Atholl Brigade and the clan regiments. The Prince followed with the second column, while Lord John Drummond marched in the centre and the Duke of Perth towards the rear, not far from the Prince. Two officers and thirty men of the Mackintosh regiment, who knew the country, went ahead of the first column as guides, while others of their clan followed behind the main force to pick up any stragglers. The night was conveniently dark and the country covered in a thick mist.

It had been agreed that the assault on Cumberland's camp should be made by both columns attacking simultaneously from different directions. This meant a longer march for Lord George, who would

192

first have to make a wide detour in order to avoid Cumberland's outposts and then attack from the North and East at the same time as the Prince attacked from the South and West. Before long, however, Lord George and his Highlanders in the leading column found themselves a long way ahead of the rest of the force and messengers had to be sent after them to ask them to halt. 'I had not marched half a mile', wrote Lord George, 'till I was stopped by a message that the half of the line were at a considerable distance, and ordered to halt till they should join. Though I did not halt, yet I marched slow, hoping that might do; but all to no purpose. I am positive I was stopped by Aid-de-camps and other officers, sent for the same purpose, fifty times before I had marched six miles.' In the end the Duke of Perth himself rode up from the rear to tell Lord George that, unless a halt was made, it would be impossible for the rear column to catch up. A halt was accordingly called and a discussion ensued between Lord George, the Duke of Perth, Lord John Drummond, Lochiel and others who by now had also caught up, as to what should be done next.

It was now two in the morning of 16 April. They had covered barely six miles in six hours and had another four miles to go to reach the enemy's camp. At this stage O'Sullivan arrived, saying that 'he had just then come from the Prince, who was very desirous the attack should be made; but as Lord George Murray had the van, and could judge the time, he left it to him whether to do it or not'.

The discussion continued, various views being expressed with varying degrees of vehemence. 'Lochiel and his brother', writes Lord George, 'said they had been as much for the night attack as anybody could be, and it was not their fault that it had not been done; but blamed those in the rear that had marched so slow, and retarded the rest of the army.' As for Lord George, his view was that 'if they could have made the attack it was the best chance they had, especially if they could have surprised the enemy. But to attack a camp that was near double their number in daylight, when they would be prepared to receive them, would be perfect madness.'

In the end it was unanimously decided to abandon the idea of a surprise attack and simply march back to Culloden, and the Duke of Perth and his brother were sent back to the Prince to inform him of this decision. The Prince's new Secretary, Hay of Restalrig who, arriving at this moment from the rear, endeavoured to dispute the decision, was given short shrift by Lord George, who held him personally responsible for the almost total lack of provisions. Thus rebuffed, Hay hurried back to make such trouble as he could by informing the Prince that Lord George had deliberately disobeyed his orders.

Finding that his army was retreating in confusion and could not now be turned back, the Prince seems at first to have reacted violently, blaming Lord George and, according to some accounts, crying out bitterly that he had been betrayed. Meanwhile the withdrawal continued, the weary, hungry Highlanders straggling back as best they could to Culloden. There they arrived in the cold, bleak light of dawn and, exhausted by the night's march and the lack of food, lay down wherever they halted. 'Everybody', says Lord Elcho, 'seemed to think of nothing but sleep.'

Distressed by his men's plight and also by the active resentment that some of them were beginning to show, the Prince, who had been amongst the last to return, sent a party to Inverness to requisition and bring back such provisions as they could find. 'The Prince,' writes the Rev. John Cameron, who was present, 'intended to give the army an hearty meal and a day's rest and to fight next morning.' That there should be a battle he was quite determined. The Marquis d'Eguilles did his best to dissuade him but, 'finding him immovable in the resolve he had taken to fight at any cost, retired in haste' to Inverness, there to burn his papers and work out a scheme to save such French troops as 'might survive'. Lochiel, Keppoch and Lord George were also against an immediate battle, though the latter kept his views to himself, as 'any proposition to postpone fighting was ill-received and was called discouraging to the army'. Charles, urged from all sides to avoid battle or seek a more favourable site, was rapidly losing patience. 'God damn it', one of his servants heard him say, 'are my orders still disobeyed? Fight where you will, gentlemen, the day is not ours.'

In the end the issue was settled by a chance remark from the commander of the Irish Picquets, Brigadier Walter Stapleton. 'The Scots', he said sourly, 'are always good troops till things come to a crisis.' The chiefs' reaction was immediate and predictable. 'I do not believe,' says Lochiel, 'that there was a Highlander in the army who would not have run up to the mouth of a cannon in order to refute the odious and undeserved aspersion.' From this moment an early encounter with the enemy on any terms and at any cost was inevitable.

During their stay at Culloden House, the Prince's officers had managed to consume sixty hogsheads of the Lord President's best claret and it was only with difficulty that Charles himself, having been assured that there was no sign of movement in the enemy's camp, managed to find some bread to eat and a dram of whisky to drink, before lying down to rest with his boots on.

He was roused barely an hour later with the news that the enemy's cavalry were now only four miles from Culloden and advancing fast. This threw the Jacobite camp into utter confusion. Only 1,000 men were ready to take the field. Officers galloped wildly hither and thither, shouting orders and trying to round up stragglers. There was no time for food, even if food could have been found. Despite the noise and uproar, many of the men were so deeply asleep that they could not be roused and simply lay where they had dropped, scattered about the grounds and enclosures of Culloden House. 'Some', writes Maxwell of Kirkconnel, 'were quite exhausted and not able to crawl.' Briefly the idea of a hasty withdrawal to the more favourable ground across the Nairn was again considered and then rejected. But already the moment for withdrawal or manoeuvre had passed. There was now nothing for it but to stand and fight.

By ten o'clock the weary Highlanders, having roused themselves, were making their way in no particular order to the actual piece of ground which O'Sullivan as Adjutant and Quartermaster-General had picked for the field of battle. This was the expanse of flat, sometimes boggy moorland which lay immediately behind and to the South of Culloden House, stretching away eastwards with occasional patches of bog towards Kilravock and Croy. Here, on O'Sullivan's orders, they were drawn up in two lines, facing North-East, with the cavalry in the rear towards the flanks and such artillery as there was out in front. On their left, in the direction of Culloden House and the Moray Firth, was an extensive patch of bog. To their right, affording, it was hoped, some measure of protection, were the stone dykes of an enclosed field and, beyond these, the fast-flowing Water of Nairn. To their rear, five miles or so away, lay the town of Inverness. To their front they looked out across the moor to where the enemy's forward troops could now be seen approaching.

By midday, after much bickering and expostulation, the Prince's army had taken up their position – 'further back than they had done the day before', wrote one of them, 'and on a much less advantageous spot of ground' – ground which there had been no time to reconnoitre. They numbered no more than 5,000. On their way to the moor they had been joined by some 300 Frasers under Charles Fraser of Inverallochy, who brought the news that a further Fraser contingent led by the Master of Lovat was on its way to Inverness from the North. Of Lord Cromartie's force there was no sign; they had in fact already been taken prisoner at Dunrobin by Lord Reay.

In the short time available the troops had been drawn up in accordance with the orders of the previous day. On the right of the line, but already complaining of their position and with the dry-stone dyke obstructing their line of advance, were the men of Lord George's Atholl Brigade, and with them some Robertsons and some Menzies. Next came Lochiel's Camerons; then the Stewarts of Appin and John Roy Stewart's Regiment; then the Frasers, the

Mackintoshes and the Farquharsons; then a combined regiment of Maclachlans and Macleans (the latter, according to Donald Mac-Donell of Lochgarry who was near them, 'as well looked men as ever I saw') commanded by Maclachlan of Maclachlan and Maclean of Drimnin; and next to them some MacLeods and Chisholms. On the far left, still seething with indignation at their removal from the right of the line, were the MacDonalds of Clanranald, Keppoch and Glengarry.

In the second line were what remained of Lord Ogilvy's, Lord Lewis Gordon's, Gordon of Glenbucket's and the Duke of Perth's regiments, with Lord John Drummond's men and the Irish Picquets on the left. The cavalry, numbering about 150, were partly stationed in the rear under Lords Strathallan, Pitsligo and Balmerino and partly on either flank of the second line. Of the Prince's few remaining cannon some were sited on each flank and some in the centre of the front line. Lord George Murray commanded the right of the first line, Lord John Drummond the centre, the Duke of Perth the left. The second line was commanded by Brigadier Stapleton and the rear by Lord Kilmarnock. After riding along the lines to encourage his men, the Prince himself took up a position on a little hill on the right to the rear of the second line with an escort of two troops of horse from the regiments of FitzJames and Balmerino.

To mark his birthday the Duke of Cumberland had the day before issued his troops with an extra ration of bread, cheese and brandy at his own expense. He had then addressed them. 'My brave boys,' he had said, speaking with a pronounced German accent, 'we have but one march more and all our labour will be at an end. Sit down at your tent doors, and be alert to take your arms.' He had then summoned his officers and told them too to do their best to encourage their men who were to encounter the enemy next day. 'Lights out' had been sounded at ten o'clock, the men being ordered to sleep with their arms beside them.

At four next morning, the 16th of April, came the shrill notes of the reveille while the drums beat the general call to arms. 'It was,' wrote Alexander Taylor of the Royals, 'a very cold, rainy morning.' On leaving his quarters Cumberland was pleased to find that his army had been drawn up in regimental order in no more than two minutes. He was no less pleased to receive reports of the enemy's disastrous night march. On his instructions every man was now issued with another tot of brandy and a ration of biscuit and cheese. Tents were struck and at a quarter past five the Duke's army marched off in three infantry columns of five regiments each with a fourth column of cavalry on the left. The artillery and baggage followed the first column on the right. Two miles ahead of the main force marched the advance guard, consisting of forty or so men of the Duke of Kingston's Light Horse and a company of Loudon's Highlanders or 'hill-skippers', as their Lowland comrades called them.

On reaching Kilravock Wood, Captain Archibald Campbell of Loudon's galloped back to report that the enemy had been sighted marching out from the Culloden enclosures. Three companies of the Argyll Militia and a squadron of Ker's Dragoons were now ordered to join him and together they continued their advance. 'Thus we moved till we ... discovered the rebels formed in a moor,' wrote Captain Duncan Campbell of the Glenorchy Company. 'We then made a halt and sent notice to Colonel Campbell. In a little time the Duke with all the general officers came up and viewed the enemy, after which they returned ... We were ordered to move on. When the enemy was formed we advanced ... The Dragoons followed us.'

Inclining southwards, the cavalry and the Argyll Militia soon reached the wall forming the eastern boundary of the Culloden enclosures. This the militia pulled down to make way for the dragoons. The Duke and his main force then followed, inclining southwards in their turn, and by about eleven o'clock the two armies were in full view of each other at a distance of some two and a half miles. Marching on another half-mile, Cumberland halted and drew up his troops in order of battle, their well disciplined ranks presenting a marked contrast to the 'confused form' of their adversaries.

On the approach march the Duke's three infantry columns had been led by the Royals, Price's and Munro's, followed by Cholmondeley's, Campbell's Royal Scots Fusiliers and Barrel's. On forming, the three latter regiments came up on the left of the three former, making a front line of six battalions. A second line of six more regiments was then formed in the same way with, behind them in reserve, a third line composed of Cumberland's three remaining infantry battalions. Each second-line regiment was posted to cover the interval between the two first-line regiments in front of it, so that 'if one column failed a second supported; and if that failed a third was ready'. On the two flanks, slightly in advance of the reserve, were Cumberland's remaining Highlanders and two squadrons of Kingston's Horse. On the left were the baggage and the dragoons, with the exception of sixty troopers of Cobham's who were sent on ahead to reconnoitre the country in the direction of Culloden House.

These movements, Cumberland was pleased to observe, 'were performed without the least confusion'. When they had been completed, the Duke, weighing almost eighteen stone and mounted on a powerful grey horse, rode slowly along the line with words of encouragement

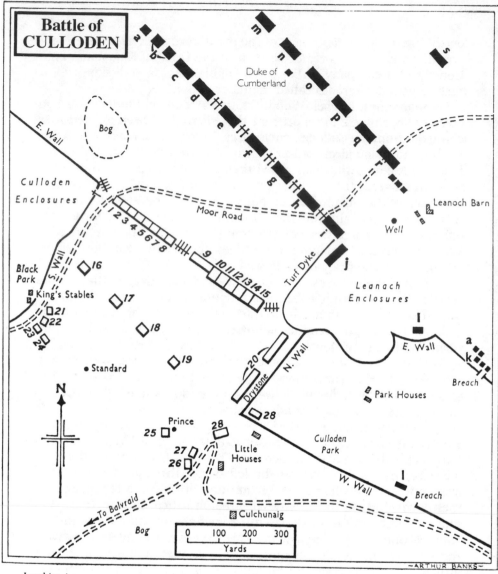

Battle of CULLODEN

Duke of Cumberland

Bog

E. Wall

Culloden Enclosures

Moor Road

Leanoch Barn

Well

Black Park

S. Wall

King's Stables

Turf Dyke

Leanach Enclosures

Standard

Drystone

N. Wall

E. Wall

Breach

Park Houses

N

Prince

Little Houses

Culloden Park

To Balvraid

Culchunaig

Bog

W. Wall

Breach

0   100   200   300
Yards

~ARTHUR BANKS~

Jacobite Army		Royal Army	
1 Glengarry	16 Irish Picquets	a Cobham's Dragoons	p Bligh
2 Keppoch	17 Royal Scots	b Kingston's Light Horse	q Sempill
3 Clanranald	18 Foot Guards	c Pulteney	r Ligonier
4 Duke of Perth	19 Ld. L. Gordon	d Royal Scots	s Blakeney
5 Glenbucket	20 Ld. Ogilvy	e Cholmondeley	
6 John Roy Stewart	21 Hussars	f Price	
7 Farquharson	22 Perthshire Horse	g Royal Scots Fusiliers	
8 Maclean and McLachlan	23 Stonywood	h Munro	
9 Mackintosh	24 Bannerman	i Barrel	
10 Fraser	25 Balmerino's Life guards	j Wolfe	
11 Appin	26 Ld. Elcho's Life Guards	k Ld. M. Kerr's Dragoons	
12 Cameron	27 FitzJames Horse	l Campbells	
13 1st Batt. ⎱ Atholl	28 Avuchie	m Battereau	
14 3rd Batt. ⎰ Brigade		n Howard	
15 2nd Batt. ⎰		o Fleming	

to his 'brave boys' and with his hat held out stiffly to salute them. 'Stand but firm', he is reported to have said, 'and your enemies will soon fly before you.' 'Flanders! Flanders! We'll follow you!' shouted the brave boys in reply, remembering Dettingen, and hoisted their hats on their bayonets to greet him.

As it was now past mid-day and there was no sign of any forward movement on the part of the enemy, one of Cumberland's staff asked whether he would give permission for the men to dine before the battle. 'No,' he replied, 'they'll fight all the better on empty bellies,' and added, no doubt for General Hawley's benefit, 'Remember what a dessert they got to their dinner at Falkirk!' After which the Duke's army marched on in order of battle with colours flying, drums beating relentlessly, 'arms secured and bayonets fixed'. 'A very uneasy way of marching', was the comment of Private Alexander Taylor of the Royal Scots. But his superiors knew better.

With the Duke of Cumberland was his ADC, twenty-two-year-old Lieutenant-Colonel the Hon. Joseph Yorke, son of the recently-ennobled Lord Hardwicke, the able attorney from Dover who had risen to be George II's Lord Chancellor. 'We marched forward so formed to meet the rebels,' young Joseph wrote to his father afterwards. 'As we drew near, I could observe that this manoeuvre of ours had caused a good deal of confusion among them and they seemed to incline more towards the Water of Nairn.'

That the Highlanders, after the experiences of the last twenty-four hours, were in a state of confusion was indisputable. 'Bad signs', we are told, 'had been multiplying throughout the morning.' 'A visable damp and dejection had spread among the troops.' 'Quite different was their appearance this day from what it had been the day before.' 'They were not the clans that had fought with such verve and vigour at Prestonpans and Falkirk.' Some had thought the bad weather might cause Cumberland to postpone his attack; but the hope was a vain one. 'He must', wrote the Chevalier de Johnstone, 'have been blind in the extreme to have delayed attacking us instantly in the deplorable situation in which we were. . . .' Without doubt the sight of the serried ranks of redcoats bearing relentlessly down on them with drums beating and colours flying was anything but reassuring. Watching them coming on, a French officer told the Prince that he 'had never seen men advance in so cool and regular a manner' and 'feared the day already lost'. 'It resembled', wrote an eyewitness of Cumberland's force as it advanced, 'a deep and sullen river, while the Prince's army might be compared to a streamlet running among stones, whose noise sufficiently showed its shallowness.' Even the Prince, for all his optimism, 'began to consider his situation desperate'. 'We are putting an end to a bad affair,' said Lord George Murray gloomily to Lord Elcho.

John William O'Sullivan, meanwhile, in his muddled way, was busily conveying the Prince's orders – or his own version of them – to the commanders and in particular to Lord George Murray. Lord George, who had already asked him angrily whether he commanded the army, found this hard to bear, and after a time answered him 'no more then if he spook to a Stone' – which seems to have accounted for at least one of Charles's orders going astray.

Certainly the results of the Adjutant-General's last-minute attempts to 'rightify' the Jacobite front line were far from happy. 'As Mr O-' Sullivan drew up the army in line of battle I cannot justly tell in what order they were drawn up,' observed Lord George later. The MacDonalds were already in a fractious frame of mind. To save time, the same order of battle was maintained as on the previous day, with the result that once again Clan Donald was deprived of its traditional place on the right of the line. This they deeply resented, the clansmen 'being far from satisfied with the complaisance of their commanders', who in the end had accepted the place allotted to them, though with bad grace. Apart from this, the accidental shooting of Glengarry's son, Angus, at Falkirk three months earlier by one of Clanranald's men and the latter's consequent execution still rankled. As a result, men from both branches of the clan had left the colours and those who remained were in a bad mood. A number of Keppoch's followers, too, had stayed on in Lochaber after the siege of Fort William had been raised, and in the North Barisdale's whole contingent had been taken prisoner along with Lord Cromartie. So that, for one reason or another, Clan Donald, by the time they reached the field of battle, were not only thoroughly disgruntled but also very much under strength.

After a further last minute attempt to claim their old position on the right, the MacDonalds next moved to the centre and then, out of spite, so far to the left that in the end Glengarry's regiment was situated near the South-East corner of the wall surrounding the Culloden enclosures. This wall and the park wall on the Jacobite right were barely seven hundred yards apart, with the result that there was not enough space between them for the regiments in the front line to deploy. Moreover the Jacobite front line was now askew and became more so when Lord George Murray ordered his Athollmen on the right of the line to advance from behind the park wall on to the open moor.

Things might even now have been put right had the Duke of Perth been able to bring the left wing forward, but the Duke, though he even declared himself ready to change his name to MacDonald if they would only move, could still not induce the MacDonalds to move any further forward. Nor did O'Sullivan make matters any better by galloping up at this juncture and blaming everything on Lord George, who, as before, maintained a stony silence. The Prince, meanwhile, was complaining of the time the clans were taking to assemble, evidently without reflecting that only a short time before he himself had despatched most of their colonels to Inverness to fetch more rations.

While all this preliminary manoeuvring was in progress, a single Highlander, detaching himself from the ranks of the Prince's army, had made his way across the moor to the enemy's front line and, throwing down his arms, had given himself up as a prisoner. He was accordingly sent back to the rear, asking, as he was passed from regiment to regiment, where he might find the Duke of Cumberland to whom, he said, he wished to surrender in person. On his way he encountered not the Duke, but young Lord Bury, Lord Albemarle's son, a friend and contemporary of Cumberland's, who was now serving on his staff. At the sight of Bury's splendid uniform, the blue and scarlet frock coat of a major in the Coldstream Guards, the Highlander felt certain that this must be the Commander-in-Chief himself. The moment for which he had been waiting had arrived. Suddenly wrenching a musket from the nearest English soldier, he fired it straight at the young man on the horse, hoping thus to rid Prince Charles of his chief enemy. But the shot missed and from his place in the ranks Private Newman of Sempill's at once shot the Highlander dead.

It was to Lord Bury, unmoved by this unpleasant incident, that the Duke now turned with the request that he ride out into the no-man's-land between the two armies to reconnoitre 'what ... appeared like a battery behind several old walls'. It was just after one o'clock and the opposing armies were now some 500 yards apart. Riding to within a hundred yards of the Jacobite right wing and then, reining in his horse, Bury stared calmly at the enemy. Upon which, the English at last broke their disconcerting silence with a cheer; the Highlanders, tossing their bonnets in the air, responded with 'alacrity and spirit'; Lord Bury, unconcerned as ever, turned his horse and rode back to his own lines; and, with a ragged discharge from the Prince's cannon, the battle of Culloden began.

CHAPTER TWELVE

The opening shots of the battle were fired from the battery of four mixed pieces of artillery sited in the centre of the Prince's front line, the other batteries on the two wings joining in later. The Jacobite gunners had been ordered to aim just to the rear of the enemy's front line, where Cumberland, a conspicuous figure on his powerful grey horse, had taken up his position, and at least two of the shots fired by the left-wing battery went very close to him.

Two minutes later the Duke's own batteries opened fire. For the first time the Highlanders now experienced the rapid and accurate shooting of trained artillerymen firing each gun once every fifteen seconds. Cumberland's batteries were manned by seven officers, six sergeants and corporals, eleven bombardiers, sixty-six gunners, sixty-two matrosses and three drummers, all under the command of Brevet-Colonel William Belford of the Royal Artillery, a young professional officer of ability and experience who had fought at Fontenoy and Dettingen. They consisted of ten 3-pounder battalion guns placed in the front line by pairs in the intervals between regiments as well as some other 3-pounders and mortars set back a little from the line on a brae to the left. They were carefully sighted and fired by their gun-crews in response to successive orders from Colonel Belford, transmitted by his second-in-command, Lieutenant John Goodwin, another regular officer of the Royal Artillery, to the fireworkers and non-commissioned officers of each battery. The rolling roar of the ten 3-pounders as their crews kept re-loading and firing continually was unceasing and their effect on the enemy altogether devastating. 'The thunder of our cannon', wrote Surgeon Grainger of Pulteney's, 'was perpetual.'

202

Before long the Prince's guns, of various calibres and ineffectually manned by untrained Highlanders, had been more or less silenced. Soon Belford's guns had made 'a strange slaughter-house' of one of the batteries, and great gaps began to appear in the Jacobite lines. 'Close up! Close up!' the Prince's officers shouted and the clansmen drew together as best they could to close the breaches made in their ranks by the enemy's round shot, as Cumberland's cannon continued to 'play very briskly upon them'.

Sometimes the shot trundled across the moor towards the front line and sometimes, following a higher trajectory, sailed over their heads to land among their comrades in the second, knocking men over like ninepins and scattering their limbs left and right. Stationed on some rising ground a little way behind the centre of his second line was Prince Charles with his standard, his personal staff and the reserve – 'so called', writes Maxwell of Kirkconnel succinctly, 'because there was no other', and consisting of some sixteen troopers of Lord Balmerino's Life Guards and not many more hussars.

Seeing the little group of horsemen around the Royal standard, Colonel Belford quickly brought two of his cannon to bear on them. They found their target and the round shot from them began to fall all round the Prince – or so it appeared to those standing near him. 'The whole fury of the enemy's artillery', wrote John Daniel of Balmerino's, 'seemed to be directed against us in the rear; as if they had noticed where the Prince was.' In a few minutes the Prince's horse was hit and his groom killed by a cannonball. It was clearly time for Charles to change his position and he rode off to the right. John Daniel from Lancashire rode after him carrying the standard. 'Frequent turns and looks the Prince made', he wrote, 'to see how his men behaved, but alas! our hopes were slender . . . We had not proceeded far when I was ordered back, lest the sight of my Standard going back might induce others to follow.'

With words of encouragement to such troops as he happened to pass, Charles now took up a position slightly to the North-East of the Culchunaig farm steadings and anything but well-suited for a command post, affording him as it did only an incomplete view of the battlefield and giving him very little idea of what was happening to his own troops. From what he could see he seems to have reached the conclusion that 'the Duke would begin the attack, as he had the wind and weather at his back'. But in this he was mistaken. Cumberland, 'finding his cannon rapidly thinning the Jacobite ranks, without experiencing any loss in return', was in no hurry to attack. Colonel Belford now ordered his gunners to load with grapeshot – 'partridge shot', an English officer called it in a letter home. This 'swept the field as with a hail storm' and the Highlanders, with no real experience of regular warfare, 'were greatly surprised and disordered by it'. 'The grapeshot made open lanes quite through them, the men dropping down by wholesale,' wrote another Englishman.

The Prince's army had by this time endured Colonel Belford's cannonade for the best part of half an hour without receiving any orders except to close their ranks, while first the round shot and then the grape ploughed through them. Their losses, partly owing to the way in which they were drawn up, had been appalling. 'Most of our shots,' wrote Surgeon Grainger appreciatively, 'took effect.' The order for which the Highlanders had from the first been waiting was 'Claymore!' the word of command for the charge, the savage onrush in which the clansmen delighted and which the red-coats had always found so hard to withstand. But this did not come. And now it began to seem as though it might soon be too late to give this or any other order. 'The regiments in the front rank', wrote Lord George Murray afterwards, 'were turned so impatient that they were like to break their ranks', and a Lowlander who served in the front line used to tell years later of the look of rage on the faces of the men who stood near him.

Most restive of all were the Mackintoshes, at the centre of the Jacobite line, and from them 'a message was sent along the line to Lochiel desiring he would represent to Lord George the necessity of attacking immediately'. To this Lochiel, in passing the message to Lord George, added another from himself to say that 'he could not hold his own men much longer'. And Lord George, realizing the need for immediate action, sent Ker of Graden to the Prince 'to know if he should begin the attack, which the Prince accordingly ordered'. On the Prince's instructions Graden now rode over to the Duke of Perth on the left, to give him the order to attack, while the Prince's ADC, young Lachlan Maclachlan of Inchconnel, was sent with the same message to Lord George and his Athollmen on the right. On his way across, a cannon-ball carried off young Lachlan's head so that his message never reached its destination. The Prince, however, to make sure his order arrived at the front line, had also sent Walter Stapleton to the right wing and Sir John MacDonald to the left.

But, before Stapleton could deliver his message, the centre, led by the Mackintoshes and the other regiments of Clan Chattan, MacGillivrays and MacBeans, had already rushed forward to the attack with their pipes playing and with yells of 'Loch Moy!' and 'Dunmaglas!' At first they could see nothing as they ran. Then a gust of wind blew the gun smoke aside and there before them, one of them remembered afterwards, was the enemy: a solid line of legs, white-gaitered with black buttons down the calves. In the absence of the Mackintosh, held prisoner at Moy by his wife, and of Lord John Drummond, who was busy conferring with his brother Perth on the left, they were commanded by the Chief of the MacGillivrays, tawny-haired young MacGillivray of Dunmaglass, who led the charge with his standard-bearer at his side. With Clan Chattan went forward the little regiment of Maclachlans and Macleans.

At the moment when Clan Chattan began their charge, Lord George Murray had been talking to Lochiel. Within two minutes he had given the word of command and the clans on the right were charging too, Athollmen, Camerons, Frasers and Stewarts, with Stewart of Ardsheil, a portly and normally lethargic man, running four or five paces ahead of his clan.

On the left, the Duke of Perth, who had been joined by Lord John Drummond, was still having trouble with the MacDonalds. Their three regiments, Clanranald's, Keppoch's and Glengarry's, amounted to no more than 1,000 men in all. Many of them had already drifted away and those who remained still bitterly resented their position on the left of the line. Earlier they had reluctantly moved up to the South-East corner of the enclosure wall and there they remained until shortly after the charge began. Now, urged on by the Duke and his brother, they finally moved forward, without however actually engaging the enemy.

Nor were the MacDonalds' immediate neighbours much more enthusiastic, but also showed 'a general disinclination to attack, which became more noticeable towards the left'. Only one company of Farquharsons joined in the charge, the other, having stopped at a farm for refreshment, were with true Highland nonchalance still dancing to their captain's fiddle when the sound of firing warned them that the battle had begun. As for Gordon of Glenbucket's and John Roy Stewart's regiments, neither, as it happened, was equipped with swords, a serious disadvantage on such an occasion.

Cumberland, a competent commander, did not allow the Highland charge to take him by surprise. He had from the first expected it and had made his dispositions accordingly. In order not to be outflanked to his right by the straggling regiments of MacDonalds, he had brought Pulteney's up from the rear and placed them to the right of the Royals, in his front line. He had also brought forward Battereau's and placed them next to Howard's on the right of the second line. This left him with no reserve in his third line save Blakeney's, but this risk he was prepared to take. On the rising ground to the right of Pulteney's he had stationed 200 of Kingston's Horse, with, on their flank, sixty of Cobham's Dragoons. Finally he had given orders that Wolfe's Regiment should be moved forward from the left of the second line and placed *en potence*, at right angles, to Barrel's on the left of the front line with their backs to the Leanach dyke, ready to take the advancing Highlanders from the flank.

More important still, Cumberland had grasped the strategic import-ance of the Culwhiniac enclosure. Culwhiniac Farm lay directly to the right of the Highland line and it had been hopefully suggested by some of the Prince's advisers that the four-foot dry-stone wall which enclosed its fields might afford a measure of protection to his right wing. 'The walls are between you and them!' O'Sullivan kept saying to Lord George who, however, was not convinced and the argument had still been in progress when the first shots of the battle were fired.

Cumberland, meanwhile, realizing that a dry-stone dyke did not present an insuperable obstacle to well-trained troops, had given orders that four companies of Campbell Militia, followed by six squadrons of Cobham's and Lord Mark Ker's Dragoons, commanded by old General Humphrey Bland, should be sent forward to some distance ahead of his left wing. 'We were advanced,' wrote one of the Militia officers, 'about one eighth of a mile before the left of the army and thus we moved from village to village along the Water of Earn till we came into hollow ground where we were out of sight of both armies except six squadrons of dragoons.'

On reaching the dry-stone wall of Culwhiniac Farm, the Militia halted. 'We came,' wrote Captain Duncan Campbell, 'to a high enclos-ure that extended to a great way to the Right and quite to the Water of Earn to the left. From this place we sent to acquaint General Bland that the Horses could go no further.' From General Henry Hawley, commanding the English cavalry, now came orders to demolish the wall. This the Campbell militiamen quickly did, making a big enough breach in it to admit a squadron of horses. After which the Campbells first went through themselves, moving across the enclosure at the run and taking up a strategic position along the north wall, and the dragoons then followed them. 'The Dragoons,' wrote Duncan Campbell, 'went out and formed at a distance, facing the rebels, and we were ordered to attack them.'

In this simple and foreseeable manner, the Prince's right wing had been successfully outflanked. Grasping this, Lord George, from his position on the right wing, at once directed the Prince's Life Guards and FitzJames's Horse to face the enemy's dragoons, at the same time giving orders to Lord Lewis Gordon's men in the second line to take up a position facing southwards immediately to the rear of his Atholl-men. For a time, Cumberland's Dragoons found their progress impeded by a deep ravine, across which a few desultory shots were exchanged with the Prince's cavalry. One Jacobite bullet found its mark in the rump of the horse ridden by Trooper Enoch Bradshaw of Cobham's. 'Twas pritty near Enoch that time', he wrote to his brother afterwards, 'but thank God, a miss is as good as a mile, as we say in Gloucestershire.'

But by now the order to charge had been given and from the right and centre of the Jacobite line the clans surged forward to the attack. The men of Clan Chattan, who led the charge, had been told to hold their fire 'until they could do certain execution', and 'on no account fling away their muskets'. But in their excitement they forgot these orders. 'Their eagerness to come up with the enemy that had so much advantage of them at a distance made them run on with the utmost violence, but in such confusion, that they could make no use of their firearms', and many 'threw them down without exploding them.'

Crowded against the park wall and the Leanach dyke, the clans on the right were in no less confusion and, with those from the centre, now rushed forward 'in a Sort of a mob, without any order or distinction of Corps'. Many of them, too, threw away their muskets without firing them for, says Kirkconnel, they were so close together 'that they could make no use of their firearms'.

And now, to make matters worse, the charging clans suddenly swerved to the right, perhaps to avoid the patch of boggy ground which lay in the hollow between the two armies. 'Their spirited advance', wrote an English soldier, 'lasted but a short time with any kind of warmth, and they shifted away to our left.' This sudden change of direction was to prove disastrous, preventing hundreds of the Prince's best troops from ever coming to grips with the enemy and bringing the advancing Highlanders under heavy fire from the centre of Cumberland's front line. It also brought the Athollmen on the right still closer to the north wall of the Culwhiniac enclosure, whence they were successfully enfiladed by the Campbell Militia, and then to the Leanach dyke, where, in accordance with Cumberland's directions, Wolfe's Regiment were waiting for them *en potence*, pouring volley after volley into them from the flank. There thirty-two officers of the Atholl Brigade and scores of clansmen were killed. Lord Nairne's men on the extreme right suffered most. His brother Robert Mercer of Aldie was shot through the head and neither his body nor that of his young son Thomas were ever found. In the end the Athollmen fell back without reaching the enemy's line.

But still the other clans came on. 'They came running upon our front line like troops of hungry wolves,' wrote Private Alexander Taylor of the Royal Scots next day in a letter to his wife. 'Those on the right with their glittering swords', wrote another eyewitness, 'ran swiftly on the cannon, making a dreadful huzza and crying *Run ye dogs!*'

'Nothing,' wrote Surgeon Grainger to his brother, 'could be more furious than their onset, which no troops but these, headed by our magnanimous hero, could have withstood.' The 350 men of Barrel's Regiment, which alone of the Hanoverian battalions had stood firm at Falkirk, and half of Munro's (which had not), met the full force of the Highland charge, holding their fire until the Highlanders were within twenty yards of them and then firing a volley from each rank in turn. 'Twas at the twinkling of an eye,' wrote an observer, 'that the fire of the small arms began from right to left, which for two minutes was like one continued thunder equalling the noise of the loudest clap.' And all the while Colonel Belford's guns kept firing their volleys of grapeshot.

No two battalions could have withstood the onrush of the eight clan regiments, numbering in all some 1,500 men. Seeing his left hard pressed, Cumberland now gave orders for Bligh's and Sempill's to be brought up in support. Soon the Hanoverian line parted and Clan Chattan and the Stewarts and Camerons broke through to the rear, inflicting 120 casualties on Barrel's alone, including their colonel, Robert Rich, both of whose hands were cut off, one with his sword still in it. Munro's, too, lost eighty men killed or wounded in their encounter with the Stewarts and Camerons.

But the clans suffered infinitely heavier casualties. 'There was scarce a soldier or officer of Barrel's', wrote one of them, 'and of that part of Munro's which engaged who did not kill one or two men each with their bayonets or spontoons.' 'The Highlanders,' wrote another English eyewitness, 'fought like furies and Barrel's behaved like so many heroes. It was dreadful to see the enemies' swords circling in the air as they were raised from the strokes: And no less to see the officers of the army, some cutting with their swords, others pushing with their spontoons, the sergeants running their halberts into the throats of their opponents, the men running their fixed bayonets up to the sockets.' The special bayonet practice on which Cumberland's infantry had concentrated while they were in Aberdeen had clearly been well worthwhile.

Clan Chattan, who were fighting on their own clan territory, bore the brunt of the battle. Of their twenty-one officers only three survived the charge, many of them dying with hundreds of their men under a hail of bullets before they could close with the enemy. Their colonel, MacGillivray of Dunmaglass, was the first to reach the enemy and the first to hack his way through them, dying in the end beyond the Hanoverian lines with his face in a spring of water. The cadet of his name who carried his standard was killed at the outset of the charge, but another clansman seized it in his place, saving it at the last by wrapping it round his body, for which he was known to the end of his days as *Donuil na Braiteach*, Donald of the Colours. Following his chief, Big John MacGillivray cut down twelve of the enemy and broke right through to Blakeney's in the third line before he was in his turn killed. Gilies MacBean, a major of Clan Chattan, had bayonet wounds in his body and arms, his face cut open from brow to chin and his thigh shattered by grape, but still he charged on to fall in his turn before the bayonets of the second line. There, too, fell Angus Mackintosh of Farr, not many hundred yards from where his fourteen-year-old son James lay in the heather watching the battle with little Archie Fraser, younger brother of the Master of Lovat, and some other friends who had played truant from school that day.

The other clans from the right and the centre, Stewarts, Camerons and Frasers, suffered equally and of the 500 or so men who broke through the enemy's lines few found their way back again. The Camerons, raked by the volleys of Wolfe's and the Campbell Militia from the right, had continued to charge, overrunning the battalion guns between Barrel's and Munro's, cutting down the gun crews and then going on to engage the infantry at close quarters in such savage hand-to-hand fighting that the clash of steel could be heard far along the line. '*Thigibh an so! Thigibh an so!*,' ran the Cameron pibroch, '*Clannabh nan con s'gheibh sibj feoil!* Come away, come away, Sons of the Dogs, and feast ye on flesh.'

Captain Lord Robert Ker of Barrel's, who three months before had shown some chivalry to a captured Highlander at Falkirk, spiked the first Cameron to reach him on the point of his spontoon, but the next split his head open to the chin. Fifty yards from the English guns lay Lochiel with both his ankles broken by grape-shot, leaning on his hands, watching his clan as they fought their way forward, until in the end four of his clansmen carried him from the field. 'Nothing,' wrote Colonel Charles Whitefoord of the Fifth Marines, 'could be more desperate than their attack and more properly received. Those in front were spitted with the bayonets: those in flank were torn in pieces with the musquetry and grapeshor.

Of the 300 Stewarts from green Appin who charged that afternoon with Ardsheil, the tutor of Appin, at their head, ninety-two were killed and more than sixty wounded. Though Ardsheil himself somehow survived, eight of his own family were killed that day, including his old uncle, Duncan, and fourteen other officers of the clan, from the families of Achnacone and Fasnacloich, Ballachulish and Invernakyle. The Stewart standard-bearer was killed beside old Duncan Stewart, but a man from Morvern named MacAntle tore the colours from the staff and, like Donuil na Braiteach, saved them by wrapping them round his own body.

On the left of Clan Chattan the little regiment of Macleans and Maclachlans charged too. Yelling 'Another for Hector!' and 'Death or Life!', they ran straight into the grapeshot of Colonel Belford's guns and the continuous musket fire of Pulteney's and the Royal Scots. The hail of bullets was so thick that as they ran forward some of the clansmen held their plaids before their eyes as though to ward off rain or sleet. Old Lachlan Maclachlan of Maclachlan, whose son Lachlan had died a few minutes earlier, was soon killed in his turn and most of his clan with him.

By now Clan Chattan had begun to retreat and old Charles Maclean of Drimnin, who had served for a time in the Royal Navy and was now leading the men of his clan against the king whose commission he had once held, found himself being swept back with them as they ran. As he sought to rally his few surviving clansmen, he encountered his son Allan, who had been wounded, and learned from him that his other son, Lachlan, was already dead. At this Drimnin turned back towards the enemy line, saying that he was going to avenge his son. Allan pleaded with him. But in vain. The old man shook him off. '*Allein*,' he said, '*comma leat misse. Mas toil leat do bheatha thoir'n arrigh dhuit fhein*: Allan, do not think of me. Take care of yourself – if you value your life.'

His own life old Drimnin clearly did not value. As he ran forward again without hat or wig to meet the enemy, two English troopers came riding at him out of the smoke of battle. One he cut down with his sword and managed to wound the other before more of their comrades rode up and finished him off. James, son of the aged Chief of Ardgour, somehow survived the charge and in due course secretly made his way back to Ardgour; fifteen years later he was killed in action at sea fighting this time for the Duke of Cumberland's nephew, King George III. Of the 180 Maclean clansmen that he and Drimnin had brought with them only thirty-eight were to return alive to Mull, Morvern and Ardgour.

While their neighbours from the centre and right were fighting their way forward, the MacDonalds on the left of the line, having reluctantly moved up to the South-East corner of the enclosure wall, again advanced, this time apparently with some intention of engaging the enemy or at any rate inducing the enemy to engage them. 'They came down there several times within a hundred yards of our men,' wrote one of Cumberland's officers, 'firing their pistols and brandishing their swords.' 'But,' he adds, 'our brave soldiers appeared as if they took little notice of their bravado.'

All this time Belford's guns had been taking their toll of the Prince's army, and now came signs of an impending threat from Cumberland's cavalry, 'which began to move forward with the evident intention of outflanking them, which the infantry regiment on the extreme right was also in a position to do'. The wisdom of the changes Cumberland had made in the disposition of his right wing at the start of the battle was fast becoming obvious. Uneasily, the MacDonalds became aware of a long line of disengaged enemy troops to their front, outflanking and outnumbering them. Then, back across the moor towards them, through the mist and smoke of battle, came running little groups of men, the clans of the right and centre, broken and in flight. The MacDonalds' immediate neighbours on the left, Perth's, Glenbucket's and Farquharsons', had already fallen back; without further ado they followed their example, many of them having never come within a hundred yards of the enemy line.

'Claymore! Claymore!' shouted the young Duke of Perth unavailingly, and his brother John tried to help him, but it was hopeless. 'Lord John Drummond did all he could to stop the Flight.... They threw down their firelocks and began to give way; on which the [enemy's] right wing advancing some paces gave their fire in so close and full a manner that the ground was covered with the bodies of the dead and wounded, and the cannon being again loaded these fired into the midst of the fugitives and made a frightful carnage.'

But though the three MacDonald regiments now 'drew off in an entire flight', the chieftains and gentlemen of the clan, who before the battle had declared that they would fight, whether their clansmen followed them or not, now proved as good as their word. '*Mo Dhia, an do threig Clann mo chinnidhmi?*' cried Keppoch, as he ran forward sword in hand towards the enemy. 'My God, have the clansmen of my name deserted me?' And a few of his clansmen were shamed into following him, to fall, as he did, almost immediately, under a hail of bullets from the long lines of enemy infantry. Young Clanranald, though shot in the head, survived; Lochgarry escaped unwounded. With Glengarry's Regiment, wearing for the occasion a tartan sash across his coat, charged the Lowland Chevalier de Johnstone, next to his friend Mac-Donald of Scothouse, who almost immediately was killed at his side with twenty of his men. 'As far as I could distinguish at the distance of twenty paces', wrote Johnstone afterwards, 'the English appeared to be drawn up in six ranks, the three first being on their knees and keeping up a terrible running fire on us.... My unfortunate friend Scothouse was killed by my side. ... I was not so keenly affected at the moment as I have been ever since.'

It was now that Cumberland's cavalry came into their own,

Cobham's sixty troopers and 200 more of Kingston's Horse riding down the fugitives from the English right flank and 'briskly falling in' with them. The withdrawal quickly became a rout. 'What a spectacle of horror!' wrote Johnstone, who himself retreated with the MacDonalds. 'The same Highlanders who had advanced to the charge like lions, with bold and determined countenance, were in an instant seen flying like trembling cowards in the greatest disorder.'

As the MacDonalds ran past their own second line, Lord Lewis Drummond's Scots Royal and Walter Stapleton's Irish Picquets, regular regiments of exiles wearing the uniform of the King of France, stood to let them pass and then, closing ranks again, took their stand in the path of the oncoming enemy cavalry, later withdrawing behind the wall of one of the Culloden enclosures in order to cover the fugitives' retreat with steady well-directed volleys which for a time successfully checked the English cavalry's advance and gave the MacDonalds more time to escape. After which, seeing the enemy's infantry advancing in strength and having already lost more than half their men, they fell back in good order on Inverness. Among the casualties was their commander, Brigadier Walter Stapleton, who later died of his wounds. It was he who had that morning somewhat sourly remarked that the Scots were always good troops until it came to a crisis.

The retreat had by this time become general. Lord George Murray, who, at the head of his Athollmen, had 'behaved with great gallantry, lost his horse, his periwig and bonnet, had several cuts with broadswords in his coat, and was covered with blood and dirt', now ran back to the second line to bring up such reinforcements as he could find. These were Lord Lewis Gordon's remaining battalion and the Scots Royal. Led by Lord George the two regiments again advanced towards the enemy in good order and exchanged several volleys with them. But, says Maxwell of Kirkconnel, 'the day was irrevocably lost; nothing could stop the Highlanders after they had begun to run'.

As they retreated, the clans on the Jacobite right wing and the Camerons in particular once again came under heavy fire from their old enemies the Campbell Militia, still safely ensconced behind the Leanach dyke. Emboldened by the English victory and yelling '*Cruachan!*', these now ventured out sword in hand from behind the wall and engaged the retreating Jacobites, losing half a dozen men and two officers in the brief skirmish that followed and so learning that even in defeat the Camerons were formidable. Again, Cumberland's foresight in securing the Culwhiniac enclosure before the battle began had been abundantly justified. 'It was evident', wrote the Chevalier de Johnstone later with the advantage of hindsight, 'our destruction became inevitable, if the English got possession of the inclosure.'

Meanwhile, not many hundred yards away, at the far end of the Culwhiniac enclosure, Trooper Enoch Bradshaw and some 500 of Ker's and Cobham's well-fed, well-mounted and well-armed dragoons were still facing a single under-strength squadron of the Prince's Life Guards led by Lord Elcho and another of FitzJames's Horse under Captain Robert O'Shea, with only the sunken road between them. Seeing the clans in full flight, the dragoons now ventured down into the ravine with the object of taking the fleeing clansmen in the rear. There they were met by the Prince's cavalry, who, though vastly outnumbered and in the end driven back with heavy casualties, managed to hold the dragoons up for long enough to give the clans on the right time to make their escape.

It was at this juncture, while the Prince's hard-pressed Life Guards and FitzJames's Horse were seeking to rally and form a square, that John William O'Sullivan galloped up from the rear in a state of high excitement. 'You see,' he shouted, addressing himself to Captain O'Shea, 'all is going to pot. You can be of no great succor, so before a general deroute wch will soon be, seize the Prince & take him off.'

Accounts of what ensued vary according to individual recollections or the point of view of the narrator. Some relate that the Prince made a last attempt to rally his troops. Others that he was only with difficulty prevented from charging the enemy alone and seeking a hero's death. And yet others that he gave way to utter panic. What is certain is that he was at first dazed by the disaster that had overtaken him and that in the end someone, O'Sullivan or O'Shea or possibly Lochiel's old uncle, Major Kennedy, seized his bridle and led him willingly or unwillingly off the field, his face wet with tears, while young Lord Elcho, who was shortly to follow his example, shouted, 'Run, you cowardly Italian!' as he went. Or so it is said. On this, too, opinions differ.

Of the Prince's other commanders, some did not attempt to leave the field. Old Lord Balmerino, urged by Lord Elcho to follow him, simply shook his head and rode back to the field to surrender, knowing full well the fate that must await him. Lord Kilmarnock, galloping up to some of Cumberland's Dragoons under the impression that they belonged to his own regiment, was made prisoner by them. As he and his captors passed the Royal Scots Fusiliers further along the enemy's line, a tall young officer came forward from their ranks to meet him and held up his hat to hide the tears of shame and mortification on his father's face. 'It was his and his wife Anne's son, Lord Boyd, who had been fighting for Cumberland. Lord Strathallan, for his part, 'resolving to die in the field rather than by the hand of the executioner', gathered forty or so troopers of his regiment and rode straight at

213

Cobham's Dragoons. He was run through the body by Colonel Howard of that regiment, the last sacrament being later administered to him in the form of whisky and oatcake by the Mackintosh chaplain, James Maitland of Careston.

Meanwhile, with colours flying and pipes playing, the Jacobite right wing, or what was left of them, carried out their retreat to the ford at Faillie and across the River Nairn 'with the greatest regularity'. That they were able to do so was due partly to the calm courage of Lord George Murray, who was one of the last to leave the field, and also to the steadiness of Lord Ogilvy and his two well-equipped, well-disciplined battalions from Angus, who, facing about again and again during the retreat, forced the pursuing dragoons to keep their distance.

Cumberland's cavalry from both wings had by now met at the centre of what had once been the Jacobite second line. While Kingston's Horse and part of Cobham's continued the pursuit under Lord Ancram and General Bland, (doing their best 'for our dear Bill', wrote Trooper Bradshaw to his brother) the remainder, under General Henry Hawley, carried out mopping-up operations on the field, hunting down and massacring any Highlanders they could find – General Hawley with especial gusto. Riding over the part of the moor where the Frasers had made their final stand, he happened to catch the eye of their commander, Charles Fraser of Inverallochy, looking up at him from the ground where he lay wounded, at which he told his Brigade Major James Wolfe to 'shoot that insolent scoundrel'. But Wolfe, to his credit, refused to do so, declaring that he would sooner resign his commission, and Hawley, much to his irritation, was obliged to send for a soldier to finish off the wounded man instead.

So far as possible, the dragoons seem to have avoided formed units of the defeated enemy and 'contented themselves', writes Kirkconnel, 'with sabering such unfortunate people as fell in their way single and disarmed'. The Jacobite wounded and what remained of the left wing offered them plenty of scope and they also enjoyed the continuing support of the artillery which went on firing long after the infantry had stopped. 'A few royals [mortars]', wrote Fusilier Edward Linn, or Lunn, of the Royal Scots Fusiliers, 'sent them a few bombs and cannon-balls to their farewell, and immediately our horse that was on the right and left wings pursued them with sword and pistol and cut a great many of them down so that I never saw a small field so thick with dead.'

Andrew Henderson, Cumberland's official biographer, who was present, has also described the scene. 'They were pursued', he writes, 'by Kingston's Light Horse and mangled terribly, while the Soldiers, warm in their Resentment, stabbed some of the wounded. A Party meeting others at Culloden House brought them forth and shot them.

... The Troops were enraged at their Hardships and Fatigues during a Winter campaign; the habit of the enemy was strange, their Language was still stranger, and their mode of fighting unusual; the Fields of Preston and Falkirk were still fresh in their memories.' And in his official despatch the Duke himself reported that he had 'made a great slaughter and gave quarter to none but about fifty French officers and soldiers'. The moor, wrote another Hanoverian eyewitness, 'was covered with blood and our men, what with killing the enemy, dabbling their feet in the blood, and splashing it about one another, looked like so many butchers rather than Christian soldiers'.

And now, as the guns of the English warships and transports at anchor in the Moray Firth fired in salute, the moment had finally come for the victorious army to take possession of the field. Riding along the line on his massive grey horse from regiment to regiment, the plump young Commander-in-Chief greeted his soldiers with words of guttural gratitude. 'Wolfe's boys, I thank you,' he cried. 'You have done the business!' To Barrel's, Pulteney's, Sempill's and Munro's too, he expressed his gracious appreciation and to the men of the Argyll Militia, as he passed them, he called out that they were 'his brave Campbells'. Wherever he rode he was greeted with thunderous cheering. 'Billy!' the troops yelled all along the line, and 'Flanders!' and hoisted their hats on the points of their bayonets. 'His presence', wrote one of them, 'was worth five thousand men.' And Trooper Enoch Bradshaw, writing to his brother back in Gloucestershire, was more enthusiastic than ever. 'Down on your knees all England,' he wrote, 'and after praise to God who gives victory, pray for the young British hero!' In due course a special medal, bearing Cumberland's effigy, was struck, to celebrate his victory and distributed to officers and other ranks alike, and for many years thereafter Culloden was included in the battle honours of the British regiments engaged.

When the Duke had finished his inspection, he rode back to the right of the line and halted. Then, pulling down his black three-cornered hat over his nose, he gave his army the order to advance. 'They run,' he cried. 'Rise up, Pulteney's and shoulder!' The order was repeated all down the line and, to the regular beat of the battalion drums, the regiments went forward, trampling the dead and dying Highlanders underfoot as they advanced.

When they reached the part of the moor where an hour before the Prince's army had stood, the battalions halted and grounded their arms. Then, as was their wont on such occasions, they gave three short sharp cheers. Not much more than a mile away, at Balvraid, where he had stopped under a tree, Prince Charles heard them. 'Do as you wish,' he said to those around him, 'only go now.'

215

PART III

BIRD ON THE WING

If Prince Charles had concluded his life soon after his miraculous
escape, his character in history must have stood very high.

Sir Walter Scott
Waverley

CHAPTER THIRTEEN

While the British infantry remained on the battlefield, enjoying a welcome meal of biscuit, cheese, brandy and rum – by courtesy of the Royal Navy – and pausing only to despatch such wounded men who sought to crawl out from under the heaps of Highland dead, General Henry Hawley's dragoons were busy scouring the country between Culloden and Inverness, riding down and sabering any surviving Highlanders and a good many civilians, including some women. A number of people had come out from Inverness to watch the battle, some even bringing picnic baskets, while others came to loot the dead. Of these many had occasion to regret the greed or curiosity which had brought them to Drummossie Moor.

The first dragoon to reach Inverness seems to have been an English volunteer from Whitehaven by the name of James Ray, who earlier that day had ridden with Kingston's Horse. On entering the town, he saw two men trying to take refuge in the well-house and, throwing his bridle to a servant girl, at once followed them in and cut their throats, emerging in due course covered with their blood. After which, pulling his horse after him, he made for the house of the Rev. James Hay, hammering on the door with the hilt of his sabre and shouting that he was a volunteer come from Cumberland to fight for religion and liberty and demanding food and lodging. 'For ministers', he said, 'always have good things.' By now the rest of Cumberland's army had formed column of route and were marching on Inverness with drums beating and colours flying, while on the Duke's instructions, the grenadier company of Sempill's under Captain James Campbell of Ardkinglas went on ahead to take formal possession of the town.

After pausing briefly at Culloden House, where a meal prepared for

Prince Charles still lay cold and uneaten on the table, Cumberland himself had ridden on into Inverness at four in the afternoon at the head of a captain's guard of dragoons. 'His Highness,' we are told, 'entered Inverness at the head of his dragoons, all bespattered with dirt and sweat and his sword in his hand. The bells were set aringing, and people gave the signal to huzza....' His first act was to order the release of the prisoners taken by the Jacobites, who were still confined in the prison. 'Brother soldiers, you are free,' he said, as they emerged, and, clapping them on the shoulder, 'ordered an entertainment for them and payment of all arrears.' Their places being almost immediately filled by such prisoners as his own troops had taken, including some survivors of the Scots Royal and Irish Picquets, to whom, as soldiers of the French King, he had agreed to give quarter.

Cumberland spent the night of the battle in Inverness at old Lady MacKintosh's house in Church Street, 'pleased', as we learn from one of his soldiers, 'to take his lodgings where young Charley had just before kept his Court.' Lady MacKintosh was less pleased. 'I've had two King's bairns living under my roof in my time,' she said later, 'and to tell you the truth I wish I may never have another.' Meanwhile, to keep her out of mischief, the Duke had her locked up in the common guardroom, while he himself spent an agreeably convivial evening with his commanders and personal staff in her best room.

As for Lady MacKintosh's daughter-in-law Anne, Lieut.-Col. Thomas Cockayne of Pulteney's had that very evening received orders to proceed to Moy House, fifteen miles to the South of Inverness, with a 'detachment of 2 Captains 6 Subs and 200 Volunteers' to arrest her. Colonel Cockayne, 'a most discreet, civil man', set out for Moy next morning, marching by Marshal Wade's fine new military road. It took him all day to get there. 'He found it,' we are told, 'impossible to restrain the barbarity of many of his party, who, straggling before, spared neither sex nor age they met with.' On finally reaching Moy, some of Colonel Cockayne's detachment were detailed to round up and drive off the Mackintoshs' livestock (a poor reward for his loyalty to King George), while the remainder went to fetch Colonel Anne, one of the officers hammering on the door and calling for 'that bloody rebel, Lady Mackintosh'. When she calmly asked them to come into the house, Colonel Cockayne's officers seem at first to have been as much taken aback by her youth and beauty as by her dignified demeanour. But soon the soldiers were busy breaking open the furniture and looting the house, even snatching a watch from the Minister of Moy, Mr Lesly, and then at once snatching the fifty guineas which Anne herself offered for its return.

On the following day Anne, wearing her blue bonnet and tartan riding habit, was ordered to mount her horse and taken under armed escort to Inverness, while, to mock her, Pulteney's drummers played the dead-beat. On her way she passed Drummossie Moor and saw the dead of her husband's clan lying in piles by the roadside. Even then she did not say a word. On reaching Inverness, Colonel Cockayne conducted her to where Cumberland was waiting for her in her mother-in-law's parlour. There is no record of what passed between them, but that night she too was committed to the guard room and there spent the next six weeks, receiving, it appears, numerous visits from some of Cumberland's young officers, who were no doubt feeling the lack of agreeable female company. 'I drank tea yesterday with Lady Mackintosh,' wrote one of them to his brother. 'She is really a very pretty woman, pity she is a rebel.' General Henry Hawley took a less favourable view of her. 'Damn the woman,' he shouted at the Commander-in-Chief's one night, when there was talk of the honour due to her. 'I'll honour her with a mahogany gallows and a silken cord.' But this he was not given the opportunity to do.

For two days, while Cumberland's troops established themselves in and around Inverness, the wounded of the Prince's army had been lying out amongst the dead on Drummossie Moor and in nearby bothies. At night the people in the neighbouring farms, at Leanach and Culwhiniac, could hear them moaning and crying out. Any who sought to crawl away were at once bayoneted or shot by the sentries who had been set to guard them. The nights were bitterly cold; many, robbed of their clothing by marauders from the hills, lay naked. The only succour they received was from three devoted women, Mrs Stoner, Mrs Leith and Mrs Leith's maid Eppy, who, in spite of everything, had somehow made their way to the moor on the afternoon of the battle.

On Thursday 17 April the Government troops sent out to bury their own dead reported that there were still some rebels alive on the moor, and that evening Cumberland's General Orders contained the following passage: 'A Captain and 50 foot to march directly and visit all the cottages in the neighbourhood of the field of battle, and to search for rebels. The officers and men will take notice that the Public orders of the rebels yesterday was to give us no quarter.' The latter assertion was in fact untrue, but this in no way detracted from its significance or impact.

The first execution squads from the Royal Scots set out for Culloden on Friday, yelling 'Billy!' as they went. With them, not altogether happily, went Lord Kilmarnock's son, Lord Boyd. They were later followed by detachments from other regiments. Among the first Jacobites the Royal Scots came on were nineteen Highland officers lying wounded in the grounds of Culloden House. These they carried to a wall to the east of the house and there, after an officer had told them to prepare themselves for death, shot them at a range of six feet. In the grieve's house they found twelve more Jacobite officers. Having induced these to come out with the story that they would be taken to a surgeon to have their wounds dressed, they shot them too. Other clansmen they found in huts and bothies about the estate. Three of these huts they burned down with the Highlanders inside, first securing the doors and then merrily echoing back the cries of agony that came from within. Eighteen wounded men were burned alive in one hut. Some beggars who happened to have taken refuge in another were burned too, for good measure. Many wounded were simply clubbed to death or bayoneted or shot where they lay in the heather. The massacre lasted through Friday and Saturday. Few escaped from the moor alive.

In Inverness, meanwhile, first the jails, then any available houses or cellars, and finally the holds of the transports lying in the Firth were filled to bursting point with Jacobite prisoners brought in by the patrols. More than 300 had been driven into the town at bayonet and sabre point on the night of the battle and these were joined every day by hundreds more, some of them men who had fought in the Prince's army and others civilians who were suspected of favouring his cause.

Among the prisoners were two or three dozen deserters from the Government forces who had gone over to the enemy. Most of these were promptly hanged on gallows erected for that purpose a mile or so outside the town, more fortunate perhaps than their companions who remained behind in the jails, herded together like animals under appalling conditions and not knowing what unpleasant fate awaited them. For forty-eight hours after the battle no food was given to the prisoners, most of whom were starving when they were brought in, and, according to the Rev. James Hay, 'it was reckoned highly criminal and very dangerous to give them anything, even water'. Finally, on the Friday, they were allowed half a pound of meal each a day, though General Hawley thought even this was too much. One of the prisoners, John Farquharson of Allargue, has described the scene: 'the wounded festering in their gore and blood, some dead bodies covered quite over with pish and dirt, and living standing to the middle of it, their groans would have pirsed a heart of stone. ...' To spare the army the trouble, beggars were employed to take away the dead. But, to save money, this was only done when there were a dozen or more bodies to be shifted. As for the prisoners on the transports in the Firth, 'numbers of them died every day, and were thrown overboard like so many dogs; and several of them before they were really dead'.

The Provost of Inverness, John Fraser, and his predecessor, John Hossack, both good Whigs, but like other inhabitants of their burgh distressed at the treatment of the wounded, decided to call on General Hawley and General Huske and urge them to mingle mercy with justice. They found General Hawley busy 'making out orders about the slaying of the wounded on the field of battle' and in no very receptive mood. 'Damn the Puppy!' he yelled impatiently as Provost Hossack hesitantly pronounced the word mercy. 'Does he pretend to dictate here?' And, amid cries of, 'Kick him out!' one of the officers present, Sir Robert Adair, spun Hossack around and kicked him smartly down the stairs and into the street. As for Provost Fraser, an officer with a party of grenadiers fetched him from his house that same evening with orders to make him muck out General Hawley's stables. In the end he succeeded in delegating the task, but thereafter Hossack and he were to be known respectively as Provost Kick and Provost Muck. Nor did Lord President Forbes himself fare much better in his appeals for clemency. 'Laws!' cried Cumberland when Forbes suggested that he should temper the laws of the country with princely mercy. 'I'll make a brigade give the laws!' And he dismissed Duncan Forbes as 'arrant Highland mad', and 'that old woman who spoke to me of humanity.'

For the rest of his stay in Scotland the Duke's policy was to be one of deliberate frightfulness designed to stamp out any remaining vestige of resistance. 'All the good we have done', he wrote to Newcastle after Culloden, 'is a little blood-letting, which has only weakened the madness, not cured it. I tremble for fear that this vile spot may still be the ruin of this island and our family.' For his own part, he trusted no one.

Even so, Cumberland was determined to do what he could. From his headquarters in Inverness orders were issued calling on all 'sheriffs, stewards and their deputies, magistrates of boroughs, Justices of the Peace, and other officers of the Law whatsoever to make diligent search for all persons of what rank soever who have been at any time in arms against His Majesty'. In every town proclamations were read out, demanding, under pain of hanging, the surrender of all arms, the laying of information against hidden rebels, and the surrender of the Young Pretender. In May 1746 the General Assembly of the Church of Scotland presented Cumberland with an obsequious address, praising his valour and conduct and referring to the 'public blessing' which his family had conferred 'on mankind'. Orders calling for the active co-operation of the Presbyterian clergy were now read before the General Assembly and before every congregation in the country. In particular, ministers were asked to furnish the names of any rebels believed to be skulking in their areas and also of any men who had been absent from their homes for long periods without adequate explanation. It was a role, which, to do them justice, some did not fancy, but others entered into with evident enthusiasm.

Other denominations fared a good deal less well. 'I have burnt two Roman Catholic meeting houses and five episcopal,' reported the staunchly Presbyterian Lord Ancram from Aberdeen, 'not forgetting two libraries of Popish and Jacobite books.'

With improving weather, the moment had arrived for Cumberland to extend the scope of his operations. Already his cavalry had been sent to the East Coast and to the Lowlands to watch for any fugitives who might be attempting to escape by sea. Two or three thousand Argyll and other Whig militiamen were getting ready to invade their hereditary enemies in Lochaber. And now in May he began to move his main body of Foot from Inverness down the Great Glen to Fort Augustus, whence, he calculated, it would be possible for him to control and terrorize the whole of the Highlands. An advance guard of three battalions left Inverness on 16 May, with Campbell militiamen scouting ahead of them. They were followed a week later by the Duke himself and eight more regular battalions, leaving General Blakeney with four battalions to hold Inverness, while Brigadier Mordaunt and three battalions went to Perth and Aberdeen. In the West General John Campbell of Mamore had begun operations in Lochaber and Appin, while the ships of the Royal Navy patrolled the West Coast, ready to intercept any French ship that sought to take off the fugitive Prince.

The news of his son's victory reached George II at St James's Palace on 25 April. It was brought to him by young Lord Bury, who had come straight from the battlefield, travelling by sea to North Berwick and thence at an unbroken gallop to London. When introduced into the royal presence, still wearing his scarlet and blue frock-coat, Bury 'behaved', the Duke of Newcastle reported back to Cumberland, 'like a Hero and a Politician' – high praise from such a quarter.

King George was much moved. 'What's become of my son?' he asked and, on being given a reassuring answer, 'Then, all's well with me,' he replied and withdrew to the far end of the room, 'unable to speak for joy'. After which, patting Bury on the back and telling Newcastle to have him given a thousand guineas, he hurried off to read his way through Prince Charles's despatch case which had been captured and by which he was fascinated. Outside, as he read, the guns were firing salutes and the bells ringing out from every steeple in London.

But a shadow clouded this moment of triumph for the House of Hanover. Though Prince Charles's army had been defeated in battle, the Prince himself was still at large and, so long as this was so, neither King nor ministers could feel themselves completely secure. From the battlefield Charles, escorted by a detachment of FitzJames's Horse, had made his way across the moor, to the ford of Faillie. There he had crossed the Water of Nairn and, dismissing his escort, had continued on his way, accompanied by Lord Elcho, Sir Thomas Sheridan, John William O'Sullivan, Captain Felix O'Neil, an Irishman in the French service newly arrived from France, and his ADC, Alexander or Sawnie MacLeod Younger of Muiravonside, whose servant Ned Burke from North Uist was to act as the party's guide.

That evening the Prince and his companions came to the house of Lord Lovat's 'doer', Fraser of Gortleg, some fifteen miles South-West of Culloden and there sought shelter. And there no doubt much to that nobleman's dismay, they found the aged Lord Lovat himself, who, having with considerable difficulty maintained his precariously balanced position until the last possible moment, had, with a decisive battle impending, thought it preferable to keep out of the way by making call on the hospitality of his clansman at Gortleg. The last thing he wanted at this juncture was to meet or, worse still, be forced to entertain the Prince.

Some weeks earlier Charles had somewhat embarrassingly expressed a desire 'to see a salmon kill'd with the rod, which he never saw before', and had hinted that the famous Beauly River might be a suitable place for this initiation. A letter written at this time by Lovat to his son, the Master, then in the North, leaves no doubt as to his feelings. 'I do not', he wrote, 'much covet that great honour at this time, as my house is quite out of order, and that I am not at home myself, nor you; however, if the Prince takes the fancy to go, you must offer to go along with him, and offer him a glass of wine and any cold meat you can get there.' 'But I fancy,' he added, 'since Cumberland is comeing so near that those fancys will be out of his head.' That had been a month before, when Charles still had some faint hopes of success. Now, without warning, Lovat suddenly found himself for the first time in the presence of his Prince, a Prince who, he now learned to his even greater dismay, had a few hours before been utterly defeated and was himself a fugitive. But even in this predicament his natural good manners and Highland sense of hospitality did not desert him.

Accounts of just what passed between the two vary. Their encounter seems to have been friendly enough, though Lovat later gave it as his opinion that 'none but a mad fool would have fought that day'. At this stage the old man no longer had any choice in the matter. His mind had been made up for him by events. Whether he liked it or not, he was now a fully fledged Jacobite, irretrievably committed to a doomed cause, with no course open to him save to seek safety in flight, leaving his lands, houses, possessions and clansmen to the mercy of Cumberland's troops.

Of the opportunities open to them the victorious Hanoverians were to take the fullest advantage. From Inverness parties of soldiers were sent out into the country round to harass the population, burn houses, drive off cattle and kill any men found bearing arms. On a fine, hot day at the end of April, a party of 400 men from the Royal Scots and Cholmondeley's under Brigadier Mordaunt set out from Inverness for Beauly where, by the banks of the Beauly River, Lord Lovat had his castle. Until a short time before, he himself had been regarded as uncommitted. Now that he had fled, the order to spare his rich estates was countermanded. Brigadier Mordaunt's instructions were to remove everything that could be moved and to destroy everything that could not, to pull down the buildings and lay waste the lands. 'All this,' wrote Volunteer Michael Hughes afterwards, 'was very cheerfully undertaken and performed. One thousand bottles of wine, three hundred bows of oatmeal, with a large quantity of malt, and a library of books to the value of four hundred pounds, was all brought to Inverness. His fine salmon weirs were destroyed; and salmon in abundance brought into the camp and divided among the soldiers.' By the time the troops had finished their work Castle Downie and the other houses and outbuildings had been burned down and reduced to rubble and everything movable carried away. For the officers and soldiers who had taken part in it the expedition had been a profitable one. By Highland standards Lovat was a rich man. There was plenty of booty. 'The traffic on the Rialto Bridge,' observed Volunteer Hughes, 'is nothing in comparison to the business that was done by our military merchants in Inverness.' Nor was Lord Lovat the only one to lose his belongings. A day or two later battalion orders contained the following entry: 'Whereas, by mistake, some soldiers took away a blue great coat with gilt buttons belonging to Brigadier Mordaunt in the plundering of Lord Lovat's house, that soldier is required to bring it to the Brigadier's Quarters and he shall receive a Crown reward.'

The Jacobites still had some 2,000 fighting men in the field and a virtually impenetrable hinterland in which to operate; with proper leadership an attempt might even now have been made to continue the campaign on guerrilla lines as a war of resistance. 'The Highlands', the Chevalier de Johnstone points out, 'are full of precipices and passes through mountains, where only one person can proceed at a time and where a thousand men can defend themselves against a hundred thousand for years; and, as it abounds with horned cattle . . . provisions would not have been wanting.' Nor had such a possibility escaped the

Duke of Cumberland, making him keener than ever to defeat the Prince's army once and for all and causing him to give orders for the neighbouring passes to be guarded immediately after Culloden. But in the event leadership was lacking. No firm plan appears to have been made by the Jacobites for a rendezvous in case of defeat, an outcome which Charles, characteristically, seems never to have contemplated. From Gortleg the Prince's aide-de-camp, Alexander or Sawnie MacLeod, had, it is true, written on the night of the battle in the following terms to Cluny Macpherson, who with his 500 Macphersons had reached the neighbourhood of Inverness only to find that the battle was already lost:

> You have [heard] no doubt ere now of the ruffle we met with this forenoon. We have suffered a good deal; but hope we shall soon pay Cumberland in his own Coin. We are to review to-morrow, at Fort Augustus, the Frasers, Camerons, Stewarts, Clanranald's, & Keppoch's people. His R.H. expects your people will be with us at furthest Friday morning. Dispatch is the more necessary that his Highness has something in view which will make ample amends for this day's ruffle. . . .
>
> We have sent an express to Lord Cromarty, Glengyle, & Barisdale, to join us by Bewly. For God's sake make haste to join us; & bring with you all the people can possibly be got together. Take care in particular of Lumisden and Sheridan, as they carry with them the Sinews of War.

But most of the surviving Jacobite troops – some 1,500 in all – had made, not for Fort Augustus, but for Ruthven in Badenoch in the belief that this was to be the rallying point. With them were Lord George Murray and most of the other Jacobite leaders, Duke William of Atholl, the Duke of Perth, Lord John Drummond, Lord Ogilvy, Lord Nairne, Stewart of Ardsheil and John Roy Stewart. On the way Lord George had encountered Cluny and his Macphersons and had invited them to cover the withdrawal of the main body. And so Sawnie MacLeod's letter was passed by Cluny to Lord George Murray, who two days later wrote on the back of it:

> Mr MacLeod's letter seems to be a state of politicks I do not comprehend, tho' I can guess it is wrote the day of the Battle; and, instead of sending any word to us, every body are ordered from Lochaber to Badenoch to cover H.R.H. from being pursued, which I wish it had taken effect. Adieu. I wish we may soon see better times.
>
> Yours, G.M.
>
> I observe the rendezvous was to be as yesterday at Fort Augustus,

227

but those who came from there last night, say H.R.H. was gone for Clanronald's country.

Clearly in Lord George's view the Prince had never intended to keep the rendezvous, if indeed he ever made one, at Ruthven, Fort Augustus or anywhere else.

But whatever his earlier intentions may have been, Charles had set out from Gortleg that same night southwards and westwards for the coast, leaving his followers a message to 'seek the means of escape as well as he can' – 'a sad and heart-breaking answer,' observes Johnstone feelingly, 'for the brave men who had sacrificed themselves for him.' Lord George Murray provides an explanation. 'Besides our defeat,' he writes, 'there was neither money nor provisions to give; so no hopes were left.' But the truth was that most if not all of them had by now lost heart.

According to Maxwell of Kirkconnel the troops who had assembled at Ruthven, 'having no orders from the Prince', simply dispersed. 'Our separation', says the Chevalier de Johnstone, 'was very affecting.... There were eternal adieus when they took leave of one another, no one being able to foresee his fate, or that his days might not be ended on the scaffold. The Highlanders sent forth screams and howlings, groaning and weeping with bitter tears at seeing their country at the mercy of the Duke of Cumberland....'

For his own part, Lord George sat down on the day after the battle and, full of pent-up bitterness gave vent to all his long-standing grievances in a lengthy, resentful letter to the Prince:

> Ruthven in Badenoch, 17the Apr. 1746
> May it please your Royal Highness, – as no person in the Kingdome ventur'd more francly in the cause then myself, and that nobody had more at stake, & in some respects not so much, I cannot but be deeply affected at our leat loss & present situation, But I declare that nixt to the safty of your R.H. person, the loss of the cause, with the present unhappy situation of my countrymen, is the only thing grieves me, for I thank God I have resolution to bear with my own and familie's ruine without a grudg.
>
> I hop, Sir, you will upon this occasion pardon me if I mention some truths which most of the Gentlemen of our army seem's sensible of.
>
> It was surely wrong to sett up the Royal Standard without having posetive assurance from his most Christian Majesty that he would assist you with all his might, and as your Royal Familie lost the Crown of these Realms by their adherence to France, the world

did (and had reason to) expect that H.M.C.M. would lay hold of the first favourable opportunity to do his utmost to restore your august Familie. As for what regards the management of your Army, we were all fully convinced that Mr O'Sullivan, whom yr R.H. trusted with the most escential things in regard to your operations, was exceedingly unfit for it, & committed gross Blunders on many occasions. He, whose business it was, did not so much as visit the ground where we were to draw up in line of Batle, and it was a fatal error yesterday to allow the enemy so fair a feild for their horse & cannon, and those walls upon their left, which made it impossible for our right to brake them, & we were expos'd both to their front & flank fire. Col. Carr can testifie that urg'd Mr. O'Sullivan to take the ground on the south side of the water of Ern, which was strong ground, & very favourable for Highlanders, & which Brigadier Stapleton and Col. Carr had visited the day before at my desire. In short, never was more improper ground for Highlanders than that where we fought. Our Atholl men & the others on the right lost Half of their Officers & men. Happy had it been for us that Mr. O'Sullivan had never got any other charge or office in our Army then the care of the Bagage & equipages, which I'm told he had been brought up to & understood. For my own part, I never seed him in time of action, neither at Gledsmoor, Falkirk, nor this last. The want of provisions was another misfortune which had the most fatal consequences. Mr. Hay, whom yr. R.H. trusted with the principle direction & superintendency of them things of leat, (& without whos orders not a Boll of Meall or one farthing of money was to be deliver'd,) has served yr R.H. most egregious ill; when I told him of the consequence of provisions, he said it was order'd, the thing was done, it would be gott &c. But yr R.H. knows the strait we were in. Had this Gentleman done his duty, which by the trust repos'd in him your R.H. had reason to expect, our ruine might have been probably prevented. The last three days (which were so critical) our army was starved, & this was a great cause of our night march proving abortive, when we possiblie might have surpris'd the enemy & defeat them at Nairn, but for want of provisions a third of our Army scater'd, & went to Inverness & other places, & those who did march went so slow that that precious time was lost. The nixt day, the fatal day, if we had got plenty of provisions, we might have not only cross'd the water of Ern, but by the strength of our position made it so dangerous for the Enemy to have atact us, that probably they would not have ventured to have done it, & by that means the rest of our Army would have had time to have join'd us, & we could have had it in our power to have atact them night or day when we pleas'd.

Mr Hay & Mr O'Sullivan had renderd themselves so odious to all the Army that they were resolved to have apply'd to your R.H. for redress if they had had time before the batle. As for my part, I never had any particular discussion with either of them; but this much I will venture to say, had our feeld of Batle been right choise, & if we had got plenty of provisions, in all Human probability we would have done by the Enemy as they have unhaply done by us.

Your R.H. knows I have no design to have continoud in the Army, even if things had succeeded, particularly leatly when I return'd from Atholl, but my Friends told me, & perswaded me, that it would be a prejudice to the cause at that juncture. I hope your R.H. will now accept of my dimission, and whatever commands you have for me in any other station you will please honour me with them, being with great zeal, Sir,

Yr R.H.'s most Dutyfull & faithfull Humble Servant,

GEORGE MURRAY

I have desire'd Mr Sheridan to leave £500 of the money he has with him with Clunie, for the use of many who are in want. We will wait for your R.H.'s directions for that and other things.

The Prince seems to have received Lord George's letter only some weeks later. Characteristically, he never forgave him for it and it effectively put an end to all communication between the two men.

Still seriously ill, Charles's former Secretary, John Murray of Broughton, had missed the battle of Culloden. On learning of the Prince's defeat, he had, like the Prince, set out for the West Coast, in the firm hope of joining him there, being carried for some of the way in a litter. On reaching Invergarry, he found the Duke of Perth, 'quite wore out with fatigue'; and not long after, on the shores of Loch Arkaig, Lochiel who had been carried home badly wounded to Achnacarry by devoted clansmen. Likewise the portly Stewart of Ardsheil and the aged Lord Lovat, now, willy-nilly himself a fugitive.

To this forlorn little group came, not long after, the news that the Prince was bound for the Outer Isles. Even so it was suggested that an attempt should be made to rally a force of clansmen who would 'keep the hills' and continue to resist the enemy. Lochiel could still put several hundred Camerons in the field. Lovat, while 'regretting that his age and infirmitys would not permitt him to Share either of the honour or the danger of the field', promised that 'his Son should bring them four hundred Frasers as his Quota'. The others there also promised to do what they could and a date was fixed for 'a Randevouse' a little to the south of Loch Arkaig.

The result was disappointing. 'When Lochiel and the other gentlemen repaired to the place, they did not find above 200 Camerons and a few M'Leans with 200 Macdonalds under Barrisdale, so difficult was it to persuade the Country people that the only method to procure their own and their familys safetys was to keep them together in a body.' Worse still, after they had waited two more days for reinforcements, 'to their great Surprise as many deserted as came in'. As for the Master of Lovat, he 'was never so much as heard of', while MacDonell of Lochgarry 'brought about 100 in place of 400 he had engaged for'. And so in the end those who had assembled simply dispersed and the project, such as it was, was abandoned.

Meanwhile, following a sharp but successful engagement with three British men-of-war, two French privateers, the *Mars* and the *Bellona*, had appeared off Arisaig, bringing with them rather belatedly 35,000 louis d'or for the support of the rising. Of this large sum Murray of Broughton, who by now was feeling better, set aside 5,000 for current expenses and then buried the rest at two different points near Loch Arkaig, where it was to serve for years as a source of constant intrigue and strife among Jacobite exiles. With other stores the two ships had brought a good deal of brandy, which provided welcome relief for those who were staying behind. While those born freebooters, Coll MacDonell of Barisdale and his men, made off with everything they could lay hands on, the Macleans took back with them to Mull 'one of the French long boats loaded with brandy and some cash'. Finally, to add to the confusion, a thoughtless Highlander let the lighted dottle from his pipe fall into a barrel of gunpowder, blowing himself to bits and starting a story that the Royal Navy had returned to the attack.

When they left again for France, the *Mars* and the *Bellona* took with them Lord Elcho, old Sir Thomas Sheridan, the Duke of Perth, 'then in dying condition' (he in fact died before reaching France), and his brother and successor Lord John Drummond. Though 'scarce able to stand upon his legs', Lochiel decided to remain where he was for the time being, feeling that, having called out his clan, it would be dishonourable on his part to abandon them. John Murray of Broughton agreed to stay behind with him.

After consulting further with Lochiel and bidding farewell to his beautiful young wife ('then bigg with child', and whom he optimistically advised to throw herself on the mercy of the new Commander-in-Chief Lord Albemarle) Murray set out across Scotland in the hope of eventually reaching the East Coast and chartering a ship to carry Lochiel and himself to Holland. His journey was a hard one. Finally, 'a party of dragoons being at his own house', he managed, a sick and hunted man, to reach after innumerable adventures his sister's house at Polmood in Peebles-shire and there at two in the morning, 'quite overcome with fatigue', went to bed. Less than three hours later he 'was wakd: the Dragoons at the Gate'.

For the Government, Murray was a rich prize. From Polmood he was immediately rushed to Edinburgh and there examined by Andrew Fletcher, the Lord Justice Clerk, who after some preliminary interrogations consigned him to the Castle. A couple of weeks later he was despatched in a coach with an escort of dragoons to London for imprisonment in the Tower, but intercepted en route by Fletcher, and under further interrogation finally weakened and in the words of Fletcher's report to the Duke of Newcastle 'said that if he could have any Hopes given him, he would discover all he Knew'.

While in the Tower, Murray, in the hope of saving his skin, did what he had promised Andrew Fletcher he would do. Though in practice his disclosures did little damage to anyone save possibly Lord Lovat, who was already heavily compromised, he nevertheless thus ensured that he would go down to history, not as one who had played an active and in some ways creditable role in the rising, but as 'Mr Evidence Murray', the Jacobite Judas. After a period of imprisonment, during which his pretty wife left him, he was released by the Government with a small pension, dying in Hertfordshire some thirty years later.

Others from the little group round the Prince were also in due course to shift their allegiance. Hardly had he reached France than Lord Elcho for one sat down to write first to the Duke of Argyll and then to the Lord Justice Clerk, assuring them of his deep loyalty to King George and begging them, unavailingly as it turned out, to take him under their protection and let him 'come home'. Likewise, not many months later we find Aeneas MacDonald, the banker, writing to the Duke of Newcastle, expressing at some length his new-found detestation of the Jacobite movement and his willingness 'to give you all the intelligence that for the future I shall be able to gather att the French Court of such or any other attempts and I dare be bold to say there is not one man belonging to the Isle of Brittain so capable of serving your Grace that way as I am'.

CHAPTER FOURTEEN

From Gortleg the Prince and his companions set out once more. Stopping briefly at Fort Augustus, where they found no one, then crossing the River Oich near Aberchalder and, following the western shore of Loch Oich, they reached Invergarry in the early hours of the morning. There they found the castle deserted, 'without meat, drink, fire or candle, except some fire-sticks'. Old Glengarry, it appeared, had gone to Inverness to try to make his peace with Cumberland; his elder son, Alastair, was a prisoner; and young Angus, who had made the Prince welcome on his earlier visit, now lay in the graveyard at Falkirk.

After breakfasting off two salmon, 'very savoury and acceptable', taken from the nets in the river, and snatching a few hours' sleep, the Prince, who had exchanged his tartan doublet for Ned Burke's shabby old coat, bid his other companions farewell. Accompanied by O'Sullivan, O'Neil, Sawnie MacLeod and Ned Burke, he set out for the house of Donald Cameron of Glen Pean, twenty-four miles away to the West at the head of Loch Arkaig. There they slept the night. Next afternoon, being still without news and seeing no signs of pursuit, they made their way 'by the cruelst road yt cou'd be seen' on foot across the hills to Glen Morar, where in the end they found shelter in 'a small sheal house near a wood'.

The following night, after resting all the day in the nearby wood, Charles and his companions moved off again, and at six on the morning of the 20 April reached Arisaig, where he had spent some days when he first landed and where he again took up his quarters at the house of Angus MacDonald of Borrodale. There was enough to eat and on arrival he had been provided with 'a suite of new Highland cloaths from Angus MacDonald of Borrodale's spouse, the better to disguise

233

him and to make him pass for one of the country'. With him, in addition to O'Sullivan, were Hay of Restalrig, Coll Ban MacDonell of Barisdale, Father Allan MacDonald, a Catholic priest who had been with his clan as chaplain, and a number of other MacDonalds, including young Clanranald. But, though there was as yet no sign of any pursuit, Borrodale was not considered safe to remain in. While Barisdale and young Clanranald urged him to skulk in the woods until the situation became clearer, O'Sullivan and Father MacDonald were in favour of his escaping to the islands. In the end it was the latter view that prevailed.

It remained Charles's firm purpose to reach France as soon as he could. Before leaving Borrodale, he addressed to the chiefs who had supported him a letter which in all probability never reached them. 'I can,' he wrote, 'at present do little for you on this side the water ... whereas by my going into France instantly, however dangerous it be, I will certainly engage the French Court either to assist us effectually and powerfully, or at least to procure such terms as you would not obtain otherways.' And he called on the Almighty to bless and direct them. 'Letter to ye Chiefs on parting from Scotland', he wrote across the back of it. But the moment for his final departure had not yet come.

Strangely enough, the Prince's own inclination at this stage was to cross to Skye and there throw himself on the mercy of MacLeod of MacLeod and Sir Alexander MacDonald of Sleat, both of whom, though once reputedly Jacobites, had since the start of the rising consistently and actively supported the Hanoverian cause. From this lunatic project he was in the end dissuaded by one Donald MacLeod from Galtrigal in Skye, whom he met secretly 'in a wood all alone'. As a Skyeman, Donald had no illusions as to the attitude or conduct of the two chiefs in question, and stoutly declined to deliver any messages to them. 'Na,' he said to the Prince, 'you mauna do't.' Both chiefs, he declared, had 'played the rogue to him altogether' and already had men out searching for him. The sooner he put himself out of their reach by leaving Borrodale the better. And so, in the end, Charles changed his mind. 'I hear, Donald,' he said, 'that you are a good pilot and you know this coast well, and therefore, I hope you can carry me safely through the islands, where I may look for more safety than I can here.' Having agreed, Donald managed to find a stout eight-oared boat which had once belonged to Borrodale's son John, killed at Culloden. And on 26 April 'they got on board, in the twilight of the evening' from 'the very spot of ground' on the shore of Lochnanuagh where Charles had first landed just nine months earlier. With Charles went O'Sullivan, Felix O'Neil, Father Allan MacDonald and, 'for pilot managing the helm', Donald MacLeod himself. The oarsmen were Ned Burke, Roderick

234

MacCasgill, John MacDonald, Duncan Roy, Alexander MacDonald and Donald's own son Murdoch, a lad of fifteen who, having run away from Inverness Grammar School and provided himself with pistol, claymore and dirk had 'took his chance in the field of Culloden battle', afterwards 'fleeing to the west coast where he found his father'.

Donald had not wished to set out that night, 'for it would certainly be a storm'. But Charles, as usual impatient, 'was positive to set out directly without loss of time', and, scoffing at Donald's fears, insisted they should start. 'All his lifetime a sea-faring man upon the coast of Scotland', Donald, not surprisingly, had been right. 'A most violent tempest arose, greater than any Donald MacLeod had ever been trysted with before.' The Prince now told Donald to steer for the shore. 'I had rather', he added, 'face cannons and muskets, than be in such a storm as this.' But, having once started, Donald refused to go back. 'Since we are here,' he said, 'we have nothing for it but, under God, to set out to sea directly. Is it not as good for us to be drowned in clear water, as to be dashed in pieces upon a rock, and to be drowned too?' After which their voyage across the dark, stormy waters of the Minch continued 'in hush and silence; not one word more among them' with neither pump, compass nor lantern.

Moidart, when Charles first landed there, had been remote enough. Now, on the mainland, with his pursuers hard on his heels, it could only have been a matter of time before they caught up with him. In the Outer Isles, sixty miles away across the stormy waters of the Minch, he would, when once there, be in another world.

The name Hebrides is said to signify Islands on the Edge of the Sea, half way, as it were, to Tir nan Og, the mythical Land of Eternal Youth which, we know, lies somewhere just beyond the sunset. They consist of a double line of several hundred islands, large and small, the Inner and the Outer Hebrides, stretching for two or three hundred miles down the west coast of northern Scotland, like two submerged mountain ranges separated from each other by the Minch, as though by a deep valley.

Of their original inhabitants little is known. More than three thousand years ago came the Celts and then, nearly two thousand years after that, the Norsemen, first as raiders, then as settlers and rulers. Four hundred years on they were followed by great Somerled, of mixed Celtic and Norse race, and his descendants, the MacDonald Lords of the Isles, who for another two centuries or so ruled in practice as independent sovereigns until in the end subdued and forfeited by the Scottish crown.

Even now the Outer Isles retain much of their remoteness and of the age-old Celtic culture and folklore that go with it. Here Gaelic still flourishes as a living language. In Charles's day it was universally spoken and English had made little, if any impact. Here the Reformation, too, had been slow to take effect. Barra and South Uist were (and still are) Catholic islands. Not until late in the eighteenth century did Protestantism reach North Uist and Benbecula.

While Skye, Mull and the Inner Hebrides are in the main mountainous, continuing, as it were, the great ranges of the Highland mainland, the Outer Isles, the Long Island, as they are known, are inclined to be low-lying and flat, marked here and there by no more than an occasional hill or ridge and forming a nearly continuous chain. While their eastern coastline is rocky and much indented, to the west, facing the Atlantic, lie open beaches with long stretches of white sand over which the great seas break ceaselessly. In the Highlands and in the Inner Isles mist and clouds gather easily in the high hills and deep glens. In the Outer Isles the relative absence of these gives the light an unusual luminous quality to be found in few other parts of the world.

Living in such natural surroundings, so remote from the less attractive features of modern civilization, with ancient traditions handed down from generation to generation, it is perhaps not surprising that the Islanders themselves possess, as they possessed in Prince Charlie's day, characteristics not readily discoverable elsewhere. In them the native ferocity of any Norse forebears is generously tempered by the subtler, more poetic, more spiritual, if sometimes less foursquare qualities of the Celt, by a natural courtesy and kindness, an instinctive hospitality which makes them by and large some of the friendliest and most agreeable people in the world.

It was first light on 27 April when Charles and his companions at long last sighted land and, 'with great difficulty, for the storm was still raging', brought their boat ashore in the secluded creek of Barra na Luinge at Rossinish near the north-eastern point of the flat, low-lying island of Benbecula, sandwiched in between North and South Uist. At Rossinish they took shelter in an empty boat. A fire of driftwood was lit and an old sail spread on the ground for Charles 'who was very well pleased with it, and slept soundly'. 'The Prince', said Donald afterwards, 'bore up most surprisingly, and never wanted spirits.'

Charles and his companions were to spend a couple of days safely hidden on the sandy little peninsula of Rossinish amid a watery labyrinth of creeks and lochs and islets, far from any road or village. Here, in Benbecula, they were on the territory of MacDonald of Clanranald, whose son had joined the Prince as soon as he landed and

236

fought with his clan throughout the campaign, though he himself had stayed at home. His house, Nunton, lay some six miles away on the far side of the island. Once, as its name indicates, a nunnery, Nunton or Baille nan Caillach was a sizeable laird's house, looking out westwards across the grassy *machair* to where the Atlantic breakers thundered on the white, sandy shore. The news that a ship had landed was brought to Clanranald by one of his herds, while he was at dinner with his children's tutor Neil MacEachain, who had been trained for the priesthood at Douai, and with the Reverend John Macaulay, Church of Scotland parish minister of South Uist and grandfather-to-be of Lord Macaulay, the historian.

In such times, the arrival of a boatload of strangers on the island was an important event and Old Clanranald at once despatched a messenger to investigate further. So, on his own account, did the Reverend John, who, being by nature inquisitive and, like his illustrious descendant, a zealous Whig, privately sent 'one of his auditors ... to learn what they were, from whence they came and where they were bound for'. A lonely Protestant among Papists, he no doubt felt it his duty to protect his own and the Government's interests. By cunningly pretending to come from Clanranald himself his emissary duly managed to elicit the startling news that Prince Charles himself was one of the party and that it was his intention to go to Stornoway as soon as the weather improved, in search of a ship to take him to France. 'Judging that he could not meet with a better opportunity to show his zeal and affection for the government' and no doubt mindful of the price of £30,000 on the Prince's head, the Rev. John now immediately sent a message to his father, the Rev. Aulay MacAulay, Minister of Harris, informing him of Charles's movements and asking him to get into touch with the Rev. Colin Mackenzie, 'established minister at Stornoway', and arrange through him with the renegade Lord Fortrose's factor to have the Prince arrested as soon as he landed there.

Old Clanranald meanwhile, having likewise learnt of the Prince's arrival, had himself hurried off with Neil MacEachain to Rossinish, where, after some discussion, it was agreed that the safest way to account for the party's arrival was to put about the story that they were the crew of a merchant ship from the Orkneys, wrecked off the Isle of Tiree and now on their way home.

Already ships of the Royal Navy were scouring the waters of the Minch in search of the Prince, which made it dangerous for them to travel by day. Accordingly, that evening, 29 April, at about six o'clock, the Prince and his companions, having taken leave of Clanranald, put out to sea again in their boat and, with Donald MacLeod once more at the helm, set course for Stornoway. An hour or two before daybreak, 'being all cold and hungry', they went ashore on Scalpa or Eilean Glas, a bleak, rocky little island at the entrance to East Loch Tarbert, between Harris and Lewis. There they remained four nights, being made welcome by the tenant of Scalpa, one Donald Campbell, who was a friend of Donald MacLeod.

As a Campbell, their host, though married to a Macdonald, was, on the face of it, unlikely to be a Jacobite. It was not long before his reliability was severely put to the test. For now, without warning, a boat full of armed men, led by the Rev. Aulay MacAulay in person, landed on Scalpa 'with a determined resolution to seize the Chevalier and secure the bribe offered by the Government'. But, when approached by Mr MacAulay, Donald, deeply aware as a Highlander of his duty as a host, 'scorned the bribe and expostulated much against the infamous attempt', indignantly informing the reverend gentleman 'that he himself would fall in his cause, rather than give up the man that intrusted him with his life, or entail shame on his posterity'. The Prince and his companions had, we are told, been 'ready to give the assailants a hot reception, had they approached; but they sneaked off from the island, ashamed, and disappointed at the loss of the money, which they already had devoured in their thoughts, and divided to every man in his due proportion'.

Next day Donald MacLeod was sent on to Stornoway in a small boat, borrowed from Donald Campbell, to try to hire a suitable vessel to take Charles to France. Three days later, on hearing that a suitable vessel had been found, Charles and his companions set out in their turn for Stornoway, travelling partly by sea and partly on foot through, what O'Sullivan calls 'the wildest contry in the universe'. But there was an unpleasant surprise waiting for them. For, when next day Donald MacLeod went back to Stornoway 'to get things in readiness', he was alarmed, on entering the town, to find a drum being beaten and large numbers of armed men forming up in front of the principal inn. These were Lord Fortrose's Mackenzies. Making his way into the room 'where the gentlemen were that had taken upon themselves the rank of officers', he innocently enquired what was happening. In reply, they 'gave him very abusive language', cursing him up and down and accusing him of having brought the Prince to Lewis with an army of 500 men. This, they said, exposed them to the 'hazard of losing both their cattle and their lives, as they heard the Prince was come with a full resolution to force a vessel from Stornoway'. The story had clearly lost nothing in the telling.

Donald now admitted (if indeed he had not, in his cups, done so already) that the Prince was indeed on the island. But with only two companions, 'and when I am there I make the third'. The secret, in so far as it had ever been one, was out. The tone of the discussion having now become quieter, the assembled Mackenzies in the end assured Donald that they 'had no intention to do the Prince the smallest hurt, or to meddle with him at present in any shape'. They were just 'mighty desirous he might leave them and go to the continent, or anywhere else he should think most convenient', though when Donald asked them to find him a pilot, his request was refused, nor would the master of the ship he had chartered now hold to his bargain.

And so, next morning, 6 May, the storm having somewhat abated, they started off again for Scalpa in the small boat Donald MacLeod had borrowed from Donald Campbell. But they had hardly gone any distance when they sighted what were undoubtedly some enemy warships and thought it wiser to land on a small island, where they spent the next four days living in a 'low pityful hut', ('like a pig-sty', says O'Sullivan).

Embarking on 10 May and keeping Donald Campbell's boat, 'because it was such a fine, light, swift sailing thing', they set out again southwards, sailing and rowing along the coast towards Benbecula. They had not gone far, however, when they sighted another enemy warship. This was HMS *Furness*, commanded by Captain John Fergussone RN, who at once gave chase. Fortunately for them, Donald Campbell's light boat drew less water than the warship. Putting on all the sail he could and bidding his six remaining oarsmen get their oars out as well, Donald MacLeod made straight for the shoal water off Rodel Point. The *Furness* tried to head him off, but by this time the tide was ebbing. Fergussone could not hope to follow him amid the rocky islets of the Sound of Harris, and in the end turned away.

Donald next set course for Lochmaddy in North Uist, only to find another Government frigate awaiting them. Again they took to their oars spending the night at sea off the broken coastline of North Uist with nothing to eat but *drammach*, oatmeal mixed with seawater, of which the Prince, says Donald MacLeod, ate 'very heartily'. Next morning, they landed in a regular gale on a little island in Loch Uskavagh or, as it is sometimes called, Loch Wiskaway, on Benbecula, and took shelter in 'a poor grass-keeper's bothy or hut'. From Loch Wiskaway Charles sent one of the boatmen to find Old Clanranald, who next day came to visit him himself, bringing him some clean clothes which he badly needed. 'When the Prince got on his Highland cloaths,' we are told 'he was quite another man. "Now," says he, leping, "I only want the itch to be a compleat highlander." ' Clanranald also brought his children's tutor, Neil MacEachain, to serve them as a guide.

From where they had landed, Neil now led them across country to a near-perfect hiding place in Glen Corradale in South Uist where the twin heights of Hekla and Benmore rise steeply on either side of a secluded inlet in the rocky coastline. As anyone who has been there will realize, it is equally difficult to reach by land or by sea. Conducted by Neil to a bothy which was near the shore, but completely invisible from the sea, Charles 'seemed extraordinary well pleased with the house, which he swore look'd like a palace in comparison of the abominable hole they had lately left'. Sitting that evening on a turf seat, he ate a supper of 'gradan bread-and-cheese and goat's milk, upon which he fed very hearty'. Afterwards he smoked a clay pipe and slept on a bed of heather and green rushes until the following mid-day. Next day Clanranald sent him wine and beer 'and a little Cassette' containing four shirts, some stockings, a pair of shoes and 'a Silver cover & a silver cup'.

Charles spent three weeks at Corradale. With the sea in front of him and the high hills at his back, he was reasonably safe against surprise and well placed to beat a rapid retreat in case of need. While he was there, he 'diverted and maintained himself with hunting and fishing', catching lyth with a hand line from a small boat and 'papping down perhaps dozens in a day of muir cocks and hens with which this place abounds; for he is most dextrous at shooting all kinds of fowl upon wing, scarce ever making a miss'.

Much of his time in Glen Corradale he spent talking to Neil Mac-Eachain, who having trained for the priesthood at Douai, knew France and the French and was of much the same age as he was. They found plenty to talk about. 'His ordinary conversation,' says Neil of the Prince, 'was talking of the army and of the battle of Culloden, and the highland chieftains whose lamentable case he deplored very much.' He told Neil how his own horse had been shot under him. Afterwards their talk 'rowlled upon the order of battle' and how he was forced to condescend to give the right hand to the Atholl-men and others, which he knew to be the MacDonald's right, and, conscious that here he was among MacDonalds, he went on to do 'a great deal of justice and honour to the Mack Donalds'. In talking of the battle, says Neil, he 'blamed always my Lord George Murray as being the only instrument in loseing the battle' and attributed the defeat 'to his infidelity, roguery and treachery'. Every day Charles spent much time watching the coast and persuading himself that the Government ships which he could see patrolling it belonged, not to the British, but to the French navy.

In Glen Corradale Charles remained remarkably well and cheerful. 'It was wonderfull,' writes Neil, 'how he preserved his health all the time. ... He had always a good appetite and could eat any meat that came in his way. . . . He took care to warm his stomach every morning with a hearty bumper of brandy, of which he always drank a vast deal; for he was seen to drink a whole bottle of a day without being in the least concerned.' And another of his companions at this time describes how 'the Prince (when resting himself) used to sit on a fail-sunk [an earthen seat], having some fog and plaids under him, and would step into a by-chamber, which served as a pantry, and (when he stood in need of it) put the bottle of brandy or whiskie to his head and take his dram without ceremony'. He also seems to have taken periodic doses of 'traicle' of which O'Sullivan kept 'a little pot' for medicinal purposes and by which he set great store. Sometimes, Neil tells us, Charles had 'melancholy fits', but 'at other times he was so hearty and merry, that he danced for a whole hour together, having no other musick but some highland reel which he whistled as he tripped along'. On fine days he would sit on a stone in front of the house looking into the sun, and when his companions tried to stop him, 'he ordered them to pack about their business, that he knew what was good for him better than they could describe, that the sun did him all the good in the world'.

Hugh MacDonald of Baleshare, whose sister was married to Donald Campbell, who had befriended them on Scalpa, has left a lively account of a visit he paid to Charles at Corradale at this time:

His dress was then a tartan short-coat and vest of the same, got from Lady Clananrald; his nightcap all patched with soot-drops; his shirt, hands, and face, patched with the same; a short kilt, tartan hose, and Highland brogues; his upper coat being English cloth.

He called for a dram, being the first article of a Highland entertainment; which being over, he called for meat. There was about a half-stone of butter laid on a timber plate, and near a leg of beef laid on a chest before us, all patched with soot-drops, notwithstanding its being washed *toties quoties*. As we had done, who entered the hut but Boisdale, who seemed to be a very welcome guest to the Young Gentleman, as they had been together above once before. Boisdale then told him there was a party come to Barra in suit of him. He asked what they were. Boisdale said they were MacDonalds and MacLeods. He then said he was not the least concerned, as they were Highlanders. . . . Then we began with our bowl, frank and free.

As we were turning merry, we were turning more free. At last I starts the question if his highness would take it amiss if I should tell him the greatest objections against him in Great Britain. He said not. I told that popery and arbitrary government were the two chiefest. He said it was only bad constructions his enemies put on't. 'Do you know, Mr MacDonald,' he says, 'what religion are all the princes in Europe of?' I told him I imagined they were of the same established religion of the nations they lived in. He told me then they had little or no religion at all. Boisdale then told him that his predecessor, Donald Clanranald, had fought seven set battles for his; yet, after the Restoration, he was not owned by King Charles at Court. The Prince said: 'Boisdale, don't be rubbing up old sores, for if I came home, the case would be otherwise with me'. I then says to him that, notwithstanding of what freedom we enjoyed there with him, we could have no access to him if he was settled at London; and [he] told us then, if he had never so much ado, he'd be one night merry with his Highland friends. We continued this drinking for three days and three nights. He still had the better of us, and even of Boisdale himself, notwithstanding his being able as a bowlsman, I daresay, as any in Scotland.

Returning at this stage, Neil MacEachain, who had been 'straggling every day about the neighbouring towns for intelligence', found the Prince's visitors 'very much disordered by the foregoing night's carouse, while his royal highness was the only one who was able to take care of the rest, in heaping them with plaids, and at the same time merrily sung the De Profundis for the rest of their souls'.

The news Neil brought was, however, calculated to bring the most drunken party to their senses: not just patrols, but large bodies of enemy troops were now searching the neighbouring islands for the Prince 'so that it seemed next to a miracle to have been able to escape'. There was no time to be lost. At once the whole party, 'committing themselves to Providence', climbed back into their boat and set off again the same night in the direction of Benbecula. Next morning, at first light, they landed on 'a desert island about three miles from Roshiness', and there lay up for some days. After which the Prince, taking with him only O'Neill and a guide, set out again for Rossinish.

From Rossinish the Prince and O'Neill seem somehow to have made contact with Lady Clanranald. But by this time the redcoats and militia were everywhere. In the end, Donald MacLeod and O'Sullivan, hearing of their predicament, crossed over to Rossinish and took them off under cover of darkness. But, as they 'rowed and sailed with vigour' in a southerly direction, they suddenly sighted two English men-of-war while, to make matters worse, 'a violent storm and a very heavy rain' drove them back on shore a couple of miles north of Corradale.

Next day, 13 June, warned of more enemy troops only two miles

Lord George Murray

Clementina Walkinshaw and (*opposite*) Prince Charles's natural daughter, Charlotte, Duchess of Albany

Flora Macdonald

Hôtel de Guéméné, Place des Vosges

Louise, Duchesse de Montbazon

Louise of Stolberg, wife of Prince Charles

Charles Edward Stuart, circa 1785

away, they again put to sea, making this time for Loch Boisdale, where they hoped to obtain help and advice from MacDonald of Boisdale, who was Clanranald's half-brother. But here things were no better. Sighting no less than fifteen enemy sail off shore and realizing that at the same time enemy troops were closing in on them on land, they were obliged to stay all day in a narrow creek and it was not until nightfall that they got into Loch Boisdale. The approach of two more warships, which Donald MacLeod took to be French, gave them a moment of hope, but it was clear that they, too, were English. With three others Charles took to the hills, while the boatmen hurriedly took their boat out of the creek 'and steered up the loch'. The English ships did not, however, enter the loch, and that night the fugitives met again by the boat and spent the next two nights in the open by the shore with nothing to eat.

The Prince now learned to his dismay that MacDonald of Boisdale had been captured. This was a serious blow. Though, when he first landed on Eriskay, Boisdale had done his best to discourage the Prince from his enterprise and advised him to 'go home', he had of recent weeks done everything he could to help him and shield him from danger, sending him secret messages and warning him of the approach of enemy troops.

Charles nevertheless now established himself on 'Stialay, a small island near the entry of Loch Boystile, within three long miles of Boystile's house'. 'It rained cruelle,' writes O'Sullivan, 'there was not a house within a mile of us, no shelter but a Rock, when the thyed was out, we got under rocks where we got some heather, tho' wet, we made use of it; we durst not set up our seal for fear of being seen from the mountains. When the tyed came in we were obliged to retir & be exposed all night long to the rain. ... We were never a day or night without rain. The Prince was in a terrible condition, his legs & thys cut all over from the bryers; the mitches or flys, wch are terrible in yt contry, devored him & made him scratch those scars, wch made him appear as if he was cover'd with ulsers.' From Stialay, the Prince sent Neil MacEachain by night to ask Lady Boisdale, failing her husband, for food – meat, if possible – and help. Called from her bed at midnight, Lady Boisdale responded nobly and, deploring 'the miserable conditions his royal highness was in', sent him by Neil such provisions as she could find.

The fugitives' situation was by now desperate. The two men-of-war lying off the mouth of Loch Boisdale effectively cut off their retreat by sea. On land about 500 redcoats and militia were within a mile and a half of them, all searching for them. And now from Lady Boisdale came news that Captain Caroline Scott and a detachment of regular troops had landed on Barra with the object of joining up with the Skye militia in South Uist. 'We see,' writes O'Sullivan, 'a man running down the hill to us as fast as it was possible to go. We go to meet him, judging there must be something extraordinary, as far as he cou'd see us, he makes a sign to us to go off, lookelly our tente was just down ... this man tells that all the boats of the seven Men of War were coming towards the land, full of soldiers, that they were not landed when he parted from Boisdels house, & that he did not doubt but they were informed of the place where the Prince was.'

There was not a minute to be lost. In a panic the boatmen were going to leave the provisions behind, but Charles, who had steady nerves and a healthy appetite, would not hear of this. ''A-Gad,' he said, 'they shall never say that we were so pressed that we abandoned our meat', and helped himself to 'a quarter of mutton and a bowl of meal'. Though now they could hear shooting, they still managed to reach the head of the loch in safety.

As old Donald MacLeod very sensibly put it, 'all choices were bad', and in the end it was decided that the Prince's party should break up, Felix O'Neil remaining with Charles, the others shifting for themselves. At this moment a boatman, whom they had sent to find out more about Captain Scott's movements, came back with the news that Lady Boisdale, her step-daughter and all their servants 'were tied neck and heel in one house, in order to extort a confession from them of the Prince's being in the country'. Their silver and other possessions the soldiers were carrying off and loading them into their boats.

Charles now took leave of O'Sullivan and old Donald MacLeod. The boat, Donald Campbell's 'fine, light, swift-sailing' boat, which had served them so well, they scuttled. Then, with tears and embraces and assurances that 'we will all joyn again', Charles 'went off with O'Neil & one of the boat men yt knew the contry, wth as soar a heart as those he left, tho' it did not appear so much'. 'It was', says O'Sullivan, 'a most dismal sight to see Sullivan in the Prince's arms; the saillors hears Sullivan crying & see the Prince go off, they all cry & roar & looks upon the Prince as lost.'

After many more adventures, O'Sullivan, no longer as plump and well fed as when he started, reached France, when James at once knighted him. Ned Burke made his way back to Edinburgh and there quietly resumed his employment as a sedan-carrier. Old Donald MacLeod, on the other hand, was taken prisoner not many days later on Benbecula by young Allan MacDonald of Sleat, taken on board the *Furness* and brought before General John Campbell of Mamore, who was cruising off the islands with Captain Fergussone. On being asked by the General whether he had been with the Young Pretender, 'Yes,' replied Donald, 'I was along with the young gentleman and I winna deny it.' 'Do you know,' enquired the General, 'what money was upon that man's head? – no less a sum than *thirty thousand pounds sterling*, which would have made you and all your children after you happy for ever!' 'What then?' replied Donald, 'thirty thousand pounds! – though I had gotten't, I could not have enjoyed it eight-and-forty hours. Conscience would have gotten up upon me: that money could not have kept it down. And though I could have gotten all England and Scotland for my pains, I would not allowed a hair of his body to be touched, if I could help it!'

'I will not say,' replied General Campbell, who by the standards of the day was a humane man, 'that you are wrong.'

CHAPTER FIFTEEN

Leaving the others on the shores of Loch Boisdale, the Prince and Felix
O'Neil now set out across the moor with Neil MacEachain as their
guide and, making for the top of the nearest hill, lay up there all day,
looking out across the low-lying country of South Uist from sea to sea.
At sunset, after eating some bread and cheese, they started off again,
heading north. It was the night of 20 June – a moonlit night and in
these latitudes a very short one.

They were making for Milton, a small estate on the west side of
South Uist, lying between the hills and the sea, and belonging to young
Angus MacDonald of Milton, a tacksman of Clanranald's. Keeping
house for Angus and caring for his cattle at a summer sheiling on
Sheaval, the hill above Milton, was his sister Fionnghal or Flora, a
'well-shaped' girl of twenty-four, related to Neil MacEachain. Reaching
Ormaclett at about midnight the three men made their way to the
sheiling.

Leaving the Prince 'at a little distance off', Neil MacEachain and
O'Neil went in and, wakening Flora, asked her whether she expected
any militia to come that way the following day. Not that day, she
replied, but the next. O'Neil then told her he had brought a friend to
see her. At which, Flora, being well informed, asked 'with some
emotion' whether it was the Prince. O'Neil said it was and whistled.
Whereupon Flora barely had time to 'throw on some of her cloaths'
before the Prince 'with his baggage on his back, was at the door, and
saluted her very kindly'. She 'brought to him a part of the best cheer
she had; among the rest was a large bowl of cream, of which he took
two or three hearty go-downs and his fellow-travellers swallowed the
rest'.

This was no chance visit. Flora's three callers had a proposition to put to her. Her own father, Ranald MacDonald of Milton, had died when she was still a child and her mother had later married Hugh MacDonald of Armadale in Skye, now a captain in one of the Government's Independent Companies, at present stationed in Benbecula. But in that time of conflicting loyalties the fact that he happened to be serving in a Government unit did not necessarily mean that Armadale was not, like most others of his clan, to a greater or lesser extent, a Jacobite in sympathy. Indeed, only a few days before this he had sent a message to Charles through 'one of the country gentlemen in whom he could repose a good deal of trust', informing him that, if he would take the advice of one who, 'though an enemy in appearance', was 'yet a sure friend in his heart', it might be possible to find means of sending him to the Isle of Skye, where, it appeared, he could, however improbably, expect help from Lady Margaret MacDonald of Sleat, daughter of Lord Eglinton and the much younger second wife of that same Sir Alexander MacDonald, on whose support Charles had counted in vain.

Sir Alexander himself, who commanded the Independent Companies in which Armadale was serving, happened at the moment to be conveniently absent, ingratiating himself with the Duke of Cumberland at Fort Augustus. Flora was a friend and protégée of Lady Margaret's, whose Jacobite sympathies were well known to her intimates, and what her stepfather Hugh now proposed was that she should 'convey' the Prince to Skye, disguised in woman's clothes as her maid and using a pass with which he, as a Militia officer, could provide her. The ostensible purpose of her journey would be to visit her mother in Skye. This scheme, says Neil MacEachain, had 'pleased the Prince mightely and he seemed very anxious to see it put in execution'. It only remained to put the idea to Flora. According to Neil's own account, it was he who 'discovered to her her stepfather's proposal and ask'd whether she was willing to run the risque', adding that she 'joyfully accepted the offer without the least hesitation'. Flora herself speaks however of her 'many qualms and objections' to the project which she at first rejected as 'fantastical and dangerous', while O'Neil, who claims that he in fact was the spokesman, records that she at first refused, though 'with the greatest respect and loyalty', on the grounds that it might 'be the instrument' of her friend Sir Alexander MacDonald's 'ruins' and might also give rise to gossip, but 'at length acquiesced, after the Prince had told her the sense he would always retain of so conspicuous a service' and O'Neil himself had, or so he says, thrown in a proposal of marriage. Be this as it may, Flora in the end agreed and, having first fixed a rendezvous with her at Rossinish

247

Point on the East coast of Benbecula, the Prince and his two companions, greatly relieved, set out together across the hills towards Glen Corradale. At first light they found themselves on the slopes of Hekla some three miles from Glen Corradale and there spent the rest of the day under a rock, taking turns at sleeping and watching and eating some bread and cheese Flora had given them.

With the idea of enlisting Clanranald's help, Flora had started soon after for his house at Nunton on Benbecula, but on crossing the ford between South Uist and Benbecula, she had been stopped on the far side by some soldiers of the Skye militia who demanded her passport. On asking what unit they belonged to and finding that her stepfather was their captain, she refused to answer any more questions until he arrived. In his absence, she was held prisoner till next morning, when he finally made his appearance and entertained her to breakfast.

From his rock on the slopes of Hekla the Prince meanwhile had sent Neil MacEachain off to Benbecula to get news. On reaching the ford, Neil was in his turn arrested on the South Uist side and not taken across until the following morning, when he arrived to find Flora having breakfast with her stepfather, who at once told the Militiamen to release him. Carefully choosing his moment, Neil managed to take Flora aside and ask her how things had gone. She replied that she had not yet been to Nunton to see the Clanranalds, but was on her way there, adding that she and 'Lady Clan' would go to Rossinish that same afternoon with food and clothes and urging him to take the Prince there as soon as possible. Neil accordingly 'posted off immediately', reaching the rock by the appointed hour to find Charles waiting eagerly for his return.

The next problem was how to get to Rossinish. As the fords were guarded, the Prince could not risk going by land, but at 'the side of Loch Skiport', near the north-eastern end of South Uist, Neil fortunately recognized four friends of his who had come there to fish in a little yaw and who now agreed to ferry them across to the Isle of Wiay, off the South-East coast of Benbecula, where Neil had hoped to meet his brother, but which they found on arrival to be deserted. It was already broad daylight and instead Neil managed to persuade the boatmen to take them to the nearest point on Benbecula. As for the Prince, he was by now so exhausted that he sat down on the first rock he saw and went to sleep.

At nightfall they again set out across country. There was no moon and in the darkness they could only see a few feet in front of them, while 'the rain was so vehement with the wind blowing directly in their teeth, that they could scarcely look where to set their foot' and were forever falling into ditches and losing their shoes in the mud. It was not until midnight that they came to Rossinish and the cottage where they had arranged to meet Flora and Lady Clanranald. Leaving the Prince and O'Neil some distance away, Neil MacEachain went in to investigate. But, instead of finding the ladies awaiting them, he was greeted by the man of the house and his wife with the news that twenty militia men had landed there two days earlier and were living in a tent only a few hundred yards away. But Neil, whose son was to become a Marshal of France, remained calm and in the end a cowherd who lodged in the cottage offered to take them to another bothy 'not far off'.

At first light the Prince, impatient as usual, wanted to send Neil over to Nunton on the other side of the island for news of Flora. But in their precarious situation Neil refused to leave him. So in the end Felix went instead.

Neil's concern for the Prince's immediate safety turned out to be abundantly justified. No sooner had Felix left for Nunton, than the woman of the house came to tell Neil that it would be dangerous for them to stay there any longer as the militia came every morning to get milk. On hearing this, they at once went down to the shore where they found a rock behind which to hide. But the rock was too small to give the Prince any protection from the rain 'which poured down upon him so thick as if all the windows of heaven had broke open', while swarms of hungry midges attacked his face and hands.

Towards evening, the guide who had gone with O'Neil to Nunton came back, bringing a welcome roast fowl and two bottles of wine from Lady Clanranald. These, after what they had been through, were good for their morale and that night, having 'supp'd very heartily', Charles slept soundly on a heather bed Neil MacEachain made up for him.

Neil now took Charles to Rueval, a hill between Rossinish and Nunton commanding an extensive view of the country round, and remained there with him, keeping a watch till evening. Next morning came signs that things were moving. To the bothy came the brothers John and Roderick MacDonald of South Uist, who had brought Charles from the mainland to Benbecula two months earlier, with the news that the boat for Skye was ready. They were cousins of Flora's and also, characteristically enough, officers of one of the militia regiments which were supposed to be searching for the Prince. Benbecula, it appeared, was momentarily clear of enemy troops and Neil MacEachain, leaving Charles in the MacDonalds's care, now hurried over to Nunton to see how things were progressing.

In Lady Clanranald's agreeable sitting-room at Nunton with its windows looking out across the *machair* to where the Atlantic breakers thundered on the shore beyond, the finishing touches had been put to the white, blue-sprigged dress which the Prince was to wear; some provisions were collected and the party were ready to start. They consisted of Lady Clanranald, her seven-year-old daughter Peggy, Flora, her brother Angus and Angus's wife. Escorted by Neil Mac-Eachain they travelled by boat from Nunton round the north end of Benbecula to Rossinish. There the Prince and O'Neil were on the shore to meet them. While the Prince conducted Lady Clan to the bothy 'O'Neil took care of Miss Flora'. In the bothy, dinner was cooked by Charles and the MacDonald brothers, who spit-roasted the 'heart, liver, kidneys etc. of a bullock or sheep'. When dinner was ready, they sat down 'very hearty and merry' with Lady Clanranald on the Prince's left and Flora, 'his young preserver', in the place of honour on his right.

But no sooner had they started to eat than one of Clanranald's herd boys rushed in with the news that General John Campbell of Mamore himself was at that moment landing near Nunton with a force of 1,500 men. Snatching up whatever came to hand they ran down to the boat and rowed across Loch Usquevaugh, landing at about five in the morning on the far side, where, says Neil, 'they ended their supper'.

On the far side of the loch they waited in the cold light of dawn for more news. At eight came the information that the dreaded Captain Fergussone of HMS *Furness* with one party of General Campbell's men had taken possession of Nunton soon after Lady Clanranald had left and had actually slept in her bed. Meanwhile Captain Caroline Scott was approaching with another large party. The latest estimate of General Campbell's total force was over 2,000 men.

At once Lady Clanranald started for home. At Nunton she was immediately brought before General Campbell and 'strictly examined' by him and by Captain Fergussone as to where she had been and why. She replied that she had been visiting a sick child, which was now much better. General Campbell said that he looked forward to dining with her, but would first like to know the child's name and where it lived. Lady Clanranald gave the most convincing answers she could think of. These were grudgingly accepted and in the end the troops withdrew, only to come back again some days later and arrest both Lady Clanranald and her husband.

For the Prince time was now of the essence. So long as he remained on the island, it could only be a matter of time before General Campbell's red-coats caught up with him. Flora's stepfather had provided her with the following letter to his wife in Skye as well as with a pass for herself and Betty Burke:

My dear Marion,

I have sent your daughter from this country, lest she should be any way frightened with the troops lying here. She has got one Betty Burke, an Irish girl, who, as she tells me, is a good spinster. If her spinning pleases you, you may keep her till she spins all her lint; or, if you have any wool to spin, you may employ her. I have sent Neil MacEachain along with your daughter and Betty Burke to take care of them.

I am your dutiful husband,
HUGH MACDONALD

Left behind, O'Neil was taken prisoner by Captain Fergussone some days later and consigned to Edinburgh Castle.

'The company being gone,' says Neil MacEachain, 'the Prince, stript of his own cloaths, was dressed by Miss Flora in his new attire, but could not keep his hands from adjusting his headdress, which he cursed a thousand times. The white, blue-sprigged gown was of calico, a light coloured quilted petticoat, a mantle of dull camlet made after the Irish fashion, with a cap to cover His Royal Highness's whole head and face, with a suitable headdress, shoes, stockings, etc.' Charles wanted to wear his pistols under the dress, but Flora would not let him, objecting that 'if any person should search them, the pistols would only serve to make a discovery'. 'Indeed, Miss,' rejoined the Prince, 'if we shall happen to meet with any that will go narrowly to work in searching as what you mean they will certainly discover me at any rate.' But nothing would move her and in the end the Prince had to content himself with a 'short, heavy cudgel, with which he designed to do his best to knock down any single person that should attack him'. It was still too early for them to start and so by the shore of Loch Usquevaugh they made a fire to dry and warm themselves while they waited for darkness to fall. Suddenly, as they were waiting, four or five boats full of enemy soldiers came up the loch, clearly searching for them. At once they dived into the heather and the boats, as luck would have it, went on their way without stopping.

The moment it was dark enough, they embarked. The boat which had been procured for them was 'a small shallop of about nine cubits, wright measure' with a mast and oars. The night was clear and calm and the Prince in good spirits, drinking some milk 'Jock-fellow-like' out of the bottle with the boatmen. Their last bottle of wine, he said, must be kept for Flora, 'lest she should faint with the cold and other inconveniences of a night passage'. There was no wind and for a time they needed to row. There could be no doubt that they had been lucky to get away when they did.

At about midnight a wind got up from the west with rain and mist. They were out of sight of land and had no compass and the boatmen, as boatmen will in the Highlands, stopped rowing and started arguing amongst themselves about which course they should take. Morale was low but Charles sang some Jacobite songs and, when the boatmen started to row again, offered to relieve whichever man was most fatigued. Flora by this time had fallen asleep in the bottom of the boat, while 'the Prince carefully guarded her, lest in the darkness any of the men should chance to step upon her', and when, at some noise or movement in the boat, she woke up, she found him bending over her with hands outstretched to keep one of the crew from stumbling over her in the darkness.

By first light on 29 June the wind had swung round strongly to the north, bringing clearer weather and slowing down their progress. They were making for Vaternish, the north-westernmost point of Skye, but, when they finally reached it, they found that it was occupied by enemy troops who fired a shot or two at them. 'They were so near the shore,' wrote Flora afterwards, 'that they saw the men armed, but luckily it was low water and the shore so rough that they wou'd not launch out their boat. They then saw some of the men running up to the house where their commanding officer lay, they suppos'd to inform him about the boat. Miss MacDonald said she was afraid they would now be taken. Don't be afraid Miss, said the prince, we will not be taken yet. You see it is low water and before they can launch their boats out over that rough shore we will get in below those high rocks and they will lose sight of us, which they did.'

Putting into a 'clift of a rock', they now rested for a time and ate some bread and butter which Lady Clanranald had given them. Then they rowed the dozen miles or so across the mouth of Loch Snizort to Trotternish and at about two that afternoon landed on the shore near Kilbride, 'within a cannon-shot' of Monkstat or Mugstot, the house of Sir Alexander MacDonald of Sleat, where it stood in a commanding position, looking out across Loch Snizort to the waters of the Little Minch beyond. Leaving the Prince in the boat, Flora and Neil Mac-Eachain at once made their way up to the house, having first told the boatmen to inform anyone who asked them that their ungainly female companion was Miss MacDonald's maid and 'curse her for a lazy jade, what was she good for since she did not attend her mistress'. On their way Flora and Neil met Lady Margaret MacDonald's maid, from whom they learned that on that Sunday afternoon Lady Margaret had visitors at Mugstot – her friend, Mrs John MacDonald of Kirkibost, her husband's factor, Alexander MacDonald of Kingsburgh, and finally Lieutenant MacLeod of the Skye militia with four of his men in the house and the rest nearby, their duty being to keep a sharp lookout for Jacobite fugitives.

Sending the maid on ahead to tell Lady Margaret that she had stopped to see her on her way home from South Uist, Flora now followed in person and was received by Lady Margaret in a room alone. She found her in a state of some agitation. Only the day before, her friend Mrs MacDonald of Kirkibost had arrived from North Uist with a story that the Prince was on his way to Skye. Moreover, though herself the wife of a captain in the Independent Companies, Mrs MacDonald had been stopped on the way across by soldiers and 'strictly examined' on the suspicion that she herself was the Prince in disguise. Good Jacobite though she was, Flora's announcement that the Prince, thinly disguised as a woman, had landed a few hundred yards from her house and was hoping for her help, filled Lady Margaret with dismay. Nevertheless she immediately sprang into action, scribbling a hurried note to her old friend Captain Donald Roy MacDonald of Baleshare. Captain Donald Roy was brother to Hugh, with whom the Prince had lately caroused at Corrodale, and also a cousin of Flora's.

Having fought with his clan at Culloden and been wounded in the foot, Donald Roy had escaped to Skye and was now living nearby. By this time, however, he had made his peace with the authorities by turning in some of his stock of old weapons, though naturally not the best of them, to his friend Lieutenant MacLeod of the Militia, now dining upstairs. More recently he had made more than one journey between Skye and the islands, carrying various messages and packages from Lady Margaret to the Prince – newspapers, two purses of twenty guineas and six of her elderly, Whig-inclined husband's very best shirts – and had returned bringing messages of appreciation and thanks from Charles. 'A tall, sturdy man about six foot high, exceedingly well shaped and about forty years of age', Donald Roy must have seemed to Lady Margaret a natural ally in such an emergency.

Meanwhile, Lady Margaret had sent Flora into the dining-room to engage Lieutenant MacLeod in conversation and at the same time had asked her husband's factor, MacDonald of Kingsburgh, a sound, sensible, middle-aged man, to come out into the garden and talk to her. As Lady Margaret and Kingsburgh reached the garden, Donald Roy came riding up on a hastily borrowed horse. 'Oh, Donald Roy,' said the young and beautiful Lady Margaret, as he dismounted, spreading out her hands in despair, 'we are ruined forever.'

After Lady Margaret had told her two companions of the news she had received, adding that, if the Prince were to be captured on their

253

land, 'they would be affronted forever', the three of them, with Neil MacEachain standing by, consulted together as to what they should do next. The problem was not an easy one. 'In a word,' says Donald Roy, 'all choices were bad, the Prince's situation having a most dismal prospect.' With enemy soldiers everywhere, it was clearly out of the question for the Prince to remain at Mugstot or indeed on the island at all. With characteristic resourcefulness, Kingsburgh at once undertook to smuggle him off it, suggesting that Charles should continue by boat round the point of Trotternish to the Island of Raasay, where the Laird, MacLeod of Raasay, was believed to be sympathetic, and thence to the mainland, where help could, with luck, be hoped for. But this, Lady Margaret pointed out, would mean passing close to a militia post on the shore at Duntulm and Donald Roy accordingly suggested that, instead, the Prince should walk the 'fourteen long Highland miles' across the island to Portree and cross thence to Raasay. Though Kingsburgh considered this a desperate venture, they decided in the end to attempt it.

From time to time while they were talking, Lady Margaret went back to the dining-room to see how things were going. This was distinctly unnerving for Flora, who 'could not help observing Lady Margaret often going in and out as one in great anxiety, while she in the meantime endeavoured to keep a close chit-chat with Lieutenant MacLeod, who put many questions to her, which she answered as she saw fit'. Alexander MacLeod of Bailemeanach was, as it happened, not just a simple soldier. Some months earlier he had served as an intermediary in some, as can be imagined, delicate negotiations between his own chief, MacLeod of that Ilk, and the latter's cousin, Simon Lovat, who described him, no doubt accurately, as 'a sneaking little gentleman'. That in the present situation he would keep his eyes wide open for the main chance was quite certain, but for one reason or another, he never noticed that anything was wrong.

Once it had been agreed that the Prince should travel overland to Portree by way of Kingsburgh, the next thing was to put the plan to him. Taking with him some bread and a bottle of wine, Kingsburgh set out to find the Prince. At first he could see no sign of him. Then he noticed some sheep moving on the hillside, and, on going to see what had disturbed them, came upon the Prince, who, taking him for an enemy, at first sprang out at him with his cudgel raised, but was soon reassured and sat down to drink the wine and discuss plans.

After a time they were joined by Neil MacEachain and 'about an hour before sunset' the three of them set out on foot for Kingsburgh's house, which was some seven miles away, due South from where they were on the shore of Loch Snizort Beag, between the road and the loch. They were soon overtaken by Flora, riding one of Lady Margaret's horses and accompanied by Mrs MacDonald of Kirkibost, who had been let into the secret and wanted at all costs to catch a glimpse of the Prince. Unfortunately the sight of Charles striding along in his skirts at once aroused the curiosity of Mrs MacDonald's maid, who had come with them and loudly declared that she had never seen a woman of such impudent appearance, adding that she must either be Irish or, worse still, a man dressed up. At this Flora hurriedly announced that Betty Burke was an Irishwoman she had known for some time and at the same time urged Mrs MacDonald to push ahead, while Neil kept whispering to the Prince 'for God's sake, Sir, take care what you are doing, for you will certainly discover yourself' and from Kingsburgh came the comment that Charles was the poorest 'Pretender' he had ever met.

To make matters worse, it was Sunday and on their way the oddly assorted little party encountered a steady stream of churchgoers all of whom were in their turn astonished by the size, impudence and uncouth appearance of Kingsburgh's companion, who walked alongside him as though she was his equal, and to whom, they were quick to notice, he seemed to be paying far more attention than to her mistress. Particularly shocking to these good folk was the immodest way in which 'Betty Burke' hitched up her petticoats every time there was a stream to cross. Despite the imminent danger, Flora, says Neil MacEachain, was 'mightily diverted' by all this. In the end, however, having prevailed on Mrs MacDonald of Kirkibost to ride on with her ahead of the pedestrians, she took leave of her at the parting of their ways and hurried on alone so as to arrive at Kingsburgh House a little in advance of Kingsburgh and the Prince.

It was late by the time the travellers reached their destination and Mrs MacDonald of Kingsburgh, who was not expecting her husband back that night, was preparing for bed, when a maid came up to say that Kingsburgh had come home, bringing some company with him.

The following is a first-hand account of what ensued.

'What company?' says Mrs MacDonald.

'Milton's daughter, I believe,' says the maid, 'and some company with her.'

'Milton's daughter', replies Mrs MacDonald, 'is very welcome to come here with any company she pleases to bring. But you'll give my service to her, and tell her to make free with anything in the house; for I am very sleepy and cannot see her this night.'

In a little her own daughter came and told her in a surprise, 'O mother, my father has brought in a very odd, muckle, ill-shaken-up wife as ever I saw! I never saw the like of her, and he has gone into the hall with her.'

She had scarce done with telling her tale when Kingsburgh came and desired his lady to fasten on her bucklings again, and to get some supper for him and the company he had brought with him.

'Pray, goodman,' says she, 'what company is this you have brought with you?'

'Why, goodwife,' said he, 'you shall know that in due time; only make haste and get some supper in the meantime.'

Mrs MacDonald desired her daughter to go and fetch her the keys she had left in the hall. When her daughter came to the door of the hall, she started back, ran to her mother and told her she could not go in for the keys, for the muckle woman was walking up and down in the hall, and she was so frightened at seeing her that she could not have the courage to enter. Mrs MacDonald went herself to get the keys, and I heard her more than once declare that upon looking in at the door she had not the courage to go forward.

'For', said she, 'I saw such an odd muckle trallup of a carlin, making lang wide steps through the hall that I could not like her appearance at all.'

Mrs MacDonald called Kingsburgh, and very serious begged to know what a lang, odd hussie was this he had brought to the house: for that she was so frighted at the sight of her that she could not go into the hall for her keys.

'Did you never see a woman before,' said he, 'goodwife? What frights you at seeing a woman? Pray make haste, and get us some supper.'

Kingsburgh would not go for the keys, and therefore his lady behov'd to go for them. When she entered the hall, the Prince happen'd to be sitting; but immediately he arose, went forward and saluted Mrs MacDonald, who, feeling a long stiff beard, trembled to think that this behoved to be some distressed nobleman or gentleman in disguise, for she never dream'd it to be the Prince, though all along she had been seized with a dread she could not account for from the moment she had heard that Kingsburgh had brought company with him. She very soon made out of the hall with her keys, never saying one word. Immediately she importun'd Kingsburgh to tell her who the person was, for that she was sure by the salute that it was some distressed gentleman.

Kingsburgh smiled at the mention of the bearded kiss, and said: 'Why, my dear, it is the Prince. You have the honour to have him in your house.'

'The Prince,' cried she. 'O Lord, we are a' ruined and undone for ever! We will a' be hang'd now!'

'Hout, goodwife,' says the honest stout soul, 'we will die but ance: and if we are hanged for this, I am sure we die in a good cause. Pray, make no delay; go, get some supper. Fetch what is readiest. You have eggs and butter and cheese in the house, get them as quickly as possible.'

'Eggs and butter and cheese!' says Mrs MacDonald. 'What a supper is that for a Prince?'

'O, goodwife,' said he, 'little do you know how this good Prince has been living for some time past. These, I can assure you, will be a feast to him. Besides, it would be unwise to be cressing a formal supper, because this would serve to raise the curiosity of the servants, and they would be making their observations. The less ceremony and work the better. Make haste and see that you come to supper.'

'I come to supper!' says Mrs MacDonald. 'How can I come to supper? I know not how to behave before Majesty.'

'You must come,' says Kingsburgh, 'for he will not eat a bit till he see you at the table; and you will find it no difficult matter to behave before him, so obliging and easy is he in his conversation.'

The Prince ate of our roasted eggs, some collops, plenty of bread and butter, etc. and (to use the words of Mrs MacDonald) 'the deel a drap did he want in's weam of twa bottles of sma beer. God do him good o't; for, well I wat, he had my blessing to gae down wi't.'

After he had made a plentiful supper, he called for a dram; and when the bottle of brandy was brought, he said he would fill the glass for himself; 'For', said he, 'I have learn'd in my skulking to take a hearty dram.'

After Mrs MacDonald and her daughter and Flora had gone to bed, the Prince and Kingsburgh sat up drinking punch, after which the Prince finally retired to the comfortable bed that had been prepared for him, the first he had slept in for many weeks.

Next morning Kingsburgh found Charles sleeping so soundly that he could not bring himself to disturb him and in the end it was decided that they should spend the rest of the day at Kingsburgh and a message was sent to Donald Roy at Portree to inform him accordingly.

That evening, after they had dined and drunk tea, it was time for the Prince to start for Portree.

On the edge of a wood, not far from the house, Charles shed his disguise and once more put on kilt, jacket and plaid. The clothes he took off were hidden under a bush and later destroyed, except for the blue-sprigged cotton gown, the pattern of which was subsequently to be copied by a milliner in Leith and to become the latest fashion for smart Jacobite ladies all over Scotland. Having accompanied the Prince thus far, Kingsburgh now bade him farewell and turned back, leaving Charles with 'one trusty man and a boy' to guide him across the hills to Portree, whither Flora and Neil MacEachain had already preceded him.

Arriving some hours later at the inn in Portree, on the island's eastern coast, in darkness and soaked to the skin, Charles found Captain Donald Roy MacDonald of Baleshare, who had managed to make contact with MacLeod of Raasay's eldest son John, who, with his younger brother Murdoch and his second cousin Captain Malcolm MacLeod of Brea, was even now waiting in the rain with a boat ready to take the Prince across to Raasay, lying directly across the narrow strait no more than two or three miles away. Captain Malcolm MacLeod was a smart, well set-up man of thirty-four, dressed for the occasion in scarlet cloth and good quality tartan. He had fought for the Prince at Culloden and been wounded in the shoulder.

On entering the Portree inn, today barely recognizable under the guise of the Royal Hotel, Charles's first demand had been for a dram. After putting on a dry shirt and Donald Roy's kilt, he sat down by the fire in the parlour – later incorporated, it is said, in the present building – to a meal of bread, butter, cheese, and roasted fish washed down by more whisky. But then came a knock and, going to the door, Donald Roy found Malcolm MacLeod come to remind them that he and his cousins were waiting in the rain with the boat.

Having paid his reckoning and bestowed about his person the comforts with which Kingsburgh had provided him – some sugar in his pocket, a bottle of brandy, four shirts and a cold hen on one side of his belt and a bottle of whisky from the inn on the other – Charles now took his leave of Flora and Neil MacEachain. Turning first to Flora, he said, 'I believe, Madam, I owe you a crown of borrowed money.' To this Flora replied that it was only half-a-crown, 'which accordingly he paid her with thanks'. Then he saluted her, saying, 'For all that has happened, I hope, Madam, we shall meet in St James's yet, where I will reward you for all you have done.' Next he bade goodbye to Neil, who was to see Flora safely to her home next day. Then he and Donald Roy left the inn, taking the opposite direction to that intended in order to throw the landlord off the scent, and then coming back by a circuitous route to where Malcolm MacLeod was waiting for them. Having arranged to keep in touch with the MacLeods, Donald Roy now took leave of the Prince. Then, at 'about the dawning of the day, Tuesday, July 1st', Charles set out across the grey waters of the loch to Raasay in the MacLeods' little boat while Donald Roy walked back to the inn.*

From the inn at Portree Donald Roy returned later that day to Kingsburgh House, where he told Kingsburgh and his wife that the Prince 'had got off in a very private way to Raasay'. From Kingsburgh he went on to Monkstat, to inform Lady Margaret 'how safely and privately things had been managed' and there found his old friend Lieutenant MacLeod, who was as always delighted to see him and took him off to his quarters for the night. Next morning early, having satisfied himself, rightly or wrongly, that MacLeod suspected nothing, Donald Roy went down to the guard-room 'to pump the common fellows'. 'In a joking way they called him a rebel, and he again called them rebels.' After which Donald Roy asked them if they knew anything about the Prince's movements. To this they replied, 'with an air of assurance', that he was still somewhere in the Long Isle 'and that he would be very soon catched, if he was not in the hands of the army already'. All boats from the Long Isle, they added, were being searched – which Donald Roy found most heartening.

For those who had helped Charles, retribution, not surprisingly, was to follow swiftly. Flora was arrested not long after and taken on board Captain Fergussone's sloop the *Furness*. Luckily for her, Major-General John Campbell of Mamore, who was there, saw to it that she was decently treated. She was later taken to London and imprisoned in the Tower, but released the following year. Kingsburgh and his daughter were also later arrested, though not Mrs MacDonald. Flora later married Kingsburgh's son Alex, by whom she had ten children. Having emigrated to North Carolina in 1774, they returned to Skye in 1779, not liking what they had seen of the American Revolution.

---

*Eleven weeks later Neil managed to escape to France, where he was to serve for some years as an officer in the French army. In France, though in fact a Maclean, he used the name MacDonald. His son Alexandre, born in France in 1765, was to become famous under the Empire as Marshal MacDonald, Duke of Tarentum.

CHAPTER SIXTEEN

The Isle of Raasay, where the Prince landed on 1 July in a downpour of rain, presented a depressing spectacle. About a month after Culloden it had been methodically pillaged and burnt by a party of sailors, marines and militiamen under one of Captain Fergussone's officers, Lieutenant Dalrymple. They had burned the laird's house and most of the other houses on the island and wantonly slaughtered all the animals they could find.

Charles and the MacLeods landed soon after daybreak on the western shore of the island, 'where they remained two days in a mean low hut'. Charles was soon on good terms with his new companions; 'friends who showed their friendship in distress were,' he said, 'the real friends.' The sight of the enemy's depredations greatly distressed him and he swore that one day he would have the burnt turf cottages replaced with proper stone houses. Of recent weeks, he said as he walked up and down on the grass in front of the hut, he had suffered a good deal of discomfort, but he would rather spend ten years like this than be captured by the enemy. 'For since Culloden I have endured more than would kill a hundred. Sure Providence does not design this for nothing.'

Soon it became clear that Raasay had nothing to offer as a place of refuge. Accordingly at about seven in the evening of 2 July they climbed back into the little boat and set off again for Skye. They reached Skye again between nine and ten that night and, landing at Nicolson's Rock near Scorobreck in Trotternish, hauled the boat up on to dry ground. Next morning John and Murdoch MacLeod and the two boatmen went back to Raasay, leaving Malcolm with the Prince.

His purpose, the Prince announced, was to make for Strath, the country of the Mackinnons. The distance, avoiding the direct road, would, Malcolm MacLeod said, be at least thirty miles and it would be unwise to set out when night was coming on. But the Prince still insisted, 'and accordingly away they went along the ridges of high hills, and through wild muirs and glens'.

At Charles's suggestion it was now agreed that he should pass as Malcolm's servant and take the name of Lewie Caw, a role for which he showed more aptitude than for that of Betty Burke, walking at a respectful distance behind Malcolm, carrying the baggage and always prepared, should they meet anyone, to sit down quietly a little way off.

As the two made their way along the ridges of the high hills, they talked of a number of things. Of the rising, and, inevitably of the conduct of Lord George Murray, who, during the two or three days before Culloden, 'did,' said Charles, 'scarce any one thing he desired him to do'. Of the dreadful things done by Cumberland and his troops after the battle, of which the Prince now learned from Malcolm with horror and which he found scarcely credible. Of Charles's habit of drinking burn-water when he was hot. 'No, no,' he replied, when Malcolm told him it was dangerous, 'that will never hurt me in the least. If you happen to drink any cold thing when you are warm, only remember, MacLeod, to piss after drinking, and it will do you no harm at all.' Finally they spoke of Charles and his destiny. 'MacLeod,' said the Prince, 'do you not think that God Almighty has made this person of mine for doing some good yet?'

From where they had landed near Scorobreck in Trotternish, a little way north of Portree harbour, they walked west of Portree village and loch, and thence through the night along Glen Varragill almost to the head of Loch Sligachan, where, to avoid the enemy garrison, they veered westwards by Lord MacDonald's Forest down to the shore of Loch Ainort and along the shore to where Strath Mor opens out. Thence, with great hills looming above them on either side, they made their way along the Strath to the head of Loch Slapin, continuing in the direction of Elgol, where, with any luck, they would find a boat to carry them across to the mainland. Daybreak found them in wild deserted country. 'I am sure', said Charles looking about him, and seeing nothing but hills all around them, 'that the Devil cannot find us out now.'

The Prince turned out at this stage to be lousy and, as this was causing him some discomfort, MacLeod set out to de-louse him, picking as many as four-score lice off him. By this time the bottle of brandy they had brought with them was almost empty and, at the Prince's instance, Malcolm finished the last drop and then hid the bottle in the

261

heather hoping to find it again, 'if the cattle have not trampled it to pieces'.

Walking through the country of the Mackinnons, many of whom had fought in the Prince's army and would know him by sight, they tried to think of ways to make his disguise more convincing. They had already exchanged waistcoats, Charles putting on MacLeod's plainer one in place of his own, which was made of scarlet tartan 'with a gold twist button'. 'I hope, MacLeod,' he said, 'to give you a much better vest for this yet.' Charles now suggested blacking his face 'with some one thing or another'. But Malcolm did not think much of the idea and in the end the Prince took off his periwig and replaced it with 'a dirty white napkin' which he wore under his bonnet. 'I think', he said, 'I will now pass well enough for your servant.' But MacLeod was still not satisfied, saying that anyone who had ever seen him before 'would still discover his face'. 'This', replied Charles, 'is an odd remarkable face I have got, that nothing can disguise it.' The truth of this was proved almost at once when they met a couple of Mackinnon clansmen coming the other way. Both had been out in the Rising and, immediately recognizing the Prince, started – for there were no stolid Anglo-Saxons – to weep bitterly, 'with hands lifted up', to see him 'in such a pickle'.

As it happened, Malcolm MacLeod's sister, who was married to John Mackinnon, 'a captain lately under the Laird of Mackinnon', lived at Elgol, and, on arriving there, Malcolm went to her house, leaving Charles outside. Mrs Mackinnon was at home and made her brother welcome, assuring him that there were no enemy troops in the area. Her husband, she said, was away but would soon be coming back. Malcolm explained that he had a servant with him, Lewie Caw, who was in the same predicament as himself and asked whether he might bring him in. Mrs Mackinnon gave her consent and the Prince then appeared carrying the baggage and, bowing, sat down at a respectful distance. Mrs Mackinnon took to the new arrival at once. There was, she said, something about the lad she liked, and she could not help admiring his looks. She then brought some bread and cheese and milk. This Charles at first refused, feigning shyness and sickness and would only take his share of the food when ordered to do so by Malcolm.

During the night Malcolm and the Prince had wandered into more than one bog and were both covered in mud up to their thighs. Accordingly Malcolm now asked a servant girl to bring some water and wash his feet and legs. While she was doing this, he said to the girl in Gaelic: 'You see that poor sick man there? I hope you'll wash his feet too.' 'No such thing!' she replied. 'Although I wash the master's feet, I am not obliged to wash the servant's. What! He's nothing but

262

a low countrywoman's son!' And it was only with the greatest difficulty that he managed to persuade this class-conscious young woman to do as she was told. Moreover, when she eventually did start to wash him, she showed but little regard for the niceties and it was not long before Charles was obliged to call for help. 'MacLeod,' he cried in some distress, 'would you desire the girl not to go so far up?'

Both men were tired after their exertions and Malcolm told Charles to get some sleep, while he kept watch and his sister climbed a knowe above the house to look out for her husband. It was not long before she came back with the news that her husband was approaching and Malcolm went out to intercept him.

After greeting his brother-in-law, Malcolm pointed to some enemy warships lying out to sea. 'What', he said, 'if our Prince be on board one of them?' 'God forbid!' replied John Mackinnon, 'I would not wish that for anything.' 'What if we had him here, John,' Malcolm went on, 'do you think he would be in safety enough?' 'I wish with all my heart we had him here,' replied John, 'for he would be safe enough.' 'Well then,' said Malcolm, 'he is here already. He is just now in your house. But when you go in, you must be careful to take no notice of him at all. He passes for one Lewie Caw, my servant.'

Captain John promised to be careful, but when he saw the Prince in his shabby kilt carrying his baby son Neil round the room and singing to him, it was more than he could bear and he turned away and wept. 'I hope,' said Charles, forgetting the pretence of being a servant, 'that this child may be a captain in my service yet.'

Charles's plan was to find a boat to take him to the mainland and it was agreed that John Mackinnon should try to hire a boatman for the ostensible purpose of carrying his brother-in-law across, without at this stage making mention of a second passenger. They likewise agreed that John should say nothing of this project or of the Prince's presence at Elgol to his chief, Mackinnon of Mackinnon, who, though 'a mighty honest, stout, good man', was felt to be too old and infirm to be involved in such schemes. But the first person John Mackinnon met on his way to find a boat was old Mackinnon himself and, when it came to the point, he soon found that 'he could not keep the matter from him'. On learning what was afoot, old Mackinnon, clearly not chief for nothing, at once took charge, announcing that he would see that a boat was found and would himself also wait on the Prince. At this Malcolm MacLeod decided that the best plan would be for him to hand Charles over to the old chief. Charles, who did not like the idea of losing Malcolm, agreed 'with much reluctancy'. At about eight or nine in the evening old Mackinnon arrived and together they went down the hillside with him to where the boat he had found was tied up. At the boat, Charles embraced Malcolm MacLeod and gave him ten guineas and a silver stock-buckle to remember him by.

Elgol commands a wide prospect out to sea southwards. Just as they were going on board, some enemy warships came in sight, threatening to cut them off, and Malcolm urged Charles to delay his departure. But Charles, claiming that the wind would change, refused to wait. 'Providence', he said, 'will take care of me, and it will not be in the power of these ships to look near me at this time.' Whereupon the wind, which was blowing 'pretty briskly', suddenly veered round to another point of the compass, the enemy ships changed course, all present were much impressed and the embarkation proceeded as planned.

With Charles went the old Chief, John Mackinnon and four boatmen. From Elgol they made their way round Strathaird Point, across the mouth of Loch Eishort to the Point of Sleat and thence across the Sound of Sleat to Mallaig, landing there at about four next morning, 5 July. The prospects at Mallaig, then no more than a cluster of huts, were not encouraging. A detachment of militiamen were encamped at Earnsaig to the south of the entrance of Loch Nevis. Nor was there anyone locally to give them shelter. For three nights they slept in the open. On 8 July old Mackinnon and one of the boatmen went off to see if they could not find 'a cave to lie in'.

While they were gone, the Prince with John Mackinnon and the other three boatmen had rashly taken the boat and rowed along the shores of Loch Nevis. Rounding a point, they almost ran into a boat tied up to a rock and at the same time saw to their dismay five men on the shore nearby with red crosses on their bonnets, indicating militiamen. These at once challenged them, calling out to know where they had come from. 'From Sleat,' John Mackinnon shouted back, but, when ordered to land, told the boatmen to row off as fast as they could. On instructions from John Mackinnon, Charles was lying in the bottom of the boat covered by the latter's plaid. His first impulse had been to land and confront the enemy, preferring, as he explained afterwards, to fight for his life than be taken prisoner, and John 'was obliged to be very positive and peremptory as to keeping the Prince in his then snug situation'. The militiamen now jumped into their boat and gave chase. Seeing this John told the boatmen to have their muskets ready, while from under the plaid the Prince kept asking how far ahead they were of their pursuers and urging John not to take lives unnecessarily. To this John replied that he would not, 'unless better could not be', adding that, should there be an engagement, 'it was necessary that none should get off to tell tidings'.

In the end it did not come to a fight. The three remaining boatmen managed to outrow the five militiamen and, turning the next point, put in to the shore, whence Charles, accompanied by John Mackinnon and one of the boatmen 'mounted nimbly to the top of the hill'. Here the hillside was 'all wood down to the water' and from where they watched the militia give up the chase and turn back. After the Prince had had a sleep on the hillside, they went back to the boat and rowed across the loch to a small island on the Knoidart side not far from the house of MacDonald of Scotus, killed at Culloden charging next to his friend the Chevalier de Johnstone. There old Clanranald, having fled from Benbecula, was now believed to be living.

While the Prince remained on the island, John MacKinnon rowed across and, coming on old Clanranald outside Scotus's house, caught him by the coat tail just as he was hurrying indoors. 'Oh, Mr MacKinnon,' said Clanranald, feigning surprise, 'is this you? I did not know you. How do you do? It is not easy to know people that come to visit us now.'

'Indeed,' replied John, 'it is hard nowadays to distinguish friends from foes.' They then took a turn together in the garden behind the house and Clanranald learned to his evident dismay that the Prince was in the neighbourhood and was looking for someone to whom he could turn. The old man's immediate reaction was one of rage and despair. 'What muckle devil', he asked, 'has brought him to this country again? I tell you, Mr MacKinnon, I know of no person into whose hands I can put him.'

'I see you are resolved', he added as they finally parted, 'not to do the smallest service to the Prince in his greatest distress and that you want only to be rid of him. Therefore you shall have no more trouble about him. But remember, Sir, that I will honestly inform him of every word that has pass'd between you and me on this subject, be the consequences what it will.'

'Well,' said the Prince quietly, when told of this conversation, 'there is no help for it; we must do the best we can for ourselves.'

With John MacKinnon, Charles now crossed the loch again to Mallaig and its cluster of huts, where they somehow managed to find something to eat. Then, as it was getting dark, they set out to walk the seven or eight miles to Cross in Morar where MacDonald of Morar was reputed to be living with his family in a bothy after the Navy had burnt down his house. Encountering some wayfarers along the road Charles resumed the guise of a sick servant lad, once more shouldering a knapsack and tying a handkerchief round his head. The disguise seems to have been effective enough, for when a guide whom they had picked up *en route* was invited to carry the poor sick lad across the River Morar, he flatly refused, observing indignantly: 'The deil on my back he comes or any fellow of a servant like him.'

When the fugitives arrived at the bothy, MacDonald of Morar was in bed. On being woken by John MacKinnon, he came to the door of the bothy to welcome the Prince and bring him inside, where his wife, Lochiel's sister, was waiting. On seeing the state Charles was in, she could not hold back her tears, but in due course managed to provide some 'cold salmon warmed again, but no bread' for her guests to eat. After they had eaten, Morar conducted them to a nearby cave where Charles, resilient as ever, slept for the next ten hours. 'None', said John MacKinnon later of their welcome, 'could be more hearty and ready to serve the Prince than Morar was.' But by next day his attitude had changed. Having set out in the morning to find young Clanranald, he returned a different man, becoming in John MacKinnon's words 'very cool and backward' and claiming that he had not after all been able to find Clanranald. 'Well, Morar,' said the Prince on being told this, 'there is no help for that; you must do the best you can yourself.' At this Morar became cooler than ever. He was, he said, sorry to tell the Prince that he 'could do nothing at all for His Royal Highness and as little did he know of any one to whose care he could commit his person'.

Morar's change of attitude shocked Charles. 'This', he replied bitterly, 'is very hard. You were very kind yesternight, Morar, and said you could find out a hiding place, proof against the search of the enemy's forces, and now you say you can do nothing at all for me.' John MacKinnon was even more outspoken, realizing that, in spite of his denials, Morar had in fact found not young, but old Clanranald and been advised by him to do no more for the Prince than he himself proposed to do.

Charles, hitherto so resilient, was distressed by these bitter exchanges and by the feeling that he had been betrayed. 'O God Almighty,' he said, 'look down on my circumstances and pity me; for I am in a most melancholy situation. Some of those who joined me at first, and appeared to be fast friends, now turn their backs on me in my greatest need. I hope, Mr MacKinnon, that you will not desert me too, and leave me in the lurch, but that you'll do all for my preservation you can.'

Though Charles was speaking to young John MacKinnon, the old chief took his remarks as being addressed to him. 'I will never', he said, with the tears streaming down his face, 'leave Your Royal Highness; but will, under God, do all I can for you, and go with you wherever you order me.' 'Oh, no,' replied the Prince, 'that is too much for one of your advanced years, Sir. I heartily thank you for your readiness to take care of me, as I am well satisfied of your zeal for me and my cause; but one of your age cannot well hold out with the fatigues and dangers I must undergo. It was to your friend John here, a stout young man, I was addressing myself.' 'Well then,' said John MacKinnon, 'with the help of God, I will go through the wide world with your Royal Highness, if you desire me.'

Charles now suggested that they should go to Borrodale again. 'I am pretty sure', he said, 'that honest old Aeneas [Angus] will be ready enough to do all he can for me.' Leaving the old chief behind, the Prince and John MacKinnon, guided by Morar's son, reached Borrodale early next morning, 10 July. Borrodale's house, like Morar's, had been burnt down by Captain Fergussone, leaving only the empty shell, and Aeneas was living in a nearby bothy. Roused by John MacKinnon, he came to the door with a blanket round him. John asked him if he had heard anything of the Prince. He replied that he had not. 'What would you give for a sight of him?' asked John. 'Time was', replied Angus, 'that I would have given a hearty bottle to see him safe; but since I see you, I expect to hear some news of him.' 'I have brought him here,' said John, 'and will commit him to your charge. I have done my duty. Do you yours.' 'I am glad of it', said Angus, 'and shall not fail to take care of him. I shall lodge him so secure that all the forces in Britain shall not find him out.' Charles knew that Borrodale's elder son had been killed at Culloden, and now, when the boy's mother was presented to him, he asked, with tears in his eyes, if she could still endure the sight of one who had been the cause of so much distress to her and her family. 'Yes,' she replied, 'although all my sons had fallen in your Royal Highness's service.'

Staying only to drink a little warm milk, John MacKinnon returned to his Chief. But already the pursuit was closing in. Next morning old MacKinnon was taken prisoner in Morar's bothy. John, who, as it happened, was hiding near the boat, managed to get away and reach his own sheiling at Elgol, only to be arrested there almost immediately by a detachment of militia. With other prisoners, he was then taken by Captain Fergussone on board the *Furness*, and there brought before General John Campbell of Mamore. On being asked by Mamore whether he had not been tempted by the price of £30,000 on the Prince's head, John had his answer ready. 'To be plain with Your Excellency,' he said, 'what a base unworthy action it would have been in me who had been in his service, had received his pay, and broke his bread, to have given him up! I would not have done it for the whole world. And had I done it, I daresay Your Excellency would have looked upon me as a monster of a wretch.' At this the General, amid murmurs of approval from the other officers in the cabin, turned to the odious Captain Fergussone. 'Pray, Captain Fergussone,' he said, 'fill up a glass for me to drink to Captain MacKinnon, and fill up another for him.' And Captain Fergussone had to do as he was told. John MacKinnon, who was afterwards to receive less generous treatment from his captors, later recorded his satisfaction at this incident and at 'Captain Fergussone's being obliged to stand and to serve him with a glass sitting'.

CHAPTER SEVENTEEN

For the next three days the Prince lay hidden at Borrodale 'in a hut in a neighbouring wood'. Thence he sent a message calling on Borrodale's nephew, Alexander MacDonald of Glenaladale, who had served as a major in Clanranald's regiment during the Rising and had thrice been wounded at Culloden, to join him. But before Glenaladale could arrive came the news of old MacKinnon's capture in Morar's bothy at Cross only a few miles away, and on 13 July it was judged prudent for the Prince to move 'four miles to the eastward, to an inaccessible cave', situated 'upon a high precipice in the woods of Borrodale', where, on 15 July, he was duly joined by Glenaladale.

The news, meanwhile, continued disquieting. On 16 July Borrodale's son-in-law sent word that it was 'whispered about the country that his royal highness was with them, and representing how dangerous it was for them to stay longer there'. Then came news from his son John, who, having been sent off 'to view the sea-coast and to learn something of the enemy's motions', announced that he 'visibly saw the whole coast surrounded by ships of war and tenders, as also the country by other military forces'. In the end the Prince 'judged it proper to remove from his grotto' and set out, accompanied by Borrodale, his son John and Glenaladale, for a fresh hiding place to which young Clanranald had offered to guide them. Next morning, however, learning that General Campbell, 'with six men-of-war, well furnished with troops', had anchored in Loch Nevis, they thought it as well to send off two men by Loch Morar to Loch Nevis 'to observe General Campbell's motions'. Then came information that the notorious Captain Caroline Scott 'had come to the lower part of Glengary's Moror' and that inland a line of camps and sentries had been established from the head of

Loch Eil to the head of Loch Hourn. From this it looked as though the enemy indeed knew that the Prince had landed in Moidart, with the result that Clanranald's country was now surrounded on all sides. Clearly Charles must move 'with the utmost dispatch'.

Leaving behind Borrodale and his son-in-law, he immediately set out with Glenaladale, his brother John MacDonald and Borrodale's son, another John MacDonald. By mid-day they had climbed to the top of Sgurr a' Mhuidhe 'in the utmost bounds of Arisaig', whence they sent Glenaladale's brother off 'to Glenfinin, the outmost bounds of Clanranald's country', for news. Early that afternoon, from their position on the neighbouring hill of Fraoch Beinn, they noticed some cattle moving. While Charles and Borradale's son stayed in hiding, Glenaladale went off to investigate, returning with the news that the beasts belonged to some of his own clansmen who were moving them out of the way of some 600 enemy soldiers who had come to the head of Loch Arkaig 'in order to inclose his royal highness in Clanranald's country, while the search was going on very narrowly within it'.

This necessitated yet another quick change of plan. Glenaladale sent one of his clansmen to fetch back his brother John from Glenfinnan and another to seek out the Prince's former host Donald Cameron of Glen Pean, with whom he had stayed immediately after Culloden and who was believed to be in the neighbourhood. He, it was thought, might know what chance there was of breaking out of Moidart in the direction of Fort Augustus. The day was 'excessively hot' and, while they were resting, a woman of the clan milked one of the cows and gave the milk to Glenaladale and to the Prince, who was passing as his servant, to drink.

The messenger who had been sent to find Glenaladale's brother John was the first to return. He had not found John, but brought the news that a hundred men of the Argyllshire Militia had already reached the foot of the hill on which they were standing. There could be no question of waiting for Cameron of Glen Pean or anyone else. They started, said one of them afterwards, 'at about sun-setting ... and travelled pretty hard till about eleven o'clock at night, when passing thro' a hollow between two hills, they observed a man coming down one of the hills ... and, as providence would have it, found it to be their intended guide, Donald Cameron.'

Donald told them what he knew of the disposition of the Government forces and declared himself ready to guide them safely through the sentries. Led by him, they then 'pursued their way through roads almost impassable even in day light' and, after travelling all night, came at four in the morning to 'the top of a hill in the Brae of Lochharkaig, called Mannyncallum'. From there they could see an enemy camp no more than a mile away, but on learning that the hill on which they were had been searched the day before, they decided to risk lying up there. And so, 'choosing the fastest place in the hill they took a little rest'. At about ten, while Donald Cameron and John MacDonald were keeping watch, they saw a man approaching and were much relieved to find that it was Glenaladale's brother John, whom they had 'given over for lost', but who, 'walking wherever Providence directed him', had somehow happened on their hiding place.

That evening at nine they set out northwards. By one in the morning, they had reached Coire nan Gall to the west of Loch Quoich, on the confines of Lochiel's country. The outlook was not promising. They had by now 'entirely run out of provisions, excepting a very small quantity of oatmeal, and as small a remainder of butter'. The enemy's camps, moreover, were spaced at intervals of about half a mile, the sentries being placed within shouting distance of one another and visited every quarter of an hour by patrols to keep them alert. It was all too clear that the Prince, if he tried to slip through between them, 'might be surely catched'.

'Being pinched in provisions', they did their best to find food, but most of the sheiling huts they came to were empty and it was three in the morning before Glenaladale's brother John and Donald Cameron eventually came back with 'two small cheeses that would not be a morsel to the piece of them'. They brought, too, the disquieting news that a hundred enemy troops were marching up the side of the hill, their purpose being 'to destroy and carry off such of the poor inhabitants as had fled to the hill for shelter'.

'The search for his royal highness being general and very narrow all round', they decided to spend the rest of that day where they were, in 'a fast place in the face of a hill at the head of Lochghuaig', whence in the bright July sunshine they could clearly see below them the Government camp at the head of the loch. In the course of the day several of the enemy's search parties passed close to them, and at eight in the evening they set off again in a northerly direction, 'his royal highness travelling stoutly till it became dark'.

Nightfall found them at the summit of a steep hill called Druim Cosaidh or Drimachosi. Straight in front of them were the fires of an enemy camp. They could distinctly hear the soldiers talking. Passing as close as they dared, they climbed the next hill, but no sooner had they reached the summit than they saw more camp fires at the foot.

Their best hope now was to make a detour through the dangerously precipitous country that lay to their west, but Charles was 'determined to penetrate through the lines at all hazards' and Donald Cameron told him 'that there was one pass with a hollow to go down a very high rock, which was exceedingly hazardous, but was the only place he could advise the Prince to attempt'. It was a dark night and they set out 'betwixt one and two o'clock in the morning'. It was now that disaster almost overtook them. The Prince was following Donald Cameron. 'But as he was coming down the hill to the top of the rock where the pass was, his foot slipped, and the hill being so steep he tumbled to the very top of the rock and would certainly have fallen one hundred fathoms perpendicular over the rock with one of his legs.' By good fortune, Charles, as he hung head downwards was caught by the next man to him and held until Donald Cameron could turn back and pull both back to safety. After which, continuing on their way, they managed in the early hours of 21 July to slip between two enemy sentries in Glen Cosaidh, through which the burn that rises on the watershed between Loch Hourn and Loch Quoich flows on its way to the latter. It had been a trying night and they were still anything but safe.

'Different nights after this', says Donald Cameron, 'they passed the other four lines of the troops, creeping on their hands and feet betwixt the sentries.' But they had at least overcome their immediate difficulties and, marching on towards the head of Loch Hourn reached, just before first light, 'a place on the Glenealg side of Loch Hourn called Corriscorrodill'. Here, in a steep glen above Kinloch Hourn, they rested all day 'in a bit hollow ground covered with long heather and branches of long birch bushes'. They were by now 'almost fainting for want of food' and the Prince was for once beginning to show signs of distress. Fortunately John MacDonald of Borrodale now managed to produce a 'leepy of groaten meal', which helped to restore morale. 'Come, come', said Charles, 'let us in God's name have a share; never were people in more need', and 'covering a slice of cheese with oatmeal . . . drank of the cold stream along with it'.

Donald Cameron of Glenpean, who had guided them thus far, did not know the country in the direction of Poolewe, where the Prince hoped he might get news of a French ship and, before they set out again, he and Glenaladale went off in search of a new guide. They came back instead with the news that there were two enemy camps 'within a canon-shot' of where they had been lying and that they had seen a company of soldiers picking out a sheep to slaughter. This caused them to change their plans once more and at about eight o'clock on 'the darkest night ever in my life I travelled', they started for Glenshiel 'in Seaforth's country', arriving there at about three in the morning 'quite exhausted with hunger and fatigue'.

The day – 22 July – was 'exceedingly hot' and the Prince and his companions spent it 'in the face of a mountain above a river that ran through Glenshiel', the Prince lying in a cave or recess beneath a great boulder. The heat gave them an appalling thirst. In young MacDonald's words, they 'were all seized with such a druth, that we were all like to perish before sunset'. The river, cool and sparkling, was only forty yards away from their hiding place, but the Prince would allow no one to fetch water from it, 'so cautious he was', and it was not till sunset that they 'went stagern to the river side'.

From Glenshiel they made for Glenmoriston, marching 'all night through these muirs till ten of the clock next morning'. 'The night was quite clear and a seren sky.' Most of next day they spent 'in a fast place' on the hillside above Strathclunie, tormented as usual by midges, the Prince being wrapped up in his plaid 'to preserve him from such troublesome guests'. At about three in the afternoon they started off again and then, hearing the sound of gunfire about a mile away, climbed to the top of a high hill 'betwixt the Braes of Glenmoriston and Strathglass', arriving there late at night in pitch darkness.

The Prince was soaked to the skin and spent the remainder of the night in 'an open cave where he could neither lean nor sleep' and where he tried ineffectually to warm himself by smoking a pipe. 'He had a bonnet on his head, a wretched yellow wig, and a clouted handkerchief about his neck. He had a coat of coarse dark-coloured cloth, a Stirling tartan waistcoat, much worn, a pretty good belted plaid, tartan hose, and Highland brogues, tied with thongs, so much worn that they would scarcely stick upon his feet. His shirt (and he had not another) was the colour of saffron.'

Next morning, 24 July, when it was light, they noticed some huts 'in the strath of the corry' and Glenaladale's brother went down to see who lived there. They turned out to be more MacDonalds, 'friends to the cause'. One, yet another John MacDonald, was asked to take up a cogful of milk to Glenaladale. On finding the Prince with Glenaladale and seeing the condition he was in, John 'changed collours, and turned as red as blood'. He then addressed Charles in Gaelic. 'I am sorry', he said, 'to see you in such a poor state, and hope, if I live, to see you in a better condition, as I have seen you before at the head of your armie, upon the green of Glasgow. All I can do is to continue faithful to you while I live, and am willing to leave my wife and children, and follow you wherever you incline going.' When this had been translated, the Prince took John's hand. 'As you are a MacDonald,' he said, 'whom I always found faithful to my cause, I shall admit you to my small party, and trust myself to you, and if ever it should be my lot to enjoy my own, you may depend upon of being equally rewarded.'

Having lost all they had, John and half a dozen companions had joined together in a band, living by their wits and pledged to continue the fight against the English. Led by one Patrick Grant and consisting of two MacDonalds, three Chisholms and a MacGregor, they were to be known to posterity as the Seven Men of Glenmoriston. Their headquarters were in a cave high in the hills, commanding an extensive view of the surrounding country. Here the whole party were 'as comfortably lodged as we had been in a Royal Pallace' and here Charles, after being 'refreshed with such chear as the exigency of the time afforded', was 'lulled asleep with the sweet murmurs of the finest purling stream that could be, running by his bedside'.

After three days spent in these pleasant surroundings, the Prince, whose morale had not of late been as high as usual, was 'so well refreshed that he thought himself able to encounter any hardships'. On 28 July, he and his party moved again 'to a grotto no less romantic than the former'. But four days later came the news that a certain Captain Campbell, 'factor to Seaforth in Kintale', was encamped with his company of militia only four miles away. Leaving one of their number in Glenmoriston 'to wait Campbell's motions' they now moved northwards by night, arriving early on the morning of 2 August 'upon the Brae of the Chisholm's country called Strathglass'. Here the Prince, having received reassuring news of Captain Campbell, installed himself in 'a neighbouring sheally hut', a shieling built by the herds as shelter for themselves in the summer and thence despatched two messengers to Poolewe, forty Highland miles away 'to know the certainty about some French vessels being there'.

From Strathglass Charles and his companions continued northwards to Glen Cannich, where they arrived on 6 August and where they spent a couple more days in another hut high up on a hill 'on the northmost side of Glencanna' while awaiting the return of the messengers from Poolewe. The news these eventually brought back was disappointing. A French ship had indeed put in to Poolewe, but had sailed away again. 'A couple of gentlemen' had however been landed and these were reported to be making for Lochiel's country in the hope of finding the Prince there. Charles accordingly decided to set out in search of them. Leaving on the night of 8 August they crossed the Cannich and early next morning arrived at Fasnakyle, where they lay up for three days in 'a very fast wood'.

From Fasnakyle, they sent out scouts to make a reconnaissance of the Braes of Glengarry and Lochiel's country and find out what was happening there. These returned on 11 August with the information that the troops searching for the Prince had gone back to Fort Augustus and early next morning Charles and his party started off 'through an unfrequented road' for the Braes of Glenmoriston, where they spent the day on a hill top. That night, just as they were setting out again, came a report that 'a strong party' was searching the Braes of Glengarry for the Prince and they decided to stay where they were in a convenient shieling.

Next morning a messenger was sent off to Loch Arkaig to summon Cameron of Clunes and another to make a further reconnaissance of the Braes of Glengarry and find out whether the enemy's troops were still there. On the following day, 14 August, on learning that 'the road was clear', the Prince and his party 'being then ten in number, set out under the advantage of a foggy afternoon'. With the Prince were Glenaladale and his brother, young Borrodale and six of the men of Glenmoriston. Passing through Glenmoriston and Glenlyne to Glengarry, they found the River Garry 'swell'd to a great height' by the rain, but forded it with the water up to their waists and spent the night a mile further on in the open 'without any cover, though it rained excessively'.

Next morning, 15 August, 'the rain still continuing very heavy', they walked on 'cross hills and muirs' as far as the Brae of Achnasaul at the eastern end of Loch Arkaig and there spent the day 'in a most inconvenient habitation, it raining as heavy without as within', waiting for news of Cameron of Clunes. In the end a message was received from him suggesting a rendezvous for the next day in a nearby wood. While they were on their way to the wood, one of them managed to shoot 'a large hart' which provided them with a badly needed meal. While they were eating this, they were joined by MacDonell of Lochgarry, who, on being told of the Prince's presence in the neighbourhood, 'came directly where his R.HS. was, and was overjoyed to kiss his hand'. Next day Cameron of Clunes arrived and Glenaladale took leave of the Prince.

Charles was now established in a wood between Achnasaul and the end of Loch Arkaig 'in a small hutt built for the purpose'. One evening, while the Prince and MacDonell of Lochgarry were walking together, Lochgarry asked him his plans, at the same time putting forward some ideas of his own. The Prince should, he said, soon be able to raise 'a flying army of about two thousand men' and the Highlanders 'were so terribly exasperated against Cumberland for his cruel behaviour that one of them wou'd be worth two before the battle'. To resume the offensive would, he believed, be the best thing the Prince could do. 'As there was now plenty of money, his army wou'd soon turn very numerous.' He himself 'engaged Glengarie's people shou'd be all ready in eight and forty hours' and personally undertook to attack and surprise Fort Augustus at their head.

The Prince, still full of hope, liked the idea, and at once sent for

Lochiel and Cluny to ascertain their views. On 20 August Lochiel's brother, Dr Archibald Cameron, through whom the summons had been transmitted, arrived with a message from Lochiel to say that he was still suffering too much from his wounds to be able to travel. The Rev. John Cameron, 'Presbyterian Preacher and Chaplain at Fort William', who came with Dr Cameron, has described the Prince as he came down to the shore to meet his visitors. 'He was,' he writes, 'then barefooted, had an old black kilt coat on, a plaid, philabeg and waistcoat, a dirty shirt and a long red beard, a gun in his hand, a pistol and durk by his side. He was very cheerful and in good health, and, in my opinion, fatter than when he was in Inverness.'

After hearing what Dr Archie had to say, Charles sent him and Lochgarry back to Lochiel and Cluny to ask for their views on another rising. But the answer Archie brought back was not encouraging. 'They answered in their opinion, as the Kingdom was so full of the enemy, it wou'd be of much worse consequence to rise in arms than doe otherwise.' And so in the end Charles decided to do nothing – 'much against his inclination, and he wou'd have rather been at the head of an army, as he propos'd'. By this time, five months after Culloden, any opportunity there might once have been, had all too clearly been lost.

Having thus abandoned any idea of a fresh rising, the Prince now decided to make for Badenoch to the east of the Great Glen, in order to consult Lochiel and Cluny, who were skulking there, as to the best way of reaching France. On 21 August he and his companions had moved to a wood called Torvault opposite the blackened ruins of Lochiel's house at Achnacarry. Here they seem to have remained hidden for some days and it seems to have been here that the Prince had a rather inconclusive meeting with the two French officers who had landed at Poolewe.

Before starting for Badenoch, Charles bade farewell to the Seven Men of Glenmoriston and their leader, Patrick Grant, to whom he gave twenty-four guineas to divide between them. Glenaladale, too, turned back at this point, leaving Charles in the care of Lochgarry and Dr Cameron. On the night of 28 August they set out on the long march to Badenoch, crossing the River Lochy at the point where the Caledonian Canal now leads into Loch Lochy. For the journey Lochgarry provided a 'trusty and brave party' of fifty Glengarry MacDonalds, who divided up into twos and threes and spread out in all directions to avoid being surprised by the enemy. Charles thus passed safely within two miles of Fort Augustus and next day reached Corrieneuir at the foot of Ben Alder.

Lochiel was at this time 'in the hills betwixt the Braes of Badenoch and Athol' and on 30 August the Prince, skirting round Benalder, met up with him by Loch Ericht on the South-Eastern slope of Benalder. Though still 'quite lean' from the wounds he had received at Culloden, Lochiel hastened forward to meet the Prince and would have knelt to him, but Charles stopped him. 'Oh no, my dear Lochiel,' he said, clapping him on the shoulder, 'you don't know who may be looking from the tops of yonder hills, and if they see any such motions they'll immediately conclude that I am here which may prove of bad consequence.'

In Lochiel's sheiling, the Prince, after travelling for three days and nights with little food and no sleep found 'more eatables and drinkables provided for his entertainment than he expected', including 'plenty of mutton, newly killed, and an anker of whiskie of twenty Scots pints, with some good beef sassers made the year before, and plenty of butter and cheese, and besides, a large well-cured bacon ham'. Food, when you are starving, has a surprising effect on morale. After he had taken 'a hearty dram, which he pretty often called for thereafter to drink his friends healths' and eaten no less heartily with a silver spoon of 'some minch'd collops dress'd with butter for him in a large sawce pan', Charles was 'gay, hearty and in better spirits than it was possible to think he could be'. 'Now, gentlemen,' he said, 'with a very chearful and lively countenance, I leive like a Prince.' As for Lochiel, he admitted that, thanks to his cousin Cluny, he was very well provided for.

Two days later, on 1 September, Cluny Macpherson, who had gone over to Achnacarry to look for Charles, returned to the shieling. When he, too, wanted to kneel to the Prince, Charles stopped him 'and kissed him, as if he had been an equal'. 'I'm sorry, Cluny,' he said, 'you and your regiment were not at Culloden. I did not hear till of very late that you was so near to have come up with us that day.' On Cluny's advice, Charles now moved, first, two miles further into Benalder, first to a 'superlatively bad and smockie' bothy, in a sheiling called Uiskchilra, where they spent some days, and then another two miles on to 'a very romantic comical habitation made out for him by Cluny . . . called the Cage'.

It was really a curiosity, and can scarcely be described to perfection. 'Twas situate in the face of a very rough, high rockie mountain called Letternilichk, which is still a part of Benalder, full of great stones and crevices and some scattered wood interspersed. The habitation called the Cage, in the face of that mountain, was within a small thick bush of wood. There were first some rows of trees laid down in order to level a floor for the habitation; and as the place was steep, this rais'd the lower side to equall height with the other; and these trees, in the way of jests or planks, were entirely well levelled with earth and gravel. There were betwixt the trees, growing naturally on their own roots, some stakes fixed in the earth, which with the trees were interwoven with ropes made of heath and birch twigs all to the top of the Cage, it being of a round or rather oval shape, and the whole thatched and covered over with foge. This whole fabrick hung as it were by a large tree, which reclined from the one end all along the roof to the other, and which gave it the name of the Cage; and by change there happen'd to be two stones at a small distance from other in the side next the precipice, resembling the pillars of a bosom chimney, and here was the fire placed. The smock had its vent out there, all along a very stonny plat of the rock, which and the smock were all together so much of a colour that any one coud make no difference in the clearest day, the smock and stones by and through which it pass'd being of such true and real resemblance. The Cage was no larger than to contain six or seven persons, four of which number were frequently employed in playing at cards, one idle looking on, one becking, and another firing bread and cooking.

In this 'romantick humble habitation' Charles remained for about a week. With him were Lochiel, Cluny, Lochgarry, Dr Cameron, Cluny's brother-in-law, Macpherson of Breakachie, Lochiel's principal servant, Allan Cameron ('a young genteel lad'), and four of Cluny's servants, including his piper and his horse-keeper.

Ever since they had received news of Culloden the French had been doing what they could to find the Prince and carry him to safety. 'It seems certain', Maurepas, the French Minister of the Navy, had written in June, 'that the Stuart Prince is on one or other of the small islands off the north of Scotland. But he is so well concealed from his enemies and from those who want to help him, that both seek him with equal lack of success.' In July a French cutter, narrowly missing the Prince, had taken off O'Sullivan. Some weeks later Maurepas was still complaining of the difficulty of finding the Prince. 'It seems that, if he is still alive, he is unwilling to let anyone know where he is hiding.' Charles, for his part, kept asking anxiously for news of a friendly ship. From the Cage, he had despatched Macpherson of Breakachie to find his friend, Colonel John Roy Stewart, 'the Body', as Charles called him, and to try for news of any French ships. But, before he came back, news was received that on 6 September two more French ships had put into Loch nan Uagh and were now anchored there. This news reached Charles on 13 September, and that same day he set out for the coast, spending the next night in the same smoky bothy at Uiskchilra. There they were joined by Breakachie and by John Roy Stewart whom Breakachie had found and brought back with him, telling him only that he was to meet Lochiel and some others.

Hearing them approaching, Charles, 'wrapped himself up in a plaid and lay down in order to surprize John Roy the more when he should enter the hut' and then, as John Roy came in, 'peeped out of the plaid'. At which, with a cry of, 'O Lord! my master', that hardened adventurer collapsed and fell in a dead faint in a pool of water in front of the door.

Much to the Prince's joy Breakachie had brought with him three of his gold and silver mounted fusees or pistols. 'It is remarkable,' he said when he saw them, 'that my enemies have not discovered one farthing of my money, a rag of my cloaths, or one piece of my arms.' All this had put the Prince in a good mood and on the march he and his companions threw their bonnets up in the air and took shots at them with the fusees, 'in which diversion his Royal Highness by far excceded'.

Starting out again, they now marched north, between Ben Alder and Loch Erricht, and then west, skirting the southernmost end of Loch Laggan towards Glen Roy. Crossing the River Lochy presented a problem. Cameron of Clunes had come to meet them with a leaky old boat, the only one of Lochiel's boats the enemy had left unburnt. Lochiel did not like the look of it, but Clunes now mentioned that he had six bottles of brandy, stolen from the garrison at Fort Augustus. 'I believe', he added, 'all of you will be the better of a dram.' At this Lochiel said to the Prince, 'Will your Royal Highness have a dram and that from Fort Augustus too?' 'Come let us have it,' said the Prince and it was not long before they had accounted for three of the six bottles. Then, they turned their attention to the river, which they crossed in relays, Clunes going first, then the Prince, then Lochiel. By now the boat was leaking badly and the brandy from the three remaining bottles, which had somehow been broken, mixed with the water in the bottom. This the boatmen scooped up and drank, saying the mixture made 'a good punch' and became 'so merry that they made great diversion to the company as they marched along'.

Marching for the most part by night, they reached Achnacarry on the night of 16 September, it 'being fine moonshine'. 'The enemy had burnt and demolished all there' and they spent the following day amid the ruins. Continuing by night, they came next day to the head of Loch Arkaig, where Cluny and Dr Cameron who had gone ahead met them with a meal of meat and bannocks.

On 19 September they reached Borrodale. Anchored in Loch nan uagh were *L'Heureux*, a privateer carrying thirty guns and a crew of three hundred, and the smaller *Prince de Conti*, both under the command of Colonel Richard Warren, another Irishman, and old Thomas Sheridan's nephew Michael Sheridan. Taking with him Lochiel, Dr Cameron, Lochgarry, John Roy Stewart and a number of other supporters, the Prince went on board *L'Heureux*. Cluny and Breakachie remained behind. Cluny knew the secret of the treasure which had been buried near Loch Arkaig and to him had been given the task of watching over it. A little before midnight the two vessels weighed anchor. The wind was favourable and soon they had cleared the loch and reached the open sea.*

For the Prince, Charlie's Year, *Bliadnha Thearlaich*, as they called it in the Highlands, was at an end. It left him in no way downcast and still utterly determined to return to Scotland as soon as he could, this time with proper French backing, and win the Three Crowns for his father.

*One reluctant passenger on this occasion was huge, fair-haired Coll MacDonell of Barisdale, who, happening to be in the neighbourhood, had been seized by the Prince's companions, accused of treachery and then shackled and dragged on board the *Prince de Conti* as a prisoner. Captured by Government troops some weeks earlier, the Highland Hercules had, it appears, been taken to Fort Augustus, where, in return for his life, he had 'touched money' and agreed to give the Government all the information he could about the Prince's movements. This, the Prince was convinced, had almost led to his capture. Imprisoned on arrival in France, Coll was not released by the French until 1749, when he returned to Scotland. There he was at once consigned to Edinburgh Castle, where he died the following year. Meanwhile Captain John Fergussone had long since bombarded and utterly destroyed the fine new mansion Coll had built himself on the shores of Loch Nevis.

CHAPTER EIGHTEEN

While Charles was being hunted from island to island and from glen to glen, the King's army had been wreaking a terrible vengeance on the Highlands. By the end of April all organized resistance had ceased and the Duke of Cumberland was able to report to the Duke of Newcastle that military operations as such were at an end. 'But', he went on, 'Jacobite rebellious spirit is so rooted in the nation's mind that this generation must be pretty well wore out before this country be quiet.' And again: 'They are now dispersed all over the Kingdom at their own homes, and nobody meddled with them except I send a military force after them ... One half of the magistracy have been either aiders or abettors to the Rebellion and the others dare not act through fear of offending the Chiefs or hanging their own cousins.'

Forbes of Culloden, it is true, still talked of mercy, but his words carried no weight with those in authority. 'Lord President', wrote Cumberland, 'has just joined me, and as yet we are vastly fond of one another, but I fear it won't last, as he is as arrant Highland mad as Lord Stare or Lord Crawford. He wishes for lenity, if it can be had with safety, which he thinks, but I don't.'

Certainly, in the weeks that followed, neither Cumberland nor his redcoats were ever to err on the side of leniency. On 16 May, just a month after Culloden, three battalions of English Foot, the Buffs, Cholmondeley's and Price's, marched out of Inverness and down the Great Glen as far as Fort Augustus. These were the advance guard. A week later, with drums beating and colours flying, came Cumberland himself and the bulk of his army – eight battalions of redcoats in all, seven English battalions, and the Royal Scots Fusiliers, with parties of Kingston's Horse riding on ahead and bringing up the rear, while the

Duke himself led the forward battalion. As they marched down the southern shore of Loch Ness, a lonely scarlet column with the beat of their drums echoing across the waters of the loch, the great hills towered bleakly above them. 'The mountains', wrote Volunteer Michael Hughes of Bligh's, 'are as high and frightful as the Alps in Spain, so we had nothing pleasant to behold but the sky. 'Tis rainy, cold and sharp weather.'

At Fort Augustus, where the River Oich flows into Loch Ness and the Great Glen broadens out into lush green meadows – 'this diamond in the midst of hell', as Cumberland called it – the Campbell militiamen, always anxious to please, had built their Commander-in-Chief a bower. 'A pretty place,' wrote Volunteer Hughes, 'with handsome green walls ... a fine hut with doors and glass windows, covered at the top with green sods or boughs, so that His Royal Highness resembled a Shepherd's life more than that of a courtier.'

In these pastoral surroundings Cumberland was to spend the next two months. The Prince's army had effectively destroyed Fort Augustus with nineteen barrels of gunpowder, and the Duke's troops pitched their tents in the meadows along the river. Here, to keep them and himself amused, the Duke would organize races for them, ridden bareback on little Highland galloways. He even offered a prize of a 'fine Holland smock' to be raced for by the soldiers' women, 'also barebacked and riding with their limbs on each side of the horse like men'. 'Eight started and there were three of the finest heats ever seen. The prize was won, with great difficulty, by one of the Old Buffs' ladies.' After which, amid loud applause, old General Hawley, now close on seventy, went thundering down the course neck and neck with Colonel Thomas Howard of the Buffs for a wager of twenty guineas, which the general won.

The Duke, a popular hero at twenty-five, was not unnaturally feeling pleased with himself. 'You must allow the Vanity of a young man to be a little blown up by such a success,' he wrote to Newcastle. 'I thank God most heartily that I was an instrument in the affair ... I really believe that a month or six weeks will enable me to do all that is necessary...'

The congenial task that lay before him was in fact to take a little longer, though certainly not from any lack of zeal on his part or on that of the troops under his command. Most of his army was now with him at Fort Augustus. Of the remainder, four battalions of foot had been left at Inverness to guard the North. Three more infantry battalions under Brigadier Mordaunt were sent to clear Perthshire and Aberdeenshire of rebels. There was a sizeable garrison at Fort William to watch the approaches to the West. Further West still, 2,000

Campbells and MacLeods under John Campbell, Younger of Mamore, were bringing fire and sword to Appin and Lochaber, while out to sea, up and down the coast, and amongst the islands, the frigates and sloops of the Royal Navy under Commodore Thomas Smith kept up a ceaseless search for the Prince and any other fugitives.

Some of these vessels, notably HMS *Furness* under Captain Fergussone, had been cruising among the Western Isles since March. Captain Fergussone, 'a fellow of very low extract, born in the country of Aberdeen and naturally of a furious savage disposition', did not confine himself to purely naval operations or to transporting parties of Campbell militiamen from one island to another. He also landed parties of sailors and marines on the coast and on the islands who, under his personal supervision, as often as not outdid the soldiers in the atrocities they committed. For a time he was also Flora MacDonald's gaoler and soon the hold of the *Furness* was full of wretched prisoners, some of whom had been there for several months.

Meanwhile every day a company or two of infantry would draw rations and ammunition and sally forth into the hills from Fort Augustus to burn and murder and plunder and rape. The discovery of the bodies of nine redcoats in a well behind the barracks had put the troops in a conveniently revengeful frame of mind. With savage enthusiasm they burned down every house they came to, large or small, carried off the contents, raped the women, old or young, and cut down or shot any clansmen they came on, without, for the most part, stopping to ascertain their loyalties or allegiance.

No one was more assiduous or more brutal in the execution of his duties than Major Lockhart of Cholmondeley's, a Lowland Scot, whom the Prince's troops had taken prisoner at Falkirk and then released on parole. It was he who, following hard in the footsteps of those renegade Jacobites MacLeod of MacLeod and Sir Alexander MacDonald of Sleat, had harried the lands and farms of the Grants of Glenmoriston, burning down anything MacLeod and Sleat had left standing, and then going on to ravage the lands of the Frasers and Chisholms in Glen Cannich, Strathglass and Glenstrathfarrer. Even Lord Loudon's men, never great fighters, now showed themselves a good deal more effective against defenceless civilians and, ranging through Badenoch, in the end subdued the Macphersons, though Cluny himself, eluding his pursuers, still held out in his cave. 'We have pretty well cleared our neighbourhood about this place,' wrote Lieutenant-Colonel Whitefoord of the Royal Marines in June and Volunteer Hughes of Bligh's was able to boast that 'for the space of Fifty Miles neither House, Man nor Beast was to be seen'.

Not unnaturally Cumberland's troops made a dead set at the Highlanders' cattle, driving them off in hundreds. Soon the fields along the River Oich were filled with vast herds of cattle, horses and sheep, which were quickly sold off to dealers from England and the Lowlands, the proceeds being distributed amongst the soldiers and their officers. 'We bring them to our camp in great quantities, sometimes about 200 in a drove,' wrote an officer in the *Gentleman's Magazine*.

Apart from the immediate financial benefit which it brought, this organized cattle-lifting was a deliberate act of policy designed to destroy the economy of the clans, whose livelihood had always depended largely on their cattle and sheep. In this it was most successful. 'The people', wrote another officer with evident satisfaction, 'are deservedly in a most deplorable way, and must perish either by sword or famine, a just reward for traitors.' Before long there gathered on the fringes of the Duke's neatly laid out camp – *an gearasdan*, as the natives called it: the garrison – groups of starving men, women and children, waiting for a chance to lick the blood and guts or chew the green hides of the slaughtered cattle or else try to barter their few remaining possessions for a handful of meal before the Provost Guard could chase them away with their halberds.

It was now known that the Prince was back on the mainland, skulking in all probability with the MacDonalds in Morar, and in May and June some 1,500 men from Fort Augustus and from Mamore's Campbell militia had been sent out to look for him. Two hundred of these, while searching for Charles, found and captured Alexander MacDonald of Kingsburgh, who was taken to Fort Augustus and charged with having sheltered the Prince for three days. It was now, too, that they took old John MacGinnis, who had rowed Charles across from Skye, and flogged him till he bled. The pursuit, they felt, was closing in. Glengarry and his wife managed to get away and hide in the heather before the soldiers arrived to burn and loot their house and drive off their cattle. Keppoch was dead, killed at Culloden, but they burned his house, too, and his wife and her new born baby barely had the time to take refuge in the hills. While Lochiel watched them from a hill above the house, 320 men of Bligh's had burnt and looted Achnacarry, destroying everything they could lay hands on. Their commanding officer, Edward Cornwallis, was, says Volunteer Hughes, 'a brave officer of great humanity and honour'.

As time went by and the Prince still remained at liberty, the methods of the searchers became more brutal. 'We hang or shoot everyone that is known to conceal the Pretender,' wrote one officer to a friend in Northumberland, 'burn their houses and take their cattle, of which we have got 8,000 head within these few days past'. And Major-General Huske suggested that the sum of £5 should be paid for the head of every rebel delivered to Fort Augustus. This particular proposal was, however, thought administratively impracticable, being liable to lead to even more indiscriminate killing and consequent waste of public money.

But all the time hunger and want were doing their work. 'There were found last week,' wrote an officer in a postcript to one of his letters, 'two women and four children dead in the hills who perished through want, their huts being burnt.' 'As the most of this parish is burnt to ashes and all the cattle belonging to the Rebels carried off by His Majesty's forces,' wrote one baffled parish minister complainingly to the *Caledonian Mercury*, 'there is no such thing as money or a pennyworth to be got in this desolate place. I beg therefore you'll advise me what steps I shall take to recover my stipends...'

After burning Achnacarry, Bligh's marched westwards to Moidart. Here they found some MacDonalds who were not inclined to surrender and 'did great execution among those who were still in arms, obstinately refusing to submit and accept a pardon'. While they were in Moidart, Bligh's were joined by Lord George Sackville, their new colonel, with another 420 men. After assuming command, Lord George, an elegant young Englishman, whose already uncertain temper had not been improved by the severe wounds he had received at Fontenoy, marched his men through Morar to Knoidart, also Mac-Donald territory. On the way, Lord George's baggage, provisions and bedding were carried off by some raiders, who suddenly swooped down on the rear of the column. For this outrage his men took their revenge on the next village they came to, first raping the women and then making them watch while their men were bayoneted and shot. In the wild hill country of Knoidart, the rugged peninsula rising steeply from the waves between Loch Nevis and Loch Hourn, Lord George fell in with a party of troops under the notorious Captain Caroline Scott of Guise's. In the months which had passed since his skilful defence of Fort William, Captain Scott had by his punitive operations in the Western Highlands won a reputation for exceptional brutality. He was now engaged on a similar mission to Lord George's: it was by such punitive forays carried out by relatively large bodies of troops marching through the heart of Jacobite country to a pre-arranged rendezvous that Cumberland planned to stamp out for good any remaining spark of rebellion.

From Knoidart, sacking and burning as they went, Lord George and his troops and the great herd of cattle they had taken now made their way back by way of Glendessary to Fort Augustus. A day's march short of their destination they camped for the night by Loch Arkaig near the charred and blackened ruins of Achnacarry. Here another minor misfortune overtook them. It was late August. Looking down on the redcoats from a cave in the hillside, was, as it happened, Prince Charles and the little group of men who accompanied him. The Prince and his companions had had no meat for a couple of days and, observing the herd of cattle Lord George had brought with him from the west, 'What would you think, gentlemen,' said the Prince, 'of lifting some? The night will favour us.' His companions objected that it was too dangerous. But Charles laughed at them, saying that, if they would not go, he would go himself. At which four of them slipped down the hill and 'brought off six cows without being in the least discovered'. There is no means of telling whether Lord George, whose subsequent career was to be an unhappy one, ever learned who had robbed him. But the story was one which the Prince was to enjoy telling for the rest of his life.

On their return to Fort Augustus, Bligh's were greeted by their comrades with the news that old Lord Lovat had at last been captured in Morar, where some of Captain Fergussone's sailors had finally found him hiding in a hollow tree on an island in the loch. A few days later he passed through Fort Augustus in a litter on his way south to stand his trial. Volunteer Hughes, who had heard a great deal about him, caught a glimpse of him as he went by in his litter. 'He had', he wrote dismissively, 'been a great courtier and a great Knave: but how abominable for ever his character is represented in England tis not half so bad as his North British countrymen make it.'

It had by this time been agreed that the Duke of Cumberland's continued presence in Scotland was no longer necessary. His reluctant successor as Commander-in-Chief in Scotland was William Keppel, second Earl of Albemarle, who had commanded the front line at Culloden and whose son, Lord Bury, had brought the news of Cumberland's victory to George II. Lord Albemarle's father, the first Earl, had come over from Holland as a page to William of Orange and soon it was being said in Scotland that a Dutchman was finishing what a German had begun. The new Commander-in-Chief liked Scotland, 'this cursed country', no better than his predecessor had done and firmly believed in the same harsh methods of government.

The Duke of Cumberland rode out of Fort Augustus on 18 July 1746. He was accompanied by three young aides-de-camp, Lord Granby, Lord Cathcart and the Honourable Joseph Yorke, and by a captain's escort from Kingston's Horse. Three months had passed since Culloden, and they had not been wasted. The Highlands could be said to have been pacified. Prince Charles was fugitive. Of the chiefs who had supported him, most were either dead, in hiding or in captivity. The clansmen were leaderless and starving and the standards under which they had fought, after being carried through the streets by a cortege of chimneysweeps, had been publicly burned at Edinburgh Cross by the Chief Hangman. A chain of five large troop concentrations at Fort George, Fort Augustus, Fort William, Castle Stalker and Dunstaffnage, now reached from the Moray Firth to the Firth of Lorne, from one end to another of the Great Glen. There were garrisons at Duart on the Isle of Mull and at Mingary in Ardnamurchan to watch the Macleans and another at Bernera on the Sound of Sleat. Over and above the regular units of the King's army, the Highlands were patrolled and policed by the Argyll militia and by eighteen independent Highland companies raised from the various Whig clans and shortly to be arrayed in scarlet tunics and in kilts of the dark green and black Government tartan worn by the Black Watch and Campbell militia. Everywhere the gaols were full to overflowing. The Highlands at last were quiet, though as Dr Samuel Johnnson was shrewdly to observe some years later, 'to govern peaceably by having no subjects argues no great profundity of politics'.

Cumberland reached Edinburgh on 21 July and York two days later, being presented by the worthies of each city with a fine gold box. At York he stopped long enough to be entertained to dinner by the Lord Mayor and Corporation. He was also treated to a lengthy address from the Archbishop, in the course of which that dignitary went so far as to say that, while the things His Royal Highness had done for the nation were 'singularly great', 'his manner of performing them was still more to be admired', thus rivalling the General Assembly of the Church of Scotland whose official address, after praising the Duke's conduct and valour, spoke in effusive terms of the 'public blessings' conferred by his family 'on mankind'. On 25 July, just a week after leaving Fort Augustus, Cumberland and his entourage galloped through Kensington and on into London itself, where every kind of rejoicing and celebration was in progress, and praises of the Martial Boy, as enthusiastic Londoners pleased to call him, were on everybody's lips. Parliament had passed a Bill to increase his annual income to £40,000. A special medal with his head on it had been struck to celebrate his victory. A new ballet entitled *Culloden*, featuring 'a prodigious cannonade', was playing before packed audiences at Sadler's Wells. A small pink and white flower had been given the name Sweet William, and just to the north of Hyde Park, Tyburn Gate, where the gallows stood and where criminals were executed, was appropriately enough renamed Cumberland Gate.

It remained to dispose of the prisoners. Since the start of the rising, some 3,500 Jacobite men, women and children had been taken. They were held in prisons and prison ships in Scotland and England, the charge against them being usually active participation in the rising, but sometimes only that they had been seen 'to drink the Pretender's health', or were 'known to wish the Rebels well' or had been heard to sing treasonable songs. Not that, from a legal point of view, it made much difference. All such actions were treasonable and all liable to attract the same ghastly penalty of hanging, drawing and quartering.

Short of mass extermination, as practised in our own scarcely more enlightened century, the disposal of so large a number of prisoners presented serious administrative and other problems. Cumberland's answer, which he was already urging on Newcastle in May, was simply to transport to the colonies several entire clans, such as the Camerons, most of the Macdonalds and several others, 'of which an exact list may easily be made'. For one reason or another, however, this simple solution did not command general approval and other means were adopted. On 23 July 1746 an order in council was issued to the effect that such of the prisoners who were not Gentlemen or Men of Estates should draw lots; that out of every twenty, one should stand trial for his life and the remainder be transported to the colonies. The lotting was carried out by the guards or jailers or in some cases by solicitors' clerks. 'About two in the afternoon,' wrote Alexander Stewart, who had been the Prince's groom and was lotted at Carlisle on 17 August, 'a rascall of the name of Gray, Solicitor Hume's man from Edinburgh, with his hatfull of tickets, presented the hat to me, being the first man on the right of all the twentie that was to draw together. I asked Gray what I was going to doe with that, and he told me that it was to draw for our lives, which accordingly I did and got number fourteen. So he desired me to look and be shure. I told him it was no great matter whether I was shure or not.'

The Privy Council had already decided that all rebel prisoners taken in Scotland should be brought to England for trial. Some made the journey on foot manacled in pairs, but most of the prisoners taken in the Highlands were brought to London by sea crammed into the holds of seven small merchantmen which had been sent into the Moray Firth after the battle of Culloden to take them on board. Five hundred and sixty-four had been loaded by the end of May, when they sailed to London in convoy under the escort of HMS *Winchelsea*. The weather was bad, and by the time they reached Tilbury three weeks later their numbers had been substantially reduced by disease, starvation and the brutality of the sailors, who as often as not got rid of the sick or the verminous by simply throwing them overboard with a stone tied to their legs – 'as they said, to drown the vermine', wrote one observer, 'but they took specell care to drown both together.'

On reaching Tilbury the prisoners were left for several months, on board the transports or the prison ship *Pamela*, to which some of them had been transferred. For Londoners that summer it became a popular pastime to take a boat down and try to get a sight of them or at any rate of the ships in which these dangerous men were confined. By September 150 of the prisoners had died and the stench from the *Pamela*'s hold was so 'intolerable' that an English surgeon sent to give an opinion on the survivors could not bring himself so much as to go below. Nor were things much better in other jails up and down the country, at York, Lancaster or Carlisle, at Newgate, Marshalsea or Southwark, where hundreds more Jacobite prisoners were held in conditions of appalling barbarity.

Even one in twenty of the prisoners represented a sizeable number and that summer, in London, York and Carlisle, the courts were kept busy trying the batches of rebels brought before them. The charge was treason and the penalty for those found guilty was, as the Judge informed them, that 'they must be severally hanged by the neck, but not till they be dead, for they must be cut down alive; then their bowels must be taken out and burned before their faces; then their heads must be severed from their bodies, and their bodies severally divided into four quarters; and these must be at the King's disposal'.

One of the first to stand his trial and meet this disagreeable end was Francis Townley, Colonel of the ill-fated Manchester Regiment to which Charles, on his retreat north, had given the hopeless task of holding Carlisle. Together with several of his officers and with David Morgan, the Welsh lawyer who had helped him raise the regiment and had been one of Charles's principal advisers on English affairs, Townley was executed on Kennington Common on 30 July. A devout, reserved, somewhat humourless Roman Catholic, he, like his companions, met his unpleasant fate with courage and dignity, wearing a new black velvet suit which he had had specially made for the occasion by a tailor in Southwark.

It was a cold, rainy English summer's day, but an immense crowd, larger than anyone could remember, had assembled on Kennington Common to see the condemned men die. Since the night before they had been gathering in the rain and at first there was much scuffling and jostling for a good view of the gallows. But, when the time came, the crowd was quieter than at most public executions, perhaps because of what was to follow the initial hanging. Finally, when the hangman had duly cut off the head and drawn out the bowels and heart of the last rebel and thrown them on the fire which burned below the scaffold, he called out 'God Save King George!' and the crowd, breaking their silence, loyally responded with the same pious prayer.

A couple of days before these first executions, which were to be followed by over a hundred more, an even greater stir had been caused by the opening on 28 July of the trials of the three Jacobite peers, Balmerino, Cromartie and Kilmarnock, who had up to now been held in the Tower of London. 'You will be in town for the eight-and-twentieth,' wrote Horace Walpole to a friend. 'London will be as full as at a Coronation.' Westminster Hall had been filled with stands for the occasion and there were special boxes for the Prince and Princess of Wales, the Duke of Cumberland and foreign ambassadors and ministers. The accused were tried by 136 dukes, earls, viscounts and barons in coronets and ermine, presided over by Lord Hardwicke, the solicitor's son from Dover, who, in addition to Lord Chief Justice, had now been appointed Lord High Steward.

On being asked how they pleaded, Cromartie and Kilmarnock simply answered guilty and were taken away. Old Balmerino, however, was inclined to make a joke of the whole trial, at first questioning the right of the court to try him at all and then insisting on making room beside him in the dock for a little boy who could not get a proper view of the proceedings. But the outcome was the same and he too was in his turn found guilty.

Two days later the three noblemen were brought back to Westminster Hall to hear their sentence. With them, in anticipation of their fate, travelled the executioner's axe. When there was some question as to which coach it should travel in, 'Come, come,' Balmerino called out, 'put it in here with me', and then as the executioner fumbled with it, 'Take care or you'll break my damned shins with that thing!'

After sentence of death had been passed, they were taken to a small room off Westminster Hall for refreshments. At this Balmerino, knowing that they were soon to be separated, suggested that they should have another, last bottle of wine together. 'We shall not meet again,' he said, 'until ...' and drew his hand across his throat. After which he did his best to cheer up Lord Kilmarnock who was showing signs of fear, by reminding him that, as peers of the realm, they had the privilege of being beheaded rather than hanged and advising him how to hold his neck to meet the axe. On their way back to the Tower, the old man, as lively as ever, insisted on stopping his coach to buy some gooseberries, or 'honey-blobs', as he called them. Not many days later the Duke of Cumberland gave a ball at Vauxhall in honour of a well-known whore named Peggy Banks, landing there from the Royal Barge amid cheering crowds to the strains of the National Anthem.

Of the three condemned men, Lord Cromartie was, thanks to his wife's successful intervention with the Royal Family, at the last moment reprieved. Kilmarnock and Balmerino were beheaded on Tower Hill on 18 August. Kilmarnock, bald, stately and entirely dressed in black, managed in the event to conquer his fear. Balmerino showed no fear at all. Indeed the way in which his aged victim walked about the scaffold and examined the axe so unnerved the executioner that in the end it took him three blows to cut off his head.

To James in Rome Balmerino left a letter in which, after recalling that he had also been out in the 'Fifteen, 'Sir,' he wrote, 'when his Royal Highness the Prince your son came to Edinburgh, as it was my bounden and indispensable duty, I joyn'd him, for which I am to lose my head on the scaffold, whereat I am so far from being dismayed that it gives me great satisfaction and peace of mind that I die in so righteous a cause . . .' In his speech from the scaffold, he called Charles 'so sweet a Prince that flesh and blood could not resist following him' and finally cried out 'God Save King James!' as he went to the block.

Two more peers remained to be executed for their part in the rising. One was Lord Derwentwater, who after thirty years of exile, had been captured at sea in November 1745 on his way from France to join the Prince. On the grounds that his title had been forfeited after his father's execution in 1715, he was tried in a court of law and not by his peers. But, though technically a commoner, he was generously granted the privilege of being beheaded and the sentence was duly carried out in December 1746.

The other was Lord Lovat who, after his eventual capture in Morar, had been brought to London, where he in his turn was tried by his peers assembled in Westminster Hall. The case brought against him rested to some extent on the testimony of John Murray of Broughton, who had saved his own life by turning King's Evidence. By now over seventy and in poor health, Lovat conducted his defence before his peers in Westminster Hall with energy and wit and, after a lifetime of equivocation, faced the inevitable sentence unflinchingly. On being asked by Lord Hardwicke whether he had anything further to say, 'Nothing,' he replied, 'but to thank your lordships for your goodness to me. God bless you all, and I bid you an everlasting farewell. We shall not meet all in the same place again, I am sure of that.'

'You'll get that nasty head of yours chopped off, you ugly old Scotch dog,' shrieked a cockney woman from the crowd, as he left Westminster Hall. 'I believe I shall, you ugly old English bitch,' he replied with admirable aplomb. On his way to Tower Hill six days later, he was told that a stand, too heavily loaded with Londoners who had come to watch him die, had collapsed, killing several of them. 'The greater the mischief, the better the sport,' was his merry reply. At one time or another while living in France he had become a Roman Catholic and in this faith he now died. Before putting his head on the block, he gave the executioner a purse. 'Here Sir,' he said, 'is ten guineas for you.

Pray do your work well; for if you should cut and hack my shoulders and I shall be able to rise again, I shall be very angry.'

More than a year after Culloden the Government had still scarcely made a start with the task of shipping to the colonies the 900 or so men, women and children who were fortunate enough to have been granted the King's Mercy of transportation and perpetual banishment; in the meantime, they were left in gaol. The problem, in a nutshell, was to find ship owners prepared to deliver them to their destination for a price which a penny-pinching Treasury was prepared to pay.

There was, it is true, every prospect of a reasonable profit from such a transaction for the ship owners concerned. Many of the prisoners were readily marketable. More than 800 of them were to go under indentures 'during the term of their natural lives' to any employer of labour who was prepared to pay for them and these indentures, made out to the shippers in the first place, could, on payment of an agreed sum, be reassigned or transferred to fresh employers on arrival.

In the end, after prolonged negotiations, the official concerned, Mr John Sharpe, the Treasury Solicitor, managed to conclude a deal with Alderman Richard Gildart of Liverpool and a Mr Samuel Smith of Cateaton Street, London, under which the latter were to ship the prisoners to the Americas for £5 a head. The first shipments began in the spring of 1747. They were still continuing two years later. For the reassignment of the indentures to their eventual employers Messrs Gildart and Smith hoped to receive another £7. This made £12 in all, to cover shipping and feeding and leave an adequate profit margin for the shipper.

As the shippers were soon to discover to their cost, there were a number of risks involved. Quite apart from natural wastage from disease and other causes, there were liable to be unexpected accidents, as when a boat ferrying eight of Alderman Gildart's rebels out to one of his ships capsized and the prisoners, being manacled together, were all drowned. Upon which the Treasury, after some acrimonious correspondence, absolutely refused to pay the £40 he claimed he was owed for them.

Mr Smith also had bad luck when his ship, the *Veteran*, on her way to Antigua with 150 duly indentured men and women, was captured by a French man-of-war and her cargo taken to Martinique and there released. Many of the prisoners thus lost to Mr Smith were clearly eminently employable on the plantations or elsewhere in one capacity or another. There was, for example, Elizabeth MacFarlane, black haired, lusty and ruddy; Daniel Macgillis, a well-made boy of twelve; John Macintosh, a sixteen-year-old fiddler from Inverness; Peter Summerall, a shoe-maker aged fourteen, slender and straight with fair hair; and a number of carpenters, shoe-makers, tailors, sempstresses, gardeners, ploughboys, drovers and others, who would have found ready takers in the colonies. But Mr Smith received little sympathy from the Government, who pointed out that the French were at present at war with Great Britain and could therefore not be made to return his property as he kept suggesting they should.

In this manner some prisoners at least regained their freedom and were able, after all they had been through, to make a fresh start beyond the Atlantic. Others were fortunate enough to find clansmen or compatriots in America who were ready and generous enough to pay the £7 necessary to buy their indentures and set them at liberty. Yet others enlisted or were drafted into one or other of the regiments stationed in North America and so soon found themselves fighting for the King against whom they had rebelled so short a time before. A few even managed to make their way back to Scotland. But most, men or women, old or young, indentured or free, stayed on in the New World and were quickly absorbed into the vigorous young civilization already springing up there.

By mid July 1746, when Lord Albemarle took over command of the King's army in Scotland, there was no further need for a strong force in the Great Glen and it was not long before he was able to move his headquarters from Fort Augustus to what must have struck him as the relative civilization of Edinburgh. The cavalry horses were once again put out to grass and most of the infantry regiments which had fought at Culloden were sent over to Flanders to face the French.

Scotland was now divided into four military districts: from Inverness and Fort Augustus to the mouth of the Spey; from Strathspey to the east coast; from Perth westwards to Fort William; and lastly all the shires south of Stirling, where Colonel Thomas Howard's Old Buffs were installed as the permanent garrison and soon made it clear by their behaviour that, as far as they were concerned, there was nothing to choose between Highland rebels and the peaceable citizens of that ancient burgh. Finally, to control access to and from the Highlands, a chain of small military posts were established westwards from Stirling to the shores of Loch Linnhe, guarding the main passes through the hills, and a fresh strongpoint was set up in MacGregor country at Inversnaid to replace the fort the MacGregors had burnt down. Henceforward the task of policing the Highlands and hunting down fugitives could confidently be left to small parties of troops commanded by junior officers or NCOs.

These patrols were reasonably successful, killing and burning in the harsh tradition established by the last Commander-in-Chief and enthusiastically continued by his successor. 'Nothing but fire and sword,' Albemarle wrote to Newcastle, 'can cure their cursed, vicious ways of thinking.' There were Government spies, too, who passed themselves off as Jacobites, in the hills or travelling through the West, passing back such information as they could collect about the movements of any suspected rebel sympathisers still at large. One, for example, a certain Donald MacDonald from Uist, had been a tailor in Edinburgh before the rising and had made clothes for most of the West Highland chiefs. What could be more natural than that he should now tour Lochaber and the west in the hope of getting some of his outstanding bills paid?

And so men were still tracked down and shot as they came out of the heather, and others caught and flogged or tortured until in the end they even betrayed their own friends. Some, however, did not. Thus Evan MacKay, caught later that year carrying letters in French and a secret cypher, was given 500 lashes to induce him to say where he was bound for, whence he had come and who had sent him. He refused. After a few days he was given 500 more lashes, but still would say nothing. He was then thrown into a pit and given a pound of coarse meal a day which he was too weak to eat. After that he was taken out and dragged to the Tolbooth in Inverness where, when he would still say nothing, he was beaten to death with musket butts and a bayonet finally thrust several times into his breast.

But still the biggest prize of all evaded the searchers. The Prince, they knew that September, was hiding somewhere in the West, but news of him never seemed to reach them in time. This Lord Albemarle found hard to endure. For the chance of laying hands on Charles he would, he wrote to Newcastle, 'with infinite pleasure walk barefoot from Pole to Pole'. It was a pleasure he was to be denied. 'Just as I imagined,' he wrote gloomily on 24 September, 'the Pretender's son is gone; the French ship's heard on ye Western Coast took him and some of his people aboard them.' Again, the news that mattered had come too late.

Even after the Prince had sailed, the English and those who worked for them still went in fear of another rising. Morale among the occupying troops was low that winter and many of the reports reaching Lord Albemarle from the Highlands were far from reassuring. There were tales of French frigates cruising among the isles and of French gold in the hills, and stories of men with swords at their waists talking boldly of fighting. The Macleans, wrote Donald MacDonald and his fellow-spy Patrick Campbell, reporting after a long tour of the West, had hopes of help from France and had hidden guns and swords against that day. And there were rumours, too, that the Camerons and some MacDonalds were ready to rise again. There were tales of Jacobite agents travelling through Fraser country in women's clothes with letters from France and talk among the Mackenzies and in the isles of a fresh rising in the spring; reports, too, that in Badenoch 'they still have plenty of arms, for when they surrendered they gave up only some rusty useless arms'.

Even in Edinburgh all was not well. Someone had had the audacity to burn down the gibbets that General Hawley had set up in the Grassmarket, And it was said that at night gentlemen went through the Wynds singing Jacobite songs and wearing white cockades. There was even a story, which seems to have originated with the Lord Justice Clerk, that the Jacobites were to hold a Ball in Leith on 20 December in honour of Prince Charles's twenty-sixth birthday at which all the women would wear white sashes and white cockades – 'a surprising, audacious, and impudent attempt to celebrate the Birthday of the Pretender's son'. This Lord Albemarle took seriously enough to march five heavily armed companies of English infantry to Leith with orders to discover and apprehend any woman or girl, of gentility or commonality, wearing a tartan gown, stockings, sash or cape, or who wore white ribbons in her hair or at her breast – only to find that the whole thing had been an elaborate practical joke.

For his own part, Albemarle had had enough of it all. 'No Englishman', he wrote, 'can wish to be in Scotland above a twelve month altogether', and he kept begging the Duke of Newcastle to let him come home. Finally in February 1747 (by when the prescribed twelve months was almost up) his request was granted. For this he was suitably grateful. 'My joy at leaving this country', he wrote, 'is inexpressible.' As for the future, he took a gloomy view of it. 'I think', he told Newcastle, 'this kingdom can never be kept in one but by a sufficient military force, and at the same time I think it is a shame that the pay of so many men should be spent among them, for it is enriching this country at the expense of England.'

But he turned out to have been unduly pessimistic. In the Highlands, the Government's harsh policy had paid off. Massacre, occupation, devastation and starvation had done their work. Only a few isolated bands of Jacobites-turned-freebooters, like the Seven Men of Glenmoriston, managed to hold out in the hills for a few more months or years. In the relatively anglicized Lowlands the only problems were those which the heavy-handed English created for themselves by going out of their way to alienate a docile, hard-working and potentially loyal population. Within a few years the Government were to find it possible to reduce still further the total number of troops in Scotland. Indeed, by increasing the strength of the existing Highland regiments and raising new ones, some from the very clans which had fought hardest against them in the rising, they made Scotland an important source of manpower for the British army.

But of the various measures taken by the Government to prevent any possibility of another rising, perhaps the most effective were those designed to destroy the clan system, notably Lord Hardwicke's Act of 1747 forbidding Highland dress and the subsequent measure abolishing the hereditary jurisdictions of the chiefs – 'one for disarming and undressing those savages', as Newcastle's brother Henry Pelham called it. 'Could we', wrote the Lord Justice Clerk and General Bland in a shrewdly reasoned memorandum to the Government, 'but at once get rid of all chiefs of clans in these barbarous and disloyal parts of the Highlands, it would facilitate all other operations both in point of difficulty and time.' And Cumberland was particularly pleased by a fresh proposal from the usually more lenient Lord President Forbes that entire clans should be transported to the American colonies.

In this they were perfectly right. The clansman's plaid and kilt, no less than his broadsword, his dirk and *sghiann dubh* were an essential part of his equipment for battle, just as they were also a symbol of his loyalty to his chief and his clan. By taking them away, the Government undermined the individual Highlander's sense of allegiance to his clan, while by abolishing the hereditary powers of the chiefs, they not only took away much of a chief's authority, but in some unhappy cases his sense of responsibility as well.

In the twelve months that followed Culloden a whole ancient civilization and way of life were dismantled. Like most others, it had had its faults and its shortcomings, but was certainly no worse than what, under different auspices, was now to replace it.

PART IV

LOCHABER NO MORE

'Glory of youth glowed in his soul.
Where is that glory now?'

Robert Louis Stevenson

CHAPTER NINETEEN

'Escaping all the Government's warships, and being in her way happily favoured by a fog', *L'Heureux* reached the little fishing port of Roscoff in Brittany on the afternoon of 10 October. There the Prince and his companions went ashore and thence he immediately made his way to the neighbouring town of Morlaix.

On reaching France, Charles's main concern was to see Louis xv as soon as he could and persuade him to send a French expeditionary force to Scotland while the spirit of resistance engendered by the rising still endured. '*Nota bene* – It is an absolute necessity I must see ye F.K. as soon as possible, for to bring things to a write head,' he wrote in a letter to his brother Henry in Paris, despatched from Morlaix the day he arrived, in which he also enclosed 'two lines' for onward transmission to his father in Rome, 'just to show him I am alive and safe'. In his letter, Charles went on to suggest that Henry 'should write immediately to ye French King, giving him notice of my safe arrival, and at the same time excusing my not writing to him myself immediately, being so much fatigued, and hoping soon to have ye pleasure of seeing him'.

The French King was most welcoming. On receiving news of Charles's landing, he at once gave orders for the Chateau of St Antoine to be put at his disposal. Meanwhile, Prince Henry, 'accompanied by several young noblemen', rode out from Paris on the morning of 15 October to meet his brother. 'He is not in the least altered,' Henry wrote to his father two days later, 'except grown somewhat broader and fatter, which is incomprehensible after all the fatigues he has endured. Your Majesty may conceive it better than I can express in writing, the tenderness of our first meeting.'

Charles made straight for Fontainebleau, where the King interrupted the Council of State over which he had been presiding to welcome him and spent the next quarter of an hour with him. '*Mon très cher Prince*,' said Louis, embracing him most cordially, I thank heaven for granting me the extreme pleasure of seeing you arrive in good health after enduring so many hardships and hazards. You have shown that all the great qualities of both heroes and philosophers are united in you and I hope that one day you will receive the just reward of such outstanding merit.'

Next Charles was hurried off to the Queen's apartments, where he was no less cordially received by his mother's friend Maria Leczinska, like her a Polish princess. He was, we are told, 'perfectly satisfied' with his reception by the French Royal family and 'they were all charmed with him'.

Gratifying as Charles's reception must have been, it had not afforded him the opportunity he sought to put to his royal host the proposition which remained uppermost in his mind, namely that he should return to Scotland at the first opportunity with the support of a strong French expeditionary force. Accordingly next morning he wrote to the King asking for a private audience. His first visit to Louis had been 'as it were incog'. Some days later a second, more formal audience was arranged for him as Prince Regent of England, Scotland and Ireland. Meanwhile, says O'Sullivan, now reunited with his royal master, he 'kept himself privet for some days in Paris': as he 'had not a second shirt nor a stoken to his foot', he needed for one thing to replenish his wardrobe. Already he was 'the subject of the Conversation of the Court & the Citty'. The fashionable ladies of the French court looked upon his discarded rags 'as so many reliques' and fought furiously among themselves to get possession of them, his bonnet going to one, his coat to another and his wig to a third who, discovering that it had been thrown away, 'wou'd have it', even though 'told it would infect her, yt was full of vermine, as really it was'. Even his old shoes and stockings and his pipe found delighted recipients. He had become, he found, a popular hero, at any rate for the time being. At the Opera, he received a standing ovation. Meanwhile Henry, whom the Marquis d'Argenson described as 'quite Italian, shy, superstitious, miserly, loving his ease and above all jealous and hating his brother', was reporting independently to their father that Charles was too much under the influence of Parson George Kelly and others and bemoaning his 'ill understood systeme of pretended popularity'.

In due course Charles's new clothes were ready and he was arrayed in them for his state visit to Louis. A perhaps slightly malicious eyewitness has described his appearance: 'His dress had in it somewhat of uncommon elegance. His coat was rose-coloured velvet embroidered with silver and lined with silver tissue; his waistcoat was a rich gold brocade, with a spangled fringe set on in scollops. The cockade in his hat and the buckles of his shoes were diamonds; the George which he wore at his bosom and the order of St Andrew which he wore also, tied by a piece of green ribbon to one of the buttons of his waistcoat, were prodigiously illustrated with large brilliants; in short he glittered all over like the star which they tell you appeared at his nativity.'

The necessary coaches, horses, coachmen and postilions having been hired – the bill for them still exists – Charles set out for Versailles some ten days after his first visit. With him in the procession were some of the surviving Jacobite leaders who had by now reached France, notably Lord Ogilvy and Old Glenbucket, Old Lochiel and Lord Lewis Gordon, while young Lochiel and some others followed on their horses. Two 'richly dressed' pages, four gentlemen of his bedchamber, some more gentlemen on horseback and ten footmen 'in the livery of the character assumed by the young Chevalier' completed the company.

Again Charles was amiably received by King Louis and 'magnificently entertained'. But again he somehow found no opportunity of saying what he had come to say and in the end committed his proposals to paper in a personal memorandum in which he emphasized how much he had been able to achieve during the rising with little or no outside help and how much more he could have achieved had such help been forthcoming. He concluded with a request for a French expeditionary force of 18,000 to 20,000 men, at the same time pointing out that, while at present he could still count on widespread and active support in Scotland, this would no longer be so once the English Government had had time to carry their policy of deliberate extermination to its logical conclusion.

But the weeks went by and there was no reply to his proposals – only a verbal message early in November from Louis' Foreign Minister, the Marquis d'Argenson, informing Charles that it was the King's gracious intention to grant him a residence and a pension of 12,000 francs a month.

This infuriated the understandably impatient Charles, who described it as 'a moste scandalous arrangement' and vented his growing indignation with the French on this and other scores in a letter to his father written from Clichy on 6 November in which he gives his state of health as a reason for not writing sooner ('an Indigestion, but I am entirely recovered, as I have all the Kiks of ye Facalty') and goes on to recount his exchanges with Monsieur d'Argenson. 'I find it and am absolutely convinced of it, that ye only way of delying with this – Government is to give as short and smart answer as one can, at the same time paying them in their own Coin by Loding them with sivilities and compliments, setting apart business, for that Kind of vermin, the more you give them the more the'l take, as also the more room you give them, the more they have to grapple at, which makes it necessary to be Laconick with them, which is the only way of pussiling them, and putting all their sheme upon their backs which they woud fairly strive to shift of by rigiros.'

This petulant communication had crossed a letter from his father written from Rome three days earlier, conveying his delight at his son's safe return. 'I cannot express to you, My Dearest Carluccio,' James had written, 'the joy and comfort I felt in receiving your letter from Morlaix of the 10th Oct^r, after all I have suffered on your account for so many months past.' And he went on, with characteristic resignation, to warn him not to expect too much of the French. 'I am affrayed,' he continued, 'you will have little reason to be satisfyed with the Court of France, and that you will not have less need of courage and fortitude in bearing and suffering in that country, than you had in acting in Brittain, and let me recommend in the most earnest manner to you patience and prudence, for by a contrary conduct you would make things worse and never better.'

James knew his son. On receiving Charles's letter of 6 November and a further letter of 21 November, since lost but which presumably touched on his and Henry's matrimonial plans, he replied as follows:

Rome December 16th 1746

I received on Monday, my dearest Carluccio, yours of the 21st Novr. I heartily wish you may succeed in your manner of acting towards the Court of France; but I am affrayd you will disgust them quite, and that by the way you are taking, not only yourself, but even those who suffer for you and have no other resource but the French, will feel the effects of them while I am no-ways in a condition to supply either them or you, for it is not a small matter that will suffice for either of you. It must be very obvious to every body that it is for the interest of our family that at least you and your brother should marry, but I don't see neither such haste in the matter. This is a very critical juncture, and if our great affairs should yet go well, you might both of you have the first Princesses of Europe, whereas perhaps now you could not have the last; and besides, naturally speaking, on all accounts methinks you should think of marrying before your brother. When you explain your idea to me I shall be better able to judge of it, and it is useless till then to say any more on the subject.

In an increasing number of ways James found Charles's conduct of

302

his affairs hard to take. '*Enfin*, my dear child,' he wrote some weeks later, 'I must tell you very plainly that if you don't alter your ways I see you lost in all respects ... I have been already too long in hott water on your occasion and that without profit or advantage to any of us.'

By the end of the year it must have been clear to Charles that in fact he had little hope of securing any active assistance from the French Government. The nearest he ever came even to discussing the matter with anyone in authority was in a completely unsatisfactory interview with Cardinal Tencin, who, as everyone kept recalling, owed his scarlet hat to James's intervention as much as to the machinations of his own fun-loving sister and was therefore generally regarded as being a friend of the exiled court. The subject of help having come up, the Cardinal casually mentioned a condition, a possible quid pro quo for France. 'What condition?' asked Charles. 'That Ireland be ceded to France,' the Cardinal coolly replied. At this the Prince flew into a rage: '*Tout ou rien!*' he shouted. '*Point de partage! Point de partage!*' The interview thus came to an abrupt end and Charles gave it as his view that the Cardinal was 'a rogue and a rascal'.

Frustrated he now turned to another quarter for help, setting out in February 1747 for Spain. But he was to get no more encouragement from the Spanish Government than he had from the French. Neither King Ferdinand nor his chief minister showed any inclination to help him. Indeed both made it clear to him that the sooner he left their country the happier they would be. 'I thought', he wrote angrily to his father, after a long bleak ride across the Pyrenees, 'there was not such fools as the French court, but I find it here far beyond it.'

By the end of March he was back in Paris. 'I am returned here', he wrote, 'in perfect health and intend to stay here some time, but absolutely in private, and iff possible to make againe another attempt to bring these people to reason.' But by now he must have known in his own heart that the prospects were not good. And now, to make matters worse, came rumours of an impending peace between France and Great Britain.

James, with what Andrew Lang calls his 'sad lucidity', had few illusions. 'I am much more concerned than surprised,' he wrote to Charles on 17 April, 'you had not a better reception in Spain, but I am in hopes your journey thither will be of no ill consequence, provided you manage your matters in a proper manner on your return to Paris, where I think you should have equally in your view the soliciting another expedition and the endeavouring to make your situation as little bad as possible in case of a pease.' And again in the same letter: 'The question is not where it might be advisable to go, but where you may be allowed to stay.'

303

Charles was still only twenty-five. Six months had passed since he had set sail from Loch nan uagh. For him they had been months of continuing frustration and disappointment and these were things which, in contrast to the hazards and hardships of the rising, he did not find it easy to endure. Nor was their effect on his character at all beneficial. As time went on, he became more resentful, more suspicious, more secretive and above all more inclined to seek solace in the bottle which had so often been a comfort to him in his wanderings.

From his father, meanwhile, came long, loving, patient letters, well reasoned, well expressed and full of sound advice. These he either answered by ill-spelt, irritable and disjointed notes or, more often, did not answer at all. His memories of the exiled court, with its huddle of intriguing hangers-on, gave him no desire whatever either to return to Rome, as his father would have wished, or to share his secrets with James's confidants, some of whom he half-suspected of being in touch with the Hanoverians. 'Nothing', he scribbled on a scrap of paper, 'to be said to Rome, where all is known.' Certainly, through Walton in Rome and Horace Mann in Florence and their various sub-agents everywhere, the London Government seem to have been quickly informed of anything of importance that happened in or around the Palazzo Muti.

James, understandably, was not happy about his son. The distance which separated them and the prolonged lack of any direct contact between them made misunderstandings even easier than they would otherwise have been. James disliked in particular Charles's choice of advisers, notably Strickland, George Kelly and, until his death in November 1746, old Sir Thomas Sheridan. He also had grave misgivings about his conduct of affairs and attitude to questions of policy. 'I see', he wrote on 7 February, 'you are misled and deluded to your great and universal prejudice by the craft of ill and designing men.' Worst of all, he suspected him of neglecting his Roman Catholic faith in the hope of thus winning favour with his Protestant supporters. All of which doubts found expression in James's letters. But Charles remained stubborn and resentful of advice.

On one subject in particular nothing would change the Prince's mind. After hiding for several months in the Highlands, Lord George Murray had in March 1747 managed to escape to Holland and thence made his way to Rome, where James had received him in audience at the Palazzo Muti. But, though James begged Charles to see Lord George and assured him that he 'never speaks of you but with great respect and *éloge*', nothing would induce Charles to receive his former Lieutenant-General. Indeed he even tried (or so Henry reported to his father) to get Lord George locked up by the French Government as a traitor. 'I hope in God', wrote James, when he heard about it, 'you will not think of getting Lord George secured after all I have writ to you about him and that you will receive him at least civilly.' But Charles would not relent and when, on eventually reaching Paris, Lord George asked leave to pay his respects, Charles simply sent him a message telling him to keep away. To this Lord George replied that he would 'punctually obey his orders' and thereafter made no further attempt to see the Prince. Even the following, characteristically reasonable appeal from his father for a little generosity failed to move Charles in his current mood of resentfulness, self-pity and suspicion:

'If he has been on several occasions of a different opinion from you or other people,' James wrote, 'I don't see what crime there is in that ... and as to what he may have failed against you personally, he has owned his fault to me and begged of me to make his submission to you for him; and I own this last part touched me, for tho' but too many people have failed towards me, yet I scarce ever remember that ever anyone made such an act of submission as he has done. All he seeks is your forgiveness, and to be restored to your favour, which you are, I am sure, incapable of refusing him. . . .'

But, though Lord George continued to correspond with James until his death in 1760, Charles was never to see him again.

Charles's relations with his brother Henry had hitherto always been close and affectionate. Now these too became clouded by mutual suspicion. In Paris, where Henry was living, the two brothers maintained separate establishments and Henry corresponded with his father on a wide range of topics quite independently of Charles, keeping him informed, as far as he could, of the latter's movements and activities. Then, one afternoon towards the end of April 1747, Henry left Paris secretly. In order, apparently, the better to disguise his intentions from Charles, he had previously invited his brother to supper, leaving his house lit up and his servants ready to receive him. At the appointed time Charles arrived to find that there was no sign of Henry and, after waiting until midnight, made his way home in some anxiety as to what might have happened to his brother. A couple of days later he was handed a letter dated Paris 29th April which the latter had left behind for him. 'I begin,' Harry had written, 'by begging you 10,000 pardons for having gone away without acquainting you beforehand.' He had done so, he went on, because of his 'great longing to pay a visit to our dear King and father, who has been nearly two years now without having seen any of uss, and my desire would be so easily convinced that I venture to say, were I only to stay with him one fortnight, it would be of inexplicable comfort to me. As far as that, I am sure you would be the first to aprove.' The journey, too, 'must naturally be of great use to my health, which you know is in bad enough condition'; and so on.

What Henry did not reveal was the real purpose of his journey. Of this Charles was only informed a couple of months later in a letter from his father dated 13 June. 'I know not whether you will be surprized, my dearest Carluccio,' this began, 'when I tell you that your brother will be made a Cardinal the first days of next month. Naturally speaking, you should have been consulted about a resolution of that kind before it had been executed; but as the Duke and I were unalterably determined on the matter and that we foresaw you might probably not approve of it, we thought it would be showing you more regard and that it would be even more agreeable to you that the thing should be done before your answer could come here and to have it in your power to say it was done without your knowledge or approbation.' Enclosed was a short note from Henry, assuring Charles of his abiding love and affection.

To Charles, already indignant at Henry's secretive behaviour and sudden departure, the news that his brother had, with their father's approval, taken this step was a cause of extreme bitterness. Henry's decision to enter the Church meant that there was now only one of them to continue the line. It also further underlined the Stuarts' continuing involvement with the Church of Rome, which had already cost them so dear and which, other things being equal, was bound to prejudice any hopes of a restoration. Both points, and also Charles's state of mind, emerge clearly from a letter written to James from Paris in July by Father Myles MacDonell, himself a Catholic priest, who frankly describes Henry's action as 'a mortal deadly stroke to the cause'. 'His R.H. the Prince,' he continues, adding, in parenthesis, ('I am told, for I don't go near him') 'has shut himself up for several hours alone upon his hearing that news. The Duke's health is no more drank nor his name mentioned at his table: he is teased about his safety, and made to believe that his life will be in danger, being now alone and unmarried.'

While Charles no longer drank to his brother's health, Henry took to his new vocation like a duck to water. Though still living at the Palazzo Muti, he made his own friends, giving lavish musical parties and even entertaining the musicians, if they were attractive enough – 'low company', his father called them. Worse still, within a year or two he had, to his father's dismay, dismissed his English *maestro di camera*, Monsignor Leigh, and substituted a good-looking, young Genoese priest, Father Lercari, thereby causing something of a scandal, even by Roman standards. And when James insisted on Lercari's dismissal, 'instead of parting with his favourite,' writes Horace Walpole gleefully, 'the young cardinal with his minion left Rome abruptly, and with little regard to the dignity of his purple'.

It was not for some weeks that Charles could bring himself to answer his father's letter of 13th June. When he did, he left him in no doubt as to his feelings on what he regarded as his brother's defection.

Had I got a Dager throw my heart it woud not have been more sensible to me than at ye Contents of yr first. My Love for my Brother and Concern for yr Ca[u]se being the occasion of it. I hope your Majesty will forgive me not entering any further on so disagreeable a subject the shock of which I am scarce out of, so shall take ye Liberty of refering to next Post anything in yours to be answered. I lay myself full of Respect & Duty at yr Majestys Feet moste humbly asking Blessing.

Your Moste
Dutifull Son
CHARLES P.

Henceforward, despite repeated and anxious attempts on the part of both his father and brother to resume their old relationship, what has survived of their correspondence shows Charles in a morose, resentful mood, which his father's long, affectionate, reproachful letters did nothing to dispel. 'Happy would I be', he wrote to his father's secretary Edgar on 24 July, 'to have happier orders and chierfull spirits, which to my misfortune my friends hinder as well as my ennemys. God forgive the last. Having not strength to say more, I remain Charles P.'

Charles had indeed little cause for happiness. The war of the Austrian Succession was clearly coming to an end and plenipotentiaries of the powers involved were already meeting at Aix-la-Chapelle to discuss peace terms. The impending peace treaty was bound to put paid to any hope he might still have of armed help from France. He already suspected the French, not without reason, of wanting to get rid of him. He was on bad terms with his father and brother. He believed himself to be surrounded on all sides by disloyalty and intrigue. He was lonely, suspicious and irritable. His relations with his few remaining supporters suffered accordingly. Lacking money, he spent it lavishly, dressing splendidly, paying 100,000 francs for a single dinner service, having medals of himself struck in silver and copper and at the same time indignantly refusing offers of financial assistance from the French Government.

At such a time what could have been more natural than for Charles to seek solace in the agreeable company of his 'second family', the Bouillons? No one had welcomed him back to Paris more joyfully than they, not least his pretty cousin, Louise de Montbazon, whose husband

Jules-Hercule was away with his regiment, leaving her at home with their twelve-month-old baby son.

Louise was by now twenty-one. A portrait painted of her at about this time in the guise of a shepherdess, shows an engaging young woman with a bold eye, a generous mouth, and, one would say, an impulsive, outgoing temperament, a natural readiness to try her luck whatever the consequences and whatever the risks.

From Scotland Charles, to whom Louise (or so she soon imagined) had long felt strongly attracted, had returned to public acclaim, a legend in his own time, more manly and better looking than ever and now endowed with an aura of romantic heroism so that any even mildly susceptible young woman was bound to find him well-nigh irresistible.

Having by the summer as good as abandoned his incognito, Charles was more in demand than ever. From a number of houses offered him by friends and admirers he had chosen for his summer residence a fine country house at Saint Ouen, placed at his disposal by a connection of the Bouillons, the Prince de Rohan-Soubise. It was, he told his father in 'a pritty situation on ye Border of ye River and within to short Leagues of Paris'. Here he was in easy reach of the capital, able to see his friends and dine there whenever he felt like it. Towards the middle of August, with Jules Hercule de Montbazon still away with his regiment, we hear of his dining with Louise and her mother-in-law, the Princesse de Guémené, at the handsome Hôtel de Guémené in the Place Royale, itself an integral part of the prestigious ensemble constructed more than a century before under the auspices of Henri IV, with the tall windows of its first and second floors looking out from above an arcaded ground floor across the spacious square to the closely matching residences of other personages of almost equal consequences.

During the weeks that followed Charles and Louise were, as was only natural, constantly thrown together in town and country alike and a week or two after dining at the Hôtel de Guémené, Charles left for a long visit to Louise's father at his great château of Navarre in the pleasant valley of the Iton, near Evreux in Normandy. Here, in the surrounding Forêt D'Evreux, he could indulge his passion for 'ye shas' and here, in one or other of the château's splendid salons with their elegant Rococo panelling or in Lenotre's elaborately laid out gardens, with their grottos and follies and Temples of Love, he could see as much of Louise as he liked.*

*Today nothing survives of the great Château de Navarre save a single grotto, perched rustically above the river. After various vicissitudes the château itself was torn down in the 1830's to make way for a factory, while a racecourse has now taken the place of its once famous gardens.

Cousinage, say the French, *dangereux voisinage*. That summer, in what Charles calls '*une maison de campagne*', either at Navarre or at Saint-Ouen, he and Louise became lovers, yielding to a powerful mutual attraction, which, if they ever sought to resist it, quickly became stronger than they were. At twenty-seven, Charles, for the first and probably the only time in his life, was deeply and passionately in love; that his love was abundantly, overwhelmingly returned, there could from the first be no possible doubt.

For Charles this was something entirely new. From those around him we know that, unlike most of his contemporaries, he was not given to casual love affairs and on the whole showed himself shy and awkward in women's company. If we can believe Drummond of Balhaldie, there is even reason to suppose that, before setting out for Scotland in 1745, he took a vow of chastity. If so, this now went by the board. By the time the lovers returned to Paris that autumn, they had arranged (in the conveniently prolonged absence of Louise's husband) to meet clandestinely almost every night, not just anywhere, but in Louise's own bedroom at the Hôtel de Guéméné, which splendid abode she shared not only with her husband when he was in Paris, but also with his formidable and vigilant mother, who lived in some style on a lower floor.

Driving in by coach from Saint-Ouen (closely watched, as we now know, by French police spies whose reports still survive in the archives of the Bastille) and stopping discreetly a few streets away, in order to give the rest of the household, including Louise's husband, if he was there, time to retire, Charles would usually wait until after midnight. Then he would make his way surreptitiously to Louise's room on an upper floor, leaving again several hours later, to return to Saint-Ouen at day-break. With the help of conniving servants, the lovers also contrived to exchange almost daily a succession of passionate love-letters, promising faithfully to burn them immediately. A promise which Louise kept, but Charles, fortunately for a lubricious and inquisitive posterity, did not.

Some of Charles's biographers have suggested that he was under-sexed or at any rate not greatly interested in women. To Louise at any rate he brought, for a time at least, unimaginable bliss.

'If you enjoyed our night together, my love,' she wrote in late November, 'I was thrilled by it and look forward to many more of them. To me they mean everything. I can't wait to hear from you. Farewell, dear heart. I feel wonderful. See you tonight – come and live in the arms of one who in the whole world only loves her dear love.'

And so it went on, night after night, all that winter. But what Charles, in spite of his love for Louise, showed all too clearly that he lacked was any degree of consideration for her, any sympathy for the problems that beset her or any real understanding of the risks she was taking on his account, with a small baby, a husband in the offing, an all too alert mother-in-law on the premises and a horde of servants whose loyalties were, to say the least of it, liable to be mixed. That in his own way he was passionately, obsessively in love with her there can be no doubt, but with the increasingly possessive passion of an impatient and self-centred man, who, as a royal prince, insisted that their affair should be conducted on his terms. Within weeks, he was constantly blaming the inconveniences they periodically encountered on her shortcomings, her obstinacy, her indiscretion, her lack of maturity, her failure to take a line of her own and stand up to husband and mother-in-law. Why, he wanted to know, could he not, as a king's son, visit his mistress whenever it suited him and spend as much time with her as he liked? Why should he bother about her husband or her mother-in-law? Again, while blaming her for indiscretion, he had on more than one occasion, when not admitted as promptly as he would have liked, himself caused a disturbance outside the Hôtel Guémené, once by actually firing his pistols in the air, the better to emphasize his point. Soon, because he could not always see her whenever he felt like it, he was accusing her of not really loving him, even of having other lovers. But Louise, though saddened and hurt by what she called his *duretés*, was far too deeply in love to do more than meekly accept his reproaches, while assuring him again and again that she loved him and would never love anyone else as long as she lived.

'I am going to be bled, dear heart,' she wrote. 'I am letting you know in advance, just in case its in my right arm . . .' And again: 'If you were angry at having to sleep alone, dear love, I can promise you I was in despair and could not sleep all night. I am still tired after being bled. Come and see me this afternoon after dinner. That will make me very happy. And tonight at midnight my ecstasy will reach its height. Tonight I shall have something to tell you. But come without fail this afternoon. Farewell, dear heart. I love you more than I can say.'

And now, to her delight, mingled inevitably with alarm, she found that she was bearing his child. Predictably pleased at the prospect of becoming a father, Charles was no less predictably upset at the thought that a convincing *raison d'être*, a more acceptable paternity, would need to be provided for the baby when Jules-Hercule next came on leave. To him the idea that his mistress should even once be unfaithful to him with her husband was intolerable. And he made her pay for it accordingly, brutally brushing aside her all too genuine assurances that she loved him and him only.

But this was not their only problem. Despite their precautions, their affair was already being talked about by more and more people in Paris and even further afield. At least one great lady, clearly no friend of Louise, complained to Charles, who, given the pattern of his life, was understandably short of sleep, that he had dozed off on her shoulder at dinner and, when he finally woke up, would only talk of the little princess, whose charms, other than purely physical, were to her way of thinking, limited. Worse still, Jules-Hercule's mother, who was no fool, had for some time been growing more and more suspicious and talking openly of the noises she heard at night, while Charles for his part became ever more unreasonable, ever more demanding and, where Louise was concerned, ever less understanding.

'I could not be more disgusted', he wrote in a letter that has somehow survived in draft form, 'by all your miserable fussing. At least it serves to diminish my love for you which was once very great. I am only ashamed to have let it all upset me as much as it has ... I will come this evening at half past eleven and not a minute sooner. If there is the slightest difficulty I shall take my revenge and make a proper scene. See you at eleven thirty or never again as long as I live.' And again, a few days later: 'You must know, woman, that you are only acceptable to me in so far as you are able to please me. This may be my last visit.'

But Louise, as usual, gave in. Anything rather than lose him altogether.

On 22 January, after a spell of leave, Jules-Hercule de Monthazon, who seems to have remained blissfully ignorant of what was happening, departed once again for the front, leaving the field, as it seemed, even clearer for the lovers.

To be nearer Louise, Charles had in December moved from Saint-Ouen to a sizeable house in the Rue du Chemin du Rempart near the Porte St Honoré. 'The Weather now', he wrote in a chatty letter to his father, 'is beginning to be Winter Like, and dissagreeable for ye Cuntry. I have just got a little house in ye scirts of ye Town, which, Tho Little, Will be very Convenient for me to see anybody privately and Lay in it when I cum to Paris.' However irritating Louise might be, he would at least now be spared the long journey by coach from Saint-Ouen.

But Louise's mother-in-law, Mme de Guéméné, had different ideas. The moment had come, she decided, for decisive action. With her son safely out of the way, she persuaded Louise's father, the Duc de Bouillon, with whom his daughter seems finally to have shared her guilty secret, that they must combine to put a stop to the affair. It was thus that at ten o'clock on 23 January, having gone to bed early, Louise, now three months pregnant by Charles, more in love with him than ever and looking forward not only to a month or two of uninterrupted happiness, while her husband was away but also to a visit from her lover that very evening, was suddenly confronted by the two of them when, invading the privacy of her room, they flatly informed her that all was discovered, that there could be no question of the affair continuing and that she must at once write to Charles telling him so. After which she was to promise faithfully never to write to him again. In the end, with all three of them distraught and in floods of tears, Louise was forced to write the letter her father now dictated to her.

'What I all too clearly foresaw has now happened,' she wrote. 'My mother-in-law knows all about us and has just been here with my father. Both of them talked to me as friends. And so I have to inform Your Royal Highness as follows. Not only must I never see you. I must receive no letters from you. If you will do me the honour to visit me from time to time, as I think you will, so as not to ruin me any more than I am ruined already, you will be received in the ordinary way. Farewell Your Royal Highness.'

'This,' she added in spite of everything, 'is a severe test of my love for you which will last as long as I live.'

Five days later Louise, careless of the promise that had been extracted from her, managed, though closely watched, to smuggle out another letter to her lover:

> I couldn't write to you before. They keep a constant watch on me.
> It was cruel of you not to answer the letter I sent you after my
> terrible experience. I was so upset I could hardly hold the pen...
> Now, dear love, I will explain to you just what happened to me on
> Tuesday – the day I wrote to you. I was waiting impatiently for
> you to arrive here an hour after midnight and thought there was
> nothing whatever to worry about. Then, at ten o'clock, who should
> arrive but my Mother-in-law who had summoned my father to
> inform him of my behaviour. She told me that she had known all
> about us for a long time, but had hoped it would fizzle out. She
> did not speak angrily – in fact she was quite friendly and promised
> not to tell a soul. But she said it must stop and I must write and
> tell you so. Death itself, when it comes, will be less of a shock to
> me than that. They made me promise never to write to you again –
> but I could not wait any longer... My life will be dreadful. They
> can't get me to take any food. My head is spinning. But whatever
> the sufferings I have to endure, they will be as nothing, if you go
> on loving me. Otherwise I shall cease to live. Remember I am bearing
> your child and that I am suffering because of you. If you stop loving
> me, it will be more than I can endure. But if you still love me, we
> will somehow keep in touch. Which will be some sort of comfort

to me in my misery. I spend my days and nights weeping, looking at your portrait and kissing a lock of your hair. I am terribly changed. If you will write to me it will bring me back to life. How happy I should be to know that you still think of your loving mistress who loves you so tenderly. I shall be yours as long as I live. One day, I swear, we shall be happy again ... I do not have the strength to write any more. Give me back my life. If you still love me, I shall be happy. Farewell, my dearest love.

Of just what had taken place at the fatal interview Charles obtained a fuller account from Anne-Françoise de Carteret, a confidante of the Prince's and a school friend of Louise, who happened to be staying with her at the Hôtel de Guémené at the time and had actually been present during the latter part of the confrontation – '*la plus horible cène*,' she called it, '*qui se soit jamais veu*'.

On returning to the Hôtel on the evening after her arrival, Anne wrote, she had found Louise's father and mother-in-law closeted together; Louise was convinced that they were talking about her. A moment or two later the two of them had appeared in Louise's room and asked her to leave them alone with Louise. From outside she had then heard terrible shrieks from poor Louise. The three of them had remained shut up together for an hour and a half, after which they had asked her to come in again. All three were in tears. 'You know', Louise's father had said to her 'of the Prince's relationship with my daughter, whom he has ruined. The Prince has shown no consideration or regard for her – no respect for himself or for her as his cousin nor the slightest gratitude for what our family has done for him since he first came to this country. On the contrary he has dishonoured her in her own house. This being so, the only thing to be done is to break off the relationship once and for all. My daughter must write to him doing this immediately.'

And Anne went on to describe to Charles the state Louise was in. Louise, she went on in a passage remarkable at once for its worldly wisdom, its depth of feeling and its restraint, was more to be pitied than blamed. Young, inexperienced and passionate by nature, with a natural imprudence which those she loved must somehow seek to make up for, she had plunged head first into their relationship, without thinking what she was doing or of the consequences. 'Your Royal Highness', she concluded, 'once loved her passionately. That is something you cannot altogether obliterate. Be sorry for her. Be kind to her. Don't simply abandon her to her despair. For God's sake have pity on her in the state to which you have reduced her.'

But, whatever its merits, Anne's letter, as was to be expected, only made Charles still angrier. To have the very real debt he owed his uncle recalled to him, to be reminded that his own behaviour in the matter might strike some as less than honourable, simply served to increase his irritation with the unfortunate Louise – in fact with all of them. How dare they try to tell him how to behave? To Louise's despairing appeals he made no reply.

Meanwhile, to disturb him still further, came in those early months of 1748 ever stronger hints of impending peace negotiations between France and Great Britain, negotiations which, if successful, would lead inevitably to his expulsion from French territory and kill for the foreseeable future any hopes of French military support for a fresh Jacobite rising. In the all too likely event of peace, what would he himself do and where would he go? These were the questions he was now having to ask himself.

As for Louise, despite her solemn promise never to try to communicate with her lover again and despite the mechanical difficulties of doing so, she continued to pour out her heart to him in long agonized letters, telling him of her despair, of her eternal love for him and of her readiness now to meet him anywhere, at any time, at whatever risk to herself – letters which he continued to ignore, as he ignored the to him frivolous and totally unacceptable request that, for the sake of appearances (for which he did not give a fig) he should now from time to time call on her socially at hours normal for such purely courtesy visits.

By this time it was more than three months since they had last met. '*Quand je pense qu'il y a trois mois,*' wrote Louise, '*la tête me tourne, je me rapelle tant d'hereux moments.*' And now Louise would go to the Opéra, to the Comédie Française, to concerts, solely in the hope of seeing her lover. But even when she saw him, he did not return her gaze. Nor, she noticed, was he any longer wearing the waistcoat she had specially embroidered for him. With all this she reproached him in more long, plaintive letters, repeating that, without him, life had no meaning for her and that she might as well end it, for herself and for their unborn child. Why, she asked, did he not simply send her a glass of poison, so that she could finish it all? '*Qu'il m'envoye un verre de poison, je le boirai avec plaisir et mon malhereux enfant perira.*' But the very next moment she was asking why they could not meet in an apartment she had at Versailles. Or, if he wanted her to, she would now even come to his house in the Rue du Chemin du Rempart, though she knew that it was watched night and day by her mother-in-law's spies.

And then Charles seems suddenly to have relented and, with the help of his devoted Irish manservant Daniel O'Brien, a meeting was arranged at midnight in a hired coach by the Pont Tournant. There, for an hour or two, she was once more in his arms, able to look at him and hear his voice, hear him tell her once again that he loved her *à la folie*, and then, a few moments later, that he loved her perhaps less than he once had done and might even look elsewhere for his pleasures. And here, somehow, there cropped up the name of her mother's cousin, more than twenty years older than her, the brilliant, beautiful and notorious Princesse de Talmond. For Charles, like other men, was inclined to feel differently on different matters at different times.

And so Louise, after they had parted again, was torn between freshly remembered bliss and the torment of fresh doubts, and could only repeat in the passionate, agonized letters she immediately sent him next day and on the two succeeding days that she loved him more than ever and begged him to meet her again in a coach or, for that matter, anywhere else. '*Dans la carosse*,' she added pathetically, '*je vous donnerai votre petit plaisir tant que vous voudrée.*' Above all she begged him not to see so much of Madame de Talmond. '*Mais, de grace, voiee moins Mde t – et ne prenee personne: J'en mourrois de douleur ... Sur tout plus tant Mde t; elle me fera mourir de chagrin.*' And why didn't he write to her, as he had promised – '*De vos nouvelles!*'

But, in reality, Charles's casually dropped hint that he might look for his pleasures elsewhere was by this time an accomplished fact. Already in April, Louise, having gone yet again to the Opéra in the hope of catching a glimpse of him, had, with grave misgivings, seen him sharing a box with the Princesse de Talmond. By the middle of May it was common knowledge in Paris that she had become his mistress.

For Louise, after their midnight encounter in the *carosse*, there were to be no more meetings with Charles in a coach or anywhere else. During the last days of May she wrote him four or five more long, loving letters, begging him to meet her; in the end she received one in return, complaining as usual of her relatives and of her supine attitude towards them. Her reply to this said everything there was to say. '*Si vous etiez libre*,' she wrote, '*vous n'auriez qu'a m'emmenee – je serais pour la vie avec vous et je ne pourrois estre contente que comme cela.*' '*Vous ne pouvez pas croire*', she added, '*a quel point je vous aime!*'

But, as she said, Charles was not free. There was nowhere in the world he could take her, even if he wanted to. Indeed, as the peace talks between France and Great Britain proceeded, it looked as though there might soon be nowhere for him to go himself. And so, after a couple more despairing letters from Louise, one regretting that Charles had been displeased by a suggestion of hers that they should meet again in the *carosse*, (*petits plaisirs* and all), the one-sided correspondence, consisting of some fifty or so of Louise's neatly written letters, so carefully preserved for all these years in the Royal Archives at Windsor, comes to an end. Possibly more secret letters passed between the cousins and for one reason or another did not survive. Or, more probably, with the emergence of Madame de Talmond, Louise simply gave up.

On 28 July her baby son was born and christened Charles Godefroi Sophie Jules Marie de Rohan. '*Madame la duchesse de Montbazon vient de nous donner un second fils*,' wrote Madame de Guéméné proudly to the titular King James in Rome, thus acquainting that long-suffering man without his ever realizing it, of the birth of his only grandson. But sadly, little Charles died less than six months later.

Louise herself was to live for another thirty-three years, to all appearances a good wife and mother, on the best of terms with her husband, who, continuing his military career, was to become a Lieutenant-General by the time he was thirty-six. On excellent terms, too, with her father, whose favourite, in spite of everything, she had always been; and even, now that it was all over, with her formidable mother-in-law. Over the years she made occasional appearances at court and in later life, seemingly deeply religious, devoted much of her time to good works. A portrait of her by Chardin, painted, probably, in her thirties, shows a good looking young woman, at peace, one would say, with the world and with herself. In a milieu where clandestine and less clandestine *affaires du coeur* were normal practice and gossip about them a way of life, there is no indication that she was ever again unfaithful to the estimable Jules-Hercule. Nor, after the death of little Charles Godefroi, did she have another child. And when, in September 1781, the time came for her to die, she was buried in Paris next to her infant son Charles at the Church of St Louis in the Convent des Feuillants, where all those years ago, his father had occasionally attended Mass. '*Aussi est-il*', wrote a contemporary, '*peu de maisons, où il y ait plus de vertu et un plus grand éloignement pour les choses du siècle.*'

Like many people in Paris, Madame de Talmond, who during that same summer of 1748 became Charles's *maîtresse en titre*, was well aware of his torrid affair with Louise and doubtless derived considerable satisfaction from having supplanted a woman half her age. With her own experience of life, she no doubt also felt, for a time at any rate, better able to cope with him. 'You want', she wrote to him in the summer of 1748, 'to give *me* the second volume in your romance of compromising Madame de Montbazon with your pistol shots.' She was, nevertheless, unlikely to prove a soothing influence on the Prince.

Everything militated against that. 'He lives', wrote d'Argenson, 'with the Princesse de Talmond; he is furious and obstinate in everything.'

Polish by birth, a cousin of his mother's and of Queen Maria Leczinska, Marie-Anne-Louise Jablonowska was well known for her charm, beauty and wit: a restless, dramatic creature, aged forty-seven. Madame du Deffand describes her as vain, like all Poles, callous, capricious, unhappy, absurd and affected. Some seventeen years before she had married Anne Charles Frédéric, Prince de Talmond, who was a good ten years younger than she was and whose interests, according to the Marquis d'Argenson, lay rather in the direction of good-looking young men and highly austere religious exercises. From the start she had been completely unfaithful to him. 'She is', writes Madame du Deffand, 'feared and disliked by all who live in her society. Yet she has truth, courage and honesty ... She pleases, she provokes, we love and hate her, seek her and avoid her.'

According to d'Argenson, she governed Charles 'with fury and folly', encouraging him whenever possible to defy the French Government. Charles, true to form, seems to have caused at least one scandal by trying to break into her house after her long-suffering husband had refused him admission. Nor was she alone in the field. '*Le Prince Edouard*', wrote d'Argenson, '*s'amuse à faire l'amour*' and he describes Madame de Talmond and the Duchesse d'Aiguillon as fighting over the Prince 'like fish-wives'. Less well informed than usual, d'Argenson also describes a 'ridiculous scene' between Charles and Madame de Guémené (who happened to be three years younger than Madame de Talmond) under the impression, apparently, that it was a lovers' quarrel, when in reality, of course, it concerned Louise.

With Madame d'Aiguillon, hostess to the *philosophes* and friend of Montesquieu and Voltaire, Charles's association may well have been platonic. She too, was anything but a soothing influence. 'Her wit', wrote Madame du Deffand acidly, 'is like her face, brilliant and out of drawing.' Dynamic and impetuous, she did nothing to calm the already disturbed and frustrated young man. Encouraged by these new intellectual associates, Charles seems even to have given some thought to literature and to the ideas and systems of the *philosophes*, and in his hastily scribbled *Maximes d'un Homme Sauvage* there are occasional, somewhat incongruous, echoes of Jean-Jacques Rousseau and of the return to nature.

Meanwhile, at Aix-la-Chapelle the peace negotiations between Great Britain and France had been continuing and in July 1748 a preliminary treaty of peace was signed and published. From this it was evident that the French were preparing amongst other things to accord formal recognition to the House of Hanover, at the same time withdrawing it from the Stuarts and in all probability depriving Prince Charles of the asylum he had hitherto enjoyed in France.

At this not unexpected change of front on the part of their former allies, both Charles and his father, acting independently, addressed vigorous protests to King Louis, both of which were printed and made public. Charles, who was becoming increasingly truculent in his dealings with the French and had probably read Voltaire's new life of Charles XII of Sweden, now went about boasting that, like his namesake, he would barricade himself into his house and resist all attempts to eject him. 'He wished', wrote d'Argenson, 'to imitate Charles XII and stand a siege in his home, like Charles XII at Bender. Madame de Talmond has dissuaded him: it is thought that a retreat will be found for him in Switzerland.'

Charles also sent a copy of his 'little work', as he called his protest, to the great Montesquieu, asking him to give it all the publicity he could, complaining that Montesquieu had not sent him a copy of his latest book on the Romans and adding that 'there should be more confidence between authors'. To this Montesquieu replied effusively, praising Charles's protest for its 'simplicity, nobility and eloquence' and for the way in which he expressed his feelings for the brave men who had followed him in victory and defeat and adding, with the hyperbole of his day, that, if Charles had not been 'so great a Prince', Madame d'Aiguillon and he would together certainly have secured his election to the *Académie Française*. But, though Charles's protest was well received by his literary friends and indeed by the French public as a whole, who felt that their rulers were treating him shabbily, it made no impression whatever on the French Government, whose chief concern was by this time simply to get rid of him.

In October 1748 the French and British plenipotentiaries met at Aix-la-Chapelle and the treaty of peace was signed. Under its terms France was expressly precluded from granting asylum to the Stuart claimant. This information was formally conveyed to Prince Charles at the beginning of November in an official note from King Louis, delivered by the Duc de Gesvres. In this the King said that he expected Charles to leave France immediately, and had too much faith in his good sense to believe that he would try to do anything else.

To this and to other less formal representations and to offers of financial inducements to leave the country and settle in Switzerland, Charles, delighting in an opportunity to annoy and embarrass the French, responded by utterly refusing to move from Paris. Indeed he ostentatiously set about renting a fine new house and ordered a splendid new silver dinner service, with which the better to entertain Madame de Talmond, who, despite her husband's warnings, continued to dine with him nightly. Nor did he pay any more attention to an agonized letter from his father warning him against the folly of breaking with France lightheartedly and ordering him 'as your Father and your King to obey the commands of his Most Christian Majesty immediately and leave his territory with good grace'.

Instead, brushing aside as idle rumours reports that he was about to be arrested and deported, Charles continued to live as ostentatiously as he could in his new house on the Quai des Théatins, opposite the Louvre, conveniently situated, as he explained to his friends, for his frequent visits amid public acclaim to the Opéra and various other places of entertainment, at which he invariably attracted far more attention and applause than the performance itself. He was also given, understandably if not very tactfully, to boasting publicly of the recent British naval victories over the French, while to the Prince de Conti, who pointed out that it was perhaps a little inappropriate that the medals which he had had struck of himself should bear on the reverse side the figure of Britannia surrounded by her warships, by which he had himself so recently been pursued, he gave short shrift. *'Cela est vrai, Prince,'* was his reply, *'mais je suis nonobstant l'ami de la flotte contre tous ses ennemis; comme je regardai toujours la gloire de l'Angleterre comme la mienne. Et sa gloire est dans sa flotte.'*

But, not surprisingly, the patience of King Louis and his advisers was fast becoming exhausted. The British Government had by now started to complain to the French that the treaty was not being observed, and in the end the decision was taken to resort to drastic measures. On 9 December Charles was given a further warning to leave the country immediately. This he ignored, and a day or two later a formal order for his arrest was submitted to King Louis for his signature. *'Pauvre Prince!'* said Louis as he signed it, *'qu'il est difficile pour un roi d'être un véritable ami.'*

On the evening of 11 December Charles, despite rumours that something was afoot, drove as usual across the river to the opera, where he had booked a box. *'Prince, retournez, on va vous arrêter. Le Palais Royal est investi,'* a voice cried from the crowd as his coach passed along the rue St Honoré, but he paid no heed.

The French Government had left nothing to chance. No less than 1,200 men of the Garde Royale under the command of the Duc de Biron, together with auxiliary contingents of police and grenadiers, were deployed all round the Opéra and in the streets leading to it. Locksmiths were mobilized and axes and scaling ladders held in readiness for fear the Prince might take refuge in a neighbouring house, while three surgeons and a physician stood by in case of casualties. But Charles simply drove on towards the entrance to the Opéra and

319

there prepared to alight.

As the steps of his coach were let down, Major Vaudreuil of the Royal Guards gave a signal and, while others took Charles by the legs, two sergeants seized him by the arms and bundled him through a narrow passage into the kitchen court of the Palais Royal and thence to the rooms of a surgeon in the service of the Duc d'Orléans. Here he was searched, relieved of his sword, a pair of pistols and a penknife and bound hand and foot with special black or, according to another source, crimson silk cord, of which ten ells had been especially provided for the purpose. '*Mon cher Monsieur*,' Charles said to Vaudreuil while all this was happening, '*vous faites la un vilain métier.*'

While his three gentlemen-in-waiting, who had also been seized, were hurried off to the Bastille, the Prince was carried 'like a corpse' head foremost into a coach. Vaudreuil and two other officers got in with him. Six grenadiers with fixed bayonets clambered upon the outside. A strong cavalry escort closed in all round, and the party set out for the Château de Vincennes. '*Ou allons nous?*' said Charles to the wretched Vaudreuil, as they stopped to change horses at the Porte St Antoine. '*Vous me conduisez à Hanover?*' And Vaudreuil mumbled something about changing horses to save time.

On reaching Vincennes, Charles was met by the governor, the Marquis de Chatelet, who happened to be a friend of his. '*Mon ami*,' he said to Chatelet, glancing down at his silken bonds, '*venez donc m'embrasser, puisque je ne puis pas aller vous embrasser.*' Feeling thoroughly uncomfortable, Chatelet at once gave orders for the cords to be removed and Charles was led off to his room. This, according to some accounts, was a wretched cell high up in the keep, but according to others a fine apartment with a comfortable bed and an excellent supper waiting for him.

The news of Charles's arrest and the way in which it had been carried out caused considerable public indignation. Even the Dauphin is said to have protested to his father the King 'in full *levée*' at this treatment of a former ally and guest of their country, and after a few days Charles was released on condition that he left France at once. From Vincennes he was escorted to the bridge at Beauvoisin on the borders of Savoy by the Marquis de Perussy, Commandant of the Musketeers, who, on reaching the frontier, bade him farewell and handed him over to two of his own gentlemen, Stafford and young Sheridan. From Beauvoisin Charles, assuming the uniform of an Irish officer in the Spanish service, made his way by chaise to the Papal city of Avignon, where he arrived at the end of December, boasting that 'his head was still on his shoulders'.

Avignon was a favourite refuge for exiled Jacobites and on arriving there Charles at once made contact with the Murrays, now out of favour with King James, and the Hays. 'I have the pleasure', wrote James Murray, titular Earl of Dunbar, to Edgar on 1 January 1749, 'to acquaint you that H.R.H. the Prince arrived here in perfect health on Friday morning at 7 o'clock. I was never more surprised than to see him at my bedside, after they told me that an Irish officer wanted to speak to me.'

Room was promptly found for Charles at the house of James Murray's sister, his father's alleged mistress, Mrs Hay, the titular Lady Inverness, where he remained until a suitable residence had been made ready for him. 'I arrived here on Friday last,' he wrote to his father from Avignon on 1 January 1749, 'and am in perfect good health, notwithstanding the unheard-of barbarous and inhuman treatment I met with.'

Although Avignon, which had been under Papal jurisdiction since the thirteenth century, did not offer Charles quite the same distractions as Paris, it was an agreeable enough place. Madame de Talmond seems to have joined him there. In due course the Papal Vice-Legate, Monsignor Acquaviva, and the Archbishop both called on him and the Vice-Legate gave a *bal masqué* in his honour, at which he met Don Philip of Spain, now on his way to take possession of his new Dukedom of Parma. Charles also tried to organize some boxing and prizefighting. This shocked the Archbishop and clergy and in the end the matter was referred to the Pope, who, not surprisingly, supported his own clergy. All of which was duly reported by the ever-vigilant Walton to his masters in London.

While in Avignon Charles seems to have embarked on a wild matrimonial project, boldly asking the Landgrave of Hesse for his daughter's hand in marriage. '*Je n'ai pas malheureusement,*' he wrote, '*une couronne a lui offrir comme elle le mérite, mais j'espère bien de l'avoir un jour.*' Put in this way, it was a proposition unlikely to appeal even to a Landgrave, especially as the lady in question happened to be already married and living happily in Rome with her husband. None of which stopped Charles from drafting a letter to Stanislas, the ex-King of Poland at Lunéville, announcing the early arrival of his bride and himself on Polish territory and referring to the Princess as '*la Princesse ma Femme*'.

But even in Avignon Charles was not left in peace. On learning of his presence there, the British Government at once protested and it was conveyed to the Pope that, if he allowed the Prince to remain there, his port of Civitavecchia would be bombarded by the Royal Navy. This was a risk His Holiness was not prepared to take and instructions were at once sent to the Vice-Legate to tell Charles that he must leave without delay. This time the Prince made no attempt to resist eviction. On the night of 28 February 1749, accompanied only by his devoted equerry Henry Goring and without revealing his intentions to a soul, he rode out of Avignon and, as far as most people were concerned, out of sight.

Charles was now in his thirtieth year. Again he had suffered a serious and in some respects deeply wounding setback. Again a period in his life had come to an end.

CHAPTER TWENTY

'What can a bird do that has not found a right nest?' Charles scribbled at about this time on a scrap of paper, 'He must flit from bough to bough *ainsi use les Irondel.*' For the next ten or twelve years, the Prince became a wanderer, flitting in disguise and under assumed names from country to country and from place to place and sometimes even baffling the British Government's spies and agents. By these he was variously reported as having been in Ireland, in Sweden, at Oxford, in London, in Kent, in Venice, in Germany and in Poland, whence the zealous Lord Hyndford wished it might have been possible to despatch him to Siberia 'where he would not have been any more heard of'.

In fact, braving King Louis's police, he seems, whatever the risks involved, to have soon made his way back to Paris. Certainly in early March 1749, only a few days after his departure from Avignon, his banker, Waters, received a message to say that he 'would call for letters'. For, though Waters evidently had no more idea of his movements than anyone else, it was important that Charles should be able to use his office as a clearing house for the secret communications which passed between him and his supporters in the Highlands and elsewhere and, in particular, for messages concerning the treasure which had been left buried near Loch Arkaig and on which he (though not only he) was now beginning to draw heavily. In Paris, too, possessive, demanding, but never boring and usually ready to help, was Madame de Talmond.

Charles did not travel directly to Paris. On 3 April 1749, he was at Lunéville in Lorraine, where ex-King Stanislas of Poland now held sway and where Madame de Talmond had her estates. At Lunéville Charles evolved (the draft, in his usual poor French, survives) an

323

elaborate and confused plan for his journey to Paris, involving Henry Goring, a travelling trunk, and a chaise, in which Charles was to travel to Paris secretly via Dijon and Ligny. On the draft plan are scribbled for future reference some names and addresses, amongst them that of Mademoiselle Ferrand, Grande Rue Varenne, Faubourg St Germain, Paris. Mademoiselle Ferrand was a Norman by birth, the daughter of Monsieur Ferrand des Marres, and a close friend of the philosopher Condillac, who bears witness to her exquisite sensibility and also to the keenness and balance of her intellect and the liveliness of her imagination. At this stage she was not, it appears, personally known to the Prince. But she was a friend of Madame de Talmond and was recommended to him in a note signed with the single letter 'T'.

Charles reached Paris by 10 April and, while there, transacted some business with Waters. Argenson believed him for some reason to be in Sweden at this time, only to discover a few weeks later that he had in fact spent a whole week in Paris, where he had been hidden by Madame de Talmond. His return, oddly enough, shocked Argenson, who was inclined to believe that Maurepas had connived at these arrangements. 'Assuredly,' he wrote, 'the prince acted very ill in breaking his word of honour to the King, when he promised to leave the realm; and he is greatly discredited by returning to a country whence he had been so brutally expelled.'

From Paris, Argenson was informed, Charles and Madame de Talmond had made their way to Lorraine, and on 26 April Charles was in Strasburg. From Strasburg he sent Henry Goring to Berlin with a message for the Earl Marischal, now in the service of King Frederick II of Prussia, asking him to meet him in Venice. Charles himself arrived in Venice on 17 May, but was ordered to leave a week later, a direct appeal to the Empress Maria Theresa having proved fruitless. As for the Earl Marischal, whose enthusiasm for the Jacobite cause had long been tempered by realism, it may safely be assumed that he never stirred from Berlin.

Argenson had barely received the news of the Prince's first return to Paris before Charles was back there on a second visit. On 3 June we find him writing to Montesquieu and by the end of the month he was once again installed there. It was now that Charles took up his introduction to Mademoiselle Ferrand. She would, he wrote, be surprised to receive a letter from him, as he was not fortunate enough to be known to her, but Mrs de Routh, the wife of an Irish officer in the French service, would explain. She was, he knew, the author of a history of Cartouche, the famous brigand, and it was for a kind of Cartouche that he now begged for her sympathy and help. Would she, he asked, act as recipient for some letters which would be addressed to Mr John Douglas and transmitted to her by Waters the banker?

For a romantically minded young woman of exquisite sensibility and pronounced literary leanings, such a request was clearly impossible to refuse. Before long Mademoiselle Ferrand, or 'Mademoiselle Luci', as Charles was soon calling her, was not merely providing an accommodation address for the Prince, but actual accommodation as well. She and her close friend Madame de Vassé, a young widow who, like her, was an intimate of Condillac and the *philosophes*, had rooms in the Convent of Saint Joseph in the rue Saint Dominique, where various ladies of fashion, including Madame du Deffand and, on occasion, Madame de Talmond, were in the habit of seeking spiritual solace and also occasionally entertaining their friends. It was here that Mademoiselle Ferrand now afforded the Prince a refuge. During the day he was able, from an alcove in her apartment, to listen, unseen, to much brilliant conversation, apparently including occasional references to himself. At night a secret staircase afforded him ready access to the rooms of Madame de Talmond, '*la Reine du Maroc*', as he now called her.

This happy arrangement seems to have lasted on and off for a year or two, while Charles's stormy affair with Madame de Talmond followed its uneven course. Just how disturbed this was, is evident from the scores of little notes which passed between the lovers. 'If you want to protect me,' writes Charles, in one of these, 'you must not make my life more wretched than it is.' And in another, proposing some kind of *modus vivendi*, he promises to 'withdraw from her territory at any hour of the day or night', if so commanded. But in the end the clash of their personalities seems to have exploded into open strife. Blows were exchanged and the uproar in their part of the convent finally became such that in the end Madame de Vassé felt obliged to send the Prince away for fear of public scandal. To make matters worse, Madame de Talmond, whose own hold on the Prince's affections had now begun to weaken, seems to have suspected poor sensitive Mademoiselle Luci of helping to alienate them. Nor, as the years went by and his treatment of her became ever worse, was she able to keep the ascendancy over him she had once briefly possessed. 'If I did not love you so much,' she wrote pleadingly, 'I would not be so wretched. The sight of me can do you no harm and the sight of you would restore me to life. I am dying. I love you too much and you love me too little.'

During this period the convent was not Charles's only hiding place. He kept on the move. In November 1749 we hear of him again at Lunéville. In December he sent the long-suffering Henry Goring to Paris, presumably from somewhere nearby to fetch 'his big muff and portfolio'. And in the spring of 1750, for a little light reading, Made-

325

moiselle Luci was asked to send to him, wherever he was, copies of *Joseph Andrews* and *Tom Jones*.

There were a number of messages, too, connected with the Loch Arkaig treasure, on which, together with money raised by Jacobite supporters in England, Charles now very largely depended. From Lochgarry, who had been in the Highlands that winter, came the information that he had seen Cluny Macpherson, now the guardian of the treasure, who said that, although much of the gold 'had been torn from him', he had kept a strict account of his disbursements and 16,000 louis d'or still remained. In the course of 1749 Major Kennedy had been sent by Charles to fetch back part of the treasure. He had been arrested and then released and had in the end brought back a considerable sum, probably £6,000, while Henry Goring, who also crossed clandestinely to England, brought over no less than £15,000 contributed by the English Jacobites. The latter had, however, made it a condition that Charles should get rid of certain members of his household of whom they disapproved, and at the same time seek a reconciliation with France.

Even now the idea of another attempt to regain the British throne was still uppermost in Charles's mind. The plans for such a venture were necessarily secret and the information that has survived is scrappy and incomplete. What is certain is that in the course of 1750 Charles made up his mind to go to London, apparently with a vague idea of himself leading some kind of Jacobite insurrection against the still unpopular House of Hanover. 'Ye Prince,' he wrote on 5 May, 'is determined to go over at any rate.... He assures that he will expose nobody but himself supposing the worst.' Arrangements were made for Henry Goring's brother, Sir Charles, to send a ship to Antwerp early in August 'and to agree where the arms etc. may be most conveniently landed, the grand affair of L [London] to be attempted at the same time'. At the same time 186,000 livres were secretly deposited with Waters the banker and a number of small silver medals bearing the Prince's profile and the encouraging inscription *laetamini cives* were ordered for distribution to his supporters, as well as a miniature to be painted by Le Brun 'with all orders'. At about this time various other small seals and medallions with Prince Charles's head on them were prepared, some with inscriptions and some without – 'coloured Glass Seals with the Pretender's Son's effigy, as also small heads made of silver gilt to be set in rings, as also points for watch cases, with the same head and this motto round "Look, love and follow"'.

And in June Charles wrote to Mr Dormer, an English merchant living in Antwerp and 'his chief medium of intelligence with England', reminding him that he had already offered, through Goring, 'to furnish

326

me with Arms necessary for my service'. 'I hereby desire you,' he continued, 'to get me with all ye expedition possible Twenty Thousand guns, Baionets, Ammunition proportioned, with four thousand sords and Pistols for horces in one ship which is to be ye first, and in ye second six thousand guns without baionets but sufficient Ammunition and Six thousand Brode sords'.

In July 1750, presumably in preparation for a landing, Charles wrote to his father in cypher, asking him to renew the Commission as Regent which he had granted him in 1745. James duly complied, but his reply was scarcely encouraging. He found Charles, he said, 'a continual heartbreak'. 'But let me recommend to you,' he went on, 'not to use other people as you do me, by expecting friendship and favors from them while you do all that is necessary to disgust them for you must not expect that anybody else will make you the return too.'

Just what Charles had in mind and just what in the event went wrong is not clear. Most probably the English Jacobites, always cautious and now warned by the sad example of the Forty-five, once again failed to show the enthusiasm expected of them. We only know that in September 1750 Charles himself did in fact go to London, crossing from Antwerp in 'an Abbé's dress with a black patch over his eye and his eyebrows black'd' and arriving in London four days later under the name of Smith. Just what he was hoping to achieve is obscure. 'Parted ye 2nd Sep.' he jotted down on a sheet of paper which still survives. 'Arrived to A [Antwerp] ye 6th. Parted from thence ye 12th Sept. E [England] ye 14th., and at L [London] ye 16th. Parted from L ye 22nd and arrived at P [Paris] ye 24th. From P parted ye 28th. Arrived here ye 30th Sept.'

As to how he spent his time in London, we have only disjointed scraps of information. He is thought to have stayed in Essex Street, off the Strand, at a house belonging to Lady Primrose, a prominent Jacobite and widow of the third Viscount Primrose. There he seems to have appeared unexpectedly while Lady Primrose was entertaining some of her friends, thus greatly startling and no doubt alarming his hostess who, however, went on playing cards, as if nothing had happened. From Lady Primrose a message went at once to Dr William King of St Mary's Hall, Oxford, a Jacobite manager, asking him to come to her house immediately. On reaching it, Dr King was astounded to be taken to Lady Primrose's dressing-room and there presented to the Prince. 'If I was surprised to find him there,' he wrote, 'I was still more astonished when he acquainted me with the motives which had induced him to hazard a journey to England at this juncture. The impatience of his friends who were in exile had formed a scheme which was impracticable. . . . No preparations had been made, nor was anything ready. . . . He was soon convinced that he had been deceived, and, therefore, after a stay in London of five days only, he returned to the place from whence he came.'

Apart from this encounter, the Prince also drank tea with Dr King, who records that his servant remarked on his visitor's resemblance to Prince Charles and, on being asked whether he had ever seen the Prince, replied that he had not, but that the Doctor's visitor was very like the busts of the Prince then on sale in Red Lion Street.

In addition to visiting Dr King, Charles held a meeting in a house in Pall Mall with some fifty leading English Jacobites, including Lord Westmorland and the Duke of Beaufort. To these he declared, no doubt sincerely, that, if they could raise even 4,000 men, he would put himself at their head and lead them in person. With the same object in view he also visited the Tower of London in company with a reliable Jacobite called Colonel Brett and, after carefully examining the approaches to it, arrived at the conclusion that in case of need one of its gates could be successfully demolished with a petard. The story is told that, on being informed of Charles's arrival in London and asked what he proposed to do, King George II remained calm. 'I shall do nothing at all,' he replied. 'When he is tired of England he will go abroad again' – in the circumstances an all too sensible answer.

Before leaving London, Charles took a step, which, if taken five years earlier, could have been of the utmost importance. Going to 'the New Church in the Strand', probably either St Mary's-Le-Strand or St Martin's-in-the-Fields, he there abjured the Roman Catholic faith in which he had been brought up and was received into the Church of England – 'In order,' he wrote some time afterwards, 'to make my renunciation of the errors of the Church of Rome the most authentick, and the less liable afterwards to malitious interpretations, I went to London in the year 1750, and in that capital did then make a solemn abjuration of the Romish religion, and did embrace that of the Church of England as by Law Established in 39 Articles in which I hope to live and die.'

Though a few leading Scottish and English Jacobites were aware of it, the Prince's conversion to Protestantism, which in the event turned out to be only temporary, was never very widely known, even amongst his supporters. His father and his brother, on the other hand, were reported to be 'ill with grief' when they learned of it.

Charles returned to Paris at the end of September. Thereafter for a time he vanished. Waters the banker he told that he should not expect to hear from him until 15 January 1751; to Mademoiselle Luci he gave instructions to forward no letters; to Madame de Talmond, with whom his relations, pending another reconciliation, were again strained, he wrote that he was leaving his *'triste solitude'*; while in October an agent of the British Government reported that 'the young Pretender is disguised in an Abbé's dress, with a black patch upon his eye and his eyebrows black'd'.

Some part of the months that followed he may have spent in a secret hiding place provided by Mademoiselle Ferrand and Madame de Vassé, which Henry Goring calls 'the château you know of, which by the description is a lonely solitary place, if you think it safe to make the journey'. But, as Goring points out, the decision was not an easy one, for 'if it should ever become publick where you are, or if more suspected, it would be almost impossible to remove and at the same time dangerous to stay'. The two ladies seem also to have offered Charles financial help, which Goring did not feel able to accept, as being 'an affair too delicate for me to meddle in without your orders', but 'thought it was my duty to acquaint you with the generous sentiments and ye noble friendship of the two Heroines, for such they are'.

In January 1751 James told the Pope in confidence that Charles was at Boulogne-sur-Mer, and we know that a month later he was in Germany, where he seems to have been received 'with great civility' by Frederick the Great, whose sister he may vainly have hoped to marry. 'Nobody whatsoever', he wrote, 'I respect more as ye K. of Prussia; not as a K. but as I believe him to be a clever man.' Frederick was certainly too clever to give his sister to such a suitor, but nevertheless remained in touch with Charles through Henry Goring and George Keith, the Earl Marischal, who was now in the Prussian service and, though understandably reluctant to compromise himself on Charles's behalf, remained at heart a Jacobite.

In March we know Charles was in Paris, where he attended a *bal masqué* at the Opéra. And not long after that, from wherever he was, he wrote to Mademoiselle Luci to ask her to send him Racine's *Athalie* and *Clarissa Harlowe* by Richardson, while she, in reply, advised him against certain psychological works which he wanted to buy, saying that they were nothing but trash. At about this time, too, he left his watch under his pillow at the convent of the English Nuns at Pontoise and young Waters was given the task of retrieving it. With Madame de Talmond his relations, in so far as he now had any, continued stormy and after one particularly violent quarrel he gave vent, for a change, to some rather incoherent political reflections. 'I have nothing at heart,' he wrote, 'but the interest of my country, and I am always ready to sacrifice everything for it. Life and rest, but the least reflection as to ye point of honour I cannot pass over.' He would, he concluded, never be a tool 'like his ansistors'.

Charles's concern and that of his adherents for the interest of his country and, more particularly, for the Stuart cause, led in the course of 1751 and 1752 to the hatching of a fresh plot against the House of Hanover. The leading spirit in this was Alexander Murray, a younger brother of Lord Elibank, who, like his elder brother, was Jacobite in sympathy, though neither of them had been out in the Forty-five.

In the summer of 1751 Alexander Murray had been charged with violence and intimidation at the famous Westminster Election of that year and, having declined to beg pardon of the House on his knees, had been imprisoned until the end of the Session when, on his release, he had been escorted by the mob in triumph to Lord Elibank's house in Henrietta Street off the Strand. In July Alexander, who was recommended to Charles as being 'most zealously attached' to him 'and in a position to raise five hundred men for the Prince's service in and about Westminster', crossed to France and during the months that followed the Elibank plot began to take shape.

The plan, in its broad lines, was that Alexander Murray, taking with him some officers of Lord Ogilvy's regiment, should cross from France to London and there secretly assemble a body of several hundred Jacobite supporters. The Prince, who evidently approved of the plan, would then join them, installing himself once again at Lady Primrose's house in Essex Street. On an agreed date Murray and his followers, armed with swords and pistols, would burst into St James's Palace and assassinate or kidnap King George II and his family, after which Charles would come forward and be proclaimed Regent. An important part in all this would be played by Alastair Ruadh MacDonell, the eldest son of John MacDonell of Glengarry, who promised to produce 'above four hundred Brave Highlanders ready at my call' as and when they were required.

Charles himself was, as usual, optimistic. Realizing, however, the importance of obtaining outside support, he now sent the faithful Henry Goring off to seek the support of the Earl Marischal, whom Frederick the Great had in August somewhat mischievously appointed Prussian Ambassador to the Court of Versailles, but who, remaining characteristically cautious and not wishing to compromise himself, would only meet Charles's envoy secretly in the Tuileries Gardens after dark and in disguise.

It was the conspirators' hope that, in conjunction with their own attack on St James's Palace, the Earl Marischal's brother, General James Keith, might somehow be induced to land in Scotland with a force of Swedish troops in support of a simultaneous rising in the Highlands led by Young Glengarry, Cameron of Fassifern, Cameron of Glen Nevis and Lochiel's younger brother, Dr Archie Cameron. But, though the Earl Marischal continued to keep in touch with the conspirators, there seems little reason to suppose that he or anyone else ever held out any serious hope of such early and direct intervention.

Whatever the truth of the matter, the conspirators had by the autumn of 1752 decided that the moment had come to put their plans into execution. In September arrangements were accordingly made by Alexander Murray for the Prince to meet Glengarry's kinsman, MacDonell of Lochgarry, and Dr Archie Cameron at the little town of Menin in Flanders. There Charles gave them an encouraging account of the situation, especially of his dealings with Frederick the Great. He had, he said, 'brought matters to such a bearing, particularly at the King of Prussia's Court, whom he expected in a short time to have a strong alliance with', but he did not now want the Highlanders to rise until General Keith and his Swedish troops had actually landed in the North of Scotland. He told them, too, that 'some of the greatest weight in England', who had hitherto been opposed to his family, 'were engaged in the attempt, and he expected to meet with very little opposition'.

Thus briefed, Lochgarry and Dr Cameron, together with Blairfelty, Robertson of Woodsheal and Forbes of Skellater, were provided with funds and despatched to Scotland, their instructions being 'to meet several Highland gentlemen at the Chef Market for Black Cattel'. Cameron of Fassifern and Cameron of Glen Nevis were for their part to serve as intermediaries between the Prince's southern supporters and Cluny Macpherson, still skulking in the neighbourhood of his cage. For the date of their assault on St James's Palace, the conspirators chose 10 November 1752.

That our information concerning the movements and plans of all concerned during the later stages of the plot becomes more and more detailed is, by a strange irony of history, due not to any records kept by the conspirators themselves, but to the fact that their every move and transaction was being regularly and meticulously reported to the British Government by one of their number, signing himself Pickle, after Smollett's Peregrine Pickle, and generally believed to have been young Glengarry, whose movements have been shown to coincide exactly with those of the British spy. Thus we know that after the meeting at Menin the Prince and Lochgarry spent two nights at Ghent, where, on instructions from London, they were joined by Pickle. On alighting from his horse, Pickle reports that he was 'accosted by the Prince's valet, Morison' and invited to 'stop for a little at the Inn'. Soon Charles came into the room and the conversation quickly turned to 'the Scheme in England'. The Prince then repeated his assurances to Lochgarry, 'but in stronger terms', adding that the Swedish troops

331

were to embark at Gothenburg. Alexander Murray, the Prince told Pickle, had been entrusted with the necessary commissions for him 'and full instructions how I was to act in Scotland'. 'The Prince,' Pickle continues, 'was so positive of his schemes succeeding, that he told me he expected to be in London very soon himself, and that he was determined to give the present Government no quiet untill he succeeded or dyed in the attempt.'

Charles, the report goes on, was particularly insistent that none of this should be passed on to the exiled court in Rome, whose security he did not trust, and Pickle had duly pledged 'his word of honour' not to do so. After which Pickle was instructed by the Prince to go to England. On arrival there he saw Lord Elibank, who much to his surprise, told him that the scheme 'was put off for some time' and that his brother Alexander had gone to Paris to inform the Prince of this.

By the beginning of November Pickle was back in France. 'You'l soon hear of a hurly burly,' he wrote from Boulogne on 2 November, 'but I will see my friend or that can happen.' As it turned out, however, there was to be no hurly burly. In the event Alexander Murray and what Lord Elcho sourly calls 'his Assassins' seem to have lost their nerve or quite possibly scented treachery and the plot – 'a Stupid Plott', says Lord Elcho – was postponed indefinitely.

It seems possible that during these weeks Charles himself again crossed to England. This is borne out by evidence from various quarters and in particular by a report sent subsequently to King James's secretary James Edgar in Rome by Young Glengarry, who, if in fact Pickle, was thus breaking yet another promise and betraying yet another trust. 'When matters came to the puish,' he wrote, 'some frivolous excuses retarded this great and Glorious blow; thank God the Prince did not venture himself then to London, tho he was upon the Coast ready at a Call to put himself at their head.'

The belief that Charles spent some time in the South of England at this period is supported by another curious piece of evidence. General Oglethorpe (whom we last saw at the battle of Clifton) owned a country house near Godalming in Surrey. In contrast to the General, his sister Eleanor, who was married to a Frenchman called de Mézières, was an ardent Jacobite and an equally keen conspirator; so keen that Charles used to say that to receive her in audience was his form of doing penance, while even his father was bored by her unflagging enthusiasm for the cause. In the autumn of 1752 Madame de Mézières came over from France and established herself in her brother's house. And here, in all probability, at the risk of being bored by his hostess, the Prince found a convenient lying-up place within easy reach of London. In addition to a local tradition that Prince Charles stayed there, there is also a story of the grounds of the house being haunted by a ghost – which likewise bears out the theory that it was here that he spent those anxious days and weeks in the autumn of 1752, restlessly pacing General Oglethorpe's grounds while awaiting news from the capital.

The British Government, though well informed on the whole subject (they may even have known of the Prince's presence in England), thought it politically advisable to keep quiet about the Elibank plot and most of those involved in it. It was no doubt for this reason that they chose to take their revenge on only one of the conspirators, the unfortunate Dr Archie Cameron, who, after the collapse of the plot, had failed to escape to the Continent with the others and, while lingering in the Highlands, was picked up in March 1753 by a party of soldiers from the rebuilt barracks at Inversnaid on Loch Lomond. Even so no mention was made of the part he had played, which the Government preferred to gloss over, and it was ostensibly for his share in the rising of 1745 that, 'undaunted and composed', he was hanged without trial at Tyburn in the summer of 1753.

With the collapse of the Elibank plot, Charles's hopes were again dashed and his life became sadder and more aimless than ever. '*De vivre et pas vivre*,' he scribbled, '*c'est beaucoup pis que de mourir.*' Despite his natural optimism, it must by now have become clear even to him that, short of a miracle, there was no longer any real hope of a restoration. In contrast to his father, Charles found adversity hard to take. To console himself, he now sought solace, not only in his old refuge, drink, but in love, love of a more domestic and therefore more binding and encumbering variety than he had found in the arms of Louise de Montbazon or Marie-Anne de Talmond.

When Charles had fallen ill at Bannockburn in January 1746, he had been nursed back to health by his host's pretty niece, Clementina Walkinshaw, a Jacobite born and bred. Indeed, according to Lord Elcho, the two had become lovers then.* Whatever the truth of this Clementina now came back into the Prince's life. Exactly what brought her to the Continent is not clear. Charles may have sent for her. Or she may have come of her own accord. (She later spoke of a promise she had given when they parted in 1746 to follow the Prince anywhere in the world – a promise, incidentally, which at that time a great many Jacobite maidens would most readily have given.) What is certain is that in 1752 she was a canoness in a Noble Chapter at Douai and that Charles, knowing her to be there, indeed, possibly having already seen

*She herself later recalled in a letter to James's secretary Andrew Lumisden that before 1745 she had lived in London 'in great plenty' and 'was between that and 1747 undone', a statement capable of various interpretations.

her there and again found her attractive, now set out to find someone who would arrange for her to be brought to him in Paris.

For a number of reasons this did not prove easy. Henry Goring, to whom he first put the proposition, refused point-blank to have anything to do with it. Such an errand was, he informed the Prince, 'only for the worst of men'. Young Madame de Vassé, when approached, likewise refused, sensibly suggesting that Sir John William O'Sullivan might be the man for the job, which he seems in fact to have been only too ready to undertake. It was not long before O'Sullivan, already knighted and soon to be elevated to the Jacobite baronetcy, was deeply involved. 'As to the personne Your Rle Hs spakes of ...', he wrote to Charles at the end of May,

> Her letter to me was from Dunkerque, where she gave me to understand yt if she had no account from yu, yt her intention to go into a convente & expres'd to me yt she was not very oppoulante ... I'l louse no time to inform myself with discretion where she is & inform her of Your Rle Hs intentions. I fancy she has a great teast for a retraite, if so really, it wou'd be worthy of your Rle Hs. & a Charity to help her, as I see with admiration it is your design. As to have her with yu, I am afraid it wou'd be too dangerouse, as well for your Hs safety, as glory, in the present jouncture.

But any doubts or scruples O'Sullivan may have had were quickly discarded. 'Be pleased, dear sir,' replied the Prince, 'to give a distinct adres how to finde Mrs Clemi.' At which O'Sullivan quickly wrote to Clementina as follows, for some reason in mediocre French: '*Depuis votre derniere lettre j'ay recu reponse ... a votre satisfaction et telle que vous pouvez desirer, et digne de la personne qu'il la faite. Il est question a present de vous rendre aupres d'elle, comme la personne en question le desir, absullement.*'

Perhaps not surprisingly, the English Jacobites thoroughly disliked the idea of such a liaison. Clementina's sister, Catherine Walkinshaw, happened at the time to be in waiting to the Princess of Wales at St James's Palace and to them it seemed all too likely that, with Clementina sharing the Prince's bed, their secrets would at once be betrayed by her to Catherine and by Catherine to her royal employers, with whom she was on the best of terms and who, in their cosy German way, would refer to her as 'our good Walky'. But Charles was not to be put off, always provided that he could get what he wanted on his own terms. 'Neither Sir John,' he wrote to Clementina, 'or anybody whatsoever must know the least thing about you or what passes between us under pain of incurring for ever my displeasure.' As for Clementina, she seems to have jumped at the offer, whatever the conditions, and in the summer of 1752 was brought, first to Paris and later to Liège, where the pair set up house as Count and Countess Johnson.

At first the relationship seems to have been a reasonably happy one. 'The Pretender,' reported Pickle, 'keeps her well and seems to be very fond of her.' At any rate in the course of 1753 Clementina gave birth to a daughter who on 29 October of that year was baptized Charlotte at the Church of Notre Dame des Fonts at Liège. But by this time, Charles, now drinking more heavily than ever, had become morose, surly and unaccountable, always ready to take offence and fly into rages. Clementina's life was a hard one; there were, as was to be expected, quarrels; and it was not long before he had decided to get rid of her. Since his conversion to Protestantism his feelings towards Catholics had, for the time being, changed, and the household which he still maintained at Avignon had been reorganized accordingly. 'I have wrote to Avignon,' he informed Goring in November 1753, 'for to discard all my Papist servants. ... My mistress,' he then adds, 'has behaved so unworthily that she has put me out of all patience, and, as she is a Papist too, I discard her also!!!' And he went on to give instructions that she should be handed over to some friends of hers in Paris. But hardly had he sent her away than he changed his mind; a reconciliation took place; and the two resumed their life together in Paris, where even O'Sullivan was shocked by a singularly ugly scene between them at a café in the Bois de Boulogne – 'a Devilish warm dispute,' he called it. But when, not long after, the English Jacobites despatched to Paris a Mr MacNamara to demand on their behalf that the Prince should get rid of her, urging him, in his own words, 'to part with an harlot, whom, as he often declared, he neither loved nor esteemed', he flew into a rage and sent him away. Although he 'had no regard for Miss Walkinshaw,' he 'would not receive directions in respect to his private conduct from any man alive'. As for Paris, now that he was there again, he hated everything about it, complaining of the 'terrible situation I am in for want of an abode, and ye impossibility of my staying here, ye Bad Blood I make in this Abominable Country, not being able to breath as much as ye fresh aire without greatest apprehension'.

Altogether this was a bad period for Charles. The arrest of Dr Cameron had distressed and also alarmed him. He was now in constant fear of being kidnapped himself. Hanoverian spies and French agents tracked him wherever he went. Travelling about with a mistress and a small child, he was, despite his disguises and assumed names, all too easy to identify. He was short of funds and had even been forced to sell his jade-handled pistols. His clothes were so shabby that, when 'an ill-dressed stranger' presented himself one day at Madame d'Aiguillon's house, her servants almost turned him away from the door.

For his father, to whom he had stopped writing, what he heard of all this was not unnaturally deeply distressing. 'I am', wrote James, 'entire stranger to all his affairs and all that relates to him and I should not so much know he were alive did I not hear from second and third hands that those who have the same share in his confidence say he is in good health; for it is now more than two years since he has writ at all here.'

By now even Charles's most loyal supporters were beginning to find his behaviour hard to endure. 'For God's sake, Sir,' Henry Goring wrote to him at about this time, 'have compassion on yourself,' and then, finding him impossible to reason with, sent in his resignation and, after years of loyal service and suffering imprisonment in the Bastille on his behalf, severed his connection with him for good. 'I have twice, Sir,' he wrote, 'been turned off like a common footman with most opprobrious language, without money or cloaths.... No, Sir, Princes are never friends it would be too much to expect, but I did believe till now that they had humanity enough to reward good services.' Incensed, Charles complained of Goring's behaviour to the Earl Marischal, suggesting that he had abused his position. But to this George Keith replied indignantly, refuting Charles's suggestion and reminding him of all that Goring had done for him and of the poor treatment he had received in return, and in his turn breaking off relations between them. To Charles, Keith's letter was a serious blow. The Earl Marischal was one of the few people in Europe who might still have helped him. 'You are the only friend that I know this side of the water,' he wrote back. 'My heart is broke enough, without that you should finish it.' But Keith would not relent. In the summer of 1754 he returned to Berlin, taking with him Henry Goring, who died not long after in the Prussian service. Two years later the British Minister in Berne reported to his Government that the Earl had utterly refused to see Charles, who, with Clementina, had moved to Basel at the end of 1755, and had spoken of him 'with the utmost horror and detestation and in the most opprobrious terms'. 'To think', he exclaimed bitterly at about this time, 'that I have sacrificed my life for that beastly family.'

In August 1755, yet another letter urging him to mend his ways was addressed to the Prince by some of his supporters over the initials CMP. This was apparently the signature of Cluny Macpherson, whom Charles had in the previous September finally authorized to leave his eight-year hiding in the Highlands and come over to France, bringing with him what was left of the Loch Arkaig treasure – treasure now unlikely ever to support a fresh Highland rising, but which might at least save Charles, his mistress and his child from starvation. But good advice, even from one who had endured so much on his behalf, made no impression on Charles, who in reply angrily invited his correspondents to mind their own business, adding that he 'despised the low malice' of his critics.

In December 1755, just ten years after his withdrawal from Derby, Charles completed his thirty-fifth year. He had reached what Dante calls *il mezzo del cammin di nostra vita*, a time when men are apt to review what they have achieved so far and to consider what the future might hold. It seems unlikely that Charles did either. In his present frame of mind one thing and one thing only remained constant: his utter, his obsessive determination to return to Britain, this time with substantial foreign support, and win the British throne for his father. That he had so far failed in this objective he chose to blame on others, chiefly the French, who six years earlier had made their position all too clear by signing a peace treaty with England and throwing the would-be Prince Regent out of their country, and on whose list of priorities a Stuart restoration still ranked low.

Even for a stronger, more resolute and more dependable character than Charles, ten years of continual frustration, of intrigues that led nowhere, of vain missions to unwelcoming foreign courts, of having to live clandestinely, of being spied on, of plotting with alleged supporters whose support, when it came to the point, never seemed to materialize, would have been hard enough to bear. In Charles it induced acute self-pity and a haunting sense of persecution, amounting almost to mania, which, taken together with the amount of alcohol he regularly consumed, made him more unreasonable, more peevish, more difficult than ever to deal with and deprived him increasingly of any sense of proportion or reality that he had ever possessed.

Until now it could be said that there had from time to time been straws to clutch at, and Charles had duly clutched at them. But ten years on, after Aix-la-Chapelle, after Elibank, after forty years of on the whole not unsuccessful Hanoverian rule, it would, even if circumstances again changed in his favour (as they were about to), have taken more than a miracle for him to achieve even a fraction of what he had so improbably achieved ten years before. Nor was Charles himself in any way the man he had been then.

'All the world,' writes Andrew Lang, 'has regretted that the Prince did not fall, as Keppoch fell, leaving an unblemished fame, that he did not ride back, if it were alone ... and die with glory.' But history is not always so kind or so accommodating. The first, the heroic part of his life had come to an end ten years before; the second, in every way less heroic, had already begun and was to continue, ever less edifyingly, for another thirty years and more.

337

CHAPTER TWENTY-ONE

During 1755 and 1756 Charles and Clementina Walkinshaw made their home at Basle, assuming, however improbably, the roles of Dr and Mrs Thompson, a retired English physician and his wife, who had come over to Switzerland with their child to enjoy the salubrious mountain air. They lived, or so the British Minister at Berne informed his Government in May 1756, 'as persons of easy fortune, but without the least affectation of show or magnificence'. To the Prince a subject of concern and much correspondence at this time was a watch he had ordered from the famous Lucien le Roy in Paris. But, though living like a person of easy fortune and ordering expensive watches, Charles was in fact in serious financial difficulties and in July 1756 found himself obliged to ask Louis xv for money. 'If I knew a Prince more virtuous than you,' he wrote, swallowing his pride, 'to him I would appeal. . . .'

Even now, Charles did not stay in one place for long. From Basle he and Clementina went back to Flanders and at the end of 1756 he was again in Paris, where he liked to be for the Carnival. In 1758 they seem to have moved to the little Château de Carlsbourg in the valley of the Semois near Bouillon, a part of the country Charles knew well, where he could shoot and fish, and where he enjoyed the company of Monsieur Thibault, President of the local court and the Duc de Bouillon's man of affairs, who quickly became a close friend and also, it would seem, a boon companion, for the Prince was drinking harder than ever and by now often needed to be carried to bed.

By this time, the resumption of hostilities between France and England in 1755 and the outbreak a year later of the Seven Years' War had given Charles a renewed importance in French eyes and

338

afforded fresh opportunities for all concerned to fish in troubled water. Even Lord George Murray, who, it might have been thought, would by now have had more than enough of the Prince and his cause, was amongst those who declared their readiness to fight for him again.

In May 1755 Charles had had meetings with Louis xv's ministers, the Duc de Richelieu and the Duc de Choiseul, but, from the reports reaching his father in Rome, it was clear that nothing had come of them and James once again drew the sad conclusion that his son's behaviour and way of life made it impossible for him to reach any kind of understanding with potentially friendly powers. Early in 1757 the French appear to have offered Charles the chance of leading their attack on Minorca, but he refused. 'The English', he said, 'will do me justice, if they think fit, but I will no longer serve as a mere bugbear.'

But, bugbear or not, Charles missed the chance of being associated with a successful millitary operation which in the event dealt a severe blow to British morale and to the prestige of the British Government, and was followed in due course by the public execution of the British admiral concerned – *pour encourager les autres*, as Voltaire slyly remarked at the time. Later in 1757, Frederick the Great, who the year before had reached a separate accommodation with the English, was informed that France was intending to invade Ireland but that Charles, still distrusting the French, had again refused to take part unless both the Austrian and Russian governments guaranteed France's proposals.

All through the spring, summer and autumn of 1759 various invasion projects were discussed, Alexander Murray and Lord Clancarty acting as intermediaries between Charles and the French, notably the Maréchal Duc de Belle Isle. Again numerous conditions were laid down and difficulties made by Charles and his associates, Alexander Murray reporting that the Scottish Jacobites would not stir unless there was a landing in England as well as in Scotland, and Charles himself, according to the ever-watchful Pickle, insisting that the objective of any invasion must be London itself.

With the appointment in December 1758 of the Duc de Choiseul as French Foreign Minister, and the possibility of a Stuart restoration with active French support was again taken seriously. In February 1759 Charles met Choiseul in the latter's garden in Paris and though very drunk was able to grasp that a strong French invasion fleet was by now already assembling in the Channel ports. Again delays ensued and relations between the French and the Jacobites became strained, following much discussion as to where in Great Britain the proposed expedition would land and whether or not Charles would accompany it. There was also some speculation on the part of the French as to whether Charles himself had 'a steady enough head' to play much of a part.

Eventually, however, according to a report sent to the British Government by another of their spies, a certain Oliver Macallester, planning was sufficiently advanced for it to be thought advisable for Charles to move to Brest, which he did, though far from enthusiastically and 'damning the Marshal's old boots which always were stuffed full of projects'. Charles meanwhile had gone so far as to draft a proclamation for use on this occasion formally announcing his 'authentick renounciation of the Church of Rome', declaring that 'the Roman Catholick religion has been the ruin of the Royal Family' and specifically denouncing 'the artful system of Roman infallibility'.

What the outcome of a full-scale French invasion would have been at this time, and what response it would have evoked in England or in Scotland, and for that matter what part Charles himself, in the condition he was by now in, might have played in it, is impossible to say. In the event a strong invasion force under the Comte de Conflans, which sailed without Charles, was utterly destroyed by Admiral Hawke in Quiberon Bay on 25 November 1759 and an end thus put for the foreseeable future to any prospect of a Stuart restoration. While Charles, for his part, went back to Bouillon to console himself with the congenial conversation of his friend President Thibault and, as so often before, with the bottle.

> Thinking not Drinking
> Drinking not Thinking
> Can not be a Tooll
> Or like a fool,

he wrote on the back of a letter at about this time.

In January 1760 Charles reached the age of forty. He had not seen his father for sixteen years. James, whose health was fast failing, continued to beg his son to come to Rome to visit him, which he claimed he could do in complete secrecy. On 3 March he even sent him 12,000 livres for the cost of the journey. Charles pocketed the money and even seems momentarily to have thought of going, but on 3 April he informed James Edgar that he was 'suffering from nerves' and could not come and again James was disappointed.

Charles's father was not the only victim of his unstable temper. Although he stubbornly refused to be parted from her simply in order to please his adherents, Charles had long made it clear to all concerned that he no longer felt the slightest affection or regard for Clementina Walkinshaw. Ever since their temporary breach back in 1753, relations between the two had continued stormy. They quarrelled bitterly over the upbringing of little Charlotte – whom Clementina

340

wanted to send to a convent in Paris, while Charles wanted to keep her with him – and much else besides. Whether from personal inclination or to keep the Prince company, Clementina was now also drinking heavily. The result was continual brawling and bickering and scenes which would often end with Charles taking a stick and beating his mistress as hard as he could; while at night, or so she told Lord Elcho, from jealousy 'he invariably surrounded their bed with chairs placed on tables, and on the chairs little bells, so that if anyone approached during the night the bells would be set a-ringing'. In the end it became more than even she could bear and in the summer of 1760 she decided to leave him.

That she should have so decided is, to say the least of it, understandable. Charles, it began to appear, took a view of the opposite sex not readily compatible with any normal domestic relationship. Men, he wrote, he could understand, but not women, 'they being so much more wicked and impenetrable'. Put in this way, the proposition leaves us wondering what could have led the Prince to this conclusion, if conclusion it was. Something he had experienced as a child at the hands of Mrs Sheldon or Mrs Hughes? Something he had observed in the tantrums of his own poor hysterical mother or, for that matter, of the titular Lady Inverness? Or, on reaching manhood and falling in love, in the behaviour of the totally besotted Louise? Or of the older and more self-possessed, but almost equally devoted Madame de Talmond? Or, in more recent years, of the long-suffering Clementina herself? All had without doubt suffered more at his hands than he at theirs. To the unprejudiced observer, surely, the fault must lie in the Prince's own character rather than in the nature of womanhood at large, and more especially in his utter inability to establish with his mistresses any kind of normal human relationship.

One day towards the end of July, when all three were at Bouillon, Clementina secretly hired a coach and disappeared, taking Charlotte with her. Her purpose seems to have been to seek refuge in a convent where her child could be brought up without interference in the religion to which, unlike her royal lover, she still clung. In a desperate, rather confused letter to her 'dearest Prince', she wrote, 'nothing but the fear of my life would ever have made me undertake anything without your knowledge. Your Royalle Highness is to great and just when you reflect not to think that you have push'd me to the greatest extremiti and that there is not one woman in the world that would have suffer'd so long as what I have done.'

As soon as Charles realized they were gone, he appealed for help to the Maréchal de Belle Isle, who was now his chief channel of communication with the French Government, but who in the middle of a war doubtless had other things to think about. He also despatched a Jesuit abbé, named Gordon, and his own servant, John Stewart, using the alias Jones, to try to find them. On 25 July the Abbé Gordon reported from Paris that he had found the fugitives and taken lodgings for them, but that Clementina absolutely refused to return to the Prince. A letter from Stewart ('Jones') shows that he fared no better:

From Jones the servant

31 July

... They (Gordon and Bodson) both came to my room and told me to go to the Lady's lodgings but she was gon out, I waited untill she came back. She seemed much surprazed at seeing me. I reasoned the matter with her but all to no purpose. She tole me that she would sooner make away with herself than go back, and as for the Chylde she would be cut to pieces sooner than give her up. I stayed in the Lady's Room until ten and a half. She sent for a coach to go out. I asked her if she would allow me to accompany her and the Chylde. She told me yes, wee set out and at a little distance from the lodgings, the coach stopt, there came a gentleman well-drest and two others ... and told the lady to come out and to go with the other coach. I came out allong with them. I asked the Lady if there was place for me; the Gentleman answered in Ruff manner, 'No Sir, go about your business if you have any'. They set off in a coach and four horses, which, Sir, seemed to me to be hired horses, the Gentleman was a Frenchman as far as one could judge. I followed them as far as I was able but lost sight of them.

Reports to the British Government from their spy Macallester show that the search for Clementina continued unavailingly for a month. Charles was genuinely distressed. 'I shall', he wrote to the Abbé Gordon, 'be in ye greatest affliction until I guet back ye childe, which was my only Comfort in my Misfortunes.' But in fact, the French Government, far from seeking to help bring back Clementina, were protecting her, and to a letter from Charles asking that his mistress should be compelled to return to him, Louis xv simply replied that 'he could not force the inclination of anybody in that situation'. Moreover not long before Charles had discovered that Clementina had appealed for help to his father and that it was James who, after constantly urging him to get rid of her, had himself furnished her with the means of escaping from him.

For Charles this was the last straw, the ultimate betrayal. Nor, needless to say, did his father's no doubt well-meant explanations do anything to improve matters between them. 'It was many months,' wrote James, 'before I had undoubted information of her desire to leave you, to satisfy her own conscience in the first place, and to stop the mouths of those to whom she knew she was obnoxious and suspected, and lastly to be able to give her daughter in a convent a Christian and good Education. O My Dear Child,' He goes on pathetically after a reference to the poor state of his health, 'could I but once have the satisfaction of seeing you before I dy, I flatter myself that I might soon be able to convince you that you never could have had a more tender Father than myself nor a truer friend, wholly taken up with all that may conduce to your temporal and Eternal Happiness.'

As for Clementina, she and Charlotte were by now safely installed at the Convent of the Nuns of the Visitation, protected by the French King and the Archbishop of Paris and in receipt of a pension from James. Thence she wrote her former lover long, part conciliatory, part reproachful letters, all guaranteed to infuriate him. 'Nothing,' she declared, 'can be more sensible to me than this fattale separation. I can't express to you my Dearest prince, how much my heart suffers on this account.... I can assure you, my Dearest prince, that I had nothing in view but your honour and glory and one principal object, which was the child's education.... She is already making great progreuss in her reading Both in lattine and french and she has a vast Desir to writ to her Dear papa.' She herself was, she wrote, 'vastly uneasie to hear about your health'. And some months later she wrote to say that reports had reached her 'that you are not yourself, that your head is quite gone ...' and again she repeated that he had pushed her 'to the greatest extremity, and even despair, as I was always in perpetual dread of my life from your violent passions'.

By now Charles was disgusted with them all, with his mistress, his father, his interfering supporters, and, as always, with the French. He would, he told himself and anyone who cared to listen to him, have nothing to do with any of them until his daughter was returned to him. Morose, suspicious and perpetually sorry for himself, he withdrew from the world to reflect on his own misfortunes and to drink more deeply than ever. And, as he drank, he would scribble down confused little rhymes on odd scraps of paper.

> To Speke to Ete
> To Think to Drink
> To ete to think
> To Speke to Drink.

Sometimes, too, he would read, though no longer books of any great intellectual value: *Venus in a Cloister or the Nun in a Chemise*, *The Brothel* and *The Art of Love in Six Cantos*. He also became the owner of 'an astronomical telescope', with which to study the stars.

From England, meanwhile, he still received occasional reports on the situation there, and exhortations from his supporters to bestir himself and reform his 'vicious habits'. 'Your Royal Highness,' wrote Alexander Murray, the Elibank plotter, whom he had dismissed for suspected complicity in Clementina's departure and who was now back in England, 'is resolved to destroy yourself to all intents and purposes. Everybody here talks of your conduct with horror, and, from being once the admiration of Europe, you are become the reverse. Think what cruel anguish these reports give to me and the few here that are truly attached to you. ... You have banished all your father's subjects.' But Charles, for his part, cared less and less.

To some Jacobites in England the death of George II in October 1760 seemed to offer an opportunity for political action and they urged Charles to join them in a scheme to print and distribute pamphlets protesting against the coronation of his grandson George III, who, having been born in England, freely declared that he 'gloried in the name of Briton'. But Charles did not seem to be interested, though strangely enough the Earl Marischal had a story, otherwise unauthenticated, that the Prince had actually been present among the spectators at Westminster Abbey when George was crowned King and had spoken to a friend of the Earl Marischal in the crowd. 'Your Royal Highness,' this friend had said to Charles, on recognizing him, 'is the last of all mortals I should expect to see here.' 'It was curiosity that led me,' Charles was said to have replied, 'but I assure you that the person who is the object of all this pomp is the man I envy least.'

For almost a year now he had been living alone. Though Clementina continued to write to him, occasionally forwarding letters from little Charlotte addressed to '*Mon Auguste Papa*' and signed '*Pouponne*', nothing would induce her to return or bring back Charlotte. As Clementina had heard, Charles was quite certainly not himself. The reports of his medical advisers bear this out. But their advice, like everyone else's, fell on deaf ears. To the Abbé Gordon, who had written, urging him for his own good to take more exercise and more solid nourishment: 'My attachment to our country is strong, he wrote, but my Scotch Blud is so high after all ye insultes to apply more to them that Refused a Little Childe in my Concine (*sic*). I shiver to think of a report that ye Scotch Regiments are to be reformed. The Olde Gengilman [his father] is ye only man that can remedy such an Infamy. Hee should I think to be father of his Subjects so to do all that is possible to pare [parry] the Stroke. Being more in power than even the first of his subjects.'

Apart from a passing concern for the fate of the Highland regiments, his letter only shows the deep-seated and unreasoning resentment of a drunkard at his real or imaginary grievances and wrongs. From the

British Embassy in Paris, meanwhile, a Mr Stanley sent back what must have been welcome news to Whitehall. 'I hear,' ran his report of 8 June 1761, 'that the Pretender's eldest son is drunk as soon as he rises, and is always senselessly so at night, when his servants carry him to bed. ... He is not thought of even by the exiles.'

In 1764 King James was taken seriously ill. The end could not be far off and in December of that year Henry wrote to his brother from Rome begging for a reconciliation. Charles replied to his letter in the third person through a secretary. He would, he said, be pleased to be reconciled to Henry, but wished neither to see nor to write to anyone. Despite this discouraging reply Henry persisted. In a letter written in February 1765 he explained the terms of their father's will and generously declared his readiness to renounce any bequests to himself in his brother's favour. In passing, he mentioned that Madame de Talmond was in Rome. 'She always speaks of your Royal Highness,' he wrote, 'with the greatest regard and respect, and really seems to be sincerely attached to you. She complains she never can hear of you, and thinks she deserves a share in your remembrance.'

In April Henry wrote again. But still there was no answer from Charles, and his brother became more and more worried about the future: where Charles would live when he succeeded his father; and what kind of reception he would get from the Pope, now Clement XIII, and everyone else if he suddenly arrived in Rome expecting royal honours. 'After al I have said and done in vain,' he wrote to a friend, 'I quite despair of everything, my only comfort is the consciousness of my having omitted nothing either to convince or persuade the Baron [Charles] to do what is for his true interest.' Finally, in October, there came a letter from Charles himself – the first Henry had received from his brother for almost twenty years. It was quite short and instructed him to get the Pope ready to acknowledge him as king in the event of their father's death.

So long as Charles remained a Protestant, this was easier said than done. On the other hand, as Henry himself was the first to point out, a sudden public re-conversion might make a bad impression. Meanwhile, in reply to representations from the British Government, the Pope, well aware of the disadvantages of offending the House of Hanover, had, through Cardinal Albani, an old enemy of the House of Stuart, already given Sir Horace Mann, the British Minister in Florence, a fairly strong hint that he had no immediate intention of recognizing Charles as king; and reports reaching London from other British embassies and legations showed that most other European governments were thinking on the same lines.

By the end of the year James was sinking fast and on 30 December

Charles at long last set out from Paris for Rome. But he did not arrive in time. On the night of 1 January 1766 Old Mr Melancholy died, 'without,' wrote his secretary Lumisden, 'the least convulsion or agony, but with his usual mild serenity in his countenance.... He seemed rather to be asleep than dead.'

James was buried at St Peter's with full royal honours, twenty cardinals in the procession and a sermon preached by the Pope. Charles, in the eyes of his supporters now King Charles III, reached Rome on 23 January. He was met by his brother Henry on the outskirts of the city and accompanied by him to the Palazzo Muti. He had had a trying journey (his coach had turned over near Bologna) and, recalling without pleasure the memories of his early life in Rome, felt far from happy to be back there. To his friend and boon companion President Thibault, happily installed at Bouillon, he wrote sadly that he 'wished he had his dear Thibault to amuse and comfort him'.

Nor was it only Rome or his immediate surroundings that irked him; it was the tacit admission that, by thus tamely accepting the part of an exiled monarch, by abandoning the more romantic, if no more effectual, role of Wanderer, he was closing the door on the heroic events of twenty years ago and finally admitting defeat.

On one thing, at least, he could count: the loyal support of his brother, with whom he was now at long last reconciled. With great generosity, Henry had already made over to Charles the substantial fortune left to him by James, amounting, according to one account, to £250,000, to which was added the pension of 20,000 crowns a year which he received from the Pope. As a Cardinal, Henry had done everything in his power to induce the Pope to recognize him as king. But Pope Clement XIII had preferred to leave the Sacred College of Cardinals to take the decision for him and, when it came to the point, the Sacred College had rejected Charles's claim and unanimously decreed that he should not be so recognized. Which Sir Horace Mann, in a despatch to the Secretary of State, readily adduced as evidence of the respect in which His Britannic Majesty's name was held, even in Rome.

Though infuriated by the Vatican's decision, Charles was at least gratified to find that, when the two brothers drove out together in the Cardinal's carriage, Henry seated him on his right, a compliment which a Prince of the Church would normally only pay to a reigning monarch. He was flattered, too, to find that, when he visited the English, Irish and Scots Colleges in Rome, he was, despite Papal instructions to the contrary, received by the rectors with royal honours and a solemn *Te Deum* sung for his early return as Charles III.

Though unwilling to recognize him as king and annoyed at the insubordination shown by the rectors in doing so, Pope Clement in May 1767 eventually agreed, under strong pressure from Henry, to receive Charles in private audience. Accompanied by Henry and announced simply as 'the brother of Cardinal York', the Prince went down on his knees and kissed the Pope's hand and, on being invited to rise, stood and conversed with the Pope 'amiably yet respectfully' for a quarter of an hour. Henry was well pleased at this. 'God be praised,' he wrote to a friend. 'Last Saturday, after a good deal of battleying upon very trifling circumstances, I carried my brother to the Pope's privately, as a private nobleman, by which means he has derogated nothing of his first pretensions and has at the same time fulfilled an indispensable duty owing to the Head of the Church. The visit went much better than I expected, the Pope was extremely well satisfied and my brother well enough content.'

Though no public announcement was ever made, it seems possible that it was on this occasion or soon after that Charles became formally reconciled with the Vatican and was received back into the Church of Rome. At any rate from now onwards no more was heard of the Thirty-Nine Articles or of his lasting attachment to them. Meanwhile, on express instructions from the Pope, Cardinal Albani had privately informed Sir Horace Mann of the audience, carefully playing down any significance it might have had.

After an interval of twenty years, Charles now settled down once again to life in Rome. Again he went shooting in the Campagna and, having always found pleasure in music, took to playing the French horn. For the rest he lived quietly at the Palazzo Muti, from whose door the Pope had in April, while he was away shooting, rather ungraciously caused the royal arms of Great Britain to be removed. Andrew Lumisden, who had succeeded Edgar as James's secretary and continued to serve Charles until eventually dismissed by him in December 1767, had declared soon after his arrival that he 'charms everyone who approaches him'. But he did not go out into Roman society, 'living', as the ever-malicious Cardinal Albani wittily put it, 'like a hermit, or rather like one affected with the plague', and avoiding in particular the company of the cardinals and of the great Roman families who readily followed the lead of the Vatican in refusing to recognize his royal status.

At his own levees and receptions he welcomed his remaining supporters and those who from curiosity or any other motive came to pay their respects. One of these visitors, an expatriate Englishwoman, a Jacobite who had known him for many years and was received by him in May 1767, passed on her impressions to Sir William Hamilton, the newly arrived British Minister in Naples, where he was to serve for the next thirty years:

> I have at last seen — in his own house; as for his person it is rather handsome, his face ruddy and full of pimples. He looks good-natured, and was overjoyed to see me – nothing could be more affectionately gracious. I cannot answer for his cleverness, for he appeared to me to be absorbed in melancholy thoughts, a good deal of distraction in his conversation and frequent brown studies. I had time to examine him, for he kept me near two hours. He has all the reason in the world to be melancholy, for there is not a soul who goes near him, not knowing what to call him. He told me time lay heavy upon him. I said I supposed he read a good deal. He made no answer. He depends entirely for his subsistence upon his brother, whom he never loved, much less now, he having brought him into the scrape.

After his audience with Pope Clement, Charles started to go out rather more, attending concerts and occasionally dropping in at receptions and balls. Another visiting Englishwoman described an encounter with him at one of these.

> The Pretender is naturally above the middle size but stoops excessively; he appears bloated and red in the face; his countenance heavy and sleepy, which is attributed to his having given in to excess of drinking; but when a young man he must have been esteemed handsome. His complexion is of the fair tint, his eyes blue, his hair light brown, and the contour of his face a long oval; he is by no means thin, has a noble person, and a graceful manner. His dress was scarlet, laced with broad gold lace; he wears the blue riband outside of his coat, from which depends a cameo antique, as large as the palm of my hand; and he wears the same garter and motto as those of the noble Order of St George in England. Upon the whole, he has a melancholy, mortified appearance. Two gentlemen constantly attend him; they are of Irish extraction, and Roman Catholics you may be sure. . . . At Princess Palestrina's he asked me if I understood the game of *Tarrochi*, which they were about to play at. I answered in the negative; upon which, taking the pack in his hands, he desired to know if I had ever seen such odd cards? I replied that they were very odd indeed. He then, displaying them, said, 'There is everything in the world to be found in these cards – the sun, the moon, the stars; and here,' says he, throwing me a card, 'is the Pope: here is the devil; and,' added he, 'there is but one of the trio wanting, and you know who that should be!' I was so amazed, so astonished, though he spoke this

last in a laughing good humoured manner, that I did not know which way to look; and as to a reply I made none.

A more regular life and rather more fresh air and exercise seem to have had a beneficial effect on Charles's health and frame of mind. For a time he drank less (Sir William Hamilton even uses the word 'sober') and was less unaccountable in his treatment of those around him. To Madame de Talmond, now, twenty years after their first meeting, old and devout and living in Paris at the Palais du Luxembourg in what Horace Walpole calls 'a charitable apartment, full of cats and chamber pots', he wrote on 15 April 1766 courteously and affectionately if not very grammatically; '*Mon tendre amitié pour vous, Madame était toujours gravé en mon coeur.*' And to other old friends he wrote kindly and even grateful letters. He also continued the few small pensions which his father had been in the habit of paying to various adherents.

This general benevolence did not, however, extend to Clementina Walkinshaw with whom he was still enraged and whose name he never mentioned. 'His passion', Lumisden wrote to her in reply to a request for help, 'must still greatly cool before any application can be made to him on your behalf.' Henry was at this time much disturbed by a rumour that his brother and Clementina had in fact been married. Whether or not Clementina herself thought she might have some kind of claim is not clear. We only know that the Cardinal, writing through Lumisden to Waters the banker, brought pressure, probably financial, to bear on her and that in due course she signed a formal declaration to say that she had never been Charles's wife.

Another ghost from Charles's past who re-emerged at this time was Lord Elcho, whom we last saw cursing Charles on the field of Culloden for a 'damned cowardly Italian' and who now came to Rome to dun the Prince for the £1,500 which he had lent him more than twenty years before and which he doubtless felt he might now have some hope of getting back. Elcho went so far as to take the matter up with Cardinal Torrigiani, the Cardinal Secretary of State, through whom he received the cool reply that Charles would repay his debt when he succeeded to the throne and a hint that if he sought to prosecute his sovereign he would find the Prince protected here in Rome 'because he is so zealous for our religion'. This was more than Elcho could bear. 'Why, only a little while ago he abjured your religion,' he retorted indignantly. 'I have heard that,' was the Cardinal's calm reply. 'But at present he is a good Catholic.' And when, not to be put off, Elcho approached Cardinal York, he received a message through a secretary desiring him not to trouble His Royal Highness further. In the end, nothing if not persistent, he applied to the Pope himself for help, only to be told that His Holiness had no influence with Charles, who had been angered by his refusal to recognize him as the King of England. Which, at long last, seems to have convinced him that his quest was a hopeless one.

It was not long before Charles had again relapsed into his former habits. He drank, as one devoted adherent put it, 'like one absent in mind when he was met with things that vex'd him, as too often was the case.' A confused letter to Henry, written in February 1767, reflects his disturbed state. In this he complains of 'my situation, that cannot be amused with quails or any diversion whatsoever. . . . What is in my breast cannot be divulged until I have occasion. God alone is Judge. I have but one view which is my Duty before God and Man.' He cannot, he adds, 'enter in innumerable things that my roving the world and experience have taught me.'

To those around him, Charles, understandably, was a constant worry. 'I have very little to say,' his brother Henry wrote to a friend at about this time,

> except to deplore the continuance of the bottle; that, I own to you, makes me despair of everything, and I am of the opinion that it is impossible for my brother to live if he continues in this strain; you say he ought to be sensible of all I have endeavoured to do for his good; whether he is or not, is more than I can tell, for he never has said anything of that kind to me; what is certain is, that he has singular tenderness and regard for me, and all regards myself, and as singular an inflexibility and disregard for everything that regards his own good. I am seriously afflicted on his account when I reflect on the dismal situation he puts himself under, which is a thousand times worse than the situation his enemies have endeavoured to place him, but there is no remedy except a miracle, which may be kept at last for his eternal salvation, but surely nothing else.

And again: 'I am persuaded we should gain ground as to everything, were it not for the nasty bottle, that goes on but too much, and certainly must at last kill him. Stafford is in desolation about it, but has no sway as, in reality no living body has with him.'

In the summer of 1770, Charles, who was now approaching his fiftieth birthday, decided, on the advice of his physicians, to take the baths at Pisa. The visit was an unqualified success. On his way he stopped in Florence, where he spent several agreeable days. Though the Grand Duke and his ministers deliberately ignored him, he was lavishly entertained by the local nobility and gentry and, in return, held levees in his own apartments, wearing, we are told, 'the Garter under his coat, and the badge of St Andrew at the buttonhole of his waistcoat'. The baths too proved beneficial and during his stay at Pisa he was able to manifest his Kingship by touching 'two or three very low people' who were suffering from the scrofula and firmly believed that they could be cured by the touch of a royal hand. All of which was duly reported to London by the diligent Sir Horace Mann.

Charles had so much enjoyed his visit to Florence that he decided to stop off there for a longer period on the return journey. But this time he found the Florentines less welcoming. Conscious of the long arm of the British Government, the Grand Duke had issued strict orders that no notice was to be taken of this controversial character. At which Charles, as stubborn as ever, announced that it was his firm intention to settle in Florence, which he greatly preferred to Rome. Nothing the Grand Ducal authorities or his friends might say could change his mind. Indeed, it was not until his brother Henry, who after all held the purse strings, gave him to understand that he would rather he moved, that he finally went back to Pisa, where he rented a villa for the winter, took another course of the baths and, in the words of Sir Horace Mann, who had been following his every move, resumed 'the same irregular life as at Rome, being totally addicted to drinking'.

Several months later, however, for all Sir Horace's vigilance, Charles succeeded in giving him the slip. For some time he had been planning a clandestine journey to Paris under the name of Douglas or, according to another version, Smith. The purpose of this expedition was surprisingly enough, matrimony. For once it was undertaken with the encouragement of the French Government, who, though by now despairing of being able to put Charles himself to any good use, were, for reasons of long-term policy, anxious that the house of Stuart should not be left without an heir.

The details of the scheme, which had the active support of the King and of the Duc d'Aiguillon, are necessarily obscure. We know that Charles left Siena on 18 August 1771 and that by the end of the month he was in Paris. There he lodged incognito at the Hôtel de Brunswick, off the rue St Honoré, in rooms let by a tailor named Didelot. About a month later Charles's presence in Paris became known in London, where the Foreign Office and everyone else finally woke up to what was happening.

Charles's sponsors were his cousin the Duc de FitzJames and a Colonel Edmund Ryan, an Irishman in the French service, who acted as his plenipotentiary and made the necessary approaches, playing much the same part as had his compatriot Wogan in finding a wife for Charles's father more than fifty years before. The first approach was made to a 'Miss Speedy', apparently the eighteen-year-old Marie-

351

Louise Ferdinande, daughter of the Prince of Salm-Kynburg. But, on the proposition being put to her, she had apparently burst into a passion of tears, not relishing the prospect of marriage to an elderly and notoriously drunken royal exile.

After this initial failure, Colonel Ryan was instructed to negotiate a marriage for Charles with any suitable princess or countess of the Empire he could find. With this aim in view he set out on his travels at the end of September. By now the British Government, fearing that Charles might have designs on the Kingdom of Poland, were thoroughly disturbed and Lord Harcourt, the British Ambassador in Paris, on learning of Colonel Ryan's mission, at once sent a secretary round to the Duc d'Aiguillon to find out what was going on and complain. D'Aiguillon, who had from the start been personally and closely involved in Charles's plans, prevaricated. He would, he said, try to find out what was happening. There seemed to be some question of a marriage. But Charles (who was in any case about to leave) would be invited to return to Italy immediately and the Duc de FitzJames (whom Charles had already picked as his companion) would be asked to accompany him. And so on, all greatly to the bewilderment and mystification of the unfortunate Secretary of Embassy.

Colonel Ryan meanwhile had not been idle. Towards the end of December 1771 he reported to Charles from Brussels that Louise Maximiliana Emmanuela, the eldest of the four daughters of the widowed (and penniless) Princess of Stolberg-Gedern was willing to marry him. Through the Bruces she had Scottish blood, was Canoness of a Noble Chapter at Mons, was nineteen years old, and had, or so the Colonel said, 'a good figure, a pretty face, and excellent teeth, with all the qualities which Your Majesty can desire'. If, on the other hand, Charles preferred a more youthful bride, her mother could offer a younger daughter who was still only fifteen. Charles replied that he would sooner have Louise and by the end of February the Duc de Fitz-James was at Versailles, trying to raise the necessary funds for the marriage.

Certain minor difficulties arose over the arrangements, which, Charles tells us, had been drawn up by no less than three theologians, two of them Cardinals. But these were quickly brushed aside by little Louise who, far from hanging back, was, we learn, 'very impatient to assume her distinguished position', and on 28 March 1772, the marriage took place in Paris by proxy, the Duc de FitzJames standing in for Charles. After which the bride and her mother set out post-haste for Italy.

Charles met his bride at Macerata, near Ancona, the house of Cardinal Compagnoni-Marefoschi, who had placed it at their disposal for this purpose. The date of the wedding, owing to the speed with which Louise and her mother had travelled and the eagerness of all concerned, fell on Good Friday 17 April. Louise was later to say that one could not expect much 'from a marriage solemnized on the lamentation day of Christendom', but at the time she certainly raised no objection. And, as her mother had specifically stipulated in the agreement that the marriage should not only be celebrated, but consummated on the day the pair first met, there was clearly no time to lose. Later that same day Charles was to report to his brother Henry that 'ye marriage was made with all ye forms', so we can presume that the terms of the contract were carried out. The wedding ring which the bridegroom gave the bride was of turquoise and carried a cameo of his own head. The accompanying posy was one of Charles's own compositions. The draft for it, in his own hand, still survives:

> This Crown is due to you by me,
> And none can love you more than me.
> Given by C. ye 3rd to his Queen, ye 17th April, 1772.

Contemporary portraits of Louise show a plump self-possessed little person, her elaborately waved and dressed hair brushed uncompromisingly back from an oval, somewhat Teutonic face, cold, alert eyes, a straight, short nose and a resolutely firm rosebud mouth and dimpled chin above a notably well filled bodice. Herr Bonstetten, a romantically inclined travelling Swiss patrician, draws a more engaging picture of her. 'The Queen of Hearts,' he writes, 'as the Queen of England was called, was of the middle height, blonde, with deep blue eyes, a nose slightly turned up, the complexion dazzingly fair, like that of an Englishwoman. Her expression was maliciously gay, but naturally not without a dash of raillery; her nature more French than German. She seemed made to turn everybody's head.' He then goes on to give a not unfriendly account of Charles: 'The Pretender was large, lean, of a kindly disposition, talkative. He delighted to speak English, and spoke much and willingly of his adventures, interesting enough for a stranger, whilst those about him might possibly have been obliged to listen to them a hundred times. His young wife laughed heartily at the history of his having been disguised in woman's clothes, considering his mien and stature.'

After a couple of days at Macerata the royal pair left for Terni to spend a few days at the house of Conte Spada, whose brother had long been attached to the exiled court. The ladies of the house were charmed by the grace and vivacity of the bride, but did not hesitate to express their astonishment that so young and beautiful a girl should think it necessary to paint her face. As for Louise, not only did she vigorously defend her own use of rouge; she also recommended it most strongly to her hostess, whose appearance, she suggested, might be much improved by it – advice which the Contessa Spada, who happened to be famous throughout Tuscany for the freshness of her complexion, clearly did not relish.

Charles and Louise entered Rome on 22 April. Henry had done his best to make an occasion of their arrival. First came four outriders. Next Charles's travelling carriage. Then the bride and bridegroom in the bride's travelling carriage, drawn by six horses. Then two more carriages with their suite. And last of all the Cardinal's own carriages. In this order they drove to the Palazzo Muti, where shortly after Henry paid a formal call on the bride and presented her with a fine snuff box set in diamonds and containing a draft for 40,000 crowns.

Once installed, Charles sent a message to Cardinal Pallavicini, the Cardinal Secretary of State, officially informing him of the arrival in Rome of the King and Queen of England. As was to be expected, no official notice was taken of this communication by the Vatican or by those who moved in Vatican circles. But it was not long before Roman curiosity outran Roman regard for the rules of procedure. Soon Charles and Louise were invited everywhere and when they themselves issued invitations to a reception, the gloomy saloons of the Palazzo Muti were invariably crowded. What is more, little Louise did not hesitate to assert her royal rights and privileges and the Romans, though doubtless laughing at her behind her back, at any rate made a show of acquiescing.

354

CHAPTER TWENTY-TWO

For a time after his marriage Charles drank less and took a new interest in Roman life. He went out more, attending parties and concerts and going for drives with his young wife, whose instant social success clearly gave him pleasure. To his mother-in-law, to Madame de Talmond, to the Duc de Bouillon and even to Louise de Montbazon, he wrote to say how fortunate he was to be so happily married. Even the arrival in Rome soon after his marriage of Clementina and her daughter does not seem to have caused him more than passing concern. Charlotte, by now almost twenty, he offered to take into his household; but he utterly refused to have anything to do with her mother and on these terms Charlotte preferred, for the time being, to stay in her convent.

Needless to say, none of this lasted very long. After eight months of a marriage of which the principal purpose had been to continue the royal line, there was no sign of an heir – a ready subject for mutual recrimination. By the end of 1773 Charles was once again resorting to what his brother Henry called 'the nasty bottle'. 'For some time after his marriage', wrote Sir Horace Mann on 11 December 'he is seldom quite sober and frequently causes the greatest disorders in his family.' Once more Charles became peevish and morose, nursing his old grievances and brooding over his wrongs, brooding in particular over the Pope's continued refusal to grant him the recognition he had granted his father.

This made life in Rome even less bearable than it would otherwise have been and, after spending part of 1774 in Siena, where he rented a villa, towards the end of the year Charles moved to Florence, where he and Louise, in the hope of finding the surroundings more congenial, now made their home, living for a time in the Palazzo Corsini, which its owner had put at their disposal.

But again they were doomed to disappointment. Having no wish to offend the British Government, the Grand Duke of Tuscany joined the Pope in withholding recognition; the leaders of Florentine society followed suit; and Charles and Louise (who attached at least as much importance to their royal status as he did) once more found themselves in a difficult and equivocal situation which Charles's own conduct did little to improve. He had always liked the theatre and night after night, having nothing better to do and nowhere else to go, would betake himself after dinner to his private box, where he would sit or, more usually, loll on a couch, refreshing himself from a flask of his favourite Cyprus wine, until in the end he became either disorderly or incapable and the gaping Florentines had the pleasure of seeing the titular King of Great Britain being carried bodily to his coach, his chin on his chest and his heels bumping down the staircase. Such conduct, needless to say, was duly reported to London with great satisfaction and a wealth of squalid detail by the assiduous British Minister to the Grand Ducal court. 'The sickness at his stomach,' wrote Sir Horace graphically, after one of Charles's visits to the theatre, 'often obliged him to retire in a hurry into the public passage, where two of his servants attended to give him assistance.'

Life with such a husband and the continual and outrageous scenes which it involved would have been hard to endure even for the most devoted, the most patient, and the most self-sacrificing of wives. Louise was none of these things, and that she should have put up with it as long as she did is in itself surprising. On the other hand, any alternative course of action, in the circumstances in which she found herself, cannot have been immediately obvious.

The following letter, addressed by her to her husband on 5 June 1775, some three years after marriage, throws an interesting light on the state of their relations and above all on the character and mentality of the writer:

> Since Your Majesty will not listen to reason and has decided to sulk because I do not wish to go walking in the month of June at the hottest time of the day, may I humbly point out to Your Majesty that my health suffers acutely from this great heat and that Your Sacred Majesty must surely be too fair minded and too kind to inflict such suffering wantonly. I well know Your Majesty's kind heart and sensitive soul and it would surely be an act of cruelty to force a poor woman to range the streets in this horrible heat simply because Your Majesty happens to feel bored indoors. As a

mitigation, you suggest I might get up at seven in the morning after we have gone to bed two hours after midnight, but clearly Your Majesty must be joking. Otherwise people will think you are in your dotage. You, Sire, are not quite as old as that yet, and it would do you no good in society if people who have always thought you quite a dashing character should decide you had gone so far down hill that you did not want to spend more than a few hours with your pretty, loving young wife. But, if Your Majesty goes on sulking, I shall be obliged to justify myself before the world and make it clear why the Royal Countenance is not quite so dazzlingly glorious as usual and its beautiful eyes not quite so radiant. I shall send all my friends a copy of the enclosed memorandum I have already sent to Your Majesty in which I set out the facts as best I can in the belief that I am in the right and that people will realize this. I am, with great devotion, Your Majesty's humble other half, Louise R.

(The *mémoire* to which the letter refers has not survived. Whether Louise ever circulated it to her friends or indeed ever wrote it, there is no means of telling.)

A week after composing this masterpiece of malice Louise despatched a no less revealing letter to her Swiss admirer Bonstetten, then in Rome. Charles's health, not surprisingly, had greatly deteriorated. 'Almost,' wrote his wife, 'yes, almost, two days ago I saw when I was to become mistress of my own destiny. Death and disease danced above the head of my lord and master.' And once more signed herself 'Louise R.'

It was not long, however, before an alternative solution presented itself. In the spring of 1777 there arrived in Florence, following a tour of the courts of Europe and at least one resounding scandal, a minor Piedmontese nobleman, Conte Vittorio Alfieri, born twenty-eight years before in the little town of Asti, famous to this day for its sparkling wine. Red-haired, heavily perfumed, good looking, talented and flamboyant, Alfieri aspired to become a poet, indeed had already achieved an early reputation as a man of letters. In the course of his travels he had also achieved a considerable reputation as a ladies' man.

Since her marriage Louise, who was anything but stupid, had blossomed physically, socially and intellectually. In Italy she had developed a pronounced enthusiasm for literature and the arts and moved when she could in literary and artistic circles. 'Her face, manners, wit, character and position,' wrote Monsieur Dutens, a visitor to Florence who also frequented her, 'made her the most interesting of women. She was of the middle height, had a beautiful figure,

357

a dazzling complexion, very fine eyes, perfect teeth, an air of nobility and sweetness, simple, gracious and modest. Her taste was cultivated by the study of the best authors, whence she has learned to understand men and works of taste.'

A portrait painted at about this time by Pompeo Battoni shows the teenage girl already grown into a mature woman. The figure is fuller, the abundant fair hair more skilfully and becomingly arranged. But the eyes are shrewder, colder and more alert than ever and there is the same resolution and concentration in the set of the mouth. Of the sweet simplicity discerned by Monsieur Dutens, there is little immediate evidence. Deeply pathetic by contrast is the companion portrait of Charles, now a sad old man, the proud features of the bonnie Prince blurred by self-indulgence and despair.

The Queen and the poet met in the late summer of 1777, as in Florence they were bound to meet. Alfieri was immediately much taken. 'A soft flame,' he wrote, 'in the darkest of eyes, coupled (which rarely happens) with the whitest of skins and fair hair, gave her beauty a power of attraction from which it was hard to escape unwounded or unconquered. Twenty-five years of age, a great inclination for the arts and for literature, and, notwithstanding her position and painful, disagreeable domestic circumstances that seldom left her happy and contented as she should have been, a golden disposition. These were not charms to be rashly encountered.' 'That autumn', he announces, 'I summoned up courage to wait upon her; nor had I gone many times before I found myself, as it were, unwittingly a prisoner.'

Soon Alfieri discovered that this, his 'fourth and last fever of the heart', was of quite a different nature from his three previous entanglements (the most recent of which had been a resounding, if not altogether satisfactory affair with Lady Ligonier, the pretty and flighty young wife of the general's nephew, who, after he had fought a duel on her behalf, had in the end thrown him over for her husband's hard-riding groom). Simultaneously he made another discovery, and, for a rising man of letters, an extremely important one: 'Instead of finding in her, as in all ordinary women, an obstacle to literary glory, a disturbance to useful occupation and a hovering of thought, I found in her a spur, a comfort and an example.' That same autumn, duly inspired, he wrote, '*Negri, vivaci, e in dolce fuoco ardenti, Occhi, che date a un tempo e morte e vita...*' (Black, vivacious and with a sweet fire burning, Eyes that bring both death and life).

In 1777 Charles, who had taken to calling himself the Count of Albany, had bought a handsome late Renaissance palace in Florence a few minutes' walk from the Duomo. The Palazzo San Clemente, formerly Palazzo Guadagni, had been built at the beginning of the previous century in the elegant, massively classical style of the period, a wing, rather larger than the original building, having been added somewhat later. Driving in through a colonnaded entrance, the coaches set down their passengers before a pair of great doors opening into a fine entrance-hall painted in the Pompeian manner. Above the door leading from the vestibule to the rest of the house Charles had, on taking possession, the British Royal Arms painted by a local artist, arms that differed from those displayed in England by his cousin George III, in that, while retaining the fleur-de-lys of France, they most definitely did not include the detested white horse of Hanover. On either side, beneath the prancing lion and unicorn, were painted two little flowers, a thistle and a white rose, and, above the whole, his own name and style, CAROLUS III MAG. BRITANIAE ET HIB. REX, and the date, 1777; while on the roof of the palace a leaden weather vane bearing the inscription CR III proclaimed the style and rank of its new occupant.

In contrast to the order observed in most Italian palaces, whose *piano nobile* occupies the first floor, the public rooms of the Palazzo San Clemente were situated on the ground floor, a succession of elegant, airy saloons, leading from the entrance one into another and ultimately into a lofty and splendidly proportioned pillared great hall, giving through the three arches of a loggia onto the formal garden beyond.

All these fine rooms, some vast and others smaller and more intimate, had not many years before been frescoed in the classical manner by a painter of considerable talent. Looking up at the ceilings or around them at the walls, Charles and his household could admire a succession of happy gods and goddesses, kings and queens, nymphs and graces, shepherds and shepherdesses, Fame blowing her trumpet, Father Time with his scythe and even the Trojan Horse. Some of these dwellers in Elysium reclined on fleecy clouds against backgrounds of purest blue. Others roamed through green classical landscapes amid grey classical ruins or peered over *trompe l'oeuil* balconies at the mortals below, while the Trojan Horse, for his part, stood stock still, his wooden head projecting enquiringly through a breach in the walls of Troy.

Even when Charles or his attendants went up the wide stone staircase to the bedrooms above or to the small gilt and red brocade sitting room which looked out on to the garden from the first floor, they were pursued by these painted personages. On the ceiling of the first landing were twin tondos, this time strictly Christian in spirit: two pairs of winged cherubs disporting themselves against an appropriate background of clouds and sky, one pair bearing aloft a scalloped and unmistakably *rococco* cross and the others a no less *rococco* crown of thorns.*

It was while Charles was living in the Palazzo San Clemente that some American colonists in Boston, of all places, tired of the House of Hanover, but still strongly attached to the monarchical principle, hit on the more or less happy idea of offering him their country's crown. But for one reason or another the idea seems not to have appealed to him and in the end, perhaps not altogether surprisingly, though he sent for a number of books and maps concerning North America, nothing ever came of it.

It was likewise in the Palazzo San Clemente that, under Charles's more or less benevolent eyes, the friendship between Louise and Alfieri took root and flourished. Alfieri, it seems, had somehow managed to make a good impression on Charles. Soon he became his constant guest and after dinner he and his hostess would sit and talk, while Charles, as often as not, drank himself into insensibility, sitting either with them or sometimes in an adjoining room. Louise had had other flirtations, including one a couple of years before with two visiting Englishmen, but Charles had raised no objection. Drunk or sober, he just made a point of always being there, thus leaving little opportunity for these romances to develop.

To the mettlesome Piedmontese this was an intolerable intrusion, and in his memoirs he recalls the distress he suffered 'to see my loved one teased by continual domestic annoyances brought about by her querulous, unreasonable and constantly intoxicated old husband ... Her sorrows were mine and I suffered the pangs of death from them. I could only see her in the evening, and sometimes at dinner at her house, but with her husband always present, or at best in the next room. Not indeed that he took umbrage at me more than others, but such was his system.'

Fortunately for him, Alfieri was a writer as well as a lover. Restless and frustrated, while waiting for his luck to change he sought and found solace in writing, pouring forth ever more poems and plays. It is to this period in his life that posterity owes such florid masterpieces in the high classical manner as *Maria Stuarda*, *Rosmunda*, *Ottavia* and *Timoleone*, the first of which, with its fairly direct allusions to these mutual frustrations, he dedicated, greatly daring, to his latest love.

How long, under these unpromising conditions, the relationship between the lovers remained platonic must be a matter for speculation.

---

*More mysterious is a fresco which still decorates the vaulted ceiling of a small, low room on the mezzanine floor; a panther couchant enclosed within a wreath of olive branches with, issuing from its mouth, a ribbon bearing the inscription: IDN: MAC: NIANCIT. How it came to be there or what its meaning can be, no one seems to know.

There may, or there may not, have been moments when Alfieri was able to take advantage of one of Charles's drunken stupors to have his way with Louise. As so often in such cases, the evidence is contradictory and inconclusive. What is certain is that from drink or from jealousy or, more probably, from a mixture of the two, Charles now became increasingly harsh and even brutal in his treatment of his wife, knocking her about and beating her just as he had once beaten and knocked about the unfortunate Clementina Walkinsaw, and rigging up round her bedstead a similar system of interconnected alarm bells. By now he was in an altogether deplorable state. 'He has,' wrote Horace Mann to Horace Walpole in May 1779, 'a declared fistula, great sores in his legs, and insupportable in stench and temper, neither of which he takes the least pains to disguise to his wife, whose beauty is vastly faded of late. She has paid dear for the dregs of royalty.'

Things were to reach a climax on St Andrew's Day, 30 November 1780, when, after an evening spent proposing and drinking copious toasts to the patron saint of Scotland, Charles burst into his wife's bedroom, accused her of being unfaithful to him, and, according to her account of what happened, then tried to ravish or strangle her or both. At this she screamed the house down until the servants, well accustomed to such disorderly scenes, came rushing in to rescue her. Within hours the whole of Florence, including the Grand Duke of Tuscany and, of course, the British Minister, were fully informed of what had or had not happened. The tale, needless to say, lost nothing in the telling and Horace Mann or Mini, as his like-minded friends called him, was soon able to regale Horace Walpole with a lively account of how Charles, after partaking of 'an extraordinary dose of wine and strong liquors', burst into Louise's bedroom and 'committed the most nauseous and filthy indecencies from above and below upon her, tore her hair and attempted to throttle her'.

This was enough for Louise. Within a week she was planning her escape. In this she had several ready helpers – Alfieri for one; also a mutual friend of theirs, a Signora Orlandini, the Irish-born widow of a general, until recently the mistress of the French Minister in Florence, but now inseparable from a good-looking young Irish adventurer named Gehegan; and last but not least Gehegan himself.

In accordance with the plan they evolved, Madame Orlandini was invited to breakfast with Charles and Louise at their palace. After breakfast Charles, as expected, invited the ladies to take the air with him in his coach. Signora Orlandini then suggested that they should drive to the nearby Convent of the *Bianchette* or Little White Sisters to see some needlework. This they did and at the entrance, as though by chance, encountered Gehegan. The ladies alighted first and quickly went up the steps and into the convent. They were followed by Gehegan who, affecting dismay, then came back to tell Charles that the nuns had most uncivilly refused him admission and had actually shut the door in his face.

Following Gehegan up the steps, Charles now 'pulled, and pushed, and kicked, and knocked' at the door. At this the Mother Superior (who was also in the conspiracy) made her appearance and informed Charles through a grating in the door that his wife, being in fear of her life, had sought asylum in the convent, where she would reside under the protection of the Grand Duchess herself. After further protests, Charles returned home, loudly offering a thousand golden sequins to anyone who would kill Alfieri for him.

A day or two later he was to receive from Gehegan an extremely formal and no less Irish communication dated 9 December, complaining that 'it has been repeatedly avowed to me that you was pleased to say at your table that you would have me shot, were it to cost you half your fortune, for no other reason that I know of than because I had the honour of handing your amiable Consort out of your carriage, and thence up a flight of stairs'. This was followed by another, longer and even more formal letter containing further references to his 'amiable Consort' and complaining this time that Charles was said 'by many persons who have the honour of dining at your table' to have called Count Alfieri a seducer, and adding that 'Count Alfieri, conscious of his innocence and justly surprised as well as irritated by such a calumny', though now in Naples, was proposing 'to return in the speediest manner to Florence to *Demand Satisfaction* for so gross an injury'. Just what, if any, was the outcome of this ridiculous challenge, is not clear, though from the contents of the second letter it seems possible that some sort of message was sent to Gehegan to let him know that Charles was not in fact arranging to have him assassinated.

Once safely under the protection of the Little White Sisters, Louise lost no time in appealing for help to her brother-in-law Henry, clearly a most useful ally if his sympathy could be enlisted, as she had every reason to believe it could. In this undertaking she was entirely successful, receiving from the Cardinal by return of post an affectionate and sympathetic reply. 'My very dear Sister,' wrote Henry from Frascati on 15 December, 'I cannot tell you the distress I suffered in reading your letter of the 9th inst. For some time past I have been anticipating what has now occurred, and the step you have taken in concert with the Court is a guarantee for the rectitude of your motives . . . . Nothing,' the silly old man continued, 'can be wiser or more appropriate under the circumstances than your petition to take shelter in a convent at Rome; therefore I did not lose a moment in going to Rome expressly to serve you and to arrange details with the Holy Father, whose kindness to me in the matter is beyond words to express... You will retire to the convent in which the Queen my mother was during the time the King my father was the victim of a certain infatuation; the establishment is better conducted than any other convent at Rome; French is spoken and some among the community are very distinguished ... God', Henry concluded, somewhat naively, 'has permitted what has occurred in order to move you to the practice of an edifying life, so that the purity of your intentions and the justice of your cause be justified in the eyes of all the world.' There followed a rather half-hearted suggestion that Charles might one day be 'converted'. And, with the assurance that he felt deeply for her, he signed himself her very affectionate brother, Henry.

An attempt by Charles to get the Grand Duke to have his wife returned to him was unsuccessful and on 30 December Louise set out in great secrecy for Rome, accompanied by a servant of the Papal Nuncio's and with Gehegan and Alfieri, disguised and heavily armed, occupying the box of her carriage. She was at once received in audience by the Pope and allocated, under a special Papal order, a pension of 6,000 crowns a year to be deducted from the 12,000 crowns the Vatican allowed her husband. Her brother-in-law made her numerous presents and it was also arranged that she should receive a pension of 20,000 crowns a year from France. 'The mould for any more casts of the Royal Stuarts,' reported Sir Horace Mann gleefully, 'has been broken, or, what is equivalent to it, is now shut up in the convent of Nuns under double lock and key of the Pope and the Cardinal York, out of reach of any dabbler who might foister in any spurious copy....'

Contrary to the expectations of Pope Clement and Cardinal York, nothing could have been further from Louise's purpose than to let herself be 'moved to the practice of an edifying life in Rome'. On arrival at the convent, she had been given leave to make use of the Cardinal's carriage 'on any very urgent occasion'. But this, says Sir Horace, 'was some disappointment to her, as she had hoped to take the air when she pleased'. But it was not just liberty to take the air that Louise was looking for; nor was it long before she got her way. 'The Countess Albanie', Sir Horace reported on 23 January 1781, 'is treated in Rome with the greatest attention. She has obtained leave to go abroad whenever she pleases without the least constraint.' The Cardinal, quite clearly, was dazzled by his charming sister-in-law. Soon she had left the convent and moved into his official residence, the magnificent palace of the Cancelleria, where her lover could and did visit her freely. Alfieri now also moved to Rome, where he rented the Villa Strozzi near the baths of Diocletian, 'a dwelling in entire harmony with my temperament, my character, my occupations', and whence, under the very noses of the Pope and Cardinal York, he would visit his beloved as often as he liked. *Psipsio* and *Psipsia*, they called each other, pet-names designed to reproduce the sound of the kisses which they were now free to exchange to their hearts' content.

Living on a painfully reduced pension and drinking less than hitherto, Charles did his best to open his brother's eyes to what was happening. Towards the end of 1782 he found in Prince Corsini an envoy willing to present his case to the Pope. Through him he asked three things: that his wife should be sent back; that his full pension should be restored to him; and that Alfieri, whom he held responsible for his wife's departure, should be banished from Rome. But to this the Pope only replied that he was perfectly satisfied with the Countess's conduct; that he intended to continue her pension; and that 'as to Count Alfieri, he wished to have many gentlemen of equal merit in Rome'. After which he sharply reproved Prince Corsini for having dared be the bearer of such a message.

Some months later, towards the end of March 1783, came the news, eagerly passed on to London by Sir Horace Mann, that Charles was desperately ill, that he had received the Last Sacrament and that his brother had been summoned from Rome. Cardinal York, Mann reported, had immediately set out, only halting at Siena to ascertain whether Charles was still alive, and on reaching Florence had taken lodgings at a convent near his brother 'with whom he passes the whole day'.

But Charles's constitution, despite the strains to which he had subjected it, was still surprisingly strong. As the days went by, the fever passed, the general state of his health improved and, from what had almost been his death-bed, he was able to give his brother an account of Louise's relations with Alfieri which belatedly convinced Henry that both he and the Pope had seriously misjudged the situation. 'The tables,' wrote Sir Horace Mann to a friend, 'are now turned. The cat, at last, is out of the bag. The Cardinal of York's visit to his brother gave the latter an opportunity to undeceive him, proving to him that the complaints laid to his charge of ill-using her were invented to cover a Plot formed by Count Alfieri.' On returning to Rome, Henry, at last realizing how blind he had been, immediately 'exposed the whole to the Pope' and an order was belatedly issued expelling Alfieri from the Holy City.

This left Alfieri with no alternative but to go, and go he did, 'like one,' he wrote, 'stupefied and deprived of his senses, leaving my only love, books, town, peace, my very self in Rome'. Without her lover, Louise consoled herself as best she could by copying out his sonnets.

'*Sonnetti di Psipsio copiati da Psipsia in Genzano, 1785, anno disgraziato per tuti due*', she inscribed them when she had finished. 'Who knows,' she wrote to a friend, 'what will happen? It is so long since the man in Florence is ill, and still he lives, and it seems to me that he is made of iron, in order that we may all die... What a cruel thing to expect one's happiness from the death of another! O God! How it degrades the soul! And yet I cannot refrain from wishing it!' But by now Charles had made a complete recovery, and was spending his convalescence travelling about Tuscany and going to race meetings.

To do her justice, Louise now only had one wish, to be reunited with her lover; to attain this end, she was prepared to sacrifice all she had: money, jewels, and, such as it was, position. In the end a solution came from an unexpected quarter. King Gustavus III of Sweden was spending the winter of 1783 in Florence and, while there, made friends with Charles, who entertained him with tales of his clandestine visits to England and other adventures. At Charles's request, the affable monarch not only helped him by intervening on his behalf with the French court and by himself providing him with a certain amount of money, but also agreed to act as a mediator between him and his wife. Travelling to Rome, he called on Louise and also on Cardinal York and on a number of other cardinals, and with them eventually succeeded in negotiating an accommodation under which Louise was granted a formal separation and the right to live wherever she pleased. In return she readily renounced her share of Charles's subsidy from the Vatican and any claim on the Sobieski jewels and plate which Queen Clementina had brought into the family on her marriage to James. For her, none of this counted for anything by comparison with her new-found freedom.

As soon as he knew that Louise was free, Alfieri hastened to make with her an assignation for, as he put it, 'perpetual joy' and, after a separation of more than a year, the two met in August 1784 at the Inn of the Two Keys at Colmar in Alsace, where they spent the next two months and more in what that somewhat naive authoress Miss Vernon Lee assures her readers was platonic bliss.

In this manner Charles had been relieved of the '*situation si cruelle, tyrannique, injuste et barbare*' of which he had once complained. Since his separation from Louise his financial position had improved (which did not, however, make him any more disposed to pay back the £1,500 he had borrowed from Lord Elcho some forty years earlier and for which that persistent nobleman still continued to dun him). His Groom of the Chambers, John Stewart, had brought him a number of family pictures from the Palazzo Muti. With these looking down on him from the crimson damask walls, he would sit in one or other of the nobly proportioned rooms of the Palazzo San Clemente and, either alone or with a friendly Italian musician, Domenico Corri, would play the harpsichord or the French horn or, when the mood took him, the pipes, bringing back the stirring memories of nearly fifty years before. Of late his health had improved, but he was now alone. And unhappy as his experience of women had been, he felt the need for female companionship.

Since her sudden departure from Bouillon twenty-four years earlier, Charles had not set eyes on Clementina Walkinshaw or on their daughter Charlotte, to whom, as a child, he had once been so attached. To numerous messages and letters asking for help or for leave to see him, he had, over the years, responded negatively and through a third party, usually Abbé Gordon, the principal of the Scots College in Paris. In March 1783, however, believing himself to be dying and being no doubt anxious to exclude Louise from any part in his inheritance, he had declared Charlotte his heir, at the same time formally legitimizing her and styling her Duchess of Albany. Now, in the summer of 1784, on recovering his health, he set about making enquiries to find out where she was and, on learning that she and her mother, now known as the Countess of Albestroff, were living in Paris at the Convent of the Visitation in the rue Saint Jacques, he wrote to Charlotte, informing her of his decision to acknowledge her as his daughter and make her his heir and asking her to come and live with him. This time neither Clementina nor Charlotte raised any objection and Charles wrote to his *chère fille*, formally inviting her to make her home with him in Florence and at the same time sending his servant John Stewart to act as her escort.

In October Charlotte arrived in Florence and took up residence at the Palazzo San Clemente, where Charles had made elaborate preparations to receive her. Since their last meeting Charlotte had grown from a little girl into a tall, dark, good-humoured, easy-going young woman of thirty-one. 'She is allowed', writes Sir Horace Mann grudgingly, 'to be a good figure, tall and well made, but the features of her face resemble too much those of her father to be handsome.' Another description comes from an itinerant Englishman writing in the Gentleman's Magazine: 'She was a tall, robust woman of a very dark complexion and a coarse-grained skin, with more of a masculine boldness than feminine modesty or elegance, but easy and unassuming in her manners, amply possessed of that volubility of tongue and that spirit of coquetry for which the women of the country where she was educated have at all times been particularly distinguished.'

Charlotte spoke only French. English she never mastered and while in Italy she picked up no more than a few words of Italian. Of her life in the intervening period little is known, though she had managed from the shelter of her convent to give birth to no less than thee children, two girls and a boy, by Prince Ferdinand Maximilian de Rohan, Archbishop of Bordeaux and later of Cambrai, who, as it happened, was the youngest son of Madame de Guémené and therefore Louise de Montbazon's brother-in-law. These, the youngest of whom, Charles Edward, had been born in that same summer of 1784, she now left to be looked after by her mother. 'My little flowers' she called them affectionately in her letters to Clementina, who also kept in touch with their father, the Archbishop.*

Delighted by his daughter's arrival, Charles loaded her with the family jewels, only recently recovered from Louise. Three times a week he gave balls in her honour, to which the *beau monde* of Florence flocked in droves and which he himself invariably attended, 'though,' wrote Mann, 'he drowses most part of the time'. Whenever he went to the theatre, his daughter, 'very richly adorned with Jewels', was at his side in their private box hung, reported Mann, 'with crimson damask, the cushions velvet with gold lace'. On St Andrew's Day, a feast he rarely failed to celebrate, he gave a state banquet in her honour and before the assembled company solemnly invested her with the green ribbon of the Order of St Andrew. And, far away in Ayrshire, the young Robert Burns, in retrospect a Jacobite, composed some lines in Charlotte's honour:

> My heart is wae, and unco' wae,
>   To think upon the raging sea,
> That roars between the gardens green
>   An' the bonnie Lass of Albany.
>
> This lovely maid's of royal blood
>   That ruled Albion's kingdoms three
> But oh, alas! for her bonnie face,
>   They've wranged the lass of Albany.

Charlotte, for her part, did what she could for her father, looking after him and trying, as far as she could, to stop him from drinking too much, using what she called her *'ton de fermeté'*. All in all she seems to have had considerable personal charm and a marked gift for human relations. Cardinal York had not been best pleased by her

---

*Charles Edward Count Rohenstart (a name ingeniously devised from Rohan and Stuart), came to Scotland in the first half of the nineteenth century, and in 1815 impressed Lady Bute by his likeness to Clementina Walkinshaw, whose portrait still hangs at Mount Stewart. He was killed in 1851 by a fall from a stage-coach and is buried in the ancient, partly ruined cathedral at Dunkeld, his tomb bearing the not inappropriate inscription, SIC TRANSIT GLORIA MUNDI. His father the Archbishop, having successfully survived the Revolution, became almoner to the Empress Josephine. After which he renounced Holy Orders and was made a Count by Napoleon, dying in 1813.

legitimization or by her assumption of the title of Royal Highness. But by taking a friendly and tactful line with him ('I deeply regret for having incurred your disgrace. Deign to read this an instant: one favourable word will reanimate my courage and fulfill my wishes'), she soon won him over and it was not long before uncle and niece were on good terms. 'I am greatly obliged to your daughter', Henry wrote to Charles, 'for interesting herself so much on my behalf. It proves the kindness of her heart, to which everyone bears witness.' And to Charlotte herself: 'Since you appear so anxious for my friendship and my confidence (which greatly pleases me) I can assure you sincerely that you have both.' By herself establishing a happy relationship with her uncle, she helped bring about a complete reconciliation between the two brothers and restore the mutual confidence which had once existed between them. She even seems to have helped steer her father back into the bosom of the Church, thereby acquiring further merit in her uncle's eyes.

For Charles, now sixty-five, this was a happier and calmer period than he had known for years. But the exertions of the Forty-five, the excesses of the last thirty or forty years and the excitement of his renewed social activities were beginning to tell on him. 'His health', reported Mann, 'decayed daily, so that he is quite incapable of transacting his own business, and his mind seems to approach that of imbecility, though he constantly goes abroad in his coach, has a small company every day at dinner, and never omits going to the theatre.' To his brother Henry, Charles himself wrote sadly: 'I am so bothered in the head...'

Charlotte did her best to protect him from disturbing influences, but every now and then something happened to upset his mental equilibrium. Thus a friend of Charles James Fox, a Mr Greathead, who was visiting Italy and out of idle curiosity called to see him, managed to steer the conversation round to the Forty-five. At first Charles seemed reluctant to discuss the subject. But, as they talked, old memories came flooding back, he grew more and more excited and finally, when he recalled the stricken field of Culloden and the slaughter that had followed it, he fell to the floor in convulsions. 'Oh, Sir,' cried Charlotte reproachfully, as she hurried into the room, 'you must have been speaking to my father about Scotland and the Highlanders. No one dares mention these subjects in his presence.' It is said, too, that that sad little melody, 'Lochaber no more', when played or sung, was enough to move him to tears.

Towards the end of 1785 Charles's health led his doctors to recommend him to take the waters at Pisa. Thence he went with Charlotte to Perugia and there they met Henry, with whom Charlotte had an immediate success. Soon uncle and niece were on the most affectionate terms and, at Henry's instance, Charlotte used her influence to get her father to travel on to Rome. Leaving Florence and taking the journey in easy stages to spare Charles's health, they reached Rome in the first half of December.

Charlotte was even able to bring about, at any rate on paper, a reconciliation between her father and her mother, to whom Charles began to send a series of friendly messages, to which Clementina readily responded. Finally in January 1787, he sent her a letter thanking her for a letter she had written him and signing it in his own hand: '*Votre bon ami. Charles R.*'

Charles did not return to the Palazzo San Clemente. The last time I visited it, its latest owners, the University of Florence, had with truly academic ruthlessness removed the royal weathercock from the roof, while rebellious students, ignorant of a king who led a braver and far more forlorn rebellion than theirs, had daubed the stately walls with red paint and out-of-date revolutionary slogans: '*Potere al Popolo*' and '*Viva Stalin*'. No one there, now that the Duca di San Clemente has sold his family's palace, had heard of its one-time occupant. But the watchmen, the *custodi*, who patrol it at night, tell of a *fantasma*, a ghost, that goes blundering through the building, bumping into things and leaving doors open behind it – an unusual phenomenon in a sunny Catholic country, where ghosts are in general frowned on or ignored.

On Charles's return to Rome, the gloomy Palazzo Muti was once again opened up and here, as in Florence, Charles gave dinner parties and concerts for Charlotte. The Pope showed himself better disposed than formerly, receiving Charles with considerable cordiality and addressing his daughter as Duchess. Taking their cue from him, the leaders of Roman society followed suit and Charlotte, as Sir Horace Mann duly reported to his Government on the last day of 1785, was most civilly received by the great ladies of Rome.

But by now Sir Horace's long series of reports and letters were approaching their end. In November 1786 he at long last died, having spent no less than forty-six consecutive years as British Minister to the Court of Tuscany and having during the whole of that period devoted a great proportion of his despatches to the affairs of Charles, his father and his brother.

For Charles, too, the end was now fast approaching. Since his return to Rome he had been afflicted by dropsy and had had more than one relapse. Then, early in January 1788, he suffered a stroke which completely paralysed one side of his body. For another couple of weeks he lingered on in a semi-conscious condition, to die at last on the morning of 31 January, cared for by Charlotte to the end. 'This morning, between the hours of nine and ten,' reported Lord Hervey, the new British Minister, 'the Pretender departed this life.'

There is a story, which seems to have originated with Lord Stanhope, that Charles in fact died on 30 January, but that those around him suppressed the news until next morning in order that it should not be known that he had died on the exact anniversary of Charles I's execution, a day of ill-omen for the House of Stuart. Whether or not this is true is impossible to say. Henry, we know, was at his brother's bedside and it is perhaps significant that the pages of the Cardinal's diary which cover these two days have been torn out.

As a final gesture of fraternal and dynastic loyalty, Henry made every effort to have Charles buried in St Peter's with full royal honours. This the Pope refused on the grounds that he had never been recognized as a sovereign. But Henry, who, as well as being a cardinal, was Bishop of Frascati, gave orders for his brother's obsequies to be celebrated with due magnificence in his own fine Cathedral there.

It seems probable that in legitimizing Charlotte and making her his heir, Charles had intended that she should succeed him as claimant to the British throne. After his death her servants continued to wear the royal livery; her carriages bore the British royal crown and cipher; and some medals which he had especially designed showed her gazing fixedly at an empty throne, while others depicted a ship approaching the British coast and bore the inscription: *Pendet Salus Spes Exigua et Extrema*. In fact, there was hardly time for the question to arise. Charlotte died of cancer the year after her father and, at her own wish, was buried without much ceremony in the Church of San Biagio. And so, whatever Charles's original intentions may have been, it was Henry who in practice succeeded him as claimant to the British throne. The medals which he now had struck bore on one side his head with the title: *Henricus nonus Angliae Rex*, and on the other: *Gratia Dei sed non voluntate hominum* – By the Grace of God but not by the will of man. As a Prince of the Church, however, Henry made no great effort to assert his rights to a terrestrial throne.

In 1789 the Paris mob stormed the Bastille and everywhere monarchs and the very institution of monarchy seemed threatened. Seven years later Napoleon's victorious armies chased the Pope out of Rome and in 1798 Henry, now in his mid-seventies, was in his turn obliged by a troop of French marauders to fly for his life from his peaceful retreat at Frascati, leaving behind everything he possessed, and seek a temporary refuge in Venice, where the long-established rule of the Doges was likewise tottering to a close. As the new century opened, a leader writer in the London *Times* of 28 February 1800 was moved to characteristic comment: 'The malign influence of the star, which had so strongly marked the fate of so many of his illustrious ancestors, was not exhausted and it was peculiarly reserved for the Cardinal of York to be exposed to the shafts of adversity at a period of life when least able to struggle with misfortune. At the advanced age of seventy-five he is driven from his episcopal residence, his house sacked, his property confiscated, and constrained to seek his personal safety in flight, upon the seas, under every aggravated circumstance that could affect his health and fortune.'

Nor was it only the *Times* that showed sympathy. In September 1799, Cardinal Borgia, who had been charged with administering the Holy See in the Pope's absence, had asked Sir John Cox Hippisley, a British Member of Parliament, to use his influence at home to help Henry. 'It is greatly afflicting to me,' he wrote, 'to see so great a personage, the last descendant of a Royal House, reduced to such distressed circumstances ... I will only intreat you to communicate this to those distinguished persons who have influence in your government, persuaded as I am that the English magnanimity will not suffer an illustrious personage of the same nation to perish in misery! But here I pause – not wishing to offend your national delicacy, which delights to act from its own generous disposition, rather than from the impulse and urgency of others ...'

Cardinal Borgia was not disappointed. On learning of Henry's predicament, King George III at once responded by making him an allowance of £4,000 a year for life. This he arranged should be remitted through Lord Minto, the British Ambassador in Vienna, who at his instance despatched a Mr Oakley to Henry with a letter so informing him. The Cardinal, for his part, was much touched by his distant cousin's generosity and wrote gratefully to Lord Minto:

> With the arrival of Mr Oakley, who has been this morning with me, I have received by his discourses, and much more by your letters, so many tokens of your regard, singular consideration and attention for my person, as obliges me to abandon all ceremony, and to begin abruptly to assure you, my dear lord, that your letters have been most acceptable to me in all shapes and regards. I did not in the least doubt of the noble way of thinking of your generous and beneficent sovereign; but I did not expect to see, in writing, so many and so obliging expressions, that, well calculated for the persons who receive them and understand their force, impress in their minds a most lively sense of tenderness and gratitude, which I own to you oblige me more than the generosity spontaneously imparted. I am, in reality, at a loss to express in writing all the

sentiments of my heart; and for that reason leave it entirely to the interest you take in all that regards my person to make known in an energetical and convenient manner all I fain would say to express my thankfulness which may easily be by you comprehended, after having perused the contents of this letter.

I am much obliged to you to have indicated to me the way I may write unto Coutts, the Court banker, and shall follow your friendly insinuations. In the meantime, I am very desirous that you should be convinced of my sentiments of sincere esteem and friendship, with which, my dear lord, with all my heart I embrace you.

HENRY, Cardinal

With the conclusion of a concordat between France and the Vatican, Henry was able to return to Rome and to the Bishop's fine fortress-like palace on its hilltop at Frascati. There he dwelt in a handsome suite of apartments, looking out across the valley to Rome in the distance, elegantly furnished and frescoed in the style of the day. The frescoes, by Thaddeus Kuntz, an eighteenth-century Polish artist of some distinction ('the Rafael of Poland!' said the caretaker enthusiastically) give prominence to his royal cypher as Henry IX and to the British royal arms. The expenses of the Cardinal's household, reported Waters the banker, were exorbitant. He lived in royal state, kept open house and 'seemed to think of nothing but enjoying himself'. In my own portrait of him, as in others, he wears over his red Cardinal's robes a pectoral cross of unparallelled magnificence, made up no doubt from his mother Clementina's famous Sobieski diamonds. Delighting in speed and possessing an excellent stable, one of his greatest pleasures was to drive across the Campagna to Rome or elsewhere at full gallop in his coach and six, with outriders and running footmen in scarlet livery, followed by another empty coach and four in case of emergency. By this time Dean of the College of Cardinals, Henry was to die at Frascati in July 1807 at the age of eighty-two.

In 1819, the Prince Regent of Great Britain, soon to succeed his father as George IV, commissioned from the famous Italian sculptor Canova, a handsome white marble monument to be erected in St Peter's at Rome. This bore in bas-relief the likeness of King James and his two sons and beneath these the following inscription:

Jacobo III, Jacobi II, Magn. Brit. Regis Filio,
Carolo Eduardo et Henrico, Decano
Patrum Cardinalium, Jacobi III, Filiis,
Regiae Stirpis Stuardiae Postremis
Anno MDCCCXIX
Beati Mortui qui in Domino Moriuntur

Meanwhile Charles's widow, Louise, had returned to Florence and once more emerged as a leader of Florentine society. From the Inn of the Two Keys at Colmar, or to be precise the neighbouring castle of Martinsbourg, she and her lover had moved to Paris, where she received a pension from the French court and where, on the strength of her former royal status, she set up in her sitting-room a throne emblazoned with the British royal arms. *Chère Souveraine*, Madame de Staël used to call her. It was in Paris that she learned of her husband's death. 'Her grief,' writes Alfieri in a not entirely convincing passage, 'was neither factitious nor forced, for every untruth was alien to this upright, incomparable soul...'

The revolution which cost Louis XVI his head and which Alfieri, as a republican in theory, wholeheartedly welcomed, eventually drove Louise from her little throne and, strangely enough, across the Channel to England, a country she had never before visited. There, she and her lover were made much of and invited everywhere. She was even, by a characteristic quirk of fortune, received at court. Horace Walpole (who better?) has described the scene. 'She was well dressed and not at all embarrassed. The King talked to her a good deal, but about her passage, the sea, and general topics; the Queen in the same way, but less. Then she stood between the Dukes of Gloucester and Clarence, and had a good deal of conversation with the former, who perhaps may have met her in Italy. Not a word between her and the Princesses; nor did I hear of the Prince, but he was there, and probably spoke to her. The Queen looked at her earnestly.' Even so, Louise's impressions were unfavourable. 'Although I knew the English to be melancholy,' she wrote, 'I could not have imagined their capital to be as melancholy as I found it to be.'

An attempt to return to revolutionary France proved unrewarding. After various adventures she and Alfieri finally escaped to Germany, whence by stages they made their way back to Florence. There they set up house in a handsome *palazzo* by the banks of Arno, and there in 1803, after twenty years of life with Louise, Alfieri died. 'I have lost all consolation, support, society, all, all!' she wrote. 'I am alone in the world which has become a desert to me.'

But Louise did not stay alone for long. For some time past she had possessed an admirer in the shape of a young monarchist exile from France, the young French painter François Xavier Fabre. Not many months after Alfieri had been laid to rest in the church of Santa Croce and the sculptor Canova had created a monument worthy of so considerable a poet, Fabre, already highly regarded in artistic circles as a portrait painter, moved in his turn into the *palazzo*.

For Louise life with Fabre seems to have been as happy and as busy as life with Alfieri had been. For another twenty years her house continued to be a centre of social, artistic and intellectual activity. There can be no doubt that, whatever her shortcomings, Louise had considerable social gifts. Everybody who was anybody came to see her and pay her their respects. When she died in January 1824, she left everything she possessed to Fabre, and he, who had remained faithful to her all this time, left everything on his death to his native town of Montpelier, save only for Alfieri's manuscripts which he bequeathed to the city of Florence.

As for the other women in Charles's life, Louise de Montbazon had since 1781 lain buried next to her infant son Charles in the church of St Louis. Madame de Talmond, the once passionate *Reine du Maroc*, had died long ago, poor and devout among the cats and chamber pots in her grace-and-favour apartment in the Luxembourg. Of Clementina Walkinshaw, titular Countess Albestroff, there is little more to record. Surviving both Charles and Charlotte, she seems to have lived on in obscurity and poverty in one convent or another until November 1802, when she too died at Fribourg in Switzerland, just fifty-six years after that wintery week in 1746, when, as she later came to believe, she and the Prince first plighted their troth at Bannockburn and she, in her own words, 'was undone'.

A SELECT BIBLIOGRAPHY

Berry, C. L., *The Young Pretender's Mistress* (London, 1977).
Blaikie, W. B., *Origins of the '45*, (1916). *Itinerary of Prince Charles Edward Stuart* (Scot. Hist. Soc., 1897).
Bongie, L. L., *The Love of a Prince* (Vancouver, 1986).
Browne, James, *A History of the Highlands and the Highland Clans* (4 vols., 2nd edition, 1845).
Burnett, Ray, Benbecula (Torlum, 1986).
Cadell, Sir Robert, *Sir John Cope*
Campbell, John Lorne, *Highland Songs of the Forty-five* (The Scottish Academic Press for the Scottish Gaelic Text Society, 1984).
Carlyle, Alexander, *Autobiography* (Blackwood, 1860).
Chambers, Robert, *History of the Rebellion in Scotland in 1745–6* (Vols I & II, Constable, Edinburgh, 1827).
Chambers, Robert, *Jacobite Memoirs of 1745* (Edinburgh, 1834).
Charteris, The Hon. E., *William Augustus, Duke of Cumberland 1721–48*.
Cunningham, Audrey, *The Loyal Clans* (Cambridge University Press, 1932).
Daiches, D., *Charles Edward Stuart*, (Thames & Hudson, 1975).
Duke, Winifred, *Prince Charles Edward and the '45* (Robert Hale, London, 1939).
   The Rash Adventurer (Robert Hale, London, 1939).
   In the Steps of Bonnie Prince Charlie (Rich and Cowan, London, 1953).
   Lord George Murray and the '45 (1938).
Dumont Wilden, L., *Le Prince Errant: Charles Edward le dernier des Stuarts* (Paris, 1934).
Eardley-Simpson, *Derby and the '45* (Philip Allan, 1933).
Elcho, David Lord, *A Short Account of the Affairs of Scotland*, ed. Hon. Evan Charteris (1907).
Ewald, A. C., *The Life and Times of Prince Charles Stuart* (Vols 1 & 2, Chapman and Hall, 1875).
Fergusson, Sir J. of Kilkerran, *Argyll in the '45* (London, 1951).
Forbes, Duncan, *The Culloden Papers* (London, 1815).
Forbes, Revd Robert, *Lyon in Mourning*, 3 vols, ed. Henry Paton (Scots Hist. Soc., 1859).
Fothergill, Brian, *The Cardinal King* (London, 1958).
Forster, Margaret, *The Rash Adventurer* (1975).
Gibson, J. S., *Ships of the '45* (Hutchinson, London, 1967).
   Prisoners of the '45.

SELECT BIBLIOGRAPHY

Henderson, Andrew, *History of the Rebellion, 1745–6* (London, 1753).
Home, John, *History of the Rebellion in the Year 1745* (London, 1802).
Hughes, Michael, *A Plain Narrative* (1746).
Jarvis, R.C., *Collected Papers on the Jacobite Risings* (2 vols, Manchester University Press).
Johnstone, Chevalier de, *Memoirs of the Rebellion* (London, 1820).
Norrie, W.D., *Life and Adventures of Prince Charles Edward Stuart* (Caxton, London, 1903).
Oman, Carola, *Prince Charles Edward* (London, 1935).
Petrie, Charles, *The Jacobite Movement* (Eyre & Spottiswoode, London, 1959).
Polnay, Peter de, *Death of a Legend* (London, 1952).
Prebble, John, *Culloden* (Secker & Warburg, London, 1961).
Ray, James, *A Complete History of the Rebellion* (Bristol, 1750).
Salmond, J.B., *Wade in Scotland* (Edinburgh, 1938).
Selby, John, *Over the Sea to Skye* The History Book Club, (London, 1973).
Shield, A., *Henry Stuart, Cardinal of York* (Longman, Green & Co., 1908).
Shield, A. & Lang, A., *The King over the Water* (London, 1907).
Sinclair-Stevenson, C., *Inglorious Rebellion: The Jacobite Risings of 1708, 1715, 1719* (Hamish Hamilton, London, 1971).
Speck, W.A., *The Butcher* (Basil Blackwell, Oxford, 1981).
Tayler, H., *The Jacobite Court in Rome in 1719* (Scot. Hist. Soc. 1938).
   Jacobite Epilogue (Nelson, 1941).
   Prince Charlie's Daughter (London, 1950).
Tayler, A. & H., *1715: The Story of the Rising* (Nelson, 1936).
   A Jacobite Exile (London, 1937).
   The Old Chevalier.
Terry, C.S., *The Rising of 1745* (Cambridge University Press, 1922).
Thomson K. & Buist, F., *Battles of the '45* (London, 1962).
Tomasson, K., *The Jacobite General* (Lord George Murray) (London, 1958).
Lang, Andrew, *Prince Charles Edward (Longman, London, 1900)*.
   A History of Scotland, vol. IV (Blackwood, 1907).
   Pickle the Spy (Longmans, 1897).
   The Companions of Pickle (Longmans, 1898).
Lees-Milne, James, *The Last Stuarts* (London, 1983).
Lenman, B., *The Jacobite Risings in Britain 1689–1746* (Eyre, Methuen, 1980).
Linklater, Eric, *The Prince in the Heather* (Hodder & Stoughton, London, 1965).
Lockhart, G., *The Lockhart Papers* (London, 1817).
MacKenzie, Compton, *Prince Charlie and his Ladies* (New York, 1935).
   Prince Charlie (London, 1932).
MacKenzie, W.C., *Lovat of the Forty-five* (Edinburgh, 1934).
McLaren, Moray, *Bonnie Prince Charlie* (1974).
MacLean, Alasdair, *A Macdonald for the Prince* (Stornoway, 1982).
McLynn, F., *France and the Jacobite Rising of 1745* (Edinburgh, 1981).
   The Jacobites (1985).
   The Jacobite Army in England (1983).
Maxwell, J. of Kirkconnel, *Narrative of Charles Prince of Wales' Expedition to Scotland in the year 1745* (Maitland Club, 1841).
Murray, John, of Broughton, *Memorials of John Murray of Broughton 1745 and After* (ed. A.H. Tayler).
The Woodhouse Lee M.S., 'A Narrative of Events in Edinburgh and District During the Jacobite Occupation, Sept–Nov 1745' (Edinburgh, 1907).
Youngson, A.J., *The Prince and the Pretender* (1985).

INDEX

383